THE MEANING OF RECOGNITION

CLIVE JAMES is the author of more than thirty books. As well as essays and novels, he has published collections of literary and television criticism, travel writing and verse, plus four volumes of autobiography, *Unreliable Memoirs*, *Falling Towards England*, *May Week Was in June* and *North Face of Soho*. As a television performer he has appeared regularly for both the BBC and ITV, most notably as writer and presenter of the 'Postcard' series of travel documentaries. He helped to found the independent television company Watchmaker, and the Internet enterprise Welcome Stranger, one of whose offshoots is a multimedia personal website, www.clivejames.com. In 1992 he was made a Member of the Order of Australia, and in 2003 he was awarded the Philip Hodgins memorial medal for literature.

BY THE SAME AUTHOR

CLIVE JAMES

THE MEANING OF RECOGNITION

NEW ESSAYS 2001–2005

PICADOR

First published 2005 by Picador

First published in paperback 2006 by Picador
an imprint of Pan Macmillan Ltd
Pan Macmillan, 20 New Wharf Road, London N1 9RR
Basingstoke and Oxford
Associated companies throughout the world
www.panmacmillan.com

ISBN-13: 978-0-330-44028-8
ISBN-10: 0-330-44028-4

1 3 5 7 9 8 6 4 2

A CIP catalogue record for this book is available from
the British Library.

Typeset by SetSystems Ltd, Saffron Walden, Essex
Printed and bound in Great Britain by
Mackays of Chatham plc, Chatham, Kent

All Pan Macmillan titles are available from
www.panmacmillan.com
or from Bookpost by telephoning +44 (0)1624 677237

To Ian McEwan

No fixed idea except to avoid fixed ideas.

Robert Musil

Acknowledgements

Some of these essays first appeared as articles in the *TLS*, the *London Review of Books*, the *Spectator*, the *Independent*, the *Guardian*, the *Sunday Times*, the *Australian*, the *Australian Book Review*, the *Los Angeles Times*, the *New York Times*, the *Atlantic Monthly*, the *New York Review of Books* and the *New Yorker*. The essay about Primo Levi's biographers was included in *As of This Writing*, a selection of my essays published in the US by W. W. Norton in 2003, but has not previously appeared in book form elsewhere. The *Independent* obituary for Sarah Raphael was reprinted along with contributions from Frederic Raphael and William Boyd in a memorial pamphlet of her drawings published in 2004. Two of the pieces began as public lectures: *Our First Book* was an address given at the invitation of the State Library of New South Wales in 2002, and *The Meaning of Recognition* was my acceptance address in Mildura when receiving the Philip Hodgins Memorial Medal in 2003. Both lectures were later printed by the *Australian Book Review*. Printed here as an essay, *Save Us from Celebrity* was a conference paper given to the Australian Commercial Radio Association on the Gold Coast in 2004. In many cases, production cuts have been restored, and in most cases a postscript has been added: a device I have taken to in recent years so as to amplify or correct a point in the light of later events, rather than, by rewriting the original piece, to confer on it a bogus prescience. If the critic can't criticize himself, he shouldn't be criticizing anything. My thanks as always to the editors and commissioners concerned. Several of the pieces, minus their footnotes, have been available on www.clivejames.com while waiting to be incorporated into this book. For help with the website, which also features radio and television interviews, I owe a special debt to my generous young cybernaut colleagues and their futuristic expertise. A multimedia website is a marvellous thing to see. The book, however, not much changed since Gutenberg, is still the breakthrough in communications technology that leaves me wondering how anybody ever thought of it.

C.J.

Contents

Introduction

Since retiring from mainstream television at the turn of the millennium – always pick the busiest moment to do a fade – I have been able to devote more time to essays and poetry. Each of the two forms, I like to think, holds territory in the other, if only through the requirement that it should be written with a care for the connection between theme and craft. Any poem which is all writing and no ideas is a pain in the neck, no matter how adroitly done; and any essay which is all ideas and no writing is dead before it hits the page. It should go without saying that a poem takes more effort to put together than the reader can guess. It is hardly ever said that an essay needs a similarly disproportionate expenditure of energy. The expenditure takes time. The essayist must be free to pause, finish reading *Joseph and His Brothers*, sleep in the afternoon, spend a whole hour on a single paragraph, watch *CSI: Miami* in the evening, and then work far into the night, until finally he produces a piece of writing that shows no more signs of strain than the easy outpouring of some dolt who bungs down the first thing that comes into his head. The essayist's fluency, however, is only apparent, like his simplicity, which is, or ought to be, a work of synthesis, and not of subtraction. To the extent that it can make a clear argument while remaining faithful to nuance, his readability, if he can manage it, is his tribute to the complexity of experience: a legitimately lyrical response to the tragic. I hope the pieces in this book, when they look simple, do so without seeming light-minded, because most of them were written with a heavy heart. After the Berlin Wall came down, many of us who were already growing old had hopes that the young would grow up in a saner world. One of the signs of a saner world would be that there would be less call to consider contemporary politics when talking about the arts. It hasn't turned out that way.

The first and last pieces in this book are concerned with the difference between celebrity and recognition. I tried to keep politics out of both of them, but it shouldered its way in, because celebrity is a frivolity, and the frivolities of Western civilization are at the centre of the question of how freedom can be defended with a whole heart when you find yourself sickened by the vices that arise from it. The answer to the question, I believe, is that those who attack liberal democracy, whether from without or within, loathe its virtues even more than its vices, and should therefore not be conceded the moral advantage even when they are granted their suicidal determination. But I don't think it's an answer that should be reached too easily, and many of the pieces assembled between the two bookends are concerned directly with just how reprehensible, even in its culture, Western civilization has been before, and still is now. There are one or two pieces that could be said to have no political dimension, unless you think that an article about Formula One motor racing might itself be a comment on the unforeseeable aftermath of World War II, evoking as it does the paradox of watching, on a Japanese television set, a German driver dominating the world at the wheel of an Italian car. Nor was Bing Crosby a notably political figure, except if you believe, as I do, that the influence of its popular culture was the one aspect of American imperialism that was neither planned in the first place nor possible to resist. But in most of these writings, politics invades every sphere, even the world of poetry. Not that poetry was ever a separate world – such a notion would have seemed very strange to Dante – but there was a time when it suited the cultivated to think it might be. Now nobody thinks that about poetry, or even about being cultivated. Politics gets into everything. It reaches even those people who have nothing to do with their lives except hope that the next distribution of food will not turn into a massacre. Especially it reaches them, leaving their bodies lying in the dust for the vultures and the television cameras. One day those birds will have electronic eyes, and the insatiable viewer of reality TV will be able to see from the inside what civilization looks like when it ends – the bloodbath before it started. Which raises the question, since the subject is so desperately serious, of whether somebody without the proper qualifications should talk about politics at all.

The answer to that question is that he must, and that the value of what he says will depend entirely on his tone of voice. Whatever the subject, whether apparently piffling or unarguably grave, his way of speaking will either be true to life or it will be a tissue of lies. There are essayists who can be faithful to the world's multiplicity even when they are writing about *Buffy the Vampire Slayer*. There are other essayists who can't report a war-crimes trial without writing flummery. In its printed form, a tone of voice is a style, and a style is a spine and a brain, not just a skin. If this book keeps coming back to poetry, it's because it starts there: because a poem without style is inconceivable, and only style can register the flow of history. Much of history's flow, alas, is the flow of innocent blood. For a while we might have tried to think otherwise, but it was wishful thinking – and wishful thinking was the fatal human characteristic with which the critical essay, a far more analytical instrument than the poem, was first designed to deal. Immured in his beloved library, Montaigne might have preferred to read instead of write. The turbulent world wouldn't let him. A gifted diplomat much sought after by his government, he tried to shut himself off from politics, but it got in through the walls. And so he invented the form we practise now, always asking ourselves what we really know, and answering with what we have learned. One thing we are bound to learn, unfortunately, is that no amount of age will bring sufficient wisdom to cover the unpredictable. There we were, fearing that our prosperous children might lose sight of the value of liberty because they would never see it threatened. Nice thought, bad guess, wrong fear.

London, 2005

THE MEANING OF RECOGNITION

If the Philip Hodgins Memorial Medal is the biggest single honour with which an Australian writer can be graced, it is because of the stature of Philip Hodgins himself. Born in 1959 and dead in 1995, he had a cruelly short lifespan in which to accomplish so much. An acceptance speech for the medal should be mainly about him and what he did. In the following speech I tried to make it so, but I thought to make a start by establishing a general context of argument. For that context, I had to draw upon my own experience more than upon his, because I didn't really know much about what it was like to be a young poet burdened with the knowledge that he was condemned to an early death. Later on, with the context established, I could bring him and his poetry to centre stage. But at the beginning, I was the man with the microphone. Well aware that I was far too comfortable in that position, I did my best to say something useful. There I was, hogging the spotlight as usual. My main subject would be a dedicated young man who had never done any such thing. How to resolve the anomaly? Well, there was a related subject: the spotlight itself. So I began with that.

*

There is a difference between celebrity and recognition. Celebrities are recognized in the street, but usually because of who they are, or who they are supposed to be. To achieve recognition, however, is to be recognized in a different way. It is to be known for what you have done, and quite often the person who knows what you have done has no idea of what you look like. When I say that I've had enough of celebrity status, I don't mean that I am sick of the very idea. As it happens, I think that the mass-psychotic passion for celebrity – this enormous talking point for those who do not really talk – is one of the luxurious diseases that Western liberal democracy will have to find a cure for in the long run, but the cure will have to be self-willed. I don't think that it can be imposed, and certainly not from the outside. I didn't much like Madonna's last television appearance in Britain. Billed as the acme of sophisticated sexiness, it featured Madonna wearing high heels, a trench coat and a beret. She crouched like a pygmy prizefighter while snarling into the microphone as if anyone listening might be insufficiently intelligent to understand her message – a hard audience to find, in my view.

I thought of this performance as an attempt to prove that a knowing sneer can be made audible while discrediting the French Resistance. But Madonna's slow paroxysm of self-regard, a flagrant example of Western decadence though it undoubtedly was, did not inspire me to fly a hijacked airliner into her house. Here indeed was a celebrity gone mad, if not celebrity itself gone mad. But she will have to realize that herself, through her sense of the ridiculous, if she still has one. A violent attack would produce nothing but more Madonnas: spiteful spores in berets. An awareness even more sophisticated than the aberration is its only cure, for her and for the phenomenon of celebrity as a whole. Until the moment when mocking laughter does its work, we will be stuck with celebrity being called a phenomenon, or, as even the journalists are now quite likely to call it, a phenomena. Really it would be just a bore if it were not so toxic. But to know that, you have to be genuinely interested in the sort of achievement whose practitioners you feel compelled to recognize in a more substantial way. The cure lies in that direction if it lies anywhere.

While we are waiting for the cure, I am quite content to go on having my life distorted by my own small measure of celebrity, which has mainly come about because my face was once on television. Your face doesn't have to be on television for long, and in any capacity, before you become recognizable not just to normally equipped people but to people who are otherwise scarcely capable of recognizing anything. You will find out why posters of the ten most wanted criminals can be so effective. How is it that the lurking presence of a fugitive master of disguise is so often detected by the village idiot? The answer has to do with a primeval characteristic of our sensory apparatus. If the human brain has the outline of another human face sufficiently implanted, that other human face can be picked out of a crowd decades in the future, whatever has happened to it. Once you have appeared on that scale, nothing is harder than to disappear. On the day you realize that you can vanish only through never emerging from your motel room, and that even then the pizza delivery man has recognized you through your floor-length facial hair, you will realize that celebrity really amounts to a kind of universal mugshot. While it resolutely misses the point of what you would like to think you have done, it is an indelible picture of who you are.

But when I say that I have had enough of it, I only mean that I have had my share, and can't complain. Some of the distortions were always welcome. That was one of the things that made them distortions. They were *too* welcome. You can very rapidly get used to the idea that the swish restaurant will always find a table for you. You can get so used to it that you think the restaurant needs a new manager on the night when the table strangely can't be found. What's needed, of course, is not a new manager for the restaurant but a new injection of fame for yourself. Now *there's* a distortion. That way madness lies, and madness would probably have arrived for me if I had ever been a famous young rock star: go to hell, go directly to hell, do not even pass through rehab. As it happened, I was never a famous young rock star. Instead I was a reasonably well-known middle-aged media man, and never became addicted to anything more destructive than Café Crème mild miniature cigars, smoked at the rate of one tin of ten a day, escalating to two tins a day the day after I passed the insurance medical. When Elvis Presley hit bottom, he exploded in the bathroom. His bottom hit the ceiling. My own nadir was less spectacular, and the world did not take note, because the world did not care.

I was in one of the smoking rooms at Bangkok Airport, on the way to Australia. I would say you should see a smoking room at Bangkok Airport, but in fact you can't see it, or anyway you can't see into it. It is not very big, and though made of glass it is opaque when viewed from the outside: opaque because of what is happening inside. The smokers are in there, jammed together like the damned on some broken-down, fog-bound trolley car designed by Dante. When a smoker, reaching for the smokes in his pocket, opens the door to enter, he realizes that he can leave the smokes where they are. All he has to do is breathe in. It was my last experience of this that made me realize that I should leave the smokes where they were permanently. Eventually, only a few months later, I did so. If what was left of my life brought stress, then I would live with it without an analgesic. I wanted to live. I was reasonably sure, of course, that I still had the choice. Others, I had finally noticed, are not so lucky. After a lifetime of self-indulgence, I was at last beginning to be impressed by the possibility that abusing your own health might be an insult to those whose health has already been abused by the Man Upstairs, who really knows how to dish the abuse out the way it should impress you most – i.e. at random. Our defence mechanisms against the anguish brought on by recognizing the arbitrariness of the Almighty are closely akin, I suspect, to the defence mechanisms of the liberal intelligentsia in declining to recognize that evil might operate without a rational motive. As a member of the liberal intelligentsia myself (how could I not be? I went to Sydney University) I try to be alert to its weak points, and that's one of them: we tend to believe that there is some natural state of justice to which political life would revert if only the conflicts between interest groups could be resolved. But whatever justice we enjoy arose from the conflicts between interest groups, and no such natural state of justice has ever existed. The only natural state is unjust: so unjust, and so savage, that we would rather not imagine it, even when, especially when, we are young and strong. Hence the defence mechanisms. Restricting perception so as to free us for action, they liberate us, but they are limiting, and sooner or later we have to examine the limitations, or the liberation will defeat itself. Facing reality ought to be an aim in life. It hardly ever is, and the pursuit of happiness can practically be defined as the avoidance of any such thing. But an aim in life it certainly ought to be. Just as long as somebody else does it.

*

Which brings us to the main subject, because Philip Hodgins faced life. He would have been the first to say that he faced it only because he was forced to, but he did it. He faced life when he faced death. For him, death lit life up. In his final time on earth he would sometimes deny this, but only in poems that lit life up like nobody else's. Lavishly talented, he would have been a major poet whatever the circumstances. If he had lived as long as his admired Goethe, he would probably have *been* Goethe. Hodgins might never have written *Faust*, but he almost certainly would have produced a vast body of work in which art and science interpenetrated each other as if all the modes of human knowledge came from the same impulse: the synthesis that Goethe was so keen on. That kind of scope needs an inexhaustible knack for putting things in an arresting manner to go with the comprehensive intensity of perception, and Hodgins had that compound gift.

Looking at it from the other direction, his circumstances would have made him emblematic whatever his talent. Put the two things together, however – the talent and the tragedy – and you've got something with a force of gravity strong enough to feel on your face. It's important to go on saying that, because his books look so slight. But they only look it. They weigh as if the language in them had been refined from pitchblende. Barely there between the finger and the thumb, when opened they put you into the world of physics whose heavy metals produced the rays that bombarded him in his illness. In his last book, sardonically called *Things Happen*, one of his last poems quotes Goethe in its title. The dying Goethe is said to have called for '*Mehr Licht, Mehr Licht*.' Hodgins' title is a translation: 'More Light, More Light'. Let me quote the first stanza. Usually when a lecturer says 'let me' he means he's going to do it anyway, but for some of what Hodgins wrote as he grappled, whether early or late, with the looming fact of his awful finale, I do feel I need your permission. I'm going to assume it, and use it as a blank cheque. When this is over, you can decide whether I've abused your trust. But enough of the pleasantries. There's no avoiding that first stanza any further. Here it comes.

> Sickly sunlight through the closed curtains
> that are white but much thicker than a sheet.
> Sunlight with all the life taken out of it,
> diminished but still there, an afterglow,
> like the presence of a friend who has died.
> You're lying still and yet you're moving fast.

Notice that by using the impersonal 'you' he shuts out the 'you' that you would use for yourself. You yourself are just reading, not even visiting. You are well. You might have seen a friend die, but you have a life you'll be going back to. Back out there in your life, the sunlight won't have all the life taken out of it. It will be ordinary, everyday sunlight. You'll be in it again. You won't be in here. But then, with the opening of the second stanza, it turns out that you might be staying. By now he has made that standard device, the impersonal 'you' that should mean only him, into a personal identification that includes the person he addresses. You are not excused after all.

> A nurse comes in to give the drip a shot.
> He opens the curtains in a moment of revelation.
> The sunlight is revitalized into an opportunist
> and instantly takes over the room like a brilliant virus,
> filling out even the places you had never thought to look.
> Your life is changed. The room is shown to you as it is,
> not as it dimly appeared to you all that time ago.
> You're moving fast and yet you're going nowhere.

And that's the whole poem. Critics shouldn't quote poems whole, I think. When they do, they turn themselves into anthologists. But we need to see this poem whole because otherwise we might miss the shift from the lifeless light that floods the first stanza to the brilliant, viral light that scorches the second, the light that turns out to be even more lifeless, the death light, like the white light Ivan Ilyich sees in Tolstoy's valedictory story, the dreadful story that tries to pretend Natasha Rostova never danced and Anna Karenina never loved. Seeing that shift of intensity, we can see the grim relationship between the poem and its title. When Goethe called for 'More light', he'd already had his share, and more than his share. He'd had enough of everything to get sick of it, which is not at all the same thing as being sick in advance. He'd had enough of fame and celebrity, for instance; enough to arrive at the accurate judgement that they don't add up to much. But it's still a lot more comfortable to arrive voluntarily at that conclusion after you've had them than to be forced to it before.

Goethe was dying of old age, which is another way of saying to die of life. What he wanted was more of what he'd spent three quarters of a century enjoying and describing. He just didn't want to leave. He could scarcely complain of never having arrived. Hodgins could. Hodgins was dying with most of his life unlived. Hodgins was dying of death. As it happened, the prognosis he had received when he was twenty-four, that he would live only three more years, was short by almost a decade. But when the end finally came he had still seen far too little of the light that left Goethe shouting for more after having bathed in it for a long lifetime. So behind the light that Hodgins makes so terrible in its truthful clarity there is the ordinary light of life that he had seen too little of. Most of the poems in the last section of *Things Happen* – the section is called 'Urban', and we can safely take it that every poem in it was written when he already knew he was a goner for sure – are, like 'More Light, More Light', terrible with the presence of the hospital's fluorescent illumination and the hum of the sad machines. I could quote details for an hour. I could quote them until you prayed for release. That was exactly what he was doing, and the words prove it.

> I watch the needle hovering over me.
> It's big. It goes in slowly and it hurts.

That's from 'Blood Connexions'. Even without reading the whole poem, you can see that the sexual connotations might be fully meant, thus to complete the work of turning the world upside down. Or try this, from 'Cytotoxic Rigor'.

> You vomit through surges of nausea and pain.
> And when there's nothing left to vomit you vomit again.

But here the critic, for once, *ought* to be an anthologist, because quoting fragments is unfair on both poet and audience. To quote fragments makes for a clumsily edited show-reel of horror, when in fact every poem is a complete film, and even when possessed by death is still full of life. The needle in 'Blood Connexions', for example, is wielded by a female nurse, with whom the narrator really does have a kind of blood connection, because both she and he had their origins in the same country, Ireland.

> The nurse unpacks a needle and a line.
> 'We're probably related,' she almost jokes,
> but wary of which side I'm on she looks
> me in the eye, just momentarily,
> a look that asks, 'Are your folks killing mine?'

One need hardly note that the poem's conventions of a romantic meeting are gruesomely transformed by the tools of intimacy. That's where the poem started: the dislocation was the inspiration. The nurse

> Undoes my catheter, makes a new connexion
> And pushes in the calming drug

But it is still a romance. It is still a determination to see the multiplicity of life, a refusal to withdraw into what would have been a very excusable solipsism, into a world bounded by the walls of a pillow when our head sinks into it. One or two of the poems in the last section don't mention his situation at all. There are postcard memories of his last trip abroad, to Venice. He is remembering, but if we assume that he is remembering with bitter regret, it can only be an assumption. There is no bitterness on the page. The poems read as if he were remembering his first delighted response. Browning arrived in Florence with no more joy than this.

> A vaporetto ducked across in front,
> taking the same date and same short route
> that Doges took for centuries
> on their way to hear the multi-choral choirs,
>
> while a pair of gondolas, as dark as submarines,
> headed down the Grand Canal,
> their prows curved up like the toes of slippers
> in a Hollywood oriental musical.

Eugenio Montale's gondolas slid in a dazzle of tar and poppies. Hodgins' gondolas are less carefree, but they still dance. I can tell you want more of those gondolas. You shall have them, because he wanted more of them too. He was sick, he knew he was sick, but he was so hungry to look, and to register what he saw.

> Below our window to the left
> about a dozen more of them
> were swaying in between thin crooked poles,
> neatly unattended and exposed,
>
> reminding me how some religions in the east
> expect that people entering a shrine
> should leave their shoes outside,
> as a mark of their respect.

From that, you would think he was going to live forever; or anyway you would think he thought so. And in fact we can stay in the same book, and merely go back a bit beyond the final section, to find magnificent poems that either fail to mention his fatal disease or else, even more remarkably, mention it as if he hadn't got it. A startling example on this point is 'A House in the Country', one of the boldest things he ever did, a poem that puts a house into world literature the way Pushkin did when he described the lights going out in the soul of Lensky. At the risk of rampant intertextuality, I'll quote the stanza presaging his final use of a further quotation that we now know he would forever make his own. But notice also what the stanza does not presage. Notice the effect that it could have employed but didn't. When we notice that, it will lead us to the most amazing thing about him. It has already been established, before this stanza unfolds, that the house is riddled by a subversive presence.

> I gazed at this miniature apocalypse
> of countless termites writhing in exposure,
> no doubt programmed to crave the opposite
> of Goethe, who had cried 'More light! More light!'
> and as the seconds dropped away as small
> and uniform as termites a feeling burrowed
> into me as bad as if I had cancer.

One 'as' after another, linked like a little chain of worry beads. How can he, of all people, be so definite about being indefinite? *As if I had cancer*. Well, we can be reasonably sure that the house has it. In the last line of the poem, the narrator is worried that for the house there might be no cure.

> I set off at a fast walk, worried about
> what was going on underneath my feet.

The house has it, but an intergalactic literary critic who stepped off a spaceship could be excused for deducing that the poet himself does not have it, or he would have written a different way. The intergalactic critic, however, would be deducing the wrong thing. At one stage I was myself the intergalactic critic, and I can remember all too well how, with regard to Hodgins' career as a poet, I got things exactly backwards. Stuck in my study in London, a long way from the Australian poetic action, I first noticed him in a little poem about a dam in the country. The poem popped up somewhere in the international poetic world: the *New Yorker* or some anthology.

(If you're serious about poetry, it's probably the best way of finding out what's really going on: when a poem hits you between the eyes even though you don't know anything about the person who wrote it, the chances are better that the person in question is the genuine article.) The rim of the dam featured a pair of ibises.

Two ibises stand on the rim like taps.

Immediately I reached the correct conclusion that Philip Hodgins had the talent to write anything. It was the only correct conclusion I was to reach for some time. By the time I read about Hodgins at length, in an essay by Les Murray now included in *A Working Forest*, Hodgins was nearing death. When I started to read Hodgins himself at length, I started in the middle and somehow convinced myself that his illness had snuck up on him, and had become a subject only towards the end, when he became aware of the threat. This was a conclusion easily reached from the seemingly untroubled richness of his central work. But it was the wrong conclusion in the biggest possible way. For a student of literature, the advantage of living abroad is that he is less likely to have his judgment pre-empted by gossip. The disadvantage is that there is always some gossip he ought to hear. Knowing about Hodgins' possible death sentence earlier wouldn't have altered my estimation of his qualities, but it would have drastically affected my appreciation of the way he brought them into action. Hodgins had known about his condition right from the beginning of his career as a poet. He had known that some periods of remission were the most he could hope for. That he had not made this his principal subject, or anyway the ostensible centre-line of his viewpoint, was an act of choice. This act of choice, I believe, must be called heroic, but before we call it that we should look at some of the results, as they are manifested in what he left behind at the start, and then in what he passed through before he returned to what he left behind, in a curving journey which contains a world.

His first volume, *Blood and Bone*, came out in 1986 and contained not only 'The Dam', which I had seen in isolation, but a cluster of poems less contemplative. In the long run, the dam and its tap-like ibises, with their effect of an Egyptian fresco discovered by flashlight, would set the poised tone for his central pastoralism. But in the first volume they were as uncharacteristic as an embrace in the middle of a battle. Most of the first poems were anguished reactions to the news the doctors had given him; news about his blood; news that gave him a new measure of time. The last three of the five tiny stanzas that make up the poem 'Room 1 Ward 10 West 23/11/83' give us a summary.

> I am attached
> to a dark
> bag of blood
> leaking near me
>
> I have time
> to choose the words
> I am
> likely to need
>
> At twenty-four
> there are many words
> and this one
> death

Though Hodgins probably did not mean us to, it is impossible for us not to think of the girl who gave her age in disbelief to the German engineer at Babi Yar as she was driven naked towards the pit. What is happening here is a wartime atrocity. Wartime atrocities happen in peacetime. Chance behaves like a homicidal maniac. It is one of Hodgins' messages, and it could have been his only message for the rest of his short career. He had the power of language to make it stick. His first book is full of moments like that. In 'Ontology' – a resonant title for someone whose existence has just been put into question – he collapses, or seems to collapse, into an inconsolable solipsism.

> The universe
> is going cold, there is no God,
> and thoughts of death have taken root
> in my intensifying bones.

He knows this is self-pity. He calls it that. He called a poem that, 'Self-pity', and put into it the pure expression of a purely personal emotion, thereby letting the rest of us taste its tears, if we dare to.

> But happiness has been serendipity. It
> happened in the ambulance on the way back
> from centrifuge. I sat up like a child
> and smiled at dying young, at all
> love's awfulness.

In the first line of 'The Cause of Death', a deadly wit got into his range of effects. 'Suddenly I am waiting for slow death'. Like the sudden sitting up and childish smile, the wit was a hint that he would find a kind of liberation in this prison. (Though Rilke was always pretty careful to keep his living conditions as comfortable as possible, the liberating prison was an idea he was fond of, so it is not strange that Hodgins was fond of Rilke, and cited him often.) But first Hodgins had to conjure the prison's stone walls and iron bars, and he went on doing it over and over. In 'Trip Cancelled' (and between the title and the first stanza we have already guessed why the trip was cancelled) he says:

> The words for death are all too clear.
> I write the poem dumb with fear.

How could he write the poem at all? And how could the poems be different from each other? In 'From County Down' he seemed to wonder that himself.

> My bad luck is to write the same poem every time.
> A sort of postcard poem
> from the rookery. *Timor mortis conturbat me.*
> I never wanted this.

We can be sure of that. But we can equally be sure that he'd seen a possibility. We might not have done, and this time by 'we' I mean I. To the extent that I know myself, I'm fairly sure that I would have given up. But Hodgins seems already to have had an inkling that he might have been handed a way back to his deepest memories if only he could keep concentrating. There are hints of this awareness even in 'Question Time', a poem that takes it for granted the clock will soon stop.

> No-one can say when.
> It's a bit like flying standby.

But there's the wit already, and at the end of the same poem is the hope that persists on surfacing through despair: the hope that something might be achieved even now.

> What you knew began with wonder
> on your father's farm
> and though it wouldn't be that good again
> you could have gone on so easily.

He never went on easily, but he did go on, into the great central period of his achievement that we can already see as one of the glories of late-twentieth-century Australian poetry. To a large extent generated by the rise of Australia to the position of an interconnected communications metropolis, a component of the global artistic hypermarket, one of the most remarkable multiple creative outbursts of modern times had the poetry of Philip Hodgins as part of its central cluster of events, and his poetry was much more pastoral than urban: it almost always had something to do with the farm. It was about a vanishing world, and it was written by a vanishing man. But in both cases, he found a way to keep the loss. One of the death poems, 'Walking Through the Crop', starts like a renunciation.

> It doesn't matter any more
> the way the wheat is shivering
> on such a beautiful hot day
> late in the afternoon, in Spring.

But it does matter, or he wouldn't be saying so. It's the writerly paradox that lies at the base of all poetry about despair, and in that paradox the young Hodgins has just received the most intense possible education. The death poems went on into his second volume, brilliantly called *Down The Lake With Half A Chook*: I say 'brilliantly' because there could have been no more economical commitment to the Vernacular Republic than to give a book of verse a title so *echt* Australian that it would need to be translated even into English. 'The Drip' is the most terrible of all the needle poems. It registers what happens when the needle comes out during the night: damage to the damage.

> The tape and gauze
> across my inside arm
> are lying there
> like dirty clouds,
> and what is underneath
> is like a gorgeous sunrise.

This is beauty as dearly bought as it can get. It would have been no surprise if Hodgins had stuck to these themes until the end, no matter how long the end might have been postponed by remissions. Most artists don't know what a winning streak is when they are on it. A few know how to follow where it leads, and only a very few, the great ones, knowing exactly what it is, get out early and look for something else. Somewhere about the time that his projected three years were up and he found himself still alive, Hodgins expanded his range into the unexpected, and began talking as if his memories of his upbringing on the farms were going to accompany him into his old age. He knew they couldn't, but he talked as if they would. 'A Farm in the High Country' is typical of his poems in this manner: typical, that is, in being pretty much a masterpiece.

> And it was easy not to notice that black snake
> sunning itself on top of some worn-out tyres
> until it melted off quickly like boiling rubber
> and flowed through a stretch of dry grass
> with the sound of the grass beginning to burn

From here until his final phase in hospital, you just have to get used to being astonished. Les Murray, himself the convener and consolidator of the post-World War II movement that surrounded Australian poetry with the vocabulary of the working land, as opposed to using the land for a mere backdrop, was clearly right to salute Hodgins as a pastoral poet without equal. The only way to evoke what Hodgins did would be to invoke it all: to become such an anthologist that one would quote almost the whole of the central hundred pages of *New Selected Poems*, which would include nearly everything in the twin touchstone single volumes of Hodgins' main manner, the booklets called *Animal Warmth* and *Up On All Fours*. There is poetry here in such abundance and intensity that the word 'great' is not out of place: in fact it refuses to be excluded. Moments of incandescent registration are so stellar in their profusion that he gives the impression of having held constellations in his hands.

Some limiting statements can be made, and if they can they should: Hodgins himself, after all, had no love for dreamland. When Hodgins rhymed solidly, he gained from it. But he seems to have found solid rhyming meretriciously neat. Deciding that, he should have avoided near-rhymes. They draw too much attention to their rattling fit even in song lyrics, and on the page, in poems, they hurt the eye along with the ear. With reference to the longest of his longer poems, the verse novel presents difficulties which make titanic demands on the poet. Murray set the fashion for the form with *The Boys Who Stole the Funeral*, and brought it to a peak with *Fredy Neptune*. He made it an Australian form, in fact: by now it is part of our literary landscape. But no amount of tactical diversion can disguise the fact that in a verse novel the characters are all saturated with the poet's mental acuity, and so all end up thinking like him, no matter how unsophisticated they are made to sound. Hodgins' verse novel, *Dispossessed*, was written at about the same time as *Fredy Neptune* but was nothing like as developed in its internal action. As much as all the others of Hodgins' rural poems put together, *Dispossessed* concentrates attention on the physical existence of the rural life that is on its way out of the world. But nothing can stop all the characters turning into poets, simply because there is so much poetic perception going on around them. Nor does the blank verse do enough to mark the local outbreaks of poetry as parts of a single poem. The book would work just as well, just as poetically, if it were prose, and I seriously suggest that somebody one day might take the dare and print it that way.

More heretically still, let me suggest that Hodgins' *terza rima* mini-epic 'The Way Things Were', one of the two big showpieces of his first great central collection *Animal Warmth*, suffers the same fate as MacNeice's *Autumn Sequel*. Marvellous though it is in its remembered observations, 'The Way Things Were' drags its feet – as, indeed, does its companion piece 'Second Thoughts on the *Georgics*', which like *Dispossessed* is cast in a blank verse all too blank. But 'Second Thoughts on the *Georgics*', whose poet can be commended for getting his hands far dirtier than Virgil ever did, merely makes too much of getting along: it doesn't irritate while doing so. 'The Way Things Were', I am afraid, does. Even MacNeice, the supreme verse technician, gave up on the idea of sustaining the *terza rima* in English with solid rhymes. But instead of reverting to the dextrously mixed and switched classical metres of its masterly predecessor *Autumn Journal*, he pushed on with the *terza rima* just to be different, and used half-rhymes just to sustain it. The result, *Autumn Sequel*, seems like a structure only to the eye, and Hodgins' rhymes in his *terza rima* piece have the same fault compounded, because they are even more loose than MacNeice's. Often a single consonant is the only thing that a triad of rhyming words have in common. I was quite a way into the poem before I realized that a gesture was being made at the *terza rima*. I thought he wasn't rhyming at all.

And in that case it would have been better if he hadn't. The truth was that he hardly needed to. Most poets lose out when they abandon overt form but Hodgins was one of the lucky few that gain. His ear was so sound that he could develop a seductively articulated texture of echo over any group of unrhymed lines. His villanelles and other systematically repetitive forms got in the road of this quality, and suggested that their main value was to help the poem get done. Flatness in Hodgins would not be so obvious if his peaks weren't so numerous: put in geographical terms, his main output would look like one of those Chinese landscape paintings in which the multiple upsurge of pointed mountains looks too extravagant to believe, until someone who has been there tells you it's all true. Anything in Hodgins that sounds willed, or manufactured to a template, is competing with poems like 'Rabbit Trap'. But the only poems like 'Rabbit Trap' are his. 'Rabbit Trap' comes from heaven. Listen to how the last stanza starts in wit and proceeds through a Montaigne-like detached sadness into a sadness no more detached than that of St Francis of Assisi.

> So sensitive and yet it is unfeeling,
> always reacting badly to slightest
> pressure on the blood-stained centre plate,
> the stage where little tragedies are played out
> while back in some warm spot the mother's young
> stare out as the world closes in on them.

Almost demanding to go unnoticed in the middle of that sumptuous progression is the linking of the trap's centre plate to a theatrical stage. Pause for a moment and you will see the trap's laid-out surrounding jaws as an auditorium. But he moves you to the next moment. Giving you more than you can dwell on at the time is one of the ways that the master poet declares himself. But I could quote from *Animal Warmth* and *Up On All Fours* until the cows come home. I could quote until the cows came home about the cows not coming home. In the Australian countryside according to Hodgins every brutal thing that can happen to an animal happens on the page. Clearly most of this uncooked vividness was remembered from childhood, but in his mature years, with the needle of nemesis always at the edge of his vision, he reinforced his memories with plenty of hands-on experience. As his football poems remind us, his illness didn't stop him being intensely physical: or anyway, that's the way he makes it sound. In the poems, he stabs pigs, dispatches wounded rabbits, watches the calf being born from an inch away. He watches afterbirth being eaten and practically gives you a taste. Except for the squeal of the boiling yabbie – there is a PhD to be written about the role of the yabbie in the poetry of Philip Hodgins, so let's hope nobody ever writes it – nothing turns his stomach. Brutality is the price of authenticity. The price of country produce that tastes of something is that an inescapable violence occurs behind it. There is violence even in the milk.

> The sweetest milk
> was lucerne in the spring

But if the cows eat the wrong stuff they bloat, and they don't come home.

> It's always a blow to lose a cow that way –
> squeezed to death from the inside,
> hugely rounded with legs jutting everywhere
> like some washed-up unexploded mine.

Those lines are from 'Second Thoughts on the *Georgics*', which I just finished saying made slow progress in its narrative drive. So it does, but one of the reasons is that it is packed with observations as good as that. The reader has to deal with almost a monotony of quality. In Hodgins' poetry about the land, you must get used to the way he brings everything out in high relief, a democracy of vividness as if the truth-telling particularity of a painter like, say, Menzel had been carried out with the fantastic allure of the Douanier Rousseau.

The narrator is always going where you don't particularly want to look, and looking hard: into the guts of a rotting sheep, into the penile lustre of a rutting bull. Not even the quality of the expression can make most of this delightful. But it is made valuable. These are tougher laws than the ones we live by in the denatured urban world. The country is a world with its own rules, and the rules are severe: even the people can die like the animals. In one poem a little boy disappears into a grain silo.

The question will always remain, now, of whether, when the little boy is sucked to his death amongst the nourishing grain, we are meant to think of the author, arbitrarily expunged in the midst of life. Was he thinking of himself? How could he not be? And yet surely the mark of his main poetry is that he is not asking for a biographical interpretation: that he is doing everything he can to avoid it. He is trying to say that real life, country life, is like this anyway; you don't have to be fatally ill to find it unsentimental and ruthless; it has those characteristics by its nature, because it is close to nature. This quarrel will go on. If I am afraid of anything in Hodgins' future, it is that he might be as much debated over as enjoyed. But he won't be *more* debated over than enjoyed, because there is too much to enjoy, and the enjoyment is too intense. It will be his immediate appeal that will lead to the annotated editions for future use in colleges across the English-speaking world. There will be footnotes to explain that 'galvo' was once Australian short-hand for galvanized iron, and the generation after next might need to be told that a 'ute' was the SUV of the past, when there were dirt roads. But Hodgins' poetry will say what the dirt roads were, and how they sounded through the floor of the vehicle.

> and there is the sound of a quarrel
> beneath you.
> Most of it is muffled and deep-throated
> but there is also a top register
> of small sharp stones
> pinging off the metal as they shoot up.
> You don't get this variety with a sealed surface.

No, you don't. On behalf of his country upbringing, Hodgins defied, as Les Murray did, the inexorable expansion of the sealed surface. There is a connection between agrarian conservatism and peeled-eyed poetic realism that can be traced through Prussia, the American south and Argentina all the way into recent times. A last-ditch stand by literati who know how to dig the ditch themselves, it has little to do with the traditional opposition of left and right. Agrarian poets, indeed, are likely to find an even bigger enemy on the right than on the left, because it is the capitalist imperative of industrial efficiency that denatures the country. And it does, after all, make life in the country more bearable for the few who remain to work their land. Most of the inventions that brought the efficiency about were devised by their forefathers, who, even when not yet dispossessed by the global reach of improvement, were already worn to a frazzle by the rigours of the life and wanted something better for their children. (One of the reasons I would like to see *Dispossessed* restored to the status of a current book is that it so bravely tells the sad truth about how a losing battle can breed narrow minds.) Something better came, but it was more bland. When everybody has enough to eat, hardly anybody cares any more about how the food gets to the table. The salt loseth its savour. Wherewith shall it be salted? From an historic dilemma comes an artistic question. It is an historic force that Hodgins' sort of poetry braces itself against.

Hence, perhaps, some of the poetic strength. But in his case the fighting courage goes immeasurably deeper, and it is at this point that I must switch into that comfortable mode of peroration by which I get the centre of attention away from him and back to me. His courage I can't measure or even identify. All I can do is comfort myself that it was only one of the factors in the recognition that came to him before his death. If valour, whether moral or physical – and his, of course, was both – were the sole criterion for recognition, most of us would have to give up on the idea, and stick with what celebrity we can get. I hasten to add that I haven't quite given up on celebrity either. It can help. Perhaps I would have had a lot more trouble getting my poems published if I had not had my face on television. It always seemed to me that it scarcely helped at all, but I might have thought that because, with being published as with being in love, rejection is more memorable than acceptance.

It isn't always to the worthless that celebrity draws attention. The world of mass enthusiasm is much more like a pure market than like a public relations campaign. In Britain, a touchingly vulnerable creature called Posh Spice has defied our expectations by remaining married to the footballer David Beckham for all these months, but she hasn't defied the law of supply and demand: she will always sell more newspapers than records, because the public, although it will read anything about a permanently pouting young woman with the voice of a moth, refuses to be fooled about the music it listens to. Completely to manage the public's taste is an ambition open only to totalitarian societies, not to free ones, and in fact not even classical communism could manage it: the Beatles still broke through. There was something I might have said about Madonna earlier on that I must say now, merely to be just: she once really got the youngsters excited, and might even have done some good. A friend recently sent me a collection of French songs sung by Carla Bruni, who is apparently celebrated for being the sort of well-connected and well-constructed young supermodel that Mick Jagger spends hours on the treadmill in order to pursue successfully. Well, good luck to him, because he would certainly be right in her case. She sings beautiful songs beautifully. If she hadn't first been a celebrity, I might never have recognized that, so the two things are bound together.

Most of the more off-putting aspects of the abundant West arise from its freedoms. The first thing we can be sure of about a free society is that it will be teeming and throbbing with things we don't like. We live in Luna Park, not Plato's Republic, and artists should be grateful that they have been given such variety to be creative about. There have been, and always will be, plenty of despots ready to give them a lot less. So welcome to the crazy house. But it does become more and more apparent that we will have to reinforce the foundations even as the edifice shakes with the urgent vigour of its productivity. It might be as difficult as getting new reinforcing rods into concrete that is being squeezed from within by the expansive oxidization of the old ones. Recognition is just such a reinforcing rod. Unequivocally, recognition is a proper aim in life. But just because it is so obviously worthy, there is no reason to think the young won't get the point. Already they find it cool to know the name that everybody else doesn't know, and there would be no credibility in that unless the unknown names were good for some-thing, even if only for an even more unintelligible version of gangsta rap. What I did to get this medal with Philip Hodgins' name on it – this outstanding emblem of recognition in a country which has so spontaneously developed an outstanding literature – never made me famous while I was doing it. As a poet, I spent two thirds of my career without even a reputation. Receiving this award, I feel like someone who has run the whole race invisible and popped into sight at the finishing line. Well, that fits. To be recognized means to be reassured that you were right to pursue a course that had no immediate rewards, and got in the road of activities that had. Poetry is something I gave at least part of my life to: a fact on which I often preened myself, at least in private. Now, to remind me that I had things easy, I have been honoured in the name of a man who gave his whole life to it, and his death as well. So the honour seems disproportionate; but I suppose an honour ought to. When a Roman general returning from his conquests abroad was awarded a triumph, a special herald rode in the chariot with him through the cheering city to whisper in his ear and remind him that he was made of dust and shadows. The occasional general no doubt said: 'Bugger off, I've had this coming for years.' At least with this triumph, with a name like Philip Hodgins on the laurel wreath, no recipient is in danger of saying that.

Australian Book Review, September 2003

Postscript

Australia figures large in this collection, and not just because, as I grow older, the country of my birth becomes steadily more important in my memory. Australia figures large because Australia is getting larger. Measured by population, it is a far smaller country than it looks on the map, but no country of its size has a comparable cultural influence on the international scale. Because Australia's busy expatriates get an unfair amount of journalistic attention, it becomes harder to remember that it's the creativity within the nation's borders that counts most, and provides the basis for everything achieved abroad. Joan Sutherland learned to sing in Sydney, and the post-war expatriate writers have done well because they were well schooled before they sailed. For decades I harboured the delusion that Sydney Technical High School had never taught me anything technical, until I at last realized that the enforced inculcation of English grammar and syntax had given me a set of constructional skills fit to annihilate twelve thousand miles of distance, and thus help me to build a career in Britain in the same way that British engineers once built bridges in Africa. Welcome to Australia's share of cultural imperialism, the imperialism that really works. In that regard, it was a duty as well as an honour to pay tribute to Philip Hodgins, whose poetry will probably never be published 'overseas' – the word that used to haunt Australian cultural life but which is now, thankfully, sinking into a long overdue neutrality of use. All serious readers of the English language, if they can, will come to Australia eventually, and when they do, they can read him there. Otherwise they can order his wonderful *New Selected Poems* from Amazon, and it will bring his hot landscape to where they live even if their windows look out on nothing but frozen tundra.

Exporting the culturally adventurous and importing them on the plane back, Australia is now joined to the world in the best possible way, by what it admires and by what is admired about it – a reciprocal contact that makes isolation a thing of the rapidly retreating past. With Australian Wagnerians visiting Bayreuth and German Wagnerians visiting Adelaide, there is no longer any cultural border worth bothering about. Which doesn't mean that a political border is without importance. On the contrary: the more the nation prospers, the more rancour it is likely to arouse, even within itself. Rancour from within, by a familiar process, is too often ready to excuse rancour from without. Australian intellectuals, taken as a class, have a tendency to blame their own country for being targeted for destruction by every disaffected person in the world who suspects that his own compatriots might like to live there. But on the whole the Australian population would prefer to elect the kind of government that will ask transients to unpack any luggage that presents a suspect silhouette to the airport scanning machine. On the way back to England, my cabin-baggage holdall did. Informed that I was carrying an unidentifiable oval metal object, I didn't know what the security officer was talking about. Had somebody planted a bomb on me? When I unpacked the bag, the mysterious article lay revealed. It was the Philip Hodgins Memorial Medal.

POLANSKI AND THE PIANIST

Roman Polanski's new film *The Pianist* is a work of genius on every level, except, alas, for the press-pack promotional slogan attributed to the director himself. '*The Pianist* is a testimony to the power of music, the will to live, and the courage to stand against evil.' If he actually said it, he flew in the face of his own masterpiece, which is a testimony to none of those things. In the Warsaw ghetto, the power of music, the will to live and the courage to stand against evil added up to very little, and *The Pianist* has the wherewithal to respect that sad fact and make sense of it. In the Warsaw ghetto, what counted was luck, and the luck had to be very good. The odds were almost impossible to beat. For the Nazis, that was the whole idea. To sum up his story in a sound bite, Polanski would have done better to borrow the two words everyone remembers from one of his previous triumphs: 'It's Chinatown.'

In *Chinatown* the bad guys did what they wanted, and so they do in *The Pianist*. The central story is about a survivor, the famous young musician Wladyslaw Szpilman. At a critical moment, his talent saves him. If this had been the only message, the film would not even have had the merits of *Schindler's List*. Steven Spielberg did his best to stave off the uplift, but inevitably he was stuck with a denial of what Primo Levi said was the real story of the Holocaust, which was not about anybody's survival, even his: the real story was about the drowned, not the saved. If Polanski had compounded the same fault by suggesting that a gift for playing Chopin could get you a free pass, he would have been in the same case as Spielberg only worse. But in fact he does an even better job than Spielberg of making sure that in watching the lifeboat we don't forget the ocean of annihilation it is trying to cross. At the end of *The Pianist* you would need to be very dense to think that Szpilman, who lived to play the piano again, had managed to do so by any mechanism except blind chance.

Spielberg offset his story of the saved by two main devices: the symbolic device of the little girl in the red coat – the only splash of colour in a black and white film – and the purely realistic device, employed with unprecedented verisimilitude, of showing the scope of the crime through violent incident. In Spielberg's camp, a Jewish woman tells the guards that they are mismanaging the construction of a new building. The Nazis agree with her suggestions but shoot her anyway, for having spoken. The incident stands out for its poisoned richness of implication. In Polanski's ghetto, such incidents arrive one after the other. They are each as powerful, and what is more they join up seamlessly, in a continuity of horror that would keep your hands over your eyes if your hands could move from the armrests of your seat. In *Schindler's List* we have to imagine how the little girl in the red coat goes to her doom; which leaves the possibility that we might not imagine it. In *The Pianist*, the little boy trying to wriggle back through a hole in the ghetto wall after a foraging expedition on the outside perishes right in front of your eyes. Szpilman is trying to pull the boy through the hole to safety. On the other side of the wall, the guards are kicking the boy to pulp from behind.

By the time Szpilman pulls him through, the boy is dead. Szpilman's sensitive face (in actuality, which he might have trouble getting back to after this, it belongs to Adrien Brody) registers the shock of an offence that goes beyond injustice. Throughout the film his face is an instrument for registering shock: first the shock of incredulity, and then, gradually but steadily, its decline into shock as a steady state, where not even the worst outrage is beyond belief. The screenplay is at its subtle best when the trapped victims are tricked by their civilized past into giving irrelevant responses to the unimaginably barbaric present. People keep saying 'It's disgraceful.' The words are comically inadequate, and that's their point.

Levi described the paralysed reaction – the stunned absence of reaction – of people bred to gentility being hit in the face for the first time in their lives. In *The Pianist*, Szpilman's father is hit in the face for walking on the same footpath as the SS. He still doesn't get it, and has to be instructed to walk in the gutter. Frank Finlay does a typically solid job of impersonating a decent man who, had he been capable of slyness, might have figured out the advisability of walking in the gutter before they told him to. But Polanski soon proves that no amount of cleverness can outfox the wolves. In the ghetto, the only smart thing left to do was join the Jewish police. Polanski is brilliant at not shirking this crucial issue. You can see how it happened, and are easily persuaded that you might have made the same choice. (A decent impulse might even have helped you make it, by convincing you that you could be useful at the right moment – and indeed it was a Jewish policeman who saved Szpilman at the very doorway of the boxcar that would have taken him to the gas chamber.) It is a pity that we are not shown the Jewish police being loaded on to the last train out, by which time most of them had realized that their complicity had bought them only a postpone-ment. But Szpilman is in hiding on the outside by then, and his viewpoint rules the movie, so he does not see the dupes being shipped off.

Duping them had been one of the Nazis' chief pleasures, because dreaming up new moral dilemmas was a Nazi sport. The idea was to create a world in which nothing a Jew could do was right. It had been so since the Nazis came to power, when among the first things they did was to concoct regulations that would face the Jews with impossible choices. Victor Klemperer's diaries give us a comprehen-sive survey of these. Punished for staying and punished for trying to leave, punished for not arriving at work and punished for boarding the tram to get there, they were reduced to neurosis. Klemperer walked more and more often to the funerals of people who had committed suicide. Speculations about when the Final Solution began are essentially a waste of breath. The massacre started in 1933. The only reason nobody noticed was that the first victims died by their own hand.

As a mechanism for duplicating hell on this side of the tomb, the Warsaw ghetto was a construction of diabolical ingenuity. Polanski is ingenious enough to match it, and show it for what it was: a torture garden whose inhabitants would become fully acquainted with a fate worse than death before they were taken away to vanish in the comparative mercy of the *Vernichtungslager*. From the view-point of the truly dedicated Jew-baiter, the drawback of the *Aktion Reinhard* extermination camps was that too many people died too quickly. Treblinka was particularly reprehensible in that regard. Auschwitz is more famous now because the gas chambers and crematoria had holding camps attached and a few people lived to tell the tale. Treblinka was a fast-track from the arrival platform to the chimney: nobody came out. For the sort of fanatic who thought that the Jews needed an education in despair, it was some compensation to know that the ghetto's atmosphere, a cocktail of fear and hope, could not be breathed for a single hour without a month of torment. Polanski breathed it in Krakow when he was a boy. We can see now that what it did to his heart and brain affected all his films on the way to this one.

But not even *Death and the Maiden* has the awful force of this one. In its masterly command of detail, weak points are hard to find. A possible one is the casting for physical appearance. Szpilman and his cultivated family might possibly have looked like film stars, but there was no need, even in filmic terms, for the SS to be such a bunch of porcine plug-uglies. They were certainly swine in real life, if you can call their life that: but here they look as if they have been raised for their bacon. The facts were otherwise. In the early days, before it started to run out of home-grown all-Aryan manpower, the SS would recruit nobody who had even one filled tooth. They were villains, but they didn't necessarily look it. Here, the SS rank and file have fat necks to fit their behaviour, which rather misses the deeper point. Against this, however, it should be said that one of the most blood-curdling acts of arbitrary violence in the movie is the casual work of a young man who looks like the offspring of Leni Riefenstahl and an Arno Breker male model after a torrid night in the pine forest. Appearing out of the blue, he selects half a dozen victims from a work detail, makes them lie face down on the pavement, and shoots them one after the other with his pistol, calmly reloading to shoot the last one. He looks magnificent doing so. You can quite see why he believes himself racially superior to anybody on earth.

The excessive good looks of another German might be less appropriate, or too appropriate: the Good German who hears Szpilman play the piano and spares his life. As Captain Wilm Hosenfeld, Thomas Kretschmann is better-looking than Klaus Maria Brandauer when young, and has the warm, deep voice of Chancellor Schroeder in boudoir mode. But it might have been true, and Hosenfeld almost certainly looked heaven-sent to Szpilman, by then only an inch from death. What we miss from the compassionate Captain, however – and we can't have it, because he would have had to supply it himself, thus straining credibility beyond measure –

is an outline of the miraculous run of luck by which it happened to be him who walked in on the huddled fugitive. Hosenfeld is a *Wehrmacht* officer, not SS, but an absence of lightning flashes on the collar was no guarantee of an absence of icy splinters in the heart. Although some of its generals later on saved their skins by pretending differently, the regular army was always well aware of what the murder squads were getting up to in the back areas. Very few *Wehrmacht* officers would have failed to turn Szpilman in, no matter how well he played Chopin. (And at his life-or-death audition, incidentally, and on a piano strangely in tune after months in the dust, he plays with the mighty force of Sviatoslav Richter: a rather unlikely show of strength for someone weak from hunger.) Hosenfeld just happened to be one of the very few. Filmically, there was no way to show this fact except with a subtitle: THE ODDS AGAINST THIS WERE A ZILLION TO ONE. It was a fact, but the fact remains an unfathomable mystery, although there are very good reasons, after the unfortunate success of Daniel Goldhagen's book *Hitler's Willing Executioners*, to reassert the ragged truth against a neat myth, and insist, by any legitimate means possible, that eliminationist anti-Semitism was far from universal among the German population when Hitler came to power. At the last election that gave him the whip hand, 56 per cent of the electorate failed to vote for him. It would be a bad case of wishful thinking, however, to believe that all those people afterwards went on being anti-Nazi to the point that they would break the law. The law against harbouring Jews was the biggest law you could break, with death as the penalty. Hosenfeld really did break it, but the film finds no means of telling us that an even more unlikely event than Szpilman surviving to meet Hosenfeld was Hosenfeld arriving to meet Szpilman. It was something that could only happen in the movies: the reason why the movie was eventually made. A more typical Polish story was that of Bruno Schulz, the greatly talented writer and painter who was protected by SS officers in the Drohobycz ghetto while he painted murals: protected, that is, until one of them shot him. No movie there. Less filmable still was the story of Arthur Rubinstein, who was born in Lodz but didn't clap eyes on its ghetto until the war was over. He had been practising his art elsewhere: the only guarantee that the power of music and the will to live might prevail.

Another weak point was probably unavoidable as long as Szpilman's eyeline defined the scope. Quite apart from Szpilman, who got to play the piano only in a restaurant for the ghetto's black-market plutocracy – another embarrassment that the film doesn't shirk – the ghetto was rich in musicians who played for all comers. Chamber music groups kept on giving concerts right up until their trains left. Modern Germany's greatest literary critic Marcel Reich-Ranicki tells the story in his autobiography. Many times he crossed the same bridge that dominates the film, the bridge between the main ghetto and its smaller annexe. People would cross that bridge just to hear music. Since the bridge could not be crossed without risk of a beating, the consolation they sought must have been magnetic in its attraction. It would have been good to see some of that, if only to offset our irrepressible trust that Szpilman's music might have had powers to soothe the savage breast. The chamber music in the Warsaw ghetto would undoubtedly have delighted Mengele and Heydrich, both of them serious music lovers. But it would not have changed their minds. That was the power of music: spiritually great but practically zero. Like the musicians in Auschwitz and Theresienstadt, the musicians in the Warsaw ghetto went to the ovens. Had we seen them go, we would have had yet more evidence of how remarkable it was that Szpilman did not, and that Hosenfeld made sure he did not. But films can't show us the whole of history. They can only hope not to distort it, and this one tries commendably hard not to.

One last possible flaw could have been fatal if left unattended. When the insurrection of April 1943 is being planned, one of the younger characters, correctly told that the rebels will have no chance, says that at least they will die with honour. No doubt pared back under the rigours of production, Ronald Harwood's script is nevertheless a work of moral subtlety at the high level we have come to expect from him on these subjects. Though crippled in the theatre by the extent of what it could not show but only say, his play about Furtwängler touched on every point that mattered, and his script for *Operation Daybreak*, the film about Heydrich's assassination, is one of the most considerable works in the genre. (If only the film had been as good as the script: but Timothy Bottoms as a Czech commando gives you an idea of what *The Pianist* might have been like if it had been made under the Hollywood conditions that the self-exiled Polanski is supposedly longing to return to. Think Brad

Pitt with a prosthetic nose.) Harwood must have known that on this point about death with honour he was courting glibness. But the visible action – and no doubt he was heavily engaged there too – protects the truth. Except as a gesture, the revolt fails terribly, giving us cause to remember that although the few combatants did indeed die with honour, the many non-combatants who died previously did not do so with dishonour. The dishonour all belonged to their persecutors.

On this point, as so often when the Holocaust is in question, one of the main opponents of sanity is our own fantasy. In the wishful thinking that saps our thinking, we can't help wondering why all those obedient victims didn't gang up at a given signal and fight back with their bare hands, as we would have. In our minds we have mighty powers, like Steven Seagal: our hands are deadly weapons. But the hands of the murderers weren't bare: they were holding rifles and machine pistols, and those really were deadly weapons. It is a tribute to the film, and a service to historical truth, that the revolt in the Warsaw ghetto is kept in perspective. In Sobibor, the breakout was led by Russian soldiers who knew what they were doing. In the ghetto, the insurgents were mainly untrained civilians. They took a heartening number of their tormentors with them, but that was it. The issue was already decided before the flame-throwers were brought in, and the tanks soon had nothing left to shoot at. Hannah Arendt took account of the uprising in Sobibor but thought she was being realistic when she said that the place to resist was in the ghetto. If only she had been right. It was too late even in the ghetto. It had been too late even before the Nazis came to power. It was too late when Hitler, still a long way from the Reichstag, preached extermination and got away with it, because the police of the Weimar Republic were dissuaded from acting against him. From then on, the Jews of Germany and of all the countries that Hitler later invaded had no chance of stopping what would happen to them, and the majority of the German people that voted against him had no chance of stopping it either. It was Chinatown.

Postscript

Before deciding to direct it himself, Stephen Spielberg offered *Schindler's List* to Polanski. In press accounts, Polanski is usually reported to have turned the job down because he believed that the lasting turbulence of his childhood memories would have affected his ability to work. Perhaps so, but another explanation might be that he didn't want to tell a story about the saved, when the real story was about the drowned. He might have been able to modify the script towards an even more intense realism of detail, while subtracting some of the uplift that marks almost every Spielberg project no matter how dedicated to a sense of tragedy. (I say 'almost' because Spielberg showed, with *Band of Brothers*, that he could seize the opportunity offered by a television series to steer clear of the hokum that marred its big-screen progenitor, *Saving Private Ryan*.) As a director, Polanski had always been able to impose his bleak vision on producers who wanted something more cheerful. For the closing scene of *Chinatown*, even the writer, Robert Towne, wanted virtue to win out – a conclusion that would have suited the studio. Polanski made sure that malevolence carried the day. But he would have been hard-pressed to do the same with *Schindler's List*, which is essentially a neo-Talmudic tale about a group of people being saved by a benevolent intervention: true to the facts, but misleadingly consoling about their context. (It should be said in haste that they were Jewish intellectuals who first and most firmly pointed out that this new Talmud of divine interventions and miraculous escapes was a blasphemy against historical experience, and not just against the scriptural tradition.) The story of *The Pianist* was about just one man being saved by a sheer fluke while everyone else was murdered. Here was a narrative much more congruent with Polanski's view, and he was able to bring all his unsentimental skill to making the most of it on screen.

FANTASY IN THE WEST WING

In America, fans of *The West Wing* are called Wingnuts. There are about twenty million of them. British Wingnuts are fewer but even more dedicated, because in order to view the programme when it goes to air, they first have to find it. Channel 4, perhaps to ward off accusations of abject subservience to American cultural imperialism, moves the programme unpredictably around the schedules in order to keep the viewing figures as low as possible. The irony here is that the White House of *The West Wing*'s fictional President, Jed Bartlet, and the White House of the actual President, George W. Bush, have little in common beyond their colour scheme and architecture. A different language is spoken in each. In *The West Wing* version of the West Wing the frantically energetic inhabitants speak modern American English in its highest state of colloquial eloquence. Crafted in the Bush administration's West Wing, a holding area for somnambulists, any speech by the President sets a standard so low that Donald Rumsfeld is elevated to the oratorical status of Edmund Burke. When the Founding Fathers were addressing the question of a national language, German and Hebrew were both considered. After they finally realized that the language in which they were discussing the matter was probably the best candidate, English won by default. Bush and the rest of the boys make you wonder how it happened. How long does it take them to wish each other good morning? Condoleezza Rice, whose gift for languages includes her own, must feel like an epidemiologist dealing with a mass outbreak of lock-jaw.

From that angle, the actual West Wing is a wildly improbable fiction. The fictional West Wing is realistic, but only in the sense of reminding you that realism is the most refined form of manufactured drama. Just how refined, in this case, is best studied by viewing the episodes one after the other. To ease the frustration of waiting for Channel 4 to peel back the camouflage on the latest instalment, the trainee Wingnut can purchase the whole of the first season on video or, even better, on DVD: twenty-two chapters of the story in a single glorious wodge. The second season will shortly be forthcoming: I haven't seen the DVDs yet, but I have been granted access to a set of time-coded tapes. So even as the third season intermittently unfolds on broadcast television, I have been able to wallow in the forty-four chapters of the first two seasons with full benefit of replay. Sometimes I watch half a dozen episodes in an evening that stretches on into the night, like Bayreuth with snappier music. Things that struck me as merely wonderful a couple of years ago are now revealed as miraculous. On a one-time basis, a typical episode is so absorbing, and flies by at such a speed, that the viewer has no time to ask how it was put together. You don't wonder how they did it. When you start seeing how they did it, you *really* wonder how they did it.

To start with, there is the dialogue. Aaron Sorkin conceived the series and supervises every line of every episode, even when he does not compose its basic story. He has absorbed the whole tradition of high-speed, counterpointed dialogue since it first emerged in 1930s screwball comedy and later on spread into drama in both the cinema and television. Before *The West Wing*, it was not unknown for straight drama to be accelerated by comic timing: Sipowicz in *NYPD Blue* would never have talked that way if his writers had not grown up watching *Sergeant Bilko*. But Sorkin has pushed the heritage to such a culmination that there is no possible further development except decadence. Even as it stands, the complexity of the exposition verges on the incomprehensible, especially if you don't know much about the American political system. (Since there aren't all that many Americans who know about it either, in its homeland the show is widely recommended by schoolteachers as a painless civics lesson.) Sometimes you have to wait for half an episode to find out that the two different sets of initials bandied about in the first scene stand for a bill and a committee that will meet each other in the last. But usually a quick reference to the Second Amendment will be expanded later on by an argument about the desirability of banning private guns, and the argument will be illustrated by somebody getting shot.

The otherwise all-inclusive talk has only one conspicuous

absence: obscenity. In the film *Wag the Dog*, David Mamet's enjoyable dialogue had the advantage that the characters were allowed to swear. *The West Wing* makes you wonder whether that is much of an advantage at all. Unlike *The Sopranos*, which as an HBO cable product enables anybody in the cast to say anything at all – try to imagine a sentence from Tony that doesn't include a four-letter word – *The West Wing* is financed and first broadcast by the NBC network and therefore rules out any swear word you can think of except 'arse', which scarcely sounds like a swear word at all when spelled and pronounced in the American way, as a perissodactyl mammal of the horse family. (Here I attempt to echo the relentless pedantry of President Bartlet, an affliction from which President Bush is notably free.) When characters refer to each other or themselves as being pissed, it doesn't even mean they are drunk. It is merely the American way of saying they are pissed off with each other, which they frequently are, even if they are pursuing the same objective. Usefully deprived of profanity as an easy shock effect, the vigour of the dialogue still depends on conflict, and thus further depends on an American cultural feature strange to us.

*

In the British version of the English language, we will go out of our way to avoid verbal confrontation even with enemies. The American version thrives on verbal confrontation even between friends. The people of *The West Wing* all adore each other, and you can tell by the way they find quarrel in a straw. The quarrel, however, is rarely a screaming match. When fighting for advantage, they up the speed, not the volume. Toby Ziegler, the Chief of Communications who is most often caught between administration policies and his personal beliefs – this is a Democrat administration, but one of the show's binding themes concerns the distorting pressure of political realities on liberal principles – is allowed only the occasional pop-eyed crescendo. When Josh Lyman, his deputy, raised his voice in the President's private office, it was because of post-traumatic stress disorder. Somebody had shot him during what looked like an armed attack on the President at the end of the first season. It also looked like the potential mass write-out that once climaxed a season of *Dynasty* so that the actors would moderate their demands in the next salary round. (Joan Collins was placed at the bottom of the pile of bodies, for purposes of encouragement to her agent.) In fact, however, *The West Wing* near-massacre was an attempt by white supremacists to nail the President's black personal assistant Charlie, who had enraged them by forming a miscegenetic alliance with the President's daughter. Enraged in his turn, Toby spent a whole episode looking for a gimmick to offset the drawbacks of the Second Amendment by finding a way around the First. He was on a personal quest to subvert the Constitution, and had to be reminded that the document had been framed against exactly that impulse. Toby did quite a lot of yelling before his colleagues calmed him down to his usual brooding mutter, but he never ceased to be articulate either way. Nobody ever does. Even the token Republicans can pack a page into a paragraph. There has never been dialogue like it, but little of it can be quoted in the form of one-liners, because there are very few of them. The wit in *The West Wing* is a lot funnier than anything in *Cheers, Friends, Frasier* or for that matter *The Importance of Being Earnest*, but most of it comes up in the interchange between serious characters. Which brings us to another trump in the show's unbeatable hand: the acting.

With a few exceptions, the standard of acting is uniformly stratospheric, but even her colleagues agree on ranking Allison Janney as beyond praise. In the role of C. J. Cregg, the White House press secretary, she is currently the most admired thespian in America. Before she was handed the script of *The West Wing* pilot, fans of Janney had to search her out in some pretty off-trail movies, and when the movies were mainstream she was rarely in them for more than a few minutes. In *American Beauty* you could see her, briefly, being downtrodden. In *Drop Dead Gorgeous* you could see her, briefly, being trailer-trash vulgar. You had to add up quite a lot of bit parts before you realized that she could do everything. Sorkin himself noticed her when she fell downstairs in *Primary Colors*, having been scared into epilepsy by the wanton attentions of a presidential candidate more like Bill Clinton than Jed Bartlet. As C.J. she can give it everything she's got, and there seems to be no limit. C.J. is a six-foot clothes horse who happens to be divinely bright and funny. Surrounded by men who specialize in the sarcastic riff, she can hold her own and often shoot them down over her shoulder while racing away from them with her elegant version of the show's typical gait, that of an Olympic walker on the point of being disqualified for breaking into a run. But she is more likely than they are to have the vapours in her office when something has gone wrong.

C.J.'s panic attacks are the sole concession to a sexual stereotype in a show that scarcely recognizes either the traditional differences between the sexes or, indeed, sex itself. By what amounts to an evolutionary change, sex is sublimated into displays of verbal bravura. This has the effect of doubling the oomph when there is a temporary relapse into what might just conceivably be a standard mating ritual. The scene when C.J. instructs Danny Concannon to kiss her is recognized among Wingnuts with an historic memory as the hottest thing since Bacall first blew smoke at Bogart. Danny is the accredited White House correspondent of the *Washington Post* and he shouldn't really be fooling with a professional enemy, but he can't resist her. It is very easy to believe. C.J. ranges between little emotional moments like that and grandstand virtuoso press conferences in which she parries the thrusts of her massed assailants with glittering wisecracks.

Janney is going to end up with a decade's worth of Emmys stuffed in her garage. Yet without this role she would have had the same kind of film career as, say, Paula Prentiss, who was the best thing in a dozen movies that nobody remembered. Janney could never have been a bankable film star. Almost exactly twice as tall as Al Pacino and with a face radiating an uncomfortable degree of nous, she just didn't look right. With due allowance for gender and altitude, the same rule applies to most of her male colleagues. Playing Toby Ziegler, Richard Schiff can fully deploy an uncanny knack for ensemble acting that was perfected through hard years of near neglect, including a stretch so far off Broadway that the adjective off-off hardly covers it. Like Janney he has never been billed above a movie's title or anywhere near it. But one of the strengths of the modern cinema in the US is the depth and strength of character acting that backs up the star system. The character actors get less to say than the stars but what they get is better. *The West Wing* was Schiff's chance to say better things at length. The DVD set of the first season carries, among its additional features, a set of interviews with the actors. Janney says something we might have guessed: that most of C.J.'s more technical dialogue has to be explained to her before she delivers it to us. Schiff says something we might not have guessed, but should take notice of: if he had stayed in movies he would never have had a chance to work like this, because movies can't do it – only an extended television series can. The same applies to Bradley Whitford, who plays Josh Lyman. Whitford is an attractive actor but not a leading man for the big screen, which is well staffed with males who set the female audience dreaming just by the way they look. In *The West Wing* he can set them dreaming just by the way he sounds.

Whether he set his secretary dreaming was an open question for at least thirty episodes. Finally the shine in Donna's eyes became unmistakable. Donna, played by Janel Moloney, has a double function: everything has to be explained to her, which makes her useful for purposes of exposition, but she also has a gift for asking the awkward question that stops the hot-shots in their tracks. In Hollywood terms Moloney is *joli laide* at most and would probably have remained a cute oddity on the feature list until time rubbed her out. Here she is where she belongs, slowly melting Josh's heart and infallibly melting ours. The never-on but never-off relationship of Josh and Donna is either safe sex carried to absurdity or a love duet from the first act of *La Bohème*, depending on your viewpoint. Judged by appearances, the currently ongoing dance between Sam Seaborn (Rob Lowe) and the in-house Republican Ainsley Hayes (Emily Proctor) is more conventional, because they are both lookers: nothing *laide* about the *joli* in either case. Lowe, indeed, was in leading-man contention for the movies, but the movies would never have given him such an extended opportunity to play it smart, and he is smart enough to know it. By now he must be blessing the unscheduled video appearance that made him available for television.

This being *The West Wing*, Sam and Ainsley have not actually touched each other yet, but when they debate the finer points of educational funding you can tell that the pheremones are flooding the air. The time seems long ago (as far back as the first few episodes, in fact) when the gorgeous Sam did anything so crass as to exploit the attractive power of his chiselled dialogue by actually getting a woman into bed, and even then she had to be a law student. She was also a call girl, but she had come to the right place. In real life, Sam would have been hounded out of his job. In *The West Wing*, his colleagues ribbed him out of countenance but finally ganged up with him to help protect his civil rights along with hers. All this was done as a sub-plot amid a tangle of other plots, some of which are still working themselves out now. Sorkin is an expert at finding out what an actor can do and projecting it far into the future, sometimes shaping a whole story line to accommodate the expansion. The younger actors accommodate best to this flexibility. The older ones are given a more predictable framework. I sometimes feel guilty at not being as thrilled by Leo McGarry, the Chief of Staff, as I am by C.J., Toby, Josh and Sam. John Spencer has had a long career of sterling work at the edge of the limelight but he still tends to show the emotion as well as having it. He has a lot of emotion to show: his wife left him, he was under investigation for his history of drink and drugs, and he had to take the rap for Bartlet's indecision in a period when the President was uncharacteristically thinking more about the opinion polls than his ideals. But Spencer shows the emotion by gritting his teeth even when the dialogue is telling the story, so the words come out crushed. The same often applies to Bartlet himself. Here I risk heresy, because by now it is established wisdom that the adulation Martin Sheen has aroused by his playing of this role would give him a real shot for office if he ever ran.

Of course it wouldn't. Martin Sheen is a radical with opinions designed to get him arrested, not elected. But as an actor in the show he copes nobly with a challenge even more uncomfortable than handcuffs: his role is the only one in the script that courts banality. Bartlet is the President as the irreproachable man of principle, and thus furthers a tradition that goes back at least as far as Henry Fonda in *Fail-Safe*. (Gore Vidal, in his script for *The Best Man*, tried to subvert the tradition by making Fonda walk away from the job because a man of principle would never do what it took to get it, but the *lèse-majesté* worked only once, and the film remains an oddity.) Having stuck himself with an impeccably guiltless hero, Sorkin dreamed up Bartlet's case of MS, so that the perfect gentle knight would have something to conceal. Wherever Wingnuts gather, there is debate about the wisdom of this initiative. My own opinion is that Sorkin could have made Bartlet as devious as LBJ and still held the story together. Making him as crooked as Nixon would have been out of the question, and to model him on Clinton would have involved one of the interns in several scenes where her dialogue went fatally silent. But sometimes when Bartlet is in the full spate of his integrity you can't help longing for a flaw – any flaw, except inarticulacy. Blessed with a total number of lines per episode exceeding his part in *Apocalypse Now* by an order of magnitude, Sheen, while often overdoing it with the scornful focus of his eyeballs, generously helps his minions sustain the exalted level of the symposium. But if they all just sat there, the symposium would look as if it had been devised by Plato. All those words would pile up in a heap if the people weren't moving: which brings us to the direction.

The direction is mainly the work of Thomas Schlamme, who can be best praised by saying that he is Sorkin's other half. The basic propulsion of the show's coruscating visual impact is the walk-and-talk, a device that the TV critics first started to notice in *ER*, whose techno-babbling medicos hurtled through the hospital at such a speed that the viewer feared there might be further injuries to people already injured. Made possible by the Steadycam, the walk-and-talk allows a television show to compensate for the visual scope it concedes to a feature film, which can afford big exteriors. Like a police procedural or a hospital soap opera, *The West Wing* is necessarily confined to interiors. The walk-and-talk turns the interiors into a speedway. Schlamme is a master of the technique. Even the overhead lights are calculated for impetus. As the heads of the hurrying characters interrupt the lighting, a strobe effect needles the viewer's subconscious, adding to the adrenalin rush. It could be said that Schlamme has pushed a gimmick to absurdity: you sometimes wonder when the walking talkers, rounding the same partition for a second time, will reach out for a bottle of water or a towel. But some of the show's best scenes have been ordinary two-hand exchanges, and among the very best was Bartlet's solo after his den-mother secretary Mrs Landingham was written out in a car crash. Alone in the cathedral, Sheen cursed God in rousing terms ('Have I displeased you, you feckless thug?') before winding up his imprecations with a passage of untranslated Latin, which the actor's expressiveness made far more intelligible than President Bush's untranslated English. Which brings us back to where we began: the quality of the language.

The answer to the question of whether there will be a movie of *The West Wing* is that there already was. Sorkin wrote *The American*

President, and the amount of his best writing that had to be left out of it gave him the idea for a television series. Annette Bening is a superb handler of dialogue, but when you compare what she got to say in the movie with what Allison Janney gets to say now you can see that a revolution is taking place. The standard three-act format of the feature film is starting to look restrictive. *Band of Brothers* had already proved that a military series could do what *Saving Private Ryan* couldn't: the movie brilliantly evoked a battle, but the series could explain a war. Politics needs more explaining than anything, and there was already reason to believe that *Washington Behind Closed Doors* had left the movies behind. After *The West Wing*, political movies are close to nowhere. Why make *Thirteen Days* as a film? Minus the exterior action, it would have done better as a series. The writing would have had room to flourish.

We are left with the consideration that America has got the writers, whereas nobody else has. Television impresarios like Sorkin and Steven Bochco might have taken the initiative away from the Hollywood film studios, but this cultural civil war is all taking place in Los Angeles. The implications for the rest of us are daunting, if not dire. When it comes to actually speaking English, America is now incontestably the centre of the English-speaking world. Britain, in particular, did itself suicidal damage when its broadcasting system was allowed to promote yob-speak as some kind of regional accent. Already there is a generation of British actors who couldn't pronounce *The West Wing* dialogue if they tried. The Australians would have a better chance: we might murder the vowels, but at least we put the consonants in. American military imperialism is a phantom. There are severe limitations to what it can do with weapons: it can't shoot John Pilger for example, although many of the regimes that he considers less lethal would not hesitate. But American cultural imperialism is a fact. Working by assent, it was hard enough to resist when it was exporting junk: American junk was always better than anybody else's. Exporting quality, it looks and sounds unstoppable. Our best hope of fighting back is to make literacy fashionable. The enemy is doing its best to help us. When I was young, American movies like *Rebel Without a Cause* were full of alienated teenagers with flick knives. The youngsters in *The West Wing* flaunt their grades and hone their rhetoric. For the example to be effective however, our yoof would have to see the show, for which Channel 4 hasn't run out of hiding places yet. The pre-breakfast slot on any Friday with an odd-numbered date is still open.

TLS, 4 April 2003

Postscript

After two more seasons, further conclusions. In the long run, *The West Wing* will probably be seen as a product of the Clinton era. President Bartlet is not a George W. Bush who can talk – as unlikely a notion as a platypus that can fly – but a Bill Clinton whose sexual requirements are fully satisfied by marriage to Stockard Channing. Aaron Sorkin could have made Bartlet promiscuous as well as clever and there would have been no great injury to his mental distinction, but the network would not have worn it. The important point is that Bartlet's intelligence, though plainly an idealized exaggeration, is not impossibly out of scale with Clinton's. As Sidney Blumenthal's bulky but civilized book *The Clinton Years* reveals, Clinton's real-life West Wing was alive with social concern and productive argument, and the man who energized the troops was Clinton himself. On the whole, the troops were up to it. There was no C. J. Cregg, alas, and a Josh–Donna combo might have been hard to find, but there was an enviably creative buzz. There might have been even more of that if so much time had not been consumed by the Whitewater investigation, which went on longer the more it became obvious that there was nothing to discover. On that theme, the malevolent Republican vigilantes in the show add up to a study in simple realism. Sorkin is careful to offset them with the adorable presence of Ainsley Hayes, the Republican angel, but on the whole the sworn enemies of Bartlet are a lot like the sworn enemies of the Clintons in real life: untiring promoters of manufactured scandals. That Clinton presented them with a real scandal remains one of the sad moments in recent political history, although it should never be forgotten that Clinton's private life, and Monica Lewinsky's, would have remained private if it had not been for Linda Tripp, who was activated ('empowered') by Kenneth Starr, the Special Prosecutor working on the Swiftian assumption that the President must be guilty of something or there would never have been a committee to investigate him.

By that measure, the Republicans in the show sin against verisimilitude only by being insufficiently malevolent. A more substantial violation of the truth is the character of the *Washington Post* reporter Danny Concannon, whose dedication to objectivity earns him many a searching kiss from Allison Janney. In reality, the *Post* was fully implicated in the Republican National Committee's long campaign to smear Clinton not just as a philanderer, which he was, but as an incompetent and a crook, either of which he wasn't. The media fables encouraged by the RNC linger to this day, impoverishing our view of recent history. One particularly damaging fable is that Clinton did nothing to prepare for the onslaught of terrorism. In fact he analysed the threat with precision, but his proposals – roving phone taps and markers for explosives were only two of them – were all defeated in a Congress heavily influenced by Republican lobbyists. The FBI, which was practically an instrument of the RNC at the time, had three hundred of its best agents chasing down the Whitewater phantom instead of checking oddball applications to flight school. Democracy wasn't working. Under the Bartlet administration it works with an unbelievable productivity – unbelievable because things are the way they are supposed to be, and not as we know they actually are. But for all its dreams and distortions, *The West Wing*, regarded as a totality, is a tremendous achievement, if only for its plenitude of dialogue scenes that give us the spoken language at an elliptical intensity seldom heard since Congreve. Not even the screwball comedies of old Hollywood had anything quite like Josh and Donna duking it out about the proper use of the change from the lunch money, or Toby Ziegler growing even more aphoristically eloquent as he blows his top. Such talk might not make us feel much better about the slovenly incoherence of Donald Rumsfeld's latest press conference, but we can't plausibly ignore the fact that it was produced in the same country.

Aaron Sorkin's coke-bust, and the resulting collapse of Josh's hairstyle in the fifth season, are subjects for another time. The first four seasons on DVD, with every episode watched at least twice, have given me enough to go on for now. Why didn't Toby's ex-wife agree to marry him again? I would have. Why did Rob Lowe bail out? Did he really think that a starring role in *The Lyons Den* would be a better bet? On the inexhaustibly enthralling topic of Allison Janney – I have never met a man whose eyes did not shine at the mere mention of her name – it remains a nice question whether *The West Wing* makes us feel better or worse about the opportunities open to female talent. In *Drop Dead Gorgeous*, Janney plays a low-rent maneater so well that she seems real. Would you have guessed that a lurching, chortling frump like that could transform herself into C. J. Cregg? *The West Wing* could offer her truest talent a home, but couldn't do the same for Emily Proctor, who sought refuge – no doubt for good financial reasons – in a long-term contract with *CSI: Miami*, where she has ten lines per episode, plus a chance to raise one eyebrow in close-up when the markings on the bullets match. (She also spends a lot of time standing sideways. So does David Caruso, but with less alluring results.) When the roles are missing, it's no use complaining that the actresses aren't there to play them. The real situation is far worse: the actresses are there, but they are being wasted. Does anybody think that Helen Hunt *wants* to act opposite a tornado, or Tea Leoni opposite an asteroid colliding with the Earth? (They might say they do, but the alternative is not to act at all.) Think of Anne Heche in *Wag the Dog*. On the strength of a performance like that, she could be Irene Dunne. All she needs is to live in a different era – or in a different version of this one, with thoughtful scripts a commonplace instead of a rarity. But that's one of the several deluding powers wielded by a show like *The West Wing*: it makes you believe there's a lot more where that came from. There is no more. What we see is all we will ever get, and we're very lucky to be getting that much.

PUSHKIN'S DEADLY GIFT

Pushkin was a stoat. There are less vulgar ways of putting it, but they wouldn't fit a sex drive like his. In his earlier amatory career, which appears to have got under way at about the same time as his chin grew its first whisker, he routinely referred to females, compliant or otherwise, as 'cunt'. On the eve of his marriage, he described, in a letter to a similarly priapic male friend, the blissful state of wedlock as 'lawful cunt', which he further defined as 'a kind of warm cap with ear-flaps'. That was about as reverent on the subject as he ever got in ordinary speech, and fastidious readers of Pushkin who find his ordinary speech hard to square with his extraordinary poetry are unlikely to thank T. J. Binyon for separating 'in all humility' the man from the myth. They should, however.

Separating man from myth is the avowed aim of this sumptuous new biography. Mr Binyon has to be commended for having shirked nothing in achieving it. But the question remains of whether it was the man we were wrong about, or the myth. Admirers of the poise, refinement and balance of *Eugene Onegin* can't help thinking of its author as poised, refined and balanced too, a paragon destined by his perfection to be rubbed out by a tyrant. The raw facts say that the man was less than that. He was a suicidal hothead, an indefatigable tail-chaser, a prolific spender of other people's money, a ranting imperialist, a gambler who could never rest until he lost, and altogether a prime candidate for perdition. But what if less than that means more than that? When genius dies young, it attracts a sentimental sympathy: we tend to think of it as an intensified virtue. Here is the evidence that Pushkin's genius was the intensification of everything, including vice. In many respects he was as vicious as a cornered rattlesnake. But on his rattles he could play a whole cascade of lyrics in which every line rings true. No wonder we wave away the smell of sulphur.

Mr Binyon has breathed it in. Luckily he has not suffered the common fate of biographers who dig up so much dirt on their subject that they feel compelled to heap some of it on his head. Previous biographers of Pushkin have admired their artist. Binyon admires him no less. But he is undoubtedly disenchanted with his man, having thought it wise to be. From the marketing viewpoint, he might have done better to put some of the enchantment back in. John Bayley's studies of Pushkin – the monograph *Pushkin: A Comparative Commentary* and the introductory essay to the Penguin edition of Charles Johnston's unmatchable translation of *Eugene Onegin* – must remain the first things to read on the subject, with Edmund Wilson's essays a close second, although the accumulated commentary in Tatiana Wolff's magnificent bran-tub *Pushkin on Literature* is still, after thirty years, the most engaging introduction of all for any prospective student who doesn't mind getting into the poet's brain before getting into his poetry. Bayley and Wilson share the elementary merit of keeping the miracle of Pushkin's poetic expression in the foreground, from which we should never allow it to be dislodged for long. Binyon, designedly not writing a critical biography in the usual sense, has declined to make a priority of crying up the poetry's uniqueness. To that end he might have done well to take it for granted. Instead, he quotes it for purposes of biographical illustration, but in translations done by himself. Scholars will probably find them faithful, but for an ordinary reader they are bound to seem a bit flat. Binyon gives us irregular, unrhymed extracts that might as well be prose. They are more approachable prose than Nabokov's bizarre rendition of *Eugene Onegin*, but they are still prose.

*

Nabokov, as one great writer serving another, wanted to give us an interlinear lexicon. Instead he gave us a pedigree dog's breakfast, but at least there was no mistaking it for anything uninspired. Binyon, providing samples not only of *Onegin* but of all the other major poetry as well, just wants to give us the sense: an aim less diffident than it sounds. In a text otherwise packed with unpredictable information, the translated extracts stand out only for their lack of pressure. A reader making a start with Pushkin is unlikely to be astonished by this material, and the book thus places itself automatically further down the track, as a tool to be employed after a first acquaintance is well established. This is an opportunity missed, because the book could easily have done a double duty if the verse had been presented with something of the appropriate formal punch. If Johnston's *Onegin* was not available for contractual reasons, those of us who admired it so volubly when it came out were often inclined to underplay the substantial merits of the Walter Arndt translation it superseded. The Arndt version sometimes dithers when it tries to dazzle, but falls less often than you might think into the usual trap of a strained sprightliness. Binyon avoids that trap by avoiding formal bravura altogether. As a consequence he can only assert Pushkin's first attraction without illustrating it. In Pushkin's poetic forms, language assembled itself as if answering the requirements of the human memory. Nabokov called the Onegin stanza 'an acoustical paradise', a term that applies just as well to every other form Pushkin employed from childhood onward. Right from the beginning, people couldn't take their ears off him. 'The rascal will crush us all,' said one of his seniors to another. Army officers otherwise unremarkable for their sensibility were quoting him by heart when he was barely out of school. Had Mr Binyon given us a fair idea of that, he might have had a more convincing back-up for his further assertion – by its nature harder to exemplify – that Pushkin was just as astonishing in real life. A twitching victim of the fidgets, he couldn't keep still for five minutes, but people couldn't stop listening either. When Pushkin the socialite was on the case, even the dumber fashionable ladies thought they were in the living presence of poetry, and the brighter ones easily assumed that his unprepossessing outer appearance might be a further guarantee of the flaming genius within.

Pushkin had black blood, but it didn't make him Denzel Washington. It might have done had he had more of it. As things were, his vestigial negritude gave him a distinct edge in the area of his mouth, traditionally one of the few physical points about a man that interest a woman at a first meeting, an occasion in which Pushkin's mouth was likely to be saying fascinating things, some of them unwarrantably familiar. From chin to eyebrows, here was a face designed to focus female attention. But the rest of him was miscast. A small man with a tall forehead and long arms, he was convinced that his yellow fingernails would be more interesting if worn as long as possible. He was almost certainly wrong about that, yet if he did not always enslave the frequently altering object of desire, he was never less than in with a chance. And the chance was there for the taking. Though the fashionable world was a marriage market in which there were few deals without a dowry, it reeked of glamorous eroticism. Physical beauty was everywhere: even the young men were peacocks, and the women were birds of paradise. A peacock who married a bird of paradise would have been disappointed if she lost her pulling power, whose continued efficacy was the warrant that he had chosen well. Like the Red Army's female soldiers in the next century, the belles of St Petersburg were back on duty within hours of giving birth: the ballroom was their front line. To look lovely was their reason for being. The susceptible Pushkin was faced with a multiple revelation every night. He was meant to be. That was the way the system worked.

Pushkin got his first taste of the St Petersburg ballrooms in 1817, when he was eighteen years old. On the road to his stamping ground he had already had plenty of practice at going nuts over a pretty skirt. It was standard operating procedure for young noblemen to get a servant girl in the family way and pay her off. Probably adding heartfelt, if temporary, words of love to the payment, Pushkin did not fail to conform. Later on, with his school years barely out of the way, there were always actresses, ballerinas, the ticket girl at the Shrovetide fair. He proclaimed his overwhelming love to all of them, which might even have helped more than it hindered: only good-looking men can afford to play it cool, and ugly poets do better to come on with a lyric in each hand. When the girls of the footlights did not succumb, there were prostitutes to compensate, and clap as a consequence. We can thank the enforced periods of laying up for some of his best early poems. When he was healthy, or thought he was healthy, he was out on the tiles. One of the many valuable aspects of Binyon's book is how it shows us that we were wrong to suppose that there was no Bohemian world Pushkin might have inhabited had he chosen to, and which might have kept him safe from the dangers of court society. The literary club that called itself the Green Lamp was not entirely a knocking shop, although much of the surviving written correspondence of its members suggests it was. Poems were written and books discussed, even as the attendant women were passed around the circle like kicking parcels. To that extent, a Bohemian world indeed existed, if in primitive form.

He might have helped make it less primitive had he continued to grace it. There was also the occasional literary salon with its resident *grande dame*, an aristocrat more interested in the arts than in her noble connections. When Pushkin died in 1837, Liszt was already four years into his liaison with the Countess Marie d'Agoult, who put her position aside in order to share his. I had always thought that Pushkin might have lived longer if the same possibility had been available in Russia. Here is proof that it was. Princess Evdokina Golitsyna, also known as the Princess Nocturne because she was rarely seen in daylight, was twenty years Pushkin's senior but held his love for months, although the negative evidence is strong that he never held her body. (The negative evidence is that Pushkin didn't claim the victory: usually his friends were informed by letter of any successful encounter immediately after it happened, if not while it was actually happening.) There was not the range of high-born bluestockings that had kept Goethe comfortable throughout his long career, but there were some. Pushkin might, had he wanted to, have found love and understanding in a life of renunciation and internal exile, although the Tsarist censorship would have had its own opinions if he had tried to publish the results. But the subject never came up, because a more exciting world beckoned.

And he really did think it was exciting. There is no point blaming him for it. If he had not been so enthralled by the radiant young beauties of the court, he would not have been able to show us Eugene Onegin being bored by them. On his first exposure to the official beauty parade, Pushkin scarcely had time to be bored himself. Experts in the Third Section having detected traces of incipient liberalism in his correspondence, he was sent south to cool off by personal order of the Tsar, Alexander I. He was lucky not to be sent east, to a far colder reception, but Pushkin already had highly placed admirers ready to speak for him. (Binyon is dauntingly good at quoting the official documents about Pushkin that Pushkin himself never saw.) Touring in the Caucasus, Pushkin was put up by, and was put up with by, a chain of consuls and highly placed officials who could contemplate, without challenging him to a duel, the spectacle of the visiting poet flashing his fingernails at their wives and daughters. He fell in love all over the map. There was thus no rust on his insinuating eloquence when he got back to St Petersburg. The duck was back in the water. A short period of banishment to his home estate at Mikhailovskoe amounted to no more than house-arrest, and, as Mr Binyon points out, it was a chance to get things actually written, instead of merely planned. Otherwise, apart from the odd sojourn in Moscow, St Petersburg was where he would live out the rest of his short life, in a succession of apartments he couldn't afford because of the succession of card games he couldn't avoid. And always waiting for him in the evenings were the gold-trimmed mirrors, the high plaster ceilings, the polished floors and the incandescent women: the million-candlepower milieu that we have been so determined to think unworthy of him. We can still think that, as long as we realize that he did not think the same. If he was broken by the life he chose to lead, he was also made by it. Our disappointment is inevitable but eventually absurd.

*

There were intelligent onlookers who were disappointed at the time. Some of them were among his censors. His liberal admirers were appalled by his dedication to frivolity. The facts say that he was never as liberal as they thought. Because his poetry breathed life, they thought it breathed liberty. They were right in one respect: raised as a future owner of the family serfs, and destined to traffic in souls because his debts outran by miles anything his work might earn, Pushkin could nevertheless see that there was something wrong with the system of bondage. In *Eugene Onegin* Tatyana's nurse is the voice and picture of the eternal Russian slave. Nabokov tried to deny that, because under the Soviet Union the text was routinely adduced as proof of Pushkin's proto-revolutionary credentials, and Nabokov was properly contemptuous of the regime's determination to rewrite literary history along with every other kind. But there is no denying it. Uncannily alert to anything in front of his bug eyes, Pushkin probably had sympathy for everyone he met, even for the merchants he cheated by not paying his bills. But he had little sympathy for people he hadn't met, especially if they were the inhabitants of strange lands that the inexorably expansionist Russia had designs on. His liberal critics were mistaken to suppose that he might take any strong exception to Russian hegemony. In *The Captain's Daughter*, the icily clear portent of the mature prose masterpieces he might have written had he lived, he unforgettably evoked the cruelties inflicted by power but never suggested even by implication that power might be cruel in itself. The censorship wouldn't have let him, of course: but there is no evidence that there was a secret text he couldn't publish, or even a secret idea that he could not develop into a text. His view on Tsarist power was to have no view.

He might have been prescient: in the long run it would not matter much what the intelligentsia thought about anything. Autocracy was a word that meant what it said: it would take Alexander II to free the serfs, his assassination to reinvigorate the spirit of absolutism, and Nicholas II's supernatural stupidity – abetted by his cretinous wife – to deny the granting of a constitution in 1905, thereby making revolution certain. What would matter in Russia, all the way to 1917, was the absence of a political class. Belinsky and his fiery friends, rendered desperate by Pushkin's conformism, were looking to a hero who had no intention of becoming a martyr. In retrospect he was right, but to those who nursed dreams of reform he looked wrong at the time, and some of his opinions would have seemed nasty at any time, even under the Roman empire. Over the question of Poland, he looked forward to the prospect of its intelligentsia being exterminated if they declined to submit: the dead claim no rights. Not much more than a hundred years later, the Soviet secret police would compete with the SS in fulfilling a vision not very different from the poet's own. Our conclusion must be that Pushkin, while incomparable at providing a full imaginative equivalent of anything he could actually see, was not especially good at imaging anything he couldn't see. He was friends with Mickiewicz, already hailed when young as Poland's national poet. The friendship was generous on Pushkin's part, because the handsome Mickiewicz, on his visits to St Petersburg, demonstrated powers of charm that were bound to overshadow even Pushkin's own. Mickiewicz, improvising poetry in French, could wow the ladies with a recitation direct from the brain. Pushkin needed pen and paper. But he loved Mickiewicz's company, and their boat-ride to Kronstadt – the playwright Griboyedov was along for the trip – is one of the occasions when you can't help thinking: yes, this is it, this is the literary company you should make your life in: stay with it. But when Mickiewicz went into exile rather than return to his threatened country, for Pushkin it was a case of someone else's fight. He loved the man and admired the poet, but had no comprehension of the patriot. Pushkin was an imperialist after the Tsar's own heart.

The Tsar by now was Nicholas I, who shared his predecessor's estimation of Pushkin's importance but with different results. Alexander had exiled him. Nicholas drafted him. Binyon is able to show that the draftee was willing enough. In a move meant to be flattering, Nicholas appointed himself as Pushkin's personal censor. It meant that everything Pushkin proposed to publish was still read by everyone who counted in the Third Section, but a decision was not taken until the manuscript reached the very top, on the desk of the supreme serf-owner, the man who owned every soul in the country. The decisions were not as oppressive as we would like to think. We would like to think of the genius being driven to his death on a short rein. And indeed one of Pushkin's masterpieces, *The Bronze Horseman* – Binyon rates it above even *Eugene Onegin*, a rare instance of an unnecessarily original judgement on the biographer's part – was never published in its author's lifetime. But the changes Nicholas had asked for were comparatively slight. Pushkin declined to make them because to do so would have been too much proof to himself that he was the Tsar's property. There was ample proof already. Apart from the standard blanket ban on any foreign travel, and the frightening prospect of being barred from reading in the Voltaire library that Catherine II had bought and installed in the Hermitage, Pushkin's greatest suffering under the Tsar was the low rank he had been awarded at court. He was a Gentleman of the Chamber: only a few steps up from a flunky. He particularly hated the unbecoming uniform that went with the grade. Sometimes he would rebel by wearing mufti instead, only to be carpeted by the Tsar and informed in front of everyone that the father of all the Russian people was not pleased with one of his favourite sons. But the miscreant had no objections to the compulsory attendance on the Tsar-blessed circuit of social events. It was where the women were.

If there were debutantes today, the smart ones might dream of Daniel Day-Lewis in *The Last of the Mohicans*: a man to bring danger into their dainty world. In imperial St Petersburg there were no movie stars. What the girls went for was poetry, and Pushkin was famous for it. (One of the myriad telling moments in Tom Stoppard's *Coast of Utopia* trilogy is when a noble daughter kisses her copy of *Eugene Onegin* as if it were the face of the man who wrote it.) He wrought havoc until it became obvious even to him that he had to settle down or fall exhausted. The girl of his choice was the loveliest in the room: Natalya Nikolaevna Goncharova. At this point the reader might care to supplement Binyon's story of a lifetime with Serena Vitale's story of a single year, *Pushkin's Button*. The single year was Pushkin's last, and the way she tells us why gives a better idea of the child bride Pushkin was crazy about, and just how crazy he went. Binyon is unbeatable on the hard details of debts and mortgages, but Vitale has a feel for the fabrics and the furniture, and it was Natalya's passion for a luxurious ambience that would have sunk Pushkin even if he had not got himself shot. Whether she was a zombie or merely enigmatic is an eternal question. Either way, she was a star, and she was high maintenance. Her family was even closer to bankruptcy than his. Pushkin relished her stardom – the thought that the Tsar himself might be after her filled him with proud outrage – and he wanted her to have the best. The debts piled up like Pelion on Ossa. They would have buried him anyway. The bullet was just a quick way out.

The bullet was fired by Baron Georges Charles d'Anthès, a standard-issue Eurotrash lounge lizard who looked snazzy in uniform: always a sore point with Pushkin. The poet had no good reason to be jealous. Like all the other husbands he placed a high value on his wife's flirting abilities, and flirting was as far as she went. The notorious anonymous letter that some pest sent all over St Petersburg suggesting the contrary had the same substance as the handkerchief in *Othello*. Unfortunately it also had the same effect. Lucky to be expelled instead of executed – duelling was forbidden by royal decree, and Nicholas had been foolish to believe that Pushkin had listened when told not to even think of it – d'Anthès lived to a rancid old age, still peddling his well-worn line to the well-born ladies and never expressing a single regret that he had killed one of the greatest poetic talents the world had ever known. But our anger is wasted, because Pushkin killed himself. He had always behaved suicidally. The duel that finished him was not his first. Why, when he had so much to live for, was he like that?

The clue is in the brilliant caricatures scattered throughout Binyon's book, many of which were scattered through Pushkin's original manuscripts. Pushkin's visual faculty was without the inbuilt dark glasses of abstraction: he never saw a type, he always saw individuals, and it is a safe bet that when he saw a beautiful woman he was looking at the Creation through an open furnace door. Binyon accepts too quickly Pushkin's written opinion that women were mentally inferior. The man who invented Tatyana could have thought anything but that. His denigration was a defence mechanism, and it is probable that his coarse language was the same. A pose of raw carnality staved off the unrelentingly repeated impact of the sublime. He was in love every time he lusted, and he was in love not because he saw less than other men but because he saw more. He could see everything, and he probably got sick of it.

TLS, 27 September 2002

Postscript

The Soviet Union's machinery of pseudo-scholarship did such a thorough job of turning Pushkin into a harbinger of proletarian consciousness that Nabokov felt bound to turn him into a reactionary. The truth, perhaps tediously, lay somewhere in the middle. Pushkin knew that there was something wrong with serfdom. On the other hand he saw nothing wrong with running up the sort of debts that only selling serfs could pay off. The life of high society called itself the *svyet*: the Light. Asking Pushkin to stay out of it would have been like locking Maria Callas in a broom cupboard. What mattered was that when he struck a liberal note he sounded as if he had a choir of angels backing him up. That was what Belinsky admired, and lamented the loss of. When this piece was first published, T. J. Binyon, a justly valued mainstay of the *TLS*, was still alive. He is dead now, so it is perhaps permissible to state a harsh truth. If his book on Pushkin had carried excerpts from Charles Johnson's translation of *Eugene Onegin*, beginners would have had the essence of a great, true story in one volume: and now they are still stuck with shopping around. I find it hard to believe that Binyon could not have done a deal. But like many a translator of Pushkin, he had convinced himself that he alone had the secret access to the central purity. Pushkin can drive people coocoo that way. Under

the Soviet Union, nearly all the Pushkin operatives in the scholarly
apparat were as mad about him as Akhmatova was: they just lacked
her talent. (For readers of Russian, Akhmatova's long essay about
Pushkin datelined 1947, when Stalin was still alive, is a daunting
example of what great poetry can mean to another great poet who
has an implacable state holding a gun to her head.) In the English-
speaking scholarship, the three voices that continue to matter belong
to Tatiana Wolff, Edmund Wilson and John Bayley, and especially
to Bayley. When young, Bayley was a poet with all of Wilson's
formal skills plus a lyrical element of his own – the ideal equipment
for a critic who wants to get somewhere near Pushkin. I don't see
how any critic without inside knowledge of the requirements of
assembling a tight poetic structure can get within rocket range, but
that might be a prejudice. And anyway, such a prejudice is dangerous, by encouraging the false notion that Pushkin might shut out
the ordinary reader. The opposite is true. His music can draw
anybody in. Tchaikovsky, in the opera of *Eugene Onegin*, was careful
to leave Pushkin's music virtually intact in the Letter Scene, thus to
accompany his own music in one of the work's most immediately
effective passages. Sing along and you're reciting Pushkin, as all the
young people did at the time, without having a clue about how his
stanzas were put together.

GREAT SOPRANOS OF OUR TIME

My four seasons of *The Sopranos* come in four neat boxes of DVDs. If I confine myself to a couple of episodes per evening, I can get through the whole disgusting saga in less than a month, and so leave a decent interval before I start again. The challenge, however, as with *The West Wing* or *NYPD Blue*, is to keep to the ration. Under the spell of such a rich, multi-plotted, invisibly directed narrative drive, there is a constant temptation to watch a third and fourth episode straight away, stretching the supposedly repellent experience deep into the night. The night, after all, is where the action is taking place, even when set in daylight. In the dark night of the soul it is often three o'clock in the afternoon on the pool terrace of a mobster's house in New Jersey. The rule of law exists only to be flouted; power to be flaunted; any scruple to be parodied. It's appalling. I love it.

Love it more, in fact, than the *Godfather* movies, which are supposedly the superior cinematic achievement, the *fons et origo* from which the mere television serial draws and dilutes its inspiration. (There is also a likelihood that it got some of its brio from *GoodFellas*, but Scorsese, in his turn, was almost certainly inspired to his hectic story by the urge to rebel against the stately progress of a common ancestor.) David Chase, the writer-producer who can be thought of as the man who made *The Sopranos* in the same way that Aaron Sorkin made *The West Wing*, was not personally involved in the *Godfather* project. Chase did his apprenticeship as a writer for *The Rockford Files* and later as a writer-producer for *Northern Exposure*. His idea of a big movie was Fellini's *Otto e mezzo*; of a crime movie, *Cul de Sac*; superior European stuff. There is no doubt, however, that the *Godfather* trilogy was on his mind, because it is on the minds of all the male characters in *The Sopranos*. Only two of its main actors were ever directed by Francis Ford Coppola: Dominic Chianese (Uncle Junior) and Tony Sirico (Paulie Walnuts) both played minor roles in *Godfather II*. But every Soprano-related male character has a frame of reference drenched with *Godfather* minutiae. Whether sitting out front at the Pork Store (their idea of the outdoor life) or lurking dimly in the depths of the Bada-Bing combined bar and strip-joint, they conduct long symposia in which Corleone family scenes are alluded to by the line and sometimes recreated almost in full, with sound effects. This is the kind of mediacultural fallout that gives respectable Italian community leaders the hump: Italo-Americans defining themselves as the heirs of gangsterism.

But these characters *are* gangsters, so why shouldn't they? What other kind of movie memories would they have on the tips of their thick tongues? *The Horse Whisperer*? *The Bridges of Madison County*? And the truth is that every American, of Italian extraction or not, knows the *Godfather* films by heart; and most of the rest of us do too. The real question here is whether the *Godfather* trilogy really is the armature of the spin-off, or whether the spin-off is bigger and better than the armature. Surely the latter is the case. We shouldn't let the size of the picture fool us. In the little picture, a lot more is going on, and it's a lot more true. Most of its many directors would probably like to make movies, because movies will make their names: one of the several ways in which the celebrity culture distorts culture. They will never work better than under Chase's guiding hand. Chase hated working in network television, but he hated it for the way it was sanitized. He has rebelled by seizing the opportunity HBO uniquely offers and making another kind of television, a kind that tells fewer comforting lies. If he had rebelled by making movies, his would probably have been better than most, but the pressure would have been on to do what the *Godfather* movies did: clean up the act.

When I first saw *The Sopranos*, my immediate candidate for an epic predecessor was *I, Claudius*, now available as yet another set of DVDs begging to be watched one after the other. If Chase had ever mentioned *I, Claudius* in an interview, I hadn't seen it. (Among the extra material in the first box of DVDs is an interview with Sorkin which reveals that he did, indeed, have *I, Claudius* in mind.) My only evidence for a direct borrowing was the name of Tony's dreadful and deadly mother, Livia. But I would have been surprised to learn that Chase hadn't taken *I, Claudius* on board. If the resemblance was a fluke, it could only be because, should you set out to draw a picture of unfettered violence shaping the destiny of an extended family, you would necessarily end up with something like the Roman empire after Tiberius consolidated the dubious achievement of Augustus in subordinating all law to the leader's will. Mussolini thought of Fascism as Rome's glory born again, but he had a debilitating habit of letting potential enemies continue breathing. The emperors were living in a bloodbath and so are this bunch.

In the last episode of the fourth season, the reliably psychopathic Ralphie (Joe Pantoliano, barking and cackling as he did when fighting off the killer dykes in *Bound*) has his brains beaten out by Tony in person. The even more psycho Christopher is whistled in as a cleaner, and we get a shot of him holding Ralphie's hand. Unfortunately for the viewer's peace of mind, the hand is no longer attached to the rest of Ralphie. Tony and Christopher are both shocked to discover that Ralphie has been wearing a wig throughout the series. Neither is shocked by the process of cutting Ralphie up. Dilettante viewers of the show who stumble on scenes like this are sometimes put off, but it takes some pretty selective stumbling. Scenes of actual violence are rare. What is always present is the *threat* of violence. The wise guys work their Thing by intimidating each other from the top of the hierarchy down, and maintain the cash-flow of their Thing by intimidating everybody else. When the soldiers toe the line and the civilians keep up their payments, life can go on peacefully from episode to episode. But if, God forbid, one of the subordinate wise guys should get ambitious, or some innocent citizen should get the idea that there is a real law beyond the one that the wise guys impose, hell briefly but effectively breaks loose. It hardly ever does, because every member of the crew, whether a made man or not, has proved in his youth that he will go on kicking and hitting until the victim expires. Murder is the nuke. It spends most of its time not needing to be used. The rubato of the show's physical action depends on this. In that respect, *The Sopranos* is unsanitized; and it was in that same respect that the *Godfather* movies were always as clean as a whistle.

Even the most fervent *Godfather* fan will agree that in the third movie the magic fell apart. It was a rush-job, and it showed: showed most fatally in the script. The lighting looked right, with all the mandatory sepia *sfumatura* that had been so revolutionary in the first movie. Fudges in the direction were mainly incidental. Coppola must have been working against the clock when Michael, suffering insulin shock during his visit to the Italian monastery, called for orange juice and candy. A factotum bearing a tray of orange juice and candy rushed straight into frame, as if a tray of orange juice and candy were always kept ready in an Italian monastery in case a visiting American regime-chief with diabetes should happen to drop by. Other directorial flat spots were inevitable. The orchestrated multiple killing to holy music had been invented triumphantly in *The Godfather*. Used again in *Godfather II*, the depraved epiphany had already been dished out once too often. In *Godfather III* the same trick is disguised by having the sacred music happening in the Palermo opera house during a performance of *Cavalleria Rusticana*, but it's transparently, and undramatically, the same trick. Directors have often repeated what they themselves invented, but the price is high, because it reminds us that the direction is being valued above the action, and perhaps always was.

What a director can't afford at all is to be unsure of where the script is going. What is Michael doing being *sincere* about going legitimate? But sentimentality had set in a lot earlier than that. It had been there from the beginning of the saga, which notionally occurs in a flashback in the second movie: but the same fudge rules the first one as well. When Vito Corleone, played by Robert De Niro in the flashback, kills Fanucci the extortionist, Vito doesn't set up a reign of extortion of his own. You would think that he flourishes solely from the olive oil business. He dispenses justice, not injustice. From the beginning of *The Godfather*, in which Vito is played by Marlon Brando, Vito is a figure of benign wisdom, busy saving the helpless Italian civilians from the indifference of ordinary American law. It's a comforting notion, but as phoney as the bumps in Brando's jaw-line: like them, it is made possible only by the plentiful introduction of cotton wool. The Corleone family, we are assured, makes its money from gambling and prostitution: the accepted human vices. At a critical moment for the plot, Vito even rules out drug-trafficking as 'a dirty business', as if the rest of his business was clean. Protection rackets are scarcely mentioned.

In his soon to be published *Cosa Nostra*, John Dickie points towards a different picture. Though meant as a serious contribution to modern Italian history, it can safely be predicted that Dickie's book will be a media sensation, not least because it has a dozen potential movies in it. (Two of them, *Salvatore Giuliano* and *Le Mani*

sulla Città, have already been made, but they will be made again.)
The news that matters, however, is about the real nature of the
Mafia's modus operandi in Sicily. As the nineteenth century turned
into the twentieth, the Sicilian grain fields were worked by peasants
whose condition was only a step up from slavery. They were left
with a cupful of the grain they reaped: the rest was taken by the
gaballoti, the overseers who had been put in by the absentee
landlords who were living it up in Palermo. It would have been nice
if the Mafia had gone into battle on behalf of the peasants. Unfortunately it was common for the *gaballoti* to be members of the
Mafia.

*

Extortion and protection were always the core business of the
Sicilian Men of Honour. In America, after the internal Mafia war
of 1930–31, *Cosa Nostra* was, in Dickie's useful term, Italianized.
In Italy, families from the different regions had had little idea of
nationality: America gave it to them. The Soprano family, who
originated in Naples, are part of this larger context. But no matter
how large Our Thing got, the petty squeezing of the helpless
remained at the heart of it, as a permanent reminder that in those
halcyon Sicilian days Robin Hood gave nothing to the poor except
grief. Modern Americanized operators such as Lucky Luciano
thought big. But there is no reason to think that the Mob has ever
dealt in big-time stuff. The crime families got big by adding small-
time deals together, and the small-time deals have always started
with protection and loan-sharking. Of the gangster movies, *Good-
Fellas* and *Donny Brasco* probably give the truest picture: an average
deal is a couple of slot machines being broken open in the back
room, and a big deal is three machines. A Mob boss gets rich from
his lion's share of the stolen and extorted money passed up to him
by the lower ranks. (Trace the rake-off upwards and you get a flow-
chart of the way the Mob's finances work: there is a pay-out at each
level, but finally the *capo* banks most of the take for doing nothing
except keeping all those below him in line. Tony banks his in the
ceiling of his house, or in a locked box out in the yard.) Muscling in
on the unions might look like a big deal, but only because every
member of the union is feeling the squeeze. There has never been
much chance of a Mob boss turning into Warren Buffet, or even

into Ivan Boesky. The stuff in *Godfather III* about taking over Immobiliare was science fiction. You could make a movie about the Mob moving in on Microsoft. Everyone would like to see how Bill Gates reacted to a horse's head in his bed. But it would be a fantasy. Mobsters are opportunist hoodlums, not business geniuses.

In *The Sopranos*, this mean reality is much more realistically portrayed. People can be friends of the family and still be soaked. Artie the restaurant owner, who is really trying to play it straight, foolishly borrows money from Tony to cash in on what looks like a sure-fire Armagnac franchise. Artie's hard-working wife, brighter than he is, is outraged. Tony guesses it's a scam, but he only warns Artie against getting into debt: he doesn't refuse the money. The moral here is that Artie, who might have got rich slowly, should never have tried to get rich quick. Once he defaults on the debt, his restaurant belongs to Tony. (The wise guys have a name for this process: they call it 'buying in'.) Artie's grieving face is an emblem for the show. Artie is still Tony's friend, but now it is no longer a case of doing Tony the occasional favour, such as letting him run up a huge tab. Now Artie must do nothing but favours: he will never be out of hock. And this is what Tony can do to a pal. What he can do to a mere acquaintance, let alone to a stranger, happens often enough per episode to remind us that his hulking charm adds an extra meaning to the word 'irresistible'. Far from helping the little guys, Tony gets the little guys in his power. He does it by terror. But usually the mere suggestion of terror is enough.

How does he feel about that? Bad enough to need an analyst, the reassuringly husky Dr Melfi, played by Lorraine Bracco, who in *Someone To Watch Over Me* was married to an honest cop. Theoretically she is on the side of the law here too, but there are complications. In *Analyse This* the mobster's shrink was played by Billy Crystal, with hilarious results. Taking over the same situation and spinning it out into a linking theme, Chase transforms a gag into a strange story of perverted love. Transference duly occurs and Tony lusts after her. She is suitably revolted. Then she gets raped in the basement car park by a pizza joint's Employee of the Month. The cops are useless. She admits the attraction of Tony's power when she tells her sympathetic but powerless ex-husband what would happen if she tipped off Tony about the rapist: her patient would 'squash him like a bug'.

Her feelings for Tony's macho strength would give a strict feminist the horrors, but they are surely plausible, and therefore disturbing. She herself is disturbed enough to seek analysis in her turn. (From Peter Bogdanovich, as it happens: showing once again, as he did in his film *Saint Jack*, what a subtle actor he is.) In the grip of the primeval instincts that it is her job to stay detached from, Dr Melfi gets more and more screwed up: a token of the grim fact that any kind of entry into Tony's orbit can have life-threatening results. As for Tony, his anxiety attacks abate, but he has told her little about the truths that matter most. He has told her what was done to him – violent father, scheming mother – but tells her nothing about what he has done to other people. A leitmotiv of his reluctant testimony to her is the question of where the ducks go in winter. This reminds us of Holden Caulfield, who wondered the same thing about fish. But Tony is no young intellectual in the making. Mixing bright broads with his usual diet of rudderless goomahs, he is spiritually drawn towards higher thoughts, but profundity can be undone in a moment by news that some idealistic agitator on a construction site needs straightening out with a baseball bat. Tony's clever brain is just another muscle.

The only but abiding complexity of Tony's character lies in the way he must bring into balance two different considerations. Outside the house, his powers are unlimited. Inside it, he can affect the behaviour of others only to a certain extent, because they know he won't kill them. Vivid as it is, this is a real conflict, genuinely subtle and complicated, continually surprising. Tony's wife, Carmela, and his children A.J. and Meadow, are forever cutting down to size the very man who would take a long knife to them if they were not his property. Michael Corleone can shut the door on his wife and children. Tony has to fight them in the kitchen for his unfair share of the lasagna. By comparison, Michael Corleone's conflict between the evil of his business and his highly developed sense of right and wrong is a mere excuse for Al Pacino to press his fingers to his weary eyes while the close-up gives us an opportunity to speculate about the improbable things that have been happening to his hair.

Tony's crew are a study in themselves, and would remain so even if Tony were to fall foul of the Rico laws and die in gaol like Al Capone. (James Gandolfini's agent has no doubt been reminded of this during discussions about his client's salary.) The supporting characters are developed and deployed through season after season. This is one of the areas in which the advantage of a TV serial over even the biggest movie really shows up. A movie is always short of time. A serial can keep the corners uncut. Paulie Walnuts isn't just a swept-back hairstyle with a few threatening lines. Paulie has insecurities. His pop-eyed humiliation when a Mob boss from the big city fails to recognize him must rank high among documents of all it means for a proud hoodlum never to make it out of Newark. Big Pussy is given time for us to know him and sort of love him before he meets his fat fate on Tony's bad-taste boat. They are all given time to be people like us, in between moments when they give terrifying proof that they are not like us at all.

It's a crowded field to stand out from, but perhaps Christopher takes the palm. He is a homicidal junkie nut who deludes himself that he might be a writer. Those of us who share the same delusion can be thankful that we grew up in a different neighbourhood. Here is a dreadful reminder that Goebbels was a novelist: evil can have an artistic sensibility. Christopher dreams of creation while working destruction. The actor who plays him, Michael Imperioli, is clever enough in real life to have written one of the best episodes of the show. (And Steve Buscemi directed another, as did Bogdanovich: a series this vital attracts talent as well as generating it.) But Christopher as a character on screen is hopelessly impulsive: it takes an armful of heroin even to slow him down. In that case it is a bit of a wonder why Tony chose him to succeed, because the choice makes Tony look stupid, which he isn't supposed to be. If the show has a needless implausibility, it probably lies there. These American small-screen geniuses are spinning stories bigger than the *Iliad*, but even Homer nods. Aaron Sorkin didn't need to give his President a case of MS, and Chase didn't need to make the stark mad Christopher a candidate for the succession. But Christopher as a future *capo* is still a lot more believable than Sonny in *The Godfather*. Even Brando, who seldom saw the script before bits of it appeared taped to the scenery (there is an industry legend that some of it was written in felt-tip on Robert Duvall's shirt), must have been surprised to find himself saying that a mere pimp 'could never have outfoxed Santino'. Your mother could have outfoxed Santino: up until that point, the movie had been busy proving almost nothing else.

As for Tony's mother, it brings us to the women, and one of the

show's most enthralling aspects. The women are terrific: some of
them in the strictest sense of the word. In *The Godfather* even
Connie is a cipher, but *The Sopranos* hasn't got a single cipher in the
line-up. Like Sian Phillips's Livia in *I, Claudius*, Nancy Marchand's
Livia in *The Sopranos* is absolute evil made absolutely believable.
Nancy Marchand played the up-market proprietress in *Lou Grant*
and afterwards got stuck with the patrician role when she made
movies: she was Harrison Ford's mother in the *Sabrina* remake and
might have lived out her career doing similar *grande dame* swan-ons
if the part of Tony Soprano's mother hadn't landed in her lap. What
she did with it will be studied by serious actresses for a long time
to come. In the nursing home, Livia retreated into a second childhood while still pushing buttons for the murder of her own son.
Was she only pretending to be senile? Her death left a gap, but
it was ably filled by Tony's sister Janice. So off-putting that she
reportedly shrank the ratings, Janice is incarnated by Aida Turturro,
who shares with her brother John the capacity to freeze your blood
with a single facial expression of crazed intensity. Janice's back-story
is composed of one dippy extravagance after another. She did time
on an ashram. She is still drawing welfare cheques for a supposed
carpal tunnel syndrome she acquired while working the steamed-
milk machine in a coffee house. Now she wreaks havoc by fulfilling
the kinkier sex fantasies of Tony's subordinates, but her real sexual
relationship is with Tony. She would like to fulfil it by getting him
killed. An hour alone with her conversation would be enough to kill
anyone. Think of your worst nightmares about females you would
prefer to avoid. Think of being trapped in an elevator with Madame
Mao. Janice is worse than that. Carmela, on the other hand, is
Tony's perfect wife, until she starts craving a more sensitive male
touch. She gets it, or dreams of getting it, from Furio, Tony's most
trusted enforcer. Where the melting Carmela is concerned, Furio
really is a man of honour. Out of respect for Tony, he fights off
temptation. Carmela, marvellously played by Edie Falco, can't bear
to be without him. Furio burns alive in the fires of thwarted passion.
Their star-crossed love is all the more believable in its tenderness
because we know that Carmela's existence depends on a perverse
disinclination to figure out where the money comes from, and that
if we ourselves owed any of it, Furio is the last man we would want
to ring our doorbell.

Like her brother A.J., Tony's daughter Meadow (Jamie-Lynn Sigler) has been growing up right there on screen. Meadow has become a beauty, and brighter all the time. By a plausible reaction to her home circumstances, she wants to be a lawyer, bringing justice to the deprived. She might do for Tony in the end, if he isn't done for by my favourite woman in the show, Adriana (Drea de Matteo). Adriana is the paradigm of the young knockout forced into a walking coma by the steadily dawning realization that she has nothing going for her but her looks. Being married to Christopher doesn't help. She is just bright enough to know he is a lunatic, but not quite bright enough to see that her insatiable taste for luxury depends on him. As stoned as he is and with even less to do – she doesn't even get to kill anyone – Adriana is an easy mark for the Feds. From her they might get the evidence they need to lock Tony away. If we find ourselves wishing that the law won't nail him, it's because he is us. Michael Corleone is us too, but only when we dream of omnipotence. Tony Soprano takes us back to the primeval forest; to instincts, not dreams. It's a different kind of vacation from the everyday drag. If you want to know just how exciting life would be if there were no law, here it is.

TLS, 30 January 2004

Postscript

In its later seasons, fans of *The Sopranos* tend to quarrel with the screen more and more often, and it is a nice question whether this means that the show is more involving than ever, or has strayed too far from its first principles. I thought Adriana's death looked like a hasty write-out, and needlessly so, because her inevitable demise had been set up years before. Or perhaps that was the point: they deliberately made the fatally determined look arbitrary. But shouldn't Steve Buscemi have given us a few more hints of lethal dementia before he finally blew his lid? And we can understand why Tony should find reasons for not facing the necessity of killing his cousin, but what about his continuing failure to realize that Christopher is unemployable even as a homicidal maniac? In TV comedy they call it jumping the shark: the tendency of a long-running show's writing team to lose faith in the established narrative precepts, and take refuge in the startling. (The term was first used after the Fonz went water-skiing, but let's not get lost in detail.) We can put up with it if Tony is in trouble. We can even understand if Tony is desperate. But if he actually starts losing his taste for power, he is too like us, and we might as well join him in watching history-channel programmes about Rommel. Nevertheless, the achievement remains. The crew that invented *The Sopranos* won through to the big prize: low-life high art, cordon bleu fast food. People argue about the show the same way that people must once have argued when walking home through the mud after seeing *Titus Andronicus*. Why couldn't the broad have picked up a knife? She didn't have any *hands*, for Christ's sake.

A MEMORY CALLED MALOUF

At an advanced point in his already prolific career, the Australian writer David Malouf has produced a book of fresh beginnings. Nominally a collection of nine short stories, *Dream Stuff* could just as easily be nine different outlines for new novels, each of them remarkably unlike any novel he has turned out before. If that sounds like a polite way of reclassifying his novels as expanded short stories, it's a stricture that he invites. His novels have always left out much of the framework and furniture that most novelists are careful to put in. On the other hand, what he puts in instead makes them read more like a poetic fermentation than a long short story.

'Everything spread quickly,' he says in the title story of *Dream Stuff*: 'Germs, butter, rumours.' He is talking about subtropical Queensland, the stamping ground of his childhood, but he could equally be evoking the luxuriant mental climate of his entire creative life. Fecund is a word that fits him as it fits few other Australian writers. Seen from space, Australia is a thin, wet edge running only halfway around a colossal swathe of hot rock. For Australia, read austere. A celebrated poem by Judith Wright addresses the largest island's anhydrous vastness in the appropriately desiccated vocative: 'Your delicate dry breasts, country that built my heart.'

Chez Malouf, however, there is scarcely a dry breast to be seen. Propagating itself like honeysuckle on a trellis, his mind exfoliates in the thin wet edge, and everything it dreams up sends out tendrils, starting new, wild gardens that you couldn't keep down with a flame-thrower. Aridity being decidedly not his thing, he is thus the least characteristic Australian writer yet to have reached world prominence, and therefore one of the surest signs that Australia's literary culture – cosseted in the long years when it scarcely existed – has by now arrived and is running nicely out of control, the way a culture should.

None of this means that Malouf is an incoherent writer. At his frequent best, and occasionally for a whole book, his prose is as tightly under control as his poetry, and often more so: his poems usually avoid the prosaic with such success that it is hard to figure out what is going on. In his narrative prose he is more likely to evoke before he implies, achieving a clarity that has helped to make obvious the main subject on which he has been reluctant to touch. That subject is sexual love, about which, on the whole, he has had less to say than almost any other serious novelist since Joseph Conrad. In Malouf's sumptuous corner of a sparse country, there is only one kind of juice that has so far failed to flow. But there are signs in these short stories that it might be finally on the move.

*

'At Schindler's', the first story in the new book, evokes a south Queensland childhood with the same enchanting clarity that he achieved in his directly autobiographical *12 Edmondstone Street* (1985), named for the house that his miraculous memory has never completely left. 'I can feel my way in the dark through every room . . .' he said in the autobiography. 'First houses are the grounds of our first experience.' In the new story, he could still be expounding the importance of early experience, with the descriptions uncannily getting sharper instead of duller as the point of view advances ever further from the object:

> There was a pool at Schindler's. In the old days Jack and his father had swum there each morning. Jack would cling to the edge and kick, while his father, high up on the matted board . . .

For any Australian who first went swimming at the end of World War II, the matted board will have the same effect as a truck full of madeleines would have had on Proust. Yes, the diving boards were wrapped with matting: he's got it exactly.

The child at the centre of the autobiography, the real Malouf, came from Lebanese immigrants on his father's side and English on his mother's. The boy in the story has nothing like so interesting a background, but something much more interesting happens in the foreground. In the autobiography he merely grows taller. In the story he grows up. It is wartime, most of the Australian young men are already overseas (too many of them, including the boy's father, as prisoners of war), and south Queensland is teeming with American service personnel, young men who have only one thing on their minds while they wait to ship out for the fighting in the north – the Australian young women.

A crucial time in modern Australian history and a crucial place are both vividly recreated. After the fall of Singapore, Australia was obliged to sideline its hallowed but fatally outdated military dependence on Britain and go all out in its new partnership with the United States – a shift of alliance, if not of loyalty, so far-reaching that its consequences are still making themselves felt today. One of the immediate consequences was that the strategically placed south Queensland became an occupied zone. It hardly needs saying that if the Japanese had been occupying it instead of the Americans the results would have been dramatic in an even more unsettling way.

Nevertheless the drama was unsettling enough. The jealousies and resentments were intense, and partly because the Americans, on the whole, behaved like gentlemen. Their good manners, added to their high pay and ready access to a PX full of otherwise unavailable consumer goods, made them hard to resist. Hard to resist didn't mean irresistible: to form a sexual relationship with an American serviceman was by no means common among Australian women already spoken for by one of our absent nationals. But fraternization in the form of friendship was. And of course the boy in the story, when his mother takes up with her charming Yank, suspects nothing more. When he walks in on them while they are making love, he hardly knows what is going on, but the story, written from his viewpoint, registers his shock. The long-term consequences are only hinted at, but clearly there will be some.

For the reader of Malouf's work, this is an uncustomary use for the word 'clearly'. The only previous instance I can think of for a potentially formative sexual event was in another short story, included in the 1985 collection *Antipodes*, In that story, called 'Southern Skies', a first-person narrator, brought up in a refugee family, recalls how when he was a boy at high school a friend of the family called the Professor took the opportunity to grope him while showing him the stars through a telescope. Since the boy has already declined the advances of his mother's mature and attractive female friend, yet does nothing to stop the Professor jacking him off while he melts with awe at the revelation of the heavens, it would be legitimate to infer that a future course is being charted. No celestial music is heard, but the favorable auspices of the heavenly bodies are hard to miss.

*

In the fictional world of Malouf's novels – a world in which childhood is a time rarely touched by sexuality and in which the same, on the whole, can be said for adulthood – the emotional relationships among men are even more fascinating for their lack of specificity than the heterosexual relationships. Apart from that one middle-period short story, there have been no instances of males sharing an explicitly sexual moment while the cosmos sparkles in approval. The heterosexual coupling in 'At Schindler's' ('nothing he had been told or imagined was a preparation for the extent to which, in their utter absorption in one another, they had freed themselves of all restraint') has a few harbingers, if only sketchily established. In his biggest novel, *The Great World* (1990), the character nicknamed Digger, a returned prisoner of war, has a years-long and quite believable Thursdays-only relationship with a widow similarly reluctant to give up her solitude. Nothing explicit is said, but at least you can assume there is a mutual sexual attraction, in the same way you can assume that the male and female protagonists in Jane Austen, upon achieving marriage, will at some time get into the same bed.

But the main relationship in *The Great World* is between man and man, and the interesting thing about it is that nothing emotional is even implied. Vic and Digger are prisoners of war together on the Thailand railway. The hellish conditions are thoroughly evoked, but one is all too aware that the source-point lies in research. The classic treatment of the subject was written by an eyewitness: Russell Braddon's *The Naked Island* (1952). Malouf, marvelous with his own memories, is never quite as good with other people's. Still, the backdrop is sharply painted. Suffering in front of it, however, Vic and Digger are wavy outlines. Vic is unbearably insensitive, yet Digger is drawn to him. There are heavy hints that their personalities are complementary: Vic has the sense of possibility, Digger the solidity. After the war, Vic gets married and goes on to be a headlong, headline-grabbing entrepreneur, while Digger lives out a quiet life with the woman who is Thursday. Yet we are given to understand that the true relationship is between Vic and Digger. They don't get on, yet they can't do without each other. But in what way?

There doesn't have to be sex: there is such a thing as chaste love between men. But if this is love, why can't it be explored? Beyond a reciprocal irritability, the thing going on between them is all implied intensity and no expressed feeling. A vacuum is not the same thing as ambiguity, which requires at least two different meanings. For the long scenes between the main men in *The Great World* it is sometimes hard to find even one meaning, and the general effect of Malouf's most ambitious novel is of being empty in the middle, a doughnut as big as the Ritz. The fault is compounded by the richness around the periphery. Malouf is touchingly right about how Australia's unemployed men during the Depression insisted on being given work to do for their handout. And among those same men there was always a tradition of self-improvement: indigent autodidacts would swallow their pride to borrow knowledge.

This tradition reached a sad apotheosis in the prison camps, whose informal oral universities Malouf conjures up with tender, admiring accuracy. He has a real feeling for the kind of friendship between males that Australians are encouraged by their nationalist cheerleaders to call 'mateship'. But Vic and Digger, never able to relax with each other or say what is on their minds, are pretty strange mates. They barely even like each other. So what gives?

*

The same question mark-shaped cloud has hung over Malouf's novels since the beginning, although it should be remembered that a dark enough cloud, as well as blocking out the sun, can provide much-needed rain. Seductively forecasting what his autobiography was going to be like, the novel *Johnno* was published in 1975. At the exact time when Brisbane was changing irrevocably into a skyscraper-studded modern metropolis, *Johnno* recreated the single-story small-town city of its author's youth, thereby providing Brisbane's current and future citizens with a vocabulary and a map by which to cherish its remnants. Malouf was already a wizard for nostalgic detail, conjuring up such ephemeral treasures as the album-cum-catalogue, celebrating the career and products of the confectioner James MacRobertson, whose colour plates 'seemed as beautiful to me then as anything I had ever seen or could imagine, a sort of colonial Book of Hours'.

But this is a fictional narrator talking, not Malouf. His name is Dante and he has a friend whose nickname is Johnno. Dante is slated for a life of order, Johnno is a *maudit*, a wild man, and ... that's it. Really they should drive each other mad, but they are involved with each other and you wonder why. Coming closer to now but sticking with the same theme, in Jay McInerney's *The Last of the Savages* we find out why the square narrator can't let go of a friend whose erratic nature scares him to death: it's love. But the ties binding Dante and Johnno are hard to trace. One thinks naturally of other books about the same sort of relationship because Johnno is such a literary performance. Though Johnno has artistic interests, he has no real talent to justify his chaotic behaviour, but boy, is he literary: he quotes the first line of the first Duino elegy in the original German without feeling the need to say that Rilke wrote it.

Unfortunately the narrator doesn't feel the need either. If it weren't my profession to spot these things, I would have been in the dark. But I spent most of the book in the dark anyway. Is the narrator called Dante because he needs a Virgil to lead him on a spiritual journey? But what kind of Virgil is Johnno, karmically predestined for a beatified self-destruction on no clear evidence of superiority? Even for J.D. Salinger's Seymour Glass it wasn't enough to read Rilke: he had to have his own poetic powers that needed Japanese forms to contain their unheard-of intensity. Johnno just haunts the downtown bars in a dozen or so of the world's capital cities while Dante checks out his performance from a distance, apparently with no particular disapproval. A mental connection between them is difficult to see, and an emotional one emphatically not in question.

*

A love between men surpassing all understanding: this theme was repeated in Malouf's bewitching short novel of 1982, *Fly Away Peter*, still the most convincing thing he has done when reaching back beyond his own time. Before World War I, an enlightened scion of the Queensland landed gentry called Ashley takes on a proletarian called Jim to help him run a bird sanctuary. The class difference between the two of them is well brought out. Though they are both living in Australia, they are from two different worlds. It takes bird-watching to unite them: that and the war, in which they both die on the Western Front. One an officer, and the other definitely not, they take separate routes to the same death, and you would think that Malouf might make something more of their last meetings in France before they get wiped out in the trenches. But he plays it down. Indeed, he throws it away. One suspects that he finds the whole idea of structure artificial, but he would have a more consistent chance of justifying such casualness if the mental connections between his main characters were perceptibly articulated. Whatever joins Jim and Ashley never fully emerges from the wetlands where they watch the birds, so there is not enough to regret when it gets lost in the mud. But, almost exceptionally in Malouf's work, you can see why they liked each other, and by no coincidence *Fly Away Peter* is sufficiently focused at the center to make the way it goes blurry at the edges seem deliberate.

If the same could have been said of *The Conversations at Curlew Creek* (1966), it would have been what the Australians call a bobby-dazzler. As it is, it is a work condemned to mere distinction. Transferred backward through time to the bad old colonial days of the 1820s, Malouf's standard two-man relationship might have had real power if it had been spelled out, but it remains a matter of suggestion. Adair and Fergus were once close friends in Ireland, where Adair was the homeless waif received into a grand family and Fergus was its scapegrace golden boy. Since Fergus will inherit everything by right, Adair lights out for New South Wales to make his own way as an officer of the law. Fergus, going all the way to the bad, ends up there too, and turns bushranger. Adair is a man of order and Fergus is a creature of impulse: Digger and Vic, Dante and Johnno, we have been here before.

Balancing two complementary halves of a single personality isn't a bad way for a novelist to search his own soul, but it helps the novel if both characters are at least present. Fergus, however, spends most of the book absent without leave. Adair isn't even sure if Fergus is in Australia. Just why Adair isn't sure is a bigger mystery than the author allows: there weren't very many people in Australia at the time, and someone billed as a 6'6" blond Irish aristocrat would have been talked about. But Malouf prefers another kind of mystery. In the end, if it is the end, Fergus turns out to have been, or possibly been,

> a figure created half out of legend to fulfil the demands of some
> for a breakaway hero, of others for the embodiment of that spirit
> of obduracy or malign intent that sets some men defiantly above
> the law, and wearing so many rags of lurid romanticism that
> every aspect of the man himself has been lost.

In real life, legends undoubtedly do grow out of events. But this sounds like an inadvertent acknowledgment that the urge to create a legend came first, and then the events were made up to fit.

*

Banishing one of the mysteriously entwined partners to the wings can be seen as a Maloufian device for ensuring that they don't have to strike up a conversation. From the reader's viewpoint, a less frustrating stratagem is to deprive one of them of the powers of speech, thus leaving the way open for a *visione amorosa* pure and simple, as the man of order is transfigured by the contemplation of feral beauty. Malouf tried this in his early novel *An Imaginary Life* (1978). The poet Ovid is in exile in a rough country, where he takes a consuming interest in a wild boy known as the Child. The reader can't fail to be reminded of *Death in Venice*, in which the aged Aschenbach is convulsed in spirit and prepared for death by his vision of the beautiful boy Tadzio paddling on the Lido. Ovid's Child paddles in less gentrified waters, but to the same effect:

> The fulness is in the Child's moving away from me, in his
> stepping so lightly, so joyfully, naked, into his own distance at
> last as he fades in and out of the dazzle of light off the water . . .

But the reader can easily fail to be reminded of the Roman world. From what we know of Ovid's eight years of killing time at the mouth of the Danube, the man at the center of Malouf's book is hard to recognize. It is true that Ovid eventually set about learning the local language, but the suggestion that he had put the old world behind him and was ready to embrace something new is absurd: the *Tristia* and the *Epistulae ex ponto* are complaints, not letters of acceptance. The *relegatio* imposed on Ovid by Augustus was only the mildest form of exile, but was still meant to be a savage punishment, and it worked. Ovid ached for Tiberius to bring him back to Rome – to bring him back to life. Malouf's Ovid hardly has Rome on his mind. His attention is fully occupied by the Child. Nothing happens, but one can't help thinking that if the author of the *Ars amatoria* had had a telescope available it well might have.

The same *enfant sauvage* theme works much better in *Remembering Babylon*, Malouf's justly praised novel of 1993. The setting is Queensland in the 1840s, and this time the wordless child is a white castaway ship's boy who walks out of the bush to join the white settlers after sixteen years with the Aboriginals. With only a few words of English, the boy is effectively a white black. In America, Mark Twain pioneered this transracial device with *Pudd'nhead Wilson*, and variations on it have proved usable all the way through to Philip Roth's *The Human Stain*; but in Australia it has rarely been exploited, not just because the country has a much smaller culture by volume but because Aboriginals, until very recently, were thought marginal if they were thought of at all. This latter point has always ranked high among Malouf's preoccupations, and through his misfit bush boy he gives us his most thorough treatment of it. The wild child ought to be a bridge between cultures, but the self-elected representatives of the dominant culture don't want a bridge; they'd rather have the river they can drown him in:

> His arms are jerked back, his head pushed down. His head, roaring into the sack, is thrust under water and the darkness in the sack turns to mud. He gasps mud.

Touch by touch, a picture of inevitable tragedy is built up which would look very like despair if there were not also, at the centre of the story, the usual unstated mutual attraction, this time between the settlers' boy from whose viewpoint we see the action and the boy from the bush whose mere existence is its principal cause.

*

Attraction might be the wrong word for what goes on between Malouf's male principals. The lack of warmth might not just be due to the invariable obliqueness of the expression, the thoroughness of the ellipsis. Perhaps what we are shown is a kind of dependence. In Malouf's Australia, the man of sensibility is walled in. He is not necessarily in a closet, but he is certainly in a cell, and without his yearning vision of someone wild in the street outside he would never dare to attack the bars in the window with that file he found in the cake. Solitude is common in Malouf's work, but it is rarely self-sufficient; although it should be said that the eponymous hero of *Harland's Half Acre* (1984) is very definitely a man on his own, a self-educated artist boiling and bristling at the center of the novel by Malouf that comes closest to being a masterpiece, and the more so because it is so unlike the others. As so often happens with prolific authors, the least characteristic work is the most fulfilled. For once the hero, instead of being drawn to another man and spending the rest of the book failing to find out why, resolves his conflicts within himself. If he has any sexuality at all, it all gets sublimated in creativity. Since the same almost certainly applied to Leonardo da Vinci, the reader can scarcely think this unlikely.

Born in poverty and ignorance, Frank Harland, through sheer strength of talent, becomes a great painter, staying true to his gift even when faced with another economic threat – prosperity. Malouf's is not the only novel to celebrate the heroically inarticulate misfit painter. Joyce Carey's Gully Jimson in *The Horse's Mouth* was there first, and Patrick White's Hurtle Duffield in *The Vivisector* must have been much in Malouf's thoughts. (Malouf wrote the libretto for the opera version of White's *Voss*.) But Malouf's Harland is a true original. It has been said that he was based on the reclusive Australian painter Ian Fairweather, but really he has taken on too much life of his own to be pinned down to one progenitor. Saul Bellow's Humboldt is said to be based on Delmore Schwartz, but he makes me think of a dozen writers who created a square mile of chaos around them for every square foot of order they created on the page; and in the same way, and for the same reason, Harland conjures up a platoon of Australian painters who came out of nowhere, followed their noses, and drew the world to their solitary hideaways. Harland in his hut on the beach could be Sidney Nolan on his country estate. Harland is the artist incarnate, the artist who has been born to it and can't stop. The theme has an incandescent focal moment when his friend Knack, a learned refugee from Europe who has survived in Australia by keeping a junk shop, shoots himself along with his mistress. The war in Europe has come to an end but the news from the concentration camps has been too much for them. Harland visits the bodies in the junk shop. There is blood all over the walls and the shape of the stains gives him the idea for a painting.

Harland's fruitful naïveté is boldly imagined, clearly defined, and psychologically true, so all of Malouf's gifts can be put to work reinforcing the center of the book instead of glamorously circumnavigating its perimeter. The best gift is his easy access to the memories of his youth, a treasury of sense impressions upon which he seems able to draw at will, with no need to check up on their accuracy. When he names the objects in his mother's sewing basket, it's doubtful whether he needs a photograph: he photographed them with his mind when the basket was on a level with his eyes. James Joyce had to write letters home to get some of his details about Dublin right, and Thomas Mann had to be in a constant process of researching his own past to pull off a tour de force like the description of the Frankfurt am Main shop windows that provide Felix Krull with his freshman year at the academy of material desire. But Malouf's inventories read as if he can just pull them out of his head. You can tell he doesn't feel the need to check up, because sometimes errors creep in. (In *Johnno* that little imported English car called the Mini is on sale a couple of years too early.) But anomalies and anachronisms are hard to spot, and it's a fair guess that they are very few.

*

In *The Great World* the prisoners of war sustain themselves by playing memory games, cherishing their personal histories. Clearly Malouf feels that way about his own. He can take his personal recollections with him into Australia's nineteenth century because the layout of the households and the surrounding scenery in the subtropical south Queensland littoral area wasn't all that different then than it was in his childhood. *An Imaginary Life* remained singular in his work because he couldn't take his memories with him into the ancient world. The supposed classical purity of that book was really just an absence of detail, and when he tried to supply some the results were strangely impalpable. (And in at least one instance disabling, as when Ovid observes that the barbaric locals ride without stirrups, the author having failed to apprise himself of the information that everybody did, since the invention of the stirrup lay six hundred years in the future.)

So far, Malouf has been at his most comfortable with his house around him. At whatever time they are set in the two hundred years of white settlement that we used to think of as the whole of Australian history, his best stories – with *Remembering Babylon*, *Fly Away Peter*, and *Harland's Half Acre* as the outstanding examples – are richly detailed transitions between wooden-walled interiors and landscapes in which every plant and living thing is catalogued by memory. Even when the house is crowded, there is a place in it for a precocious boy. Frank Harland and his brothers are brought up in a single room, sleeping several to a bed, but Frank ends up getting the single bed against the wall, the way to the world. And there is always a space under the house, which is the way to adventure. Not just in the autobiography but in a surprising number of the novels as well, the dark, wedge-shaped space under the house is where the protagonist goes to be alone and to find his way forward, up to the limit set by the line of light where the front of the house almost meets the ground. (In Queensland the old weatherboard houses usually had a moat of air between themselves and the ground, thus to stave off the white ants, a species of termite fanatically dedicated to the demolition business.) In the title story of the new book he is still under the house, still feeling its weight on his shoulders, still mesmerized by that line of light.

But there is a difference. The old entrapment has, at long last, been reduced to something merely formative, rather than definitive. 'Dream Stuff' is a story about someone who has been out into the light and let it change him: it is the story, in fact, of an internationally successful writer who has taken his risks, including the risk – perhaps the scariest of all for an Australian expatriate – of going home. Thus to draw on his adult experience is a rare thing for Malouf and one can only hope for more of it. On the evidence of his new book, there is a new expressive impulse that will be hard to deny. Probably it was always there, but he kept the lid on it. In *Antipodes* there is a beautiful story, 'That Antic Jezebel', about the Sydney community of European *beau monde* refugees. A one-time all-conquering beauty dresses up in her old finery to go to the new opera house, where she is disturbed to find that one of her ex-lovers fails to take his regular seat. He has died of old age, and soon she will too.

From someone who could write a story like that, it would have been legitimate to expect a string of books that dramatized the complex postwar interchange between Australia and Europe, but apart from a few pages about Tuscany appended to the autobiography, Knack's suicide in *Harland's Half Acre* was the only further sign of such interests. (Malouf lived in Tuscany at one stage and still spends part of each year there: he has been frank about finding the Australian arts world too attentive. Though pleased enough to be accepted, he is not the type to relish being found familiar.) More often than not, and certainly more often than a man with his qualifications might have, Malouf has written novels as if he were setting out to meet the demands of an unreconstructed Australian nationalist for reliably indigenous yarns with as few cosmopolitan overtones as possible. They are complex, many-layered books, but with rare exceptions they are not many-layered in the social sense, and even his sole truly large-scale work, *The Great World*, has not much in it of Australia's actual social workings. As in a film script, there is a high-concept contrast between rich man and poor man, but there are no real social divisions, and to carry on as if Australia does not possess social divisions is worse than uninformative, it is sentimental.

*

In Australia, as in America, there is a world where money grows old, power is preserved, and customs are refined beyond the easy reach of the common people. Australia isn't England, but it isn't Illyria either. Though democratic, prosperous, and egalitarian beyond all historic precedent, it is still a complex society, with highly sophisticated, self-protecting elites that Malouf in his years of success has learned a lot about. That there could be startling results if he puts this knowledge to use is proved by 'Great Day', the last and longest story in the new book, in which the members of a distinguished family gather at their country seat, where the patriarch, an erstwhile political grandee called Audley, is living in the afterglow of his influence on public life. He is still consulted as an oracle by the media and the new crop of politicians, but his children, all grown to adulthood, have their own ideas about his infallibility, and are working out their destinies according to their own desires.

The women's roles are particularly finely detailed – a new departure for Malouf. Audley's daughters could be Russian sisters longing for Moscow, except that they are already there, and find themselves unsettled. For tone, pace, and sense of nuance, a comparison between 'Great Day' and a Chekhov long short story – 'Anna Around the Neck', for example – would not be too far-fetched. And as with Chekhov, the reader finds the end of the story looming far too soon. 'Great Day' cries out to be a novel: the novel Malouf has not yet tried, the novel about now.

Malouf has a reason for disliking the present: it wants to murder his memories. In 'Great Day' a folk museum – one of those typically Australian amateur collections of *bricolage* and natural wonders – burns to the ground, obviously as a symbol of the modern world having its way. In 'Jacko's Reach' he is explicit about what he has spent so long saying goodbye to:

> The last luminous grains of a freer and more democratic spirit, that the husbands and wives of my generation still turn to dreams. . . . It is this, all this, that will go under the bars of neon lights and the crowded shelves and trolleys of the supermarkets, the wheels of skateboards, the bitumen walks and solid, poured-concrete ramps.

It would be a more persuasive threnody if he could first persuade himself, but there are encouraging signs that he can't, quite. Australia's future is unlikely to be settled on such predictable lines, and one of the reasons is the country's by now firmly established status as a creative powerhouse. Though the Gold Coast of Malouf's beloved Queensland looks more like Las Vegas every year, Australia is not in much danger of becoming too Americanized while there are writers like him around. Its cosmopolitan artists, of whom some of the most prominent have spent their lives abroad, have served their country well by pursuing their own ends. An insulated nationalist culture would have been no culture at all, and very easily displaced by the American mass-media influence that Australia's intellectuals, with some reason, fear can leap oceans at a single bound.

Instead, we have been given what we scarcely expected, or we would not have hoped for it so vocally: a world-embracing cultural identity, stated in our own version of the English language, with a vocabulary enriched by the collective memories of a population that came from everywhere, the earliest part of it across thousands of years of time. This is the uniquely vivid language that David Malouf speaks with such fluency, although I wish, when he so deliciously evokes the mid-century childhood some of us shared with him, that he wouldn't say 'all over' to mean 'everywhere'. We used to say 'everywhere'. 'All over' – he may remember – is what the Yanks said.

New York Review, 21 December 2000

Postscript

Critics can't influence the course of artists, and look foolish trying. There is no magnet that powerful. If I could alter the course of an artist like David Malouf, however, I would bring the focus of his attention closer to here and now. His historical novels and stories are richly imagined, but they are all too easily employed as referential ammunition in sterile battles fought about the supposedly formative experiences of colonial Australia. The experiences undoubtedly did happen, but it was minds, not events, that were formative. It didn't take unusually sensitive young men on the land, for example, to realize that there was something wrong about killing Aboriginals: Governor King knew it before he arrived in Sydney, and one of his first initiatives was to post a law that said so. There is an element, in much of Malouf's work, of being mired in Arcadia. Imagine, for an equivalent, a modern American literature in which Saul Bellow wrote about General Custer, Philip Roth wrote about the Gold Rush, and even Gore Vidal wrote less about Lincoln and Aaron Burr than about the Lewis and Clark expedition. The mismatch of time and attention is made all the more piquant by Malouf's startling gift for talking about the complexities of modern history. If I were to say that he was hiding in the far past, however, it might well be an impertinence. A talent does what it must, and Malouf is as talented as a writer need be. His memory, in particular, is a poetic instrument which I tried to praise in this piece but still didn't praise enough. In my own book *Unreliable Memoirs* I thought I had done something to evoke the house I grew up in. Then I read Malouf's *12 Edmondstone Street* and realized I had got no further than the bricks and mortar. Malouf gives you the feeling of the carpet under your sunburned bare feet, the itch of blistered skin about to peel. I think it fair to say that he would have been less sensitive to these nuances if he had not had an immigrant background, and that the emergence of the post-World War II multicultural Australia, with all its new concentrations of power and social prestige, is the even greater tale that remains for him to tell. There are touches of it in his short stories, especially the autobiographical ones, but so far the novels have been informed by it more in the rind than at the core. There is always the chance, of course, that Malouf's next book will render this footnote nonsensical at a stroke. I look forward to that.

THE HIDDEN ART OF BING CROSBY

From its bare billing in *Radio Times*, *Bing, the Greatest of Them All* doesn't sound like the kind of event that might win gangsta rap fans away from their alleged interest in gun crime. But for anyone who has ever wondered how a simple-seeming song lyric can invade the mind with such poetic force, here is some essential listening. Going to air in three parts on BBC Radio 2, the series manages to raise most of the issues about what happens when a superficially ordinary, non-operatic voice shapes and guides the words of a song so that they get into your head and stick there. The most niggling issue of all is raised by the choice of presenter. In the enforced absence of the actual Bing, his story is told by Pat Boone. It would be fair to say that Boone himself is by now heading for the last round-up, yet his voice still sounds young. It always did. When he was on top of the hit parade half a century ago, his voice spelt unspoiled youth. It was pure and pretty: far prettier than Bing's. So what did Bing's voice actually do, if it couldn't do the whole job just by itself?

The answer is that a popular singer's voice should have a lot more going for it than just its quality. Too much natural beauty, indeed, can get in the way, flooding the aural reception system of the listener before the actual song gets a chance to register. Pat Boone was lucky with his biggest hit, *Friendly Persuasion*: the archaic diction ('Thee I love') injected some aural roughage into his usual effect of squirting the audience with perfume. Leaving even Boone sounding rugged was Johnny Mathis, who made angelically soaring journeys up the charts in the fifties with the kind of big ballad that enabled him to show off his effortlessly gorgeous upper register. (In its land of origin, the Mathis approach fell into the category of 'make-out music', meaning that it could be safely left to sound vaguely romantic in the background without diverting any of the attention necessary for the unhooking of a bra.) By the time I was old enough to be in control of the Bakelite knobs on our lounge-room radio in Sydney, Bing, across the Pacific in Los Angeles, was getting into his next to final phase. After more than twenty years of averaging three movies and forty records a year on top of a radio show every week, he was finally slowing down enough to look like the lazy son-of-a-gun he had always cannily pretended to be. But I didn't have to do much research to find out what he had that the newer fellows hadn't: or, rather, what they had that he wasn't burdened with. They were doing it the pretty way. He was just doing it, although 'just' is a word we will need to dismantle with care.

'I have just an ordinary voice,' he said in one of his carefully uninformative interviews. 'Anyone who can carry a tune thinks he can sing as good as I do.' His use of the word 'good' for 'well' is a tip-off that his gift for the common touch could sometimes lapse into the common lunge. Sinatra was a more typical band singer in having no book-learning to speak of, or with. In high school Crosby learned elocution from the Jesuits. He went on to a college education. He was so at home with a twelve-cylinder vocabulary that his radio and film writers later poured on the polysyllables in full confidence that he could handle anything. But he was saying exactly what he meant when he said he had an ordinary voice. He could do extraordinary things with it, but regarded as a mere sound it was just the noise of a nice man speaking. He put most of his art into making sure that he still sounded like that even when he was performing prodigies. The secret of great success in the popular arts is to bring the punters in on the event, and you can't do that if you are manifestly doing something they can't do. You have to be doing something they can do, so that they can dream. It's just that you do it better, so that they can admire. Essentially they are admir-ing themselves: it's a circuit, and too much obvious bravura will break it.

Bing had the bravura, but except in his early days it wasn't obvious. Starting his career in the 1920s, he was the man on the spot when the microphones got good enough to be canoodled with, as if they had hair to be stroked. Released from the necessity to project, he could concentrate on shaping a sung note so that it sounded like speech. Other singers were slower to catch on, and some of them never caught on at all. In any film musical starring Dick Powell you can hear – and what is almost worse, see – what happened to a

singer when, even if miming to playback, he continued to project as
if he weren't being amplified. He looked as if his vocal cords hurt
like piles. Bing went in the other direction, as if the microphone
could hear him think. In this endeavour, he was lucky with the
natural attributes of his voice. Often characterized as a pleasant light
baritone, it had a tenor top to it, conferring the precious gift of
allowing him to relax into the upper register. A singer can have a
note-perfect two and a half octave range and no flexibility at all.
What counts is the capacity to negotiate the tricky intervals, and
Bing could do an instantaneous octave jump that left the second
note ringing as clear and open as the first.

Admirers of the cornet player Bix Beiderbecke would describe
the resonating clarity of his attack as bullets hitting a bell. Bing
could do what Bix did and often did it with him. They were both
in Paul Whiteman's huge jazz band. Often derided in retrospect by
jazz purists as a lumbering rip-off of the black man's heritage, the
Whiteman organization had some funkier components than its name
taken literally might suggest. An outfit within the outfit was called
the Paul Whiteman Rhythm Boys. Singing sprightly tongue-twisters
with the Rhythm Boys, Bing proved that he could string notes
together like Bix playing a triple-tongued glissando. 'There Ain't
No Sweet Man Worth the Salt of My Tears' was supposed to be a
woman's song but Bing turned it into an athletic event. Sometimes
he and Beiderbecke performed together, like two instruments, or
two voices, vying for supremacy. Bing showed that he could smear a
note without blurring it. He could make it dip in the middle like
a Chinese vowel, and it would still sound as if it had been spoken.
These were prodigious amounts of know-how for a crooner to have,
and they were the real secret behind the later success in which he
seemed to repudiate them. You have to have it before you can throw
it away.

Later on, Bing was as careful not to attract attention with his
technique as a hired assassin is with his luggage. He attracted
attention to the song, and there he was lucky in his timing, because
the American song was in the full flight of its creative energy, still
establishing the repertoire whose presence does most to explain the
absence of a considerable modern American opera. (Sondheim is
exceptional only in proving the rule to its limit: his work is not the
dilution of opera, but the furthermost development of the musical

show.) Tin Pan Alley, Broadway and the big jazz bands added up to a powerhouse working flat out to supply its own demand for product, and the product was a solidly rhyming, singable lyric personal only in the sense that a singer could adapt it to his or her style. When Crosby sang direct from the Coconut Grove at the Ambassador Hotel in LA, his audience, stretching up beyond San Francisco on the West Coast, weren't hearing the barely articulated words of a personal anguish as they would be today, they were hearing a skilful interpretation of a national literature. The same would later be true for Billie Holiday. 'Strange Fruit' was rare in her repertoire for expressing the black condition. More typical was 'Pennies from Heaven', which expressed anybody's condition. Bessie Smith and the other blues singers had sung the stock songs of black experience, but although the black experience was almost incomparably awful when set beside the white experience, the stock was restricted. The white repertoire of lovelorn standards dealt with a far narrower range of suffering, but offered a far wider range of opportunity to sing a commercial hit. In anticipation of Ella Fitzgerald, Billie Holiday sang mainly from the standard song-book, and worked few variations that could be called black. She hardly even bent the notes. She is hard to parody because she had few mannerisms. Today, Mariah Carey, the culmination of a soul-shouting line that began with Aretha Franklin and started going haywire with Dionne Warwick, gives us nothing but mannerisms: the song is a notional presence in a cloud of melisma.

Clean-cut respect for the song was also the mark of Nat King Cole. A jazz man of stature whose voice was as well schooled as his piano style, Cole won enough general acceptance to live in a white neighbourhood without getting lynched. But he remained a white man's ideal black. He was so keen to keep up orderly appearances that when he put on his trousers in the dressing room of his TV show he wouldn't sit down again until he was on the set, in case he broke the crease. Almost all his material came from the repertoire of the romantic song. Treating the bathroom mirror to my version of his monster hit 'Mona Lisa', I copied the articulation of his lips, not because I hankered after a black style but because I thought that was how he was getting his mellow tone, from the movement of his mouth rather than from the subtle flexing of his abdomen. Similarly

I hoped to get Crosby's tone by letting my mouth hang loose at the corners. I rather wished that my ears stuck out, like his.

But the great role model of my first bathroom period was Frank Sinatra. He, too, sang from the standard repertoire, but by selection and presentation he dragged it towards the forbidden. One of my fellow study-circle leaders in the Kogarah Presbyterian Church Fellowship was a secret collector of Sinatra records. He possessed the first copy of *Songs for Swinging Lovers* I ever heard. I helped him to wear it out. I also helped to wear out several seats at the local Odeon, where I watched *The Tender Trap* over and over. Only much later in life did I realize what Sinatra was doing from the technical angle. The standard item of praise is 'breath control' but every professional singer has a certain amount of that. What Sinatra really had was enunciation control. In that department he went beyond Crosby, who even when feigning heavy-lidded gloom was always reassuringly joyful, as if the very act of singing was a guarantee of buoyancy. Sinatra could get the tone of bitter speech into singing words. Almost to its outer limit, he increased the range of naturalistic enunciation, making a song into a spoken statement. (If his voice had been as pretty as his epigone Vic Damone's, he would have found that a lot harder.) The only realistic element he did not include was inarticulacy.

Though they have never come up with anything quite so slovenly as Estuarine English, even the Americans occasionally swallow their final consonants when speaking. Uniquely among the crooners, Dean Martin adapted the suppression of terminal consonants to his singing style. In London at the moment, an Italian restaurant called Da Paolo in Charlotte Place plays Dean Martin tracks one after the other as background music to the evening meal. For those of us who grew up marvelling at Dino's ability to exhale a satiated moan along with the fumes of the third cocktail, here is vivid evidence that our memories are exact: he really did keep missing out on the final 's' as if the olive had got into his mouth along with the gin, and he really did bring English into line with Japanese by eliminating the difference between the singular and the plural. Sometimes the consonant before the 's' vanished along with it: 'Make my dree come true.' At other points, if you put the 's' back on one word as the sense seemed to demand, it turned out that the rhyme word up ahead of it needed an 's' too. ('Thrill me with your charm/ Take me in your arm'.) In his own words, it was a magic technee. ('When we kiss I grow wee.') Admittedly most of the songs victimized by Dino were already victims. Far from being refined examples of the upmarket repertoire, they were Italian hits translated into an English so indifferent that it was asking to be assaulted. But his calculated maltreatment of received elocution was more creative than I was ready to admit at the time. Only today am I ready to see the sophistication of his approach. Sleepy but unsleeping, he was transmitting the sweetly painful post-coital admission that desire could never be satisfied, but only, temporarily, allayed. Admissions like that weren't very common around the Kogarah Presbyterian Church Fellowship. No wonder I didn't get it. Sinatra was more than enough for me.

Every inflection Sinatra sang came from the spoken language. By no paradox, he did the same for screen dialogue. His sense of the music inherent in speech – not the music that can be imposed on it, but the music already in it – made him a revolutionary screen actor. Alas, he was too impatient to become the screen giant he might have been. (In the recording studio he would volunteer for another take: in the film studio never.) Crosby in his screen heyday was number one box office star in the world five years running. Sinatra would have thought that was a stretch in prison. It was one of the differences between them, and you could see all the differences in *High Society*, one of the great cinematic experiences of my first youth. For *High Society* I moved into the cinema and stayed there, as if constant attendance would get me an audience with Grace Kelly.

In *High Society*, Bing, old enough to be her grandfather, and Sinatra, merely old enough to be her father, vie for Grace Kelly's blessing. Frank got close, but the matter was settled in Bing's favour after he and the spun-gold goddess sang 'True Love' together. A song so undemanding that even I could sing it, 'True Love' was constructed by Cole Porter especially for the movie after it was noticed that Kelly could not manage three notes in a row unless two of them were the same and the third not very different. For the standard romantic ballad, 'True Love' was a symbolic indulgence so overwhelming that it invited rebellion, like the rumours about Marie-Antoinette's necklace. Sinatra had been doing his best for years to divert the traditional repertoire in the direction of actual sexual passion, rather than well-behaved self-control. Bing stood for adulthood, with all its renunciations. Sinatra stood for adultery. He could sing 'One For My Baby' with a whole heart. When, in 'Love and Marriage', he sang that they went together like a horse and carriage, you could tell he thought that the sentiment was a natural product of the horse. Bing, always a great one for the ladies until his second marriage settled him down (I prefer to leave out his off-screen success with Grace Kelly: the matter is still too painful), would probably have agreed with Sinatra on the subject but would never have let himself be caught uttering a non-conformist nuance. Sinatra's problem was that nuances were as far as he could go. In the world of the well-made song, illicit love, no matter how delicious, was a crime, and the compulsion to sing about it was the punishment. The standard song catalogue was a thousand modulations on the theme of anguish. Rock and roll was the shout of guiltless joy.

Rock and roll took over the hit parade, which would eventually cease to be a show-case for the well-made song, although the period of overlap lasted longer than we tend to remember. Elvis Presley and Sammy Davis Jr were sometimes up there one after the other, Elvis instructing us that we were nothing but a hound dog and Sammy driving the last nails into the coffin of some helpless big ballad chosen to prove that he bought his shirts and shoes in the same store as his friend Frank. But on the whole, and irreversibly, the popular music of the hit parade turned into something only the young could love. The popular music that could still be enjoyed by older people took up a shadow existence, with the album charts as the nearest approach to the glare of daylight. Broadway shows and film soundtracks continued to be written, however, and although Elvis Presley's album sales soon rivalled the astronomical figures Judy Garland had attained before youth usurped the business, so did the album sales of Barbra Streisand. The rock numbers and the well-made song could co-exist. Some of the rock numbers, indeed, were themselves well made, and not just as calculated throwbacks to the old music industry traditions but as spontaneous products of its tenaciously surviving vestiges. (The Leiber-Stoller numbers in the Elvis opus *Jailhouse Rock* were put together with a precision that would have been approved of by George and Ira Gershwin.) What really hurt the tradition of the well-made standard was the rise of the singer-songwriter: the very aspect of the sixties popular music revolution that we were supposed to be most happy about. No more mass production! Personal inspiration at last! But it turned out that some of the mass production had been pretty good, and that a lot of the personal inspiration was dire.

If criticism could be divorced from economics, the breakthrough of the singer-songwriters would look like the triumph of expression over music business logic. Actually, music business logic was the first thing the breakthrough expressed. The Beatles, apart from proving that Britain was a good offshore base from which to revitalize the American song, also proved that a singing act of any size would make more money if it wrote its own stuff. The act would get paid twice: once for performing, and again for what it wrote. It was an irresistible dynamic that spelled lingering death for the independent professional songwriter who wrote for all comers. This would be the age of gifted amateurs who wrote mainly for themselves. If someone else later recorded their songs they would be paid a third time, but the fact that they had already been paid twice was what drew new recruits to the ranks. Gifted amateurs proliferated.

Inevitably some of them were less gifted than others. The first thing to say about the rise of the singer-songwriters was that, in depth if not in breadth, it paid off artistically, even by the parameters of the tradition it superseded. Bob Dylan didn't further that tradition and didn't mean to, but there were many who did. The best songs that came out of California – John Sebastian, the Mamas and the Papas, and The Lovin' Spoonful were only some of the active names – weren't like Broadway show tunes, but they were neatly constructed and full of a new kind of life. Later on, the Eagles showed that millions could be made out of a group sound that didn't necessarily sound like a song: but the words, when you could figure them out, were often wittier than they needed to be ('Everybody wants to touch somebody / If it takes all night'). When we talk about a rock classic, we usually mean that it goes on yielding satisfaction beyond the initial impact it must always have. Randy Newman turned out to be a master songwriter, although you had to listen hard. His elliptical mumble set Enigma standards of encryption. But Newman's rhymes were solid, pure and cunning, even if, when he enunciated them, he compounded Dean Martin's missing consonants by turning most of the vowels into a common groan. Newman was an extreme version of the singer-songwriter who wrote classic songs but delivered them with such a personal stamp that they were hard to borrow. Alan Price took a few of them over and got away with it. But when Joan Baez did a cover version of the Band's wonderful anthem 'The Night They Drove Old Dixie Down', it didn't sound wonderful. It sounded ludicrous, even though Baez's voice was as pretty as ever. Expressing themselves as nobody had ever done since the first days of the blues, the singer-songwriters had achieved a unity of material and delivery that paradoxically yielded scattered results when it came to building up a new catalogue of standards. It was a literature, but it wasn't a repertoire.

The country musicians did best: the average country song could be covered by the average country singer, because they were all wearing the same boots and hats, even the women. (*Shania Twain sings Merle Haggard* is an unlikely album title, but not impossible.) But the average singer-songwriter, for whom individuality was everything, ran a double danger through self-enthralment. Even if the song was any good, it would have small chance of independent life. And the chances were very good that it would be bad.

Popular music has never run out of music. But it has, pretty well, run out of words, and lately there is a widely recognized awareness that the business of writing considerable songs might be a bit more complicated than just bunging down a few thoughts. At the moment, Ravi Shankar's daughter Norah Jones is selling albums by the million. Her voice is as lovely as her face. It would be too much to say that she can write melodies to match, but they are never less than pleasant. Her lyrics, however, rarely rise to the level of drivel, which is at least clear. On her new album *Come Away With Me* she sensibly puts in some songs by other people. On Robbie Williams' new album *Swing When You're Winning* all the songs are by other people, most of them long dead. So is the album's acknowledged hero, Frank Sinatra. Robbie wants to be Frank. It is a laudable aim, but he has a long way to go. On one track, by electronic trickery, he actually sings a duet with his idol, thus cruelly revealing what he can't do: give the words their value. I should hasten to say that Norah and Robbie have both been doing something right. They make money by the shed-load, whereas I and my collaborator Pete Atkin are in no danger of corruption through affluence. But tonight, when we play the first date of our new song-show tour, we will have our eye on something that must be more satisfactory than cash, or we would have given up years ago. Not that having a budget wouldn't be nice. (When I say that his new album, *Winter Spring*, is available through his website at www.peteatkin.com, I am mounting our entire advertising campaign in one parenthesis.) For me, however, the writer of the words, what comes first is the return to the source. Listening to the hit parade when I was a kid was how I started to be a writer. In amongst the cheap artifice there was expensive artifice; in amongst that there was art; and ever since I have always liked the idea of finding sapphires in the mud. Anyone can find them in Tiffany's.

Postscript

This piece was something of a departure for the *TLS*, but there were no protests, and there were several letters of support from impeccably qualified literary people who were glad to see the tradition of the showbiz song lyric receiving its due honour. One such correspondent was disappointed that I singled out Bix Beiderbecke, rather than Louis Armstrong, as the young Bing's jazz alter ego. I did it because it was true. Bing's duet with Satchmo in *High Society* might have been the great and lasting sign that the racial barrier in popular culture was broken for ever, but before the war, though the two men did occasionally appear together, it was always a novelty act. In the music business, de facto segregation continued far into the age of rock and roll, even on radio. Pat Boone's cover version of 'Tutti Frutti' got more airplay than Little Richard's original because Boone *sounded* white. Jim Crow was that hard to beat. One of the measures of the iconic status reached by the American entertainers is that we retroactively credit them with powers of influence. But they possessed the influence only on the understanding that it was seldom exercised. Humphrey Bogart was unusual in marching against McCarthyism even once, whereupon he was persuasively informed that his charisma had no existence apart from his career. After that, he campaigned for Adlai Stevenson – a radical enough allegiance for the time – but he did no more marching. Bing, still selling orange juice far into his old age, never forgot that he was only a performer, and lucky to be one.

Permit me to add that *Winter Spring* is still very much available from the Pete Atkin website. During a recording session for BBC radio's *Loose Ends* I thrust a copy of our cruelly neglected disc on Tony Bennett. Ever the gentleman, he examined its cover carefully, in the manner of a Japanese executive taking pains not to insult the owner of a proffered business card by putting it into his pocket after too brief an interval. For all his politeness, it was a doomed move on my part, which I could have compounded by telling him that I had managed to write a whole article about popular singers without even once mentioning him, the most scrupulous technician of the lot. Katie Melua was in the studio too. It was the first time I had heard her sing, and her way with the words made my tiny eyes moist with gratitude. Diana Krall had already affected me the same way. On a flight to Australia I watched a video of Krall's Paris concert three times in a row. The following year she sold out the Albert Hall for a week. How marvellous that what we thought was gone should come back with confidence, and find an audience even among the young.

LARKIN TREADS THE BOARDS

Before explaining my belief that Jack Nicholson is the only choice to play Philip Larkin on screen, I should pay tribute to how well Tom Courtenay plays him on stage. A one-man show that had the audience at the Comedy shouting its approval on opening night, *Pretending To Be Me* has a booby-trap for a title. When Larkin coined that phrase, he wasn't saying that he was short of a personality. He only meant that he didn't want to waste his time, effort and creative energy on making public appearances to bolster the career of the famous name he had accidentally become by writing poems quietly at home. (Now, post mortem, someone else is doing it for him: a paradox we might have to examine.) Luckily Tom Courtenay, the principal deviser of the show, is well aware that Larkin, whatever else he was short of, was never short of a sense of self. If he wound up as a reclusive curmudgeon, it was a role he chose for himself and studied with relentless application from quite early on: an act of assertion if ever there was one. With appropriate decisiveness if implausible aplomb, Courtenay's Larkin is up there like Judy Garland at the Palladium. After the third encore, Judy would promise, or threaten, that the evening wasn't over yet ('I could sing all night!') A two-hour monologue from Larkin, all of it drawn from his marvellous prose except when studded with his incomparable poetry: what could be more riveting? And what could be less likely?

There, of course, lies the show's first and most glaring problem with verisimilitude. In real life, holding forth at length always rated high on the list of things Larkin could never be imagined doing. A weekend in Acapulco with Julie Christie: perhaps yes. But a long uninterrupted speech? Not a chance. The only reason he would ever talk for more than two minutes at a stretch was his fear that if you said something he wouldn't understand it. He was deaf. The life that had begun with difficulties in speaking ended with difficulties in hearing. Courtenay retains a hint of the stammer, but uses it as a device for varying the pace and emphasis in a flow of speech that Larkin could never have contemplated. His prose gives us the sense that he could talk like that, but good prose always does, and great prose can almost be defined as the illusion of what can be said concentrated until it sings. Larkin wrote the way he did because he could never talk that way. So the piece rests on an anomaly: reticence on the rampage.

Luckily the theatre, despite Brecht's best efforts, remains a place where we are content to fool ourselves by accepting the patently anomalous. The experimental writer B. S. Johnson once told me that he didn't think Shakespeare's plays were up to much, because real people do not speak poetry. B. S. Johnson is no longer with us, and Shakespeare remains the experimental writer that counts. Similarly, nobody in real life speaks continuously for hours on end unless he is Fidel Castro: but whereas Havana is full of people who wish he wouldn't, and Miami full of people who wish he hadn't, we wish that other people would. Larkin was already near the head of that wish-list before we first-nighters entered the theatre, some of us well armed with memories of every word he had written; but others, presumably, not.

The curtain opened on a set consisting of nothing except a few boxes pretending to be the packed goods Larkin had just moved from one Hull house where he was reasonably content to another Hull house that he hated on sight. Postponing the task of unpacking the 'specially chosen junk' that he once evoked in a poem, he began by speaking prose. Clearly he would speak the prose well. How well he would speak the poetry remained to be heard. The prose was cunningly spliced together from articles, interviews and letters. I could spot nothing that had been posthumously invented for the occasion. This was a mercy, because it would have stood out like a Big Mac at the Last Supper. Courtenay brought to the prose a commendable respect for its tone and rhythm. He varied both without notably distorting either, and apart from a few physical effects he held the attention by the quality of the words alone. (Except for one member of the audience who had attended the event in order to die of diphtheria, there was scarcely a cough all evening.) Admittedly some of Courtenay's physical effects were a bit weird.

Prominent among them was his periodic adoption of a wide-legged, knee-trembling, goal-covering stance as if he had suddenly been required to save a penalty from David Beckham. But the only real question about his delivery arose over the poems, and even that question, except at one telling point, was not about the way he spoke them. Last week in this paper Hugo Williams, who had attended a preview, properly raised a general objection to the way actors recite poems. No mean reciter himself, he was well qualified to speak, and he was right. Most actors do bury the rhymes, mangle the rhythms, and comprehensively ruin the poem by trying to put emotion in instead of just contenting themselves with getting it out. But Williams left it politely vague as to whether Courtenay himself was included in this indictment.

I think he should have said specifically that Courtenay wasn't. All of Larkin's poems invite recitation. Even the big poems whose long stanzas would resist being spoken in a single breath always invite you to try. Courtenay was good even with 'The Whitsun Weddings', which is a very hard number to read aloud, because it stretches single sentences over rhymed and rhythmic frames to an extent that Yeats himself, though he pioneered the practice, never pushed quite so far. While making every poem flow like a spontaneous utterance, Courtenay was careful to respect the punctuation, which includes the line-endings, each of them doubling as the phantom comma that a thespian in quest of conversational naturalism typically leaves out. Courtenay's respect for syntax was immaculate, sometimes to the point of pedantry. On the last line of 'An Arundel Tomb' ('What will survive of us is love') he hit the word 'us' as if we who are alive were being contrasted with the figures on the tomb. Professor Ricks has made a case for this possible stressing as part of the last line's putative complexity. But if Larkin had meant that, he would have found a way to stress the point that left less room for Professor Ricks to crash the party. The word to hit is 'survive', because we are being included, along with the effigies, in the contention that our only immortality might consist of a remembered gesture. (The 'might' is covered in the penultimate line: it's only *almost* an instinctive belief, and it's only *almost* true.) But an actor who can get your mind working about textual points like that isn't doing too badly, and we can be sure that for listeners coming fresh to Larkin it wasn't the quibbles that mattered: it was the imagery, sent over the footlights like an arrow shower, and right there becoming rain. On the whole Courtenay read the poems better than I ever hoped to hear them read. That wasn't the problem.

The problem with the poems – the second problem of verisimilitude dogging the production – was with the spontaneity, not the utterance. Mercifully never preceded by a drum-roll or postluded by a curtsey for applause, each poem seemed to arise from the surrounding prose, which Courtenay was successfully endeavouring to make sound as if it was being thought up on the spot. The result was that the poems sounded as if they were being thought up on the spot too. If Larkin had been capable of that, either his entire poetic output as we now have it would have been composed in a fortnight, or else he would have spent his lifetime making the torrential Victor Hugo look like the parsimonious Ernest Dowson. But Larkin had to work hard at his craft, and the demands of that work defined his life. In Courtenay's all too accomplished readings, the poetry was respected but the real career, that of poet, was diminished. A poet with Larkin's fanatical standards of quality control must spend a lot of time waiting. Even while he works, he might spend hours trying to fit a single phrase in the right spot. Sometimes Larkin spent decades trying: a long patience. There could be no activity less dramatic, but some attempt might have been made to dramatize it. Courtenay could scarcely have paused for a month or so before reciting each poem. A less impossible device might have been for him to recite one of the poems that Larkin eventually abandoned for want of a single line, and then to supply an appropriate line of prose that might point that fact out. But even in the absence of any means to show the length of time involved in composition, it should have been possible to indicate that the poems had been composed in a way the prose wasn't. (Actually the prose took time too, but much less of it.) Lighting effects are the obvious answer, and at the climactic point, near the end of the show, when Courtenay's recital of the magisterial 'Aubade' marked the oncoming finale of a night out and of a man's life, a lighting effect was actually used. Everything went dark around him, to make him look isolated, instead of just alone.

The upside of this was that one of Larkin's supreme achievements was put in a separate frame. The downside was that Courtenay felt inspired to go for broke. For one almost fatal moment the extraordinary actor became an ordinary actor. Suddenly transforming himself into a human loud-hailer, he ranted a phrase that was begging to be whispered. I won't mention which one it was, because I very much hope that he changes his mind about this initiative, which added colour to the poem only in the way that the uninvited arrival of a circus barker would add colour to a funeral. By then, luckily, the success of the evening was beyond sabotage even from himself. Against all the odds, he had given us the old curmudgeon's tough love of language, the deep secret of his acerbic charm. The question of whether some of the uncharming stuff had been disingenuously left out, however, lingered in the air, even as we stomped and cheered. This was the third problem of verisimilitude, and the one that mattered most.

If some of the critics have been tepid about the show, this problem was their main reason. They have a point. There are cats out of the bag, and Courtenay put them back in. Larkin the pornophile is only fleetingly present, and funny when he is. He complains with disarming bitterness about the way his new television set fails to provide the flood of filth he was threatened with before its purchase, and there is a suggestion that his interest in well-developed schoolgirls might include their corporal punishment. But the pile of treasured top-shelf publications that he might have produced from one of the crates – just to check that they had not been injured in transit – is not forthcoming. As for his racism, the point is raised only by implication, and solely in his favour. He plays records by Louis Armstrong and Billie Holiday on his obsolescent radiogram, and dances about in silent ecstasy to the music. The implication – and it would have been the right inference to draw – is that the man who was supposed to dislike blacks was grateful to black musicians for having made his life more bearable.

But to deal with the point fully would require at least two more elements. One of them would be a recital of his poem 'For Sidney Bechet', in which the great saxophonist is saluted as the exemplar of all joyous creativity, the man of genius to whose eminence Larkin the mere poet can only aspire. No true racist would be capable of such homage. But in fairness to all the black Britons who do not play jazz, there would have to be a set of quotations from the bigotry that cropped up in letters he wrote to close friends. I think a fair view of Larkin's prejudices is that he disliked multiculturalism because it altered his bolt-hole version of England, and that he could no more stand alteration than an institutionalized prisoner can stand being issued with a new cup; but there can be no doubt that the way he said so is unpleasant to read, and doubly so because it comes from him. If those remarks were quoted, however, you would also need a disembodied voice to explain that among his circle of unshockable correspondents, to write shocking things was a sport, and that in his public life as a librarian and a literary figure it was unknown for Larkin to be less than courteous to anybody of whatever gender, creed or colour. The disembodied voice, which would need more time on the public address system than Courtenay has on stage, would have to go further, raising the issue of whether or not Larkin made a mistake when he failed to engineer the bonfire of his private papers that he often contemplated. He was an archivist by nature, but he might have foreseen that his impulse to preserve would injure his reputation as a poet after his death. He didn't care about his career in the usual sense of the word, but about his poetic reputation he cared passionately. Yet he would have had to be clairvoyant to guess that his literary executors, by showing us his prejudices, would open the door for a rush of dunces.

The diligence of the executors was perhaps foreseeable. The zeal of the dunces was something else. Invited to attack the man, they have downrated the poet as well, and though the absurdity of this disparagement must eventually become apparent, in the meantime it will serve to ensure that the world's path to the better mousetrap he built becomes an obstacle course. As Hugo Williams noted last week, Bonnie Greer, *per media* the *Mail on Sunday*, recently instructed us to stay cool on the subject. In her view, there was no need to worry about Larkin the racist, because Larkin the poet was not very good anyway. So in her view there was no real problem. Bonnie Greer's sensitivity to poetry could be assessed when she appeared in an episode of BBC 2's *Essential Poems (To Fall In Love With)* and gave her assigned poem the kind of working over calculated to make Hugo Williams take up gardening. Nevertheless, or all the more, she needs to be told that there is a problem after all. Philip Larkin really was the greatest poet of his time, and he really did say noxious things. But he didn't say them in his poems, which he thought of as a realm of responsibility in which he would have to answer for what he said, and answer forever. He also thought there was a temporary and less responsible realm called privacy. Alas, he was wrong about that. Always averse to the requirements of celebrity, he didn't find out enough about them, and never realized that beyond a certain point of fame you not only don't have a private life any more, you never had one. But for treating these themes in *Pretending To Be Me* there is neither time nor room. They would have to be raised in class. Ideally it would be a literature class in which race relations might occasionally be discussed, but the rule of dunces may soon ensure that it will be a race relations class where literature is occasionally discussed, and only as evidence for the prosecution.

On stage, the women who loved Larkin in real life are neither present nor specifically referred to, except perhaps in the beautiful poem about the footprints in the snow, which has recently cropped up even in some of the tabloids, with the addressee duly named and shamed. Normally the tabs are not open to poetry, but all evidence of Larkin's amatory duplicity can now be assured of maximum exposure. This, again, is a huge subject that would be hard to fit on stage even in skeletal form. Just as the man who complained about his shy diffidence was actually an efficient bureaucrat at the top of his profession, the man who complained so often about missing out on love was actually surrounded by it. If Larkin was not exactly Warren Beatty, he certainly bore, in his multiple liaisons if not in his personal appearance, a striking resemblance to Albert Camus. In the week before Camus met his death in a suitably glamorous car-crash, he wrote to five different women pledging eternal fealty to each, and he was probably telling the truth every time. Larkin had a similar network of affectionate loyalties, but always with the proviso that his life had to remain undivided. Not even Monica Jones, who was the closest to being a companion, got a share of his solitude. When he said 'Deprivation is for me what daffodils were for Wordsworth' he left open, beyond the simple statement, the complex implication that if he had not been granted sufficient deprivation he would have had to seek more of it. The play depends on the assumption that the life shaped the work. The proposition that the work shaped the life would be too difficult to discuss in the theatre, and would be hard enough to discuss for a panel of professors locked up together for a year. If we accept all these limitations as inevitable, *Pretending To Be Me* can be hailed for what it is. It gives us a bravura performance by an actor who understands that bravura must be in service to emotion, and not just a display of technique. It shows a curmudgeon doing what curmudgeons do best: being sardonically funny about life. Above all it brings to the theatre the primal exultation of language; the very thing that has made the English theatre thrilling since Mercutio first told Romeo about Queen Mab; the thing from which it can stray only so far before ceasing to be substantial.

The only question now is who will play Larkin next. Courtenay can't keep it up forever: for only one set of vocal cords, the piece must be like trying to sing the whole of *Aida* on your own. The perfect lookalike, Eric Morecambe, is sadly not available, and anyway he was too merry. Alexei Sayle could do it: he's the wrong shape, but he can do the right kind of humour, which is the curmudgeon's humour, and thus not very merry at all, because it makes jokes about the world falling apart only on the understanding that the man making them is falling apart as well.

Recasting the leading role in your own mind is a good sign: it means you think the script is alive. Recasting it for Hollywood is a bigger challenge, but it will have to be faced. Courtenay has been a fine film actor at every stage of his career (if you think nothing could be better than his appearance in *Billy Liar*, see him in *The Dresser*) but Miramax will probably want an American. Miramax won't relocate Larkin from Hull to Harvard: Harvey Weinstein knows by now that British literary life has a solid appeal on the art-house circuit and a pipeline to the Oscars. But Weinstein will want a bankable star. According to my own sources, Robert De Niro has already declared his interest, but to prepare himself for the role he wants to spend fifty years in a library. Bruce Willis wants the library to be taken over by terrorists. Seriously, it has to be Jack Nicholson. Jack has been in training as a curmudgeon since the campfire scene in *Easy Rider*. Remember *Five Easy Pieces*? 'Hold the mayo.' The scorn, the bitterness! Nobody does sardonic better. There is nobody like him for disillusioned. When Jack gives it the bared teeth and the arched eyebrows, he could recite his own death sentence and still sound funny.

The beauty part is that Jack has just played an irascible old bastard and will probably get an Oscar for it. In *About Schmidt* he's Philip Larkin without the bifocals. Admittedly Schmidt doesn't write poetry or do anything very much. The movie, which you should see unless you have a chance to visit a molasses factory, asks us to believe that Schmidt has wasted his life in an insurance office. But since there is no residual evidence of any personal qualities that he might have wasted, Jack is left to convey little except an unspecific sense of having achieved nothing. To put it another way, he is left to convey nothing. He does this by impersonating a stunned mackerel with a comb-over. But at least there are no mannerisms. Jack is ready to begin again, after Stanley Kubrick set him on the wrong track by convincing him that there could be an acting style beyond naturalism. There is no acting style beyond naturalism except ham, as Jack proved in *Prizzi's Honour*, where he pioneered his latterday schtick of clenching his lips with difficulty over an object he was reluctant to identify. By the time he got to *As Good As It Gets*, you would have thought he was concealing a live mouse in his mouth. But when he bared his teeth at Helen Hunt like a wolf with its eye on a new-born lamb, we got a reminder of what this man could do, and can still do. That killer drawl is ready for its greatest workout. And he only wants a few changes. 'Your mom and pop, heh heh. They fuck you over, right?' Coming soon to a multiplex near you.

Postscript

Ian McEwan said that he would never forgive me for having written this piece, because it persuaded him to break his personal rule of staying away from the theatre. Choosing his words with care, he told me that he had disliked the evening very much, and that he thought me demented, if not criminal, for having encouraged people into the theatre with my review, instead of standing outside the theatre and encouraging them to go home. Speaking as one who loved Larkin's poetry at least as much as I did, he wanted to know how I could be a party to a theatrical presentation that might have been designed specifically to render the poetry less meaningful, by promoting the idea that such a concentration of emotion needed acting out. I tried to tell myself that Courtenay's performance might have gone off a bit since I first saw it, but on second thoughts I had to admit that McEwan might have had at least the ghost of a point. Hadn't I, while watching the play, been thinking that it would be a good introduction to Larkin's poetry for young people who had never read it? And hadn't I, who knew his work well, also been thinking that to hear even the best actor read the words aloud was nothing like as good as becoming acquainted with them in the silence of print? In other words, I had been thinking of what might be good for others: a sure-fire formula for distorting one's initial response. But my first thoughts were the ones I wrote down in that same week, and I was glad to have done so. One young lady said that my review led her to the play, that the play led her to Larkin, and that his poetry became part of her life. She recited the last lines of 'Dockery and Son' to prove it. There had to be something good about that chain of events, at a time when accredited arts experts were lining up in print, on radio and on television to insist that the old fool had never been worth bothering with.

Now it can be revealed: the phrase of 'Aubade' that Courtenay hammered was 'This one will', and it had the effect of dropping a mortar bomb into the adagio of Schubert's C major string quintet. The anomalous uproar was especially unfortunate because 'Aubade' is the poem that so many of Larkin's literary admirers think of when they hear the creaking of death's door. 'Aubade' unites other writers in a common worship. People agree about its quality who agree about nothing else. Harold Pinter can recite the whole poem from memory while seated at the dinner table. The poem is a point of reference in Simon Gray's *The Smoking Diaries*. Very few poems have that kind of currency. Tom Courtenay probably thought the same: the reason that he gave it special treatment. He should have copied Pinter, who dials down the histrionics. But finally the poem outclasses even the most beautiful voice that tries to recite it. One is reminded of what Schnabel said about Beethoven's late piano sonatas: music better than can be played.

THE IRON CAPITAL OF BRUNO SCHULZ

As a writer, a painter and a man, Bruno Schulz believed that the aim of life was to mature into childhood. In the peachy light of the recent me-speak compulsion to get in touch with one's inner child, Schulz's belief might look like yet another reason for not getting in touch with him. He didn't write a lot, and a lot of what he did write was in a Polish difficult even for Poles: he is hard to translate. Nearly all of what he painted went missing. He is one of those creative spirits from what Philip Roth called 'the other Europe', the Europe beyond the Elbe, whose reputations tend to stay there because it is hard to airlift them out. If we add to all that the notion that he was a toy-cuddling advocate of infantilism, he could be lost to us indeed. But the truth of his mentality was anything but infantile: it was a penetrating realization that the perceptual store of our early childhood forms what he called 'the iron capital' of the adult imagination.

The realization was itself realized in his two little books of short stories, *Cinnamon Shops* (otherwise known as *The Street of Crocodiles*) and *Sanatorium Under the Sign of the Hourglass*: the two little books that constitute the bulk of his writing as it has come down to us, and which are enough by themselves to make him a weighty figure. Nobody quite matches him for seeing everyday objects in three dimensions, and evoking them as if the fourth dimension, time, had been erased. Making a mythology from the actual, he convinces us that the actual is made from myths. Reading him, we feel as our own children must feel when we are reading them the words of Maurice Sendak while they are looking at the pictures. Colours breathe. Textures pulse. The butcher, the baker and the candlestick maker loom like totem poles. And it is all done in such a short span, in paragraphs worth chapters, and chapters worth a book. There might have been another, longer work – the novel usually called *The Messiah* – but if the manuscript ever existed it vanished like the paintings; and all other possibilities of future work vanished along with his future. On a scale measured by his potential achievement, he died young.

In fact he had already turned fifty when he was murdered, but we are right to think of him as still beginning, because it was always the way he thought of himself. So it was an untimely end, as well as a terrible one. If only it had been uniquely terrible. Alas, it was a commonplace. He was one more Jew rubbed out by the Nazis. The circumstances, in his case, were merely unusual. In the Drohobycz ghetto, a Gestapo officer with good taste, one Felix Landau, had made a pet of him so that he could paint murals. In November 1942, on a day of 'wild action' – that is, a day when the Nazis ran around shooting people at random instead of rounding them up to be shipped off in batches, as on an ordinary day – Schulz's protector took his eye off his human property. Landau had a jealous rival, another Gestapo officer called Karl Günther. Landau had once shot Günther's pet dentist, so Günther took the opportunity to get square. He put two bullets through Schulz's head. If we find ourselves hoping that the first bullet did the job, it is because it is so hard to bear the idea that Schulz might have had even a split second to reach the false conclusion that his life had come to nothing.

It was a conclusion he had always been apt to reach even in normal circumstances. One of the many ironies of his life was that the Nazis made actual the torment of uncertainty in which he had lived and worked since his adolescence. Insecurity, indecisiveness and diffidence were marks of his personality. He was one of those geniuses blessed with an uncanny creative ability and cursed with an almost equally uncanny inability to do anything practical about it. From Jerzy Ficowski's biography this pitiably tentative personality emerges so sharply that it is likely to make us impatient, but decency and a sense of proportion demand that we should rein our impatience in: it was after all the condition for his inventiveness, which was the opposite of tentative, and indeed looks bolder as time goes by. By extension, it would be wise not to become impatient with this biography. It has been a long time getting to us. The first version was published in 1967. This translation is of an expanded version, but it still has some of the marks of a thesis. 'The attainment of the Schulzian artistic postulate led me to a state of feverish ecstasy' is not a heartening sentence to meet early on.

Luckily there are better sentences to be met later, when we are told that Schulz's jeweller's glass was a kaleidoscope, and that he had a way of being mathematically precise about myth. If such statements are not perfectly transparent, they are at least usefully suggestive, and thus fall into the realm of true criticism. A more worrying feature is not the presence of jargon, but the absence of a complete historical context. The Nazis are on parade but the Communists are not. Introducing the book, which she translated, Theodosia Robertson tells us that Ficowski kept Schulz studies alive in Poland during the 1950s and 1960s despite 'enormous obstacles', but she doesn't tell us what those obstacles were. More remarkably, Ficowski doesn't tell us either. We presume that the obstacles were political. Communist Poland found it hard to be proud of the great modern Polish writers, because they would not cooperate. There were attempts to lure Gombrowicz home, but they failed. Czeslaw Milosz remained resolutely unavailable and indeed his masterly long essay *The Captive Mind* can now be seen as one of the first wedges driven between the planks of the Warsaw Pact. Schulz, being safely dead, might have been more pliant, but there was something subversive about him. Any graduate of the Polish film and acting schools in the 1970s can tell you what it was. 'What we got from him,' says a Polish actress of my acquaintance, 'was luxury.' She didn't mean the high life. She meant the way he brought out the riches of the ordinary life he led in the few hundred square yards of Drohobycz that he knew intimately and almost never left. He brought out the quality of things: things to eat, chairs to sit on, curtains of different weaves, the cart rattling out of the dark. And he brought out the diversity of people, all observed minutely as individuals, sometimes elevated to the status of mythical beings, but never classified as types or members of a class. He was about as far from socialist realism as you could get. In preserving and furthering Schulz's reputation, Ficowski was ploughing a lonely furrow. Active in the intellectual movement that helped prepare the advent of Solidarity, he himself was an underground writer from 1977 onward. He is amply qualified to tell the story of the Communist state's attitude to his touchy subject, but he doesn't.

Perhaps he is worn out from trying to ride two horses at once. After it turned out that a few of Schulz's murals had survived after all, Ficowski was on the spot, and understandably put out, when agents of Yad Vashem intervened to pack up some of the most precious fragments and ship them back to Israel. A cultural version of the Raid on Entebbe, the caper raised not only a scandal but a false question: had Schulz been a Pole or a Jew? Ficowski, surely rightly, wants Schulz to be both, but runs a danger of tipping the balance if he puts too much emphasis on the possibility that his country might have been, in the recent past, a bad host to the writer's memory. It isn't now, of course, but the recent past refuses to lie down and die, and for the less recent past that goes double. Doomed to the margins in an anti-Semitic culture, weren't the Jews oppressed even before the Nazis got there? Wasn't Schulz a born victim?

He probably was, but not in the historical sense. Frustratingly missing in the area already noted, Ficowski's sense of history is present and correct where it matters most: he sees the Drohobycz *shtetl* of Schulz's childhood as a creative incubator, and not just as a trap. Drohobycz was in the old Galicia, so Schulz was born and raised under the Austro-Hungarian Empire. Until the Russians moved in and made it part of the Ukraine, his home town was part of a civilization. For Jews, that civilization certainly had its difficulties, but the coming nightmare kept nobody awake, because it seemed unthinkable. Jews had a future. Schulz's helpless fatalism has to be sought in his personality, and it is too much to assume that his personality was determined by his circumstances, or else we would have to say that his talent was too. The fatalism and the talent went together.

Part of the fatalism was a counter-productive propensity to be a good man at every moment, with never a thought for his own long-term interests. The boy who was caught by his mother feeding flies so that they would be safe for the winter grew to be the man who would give all he had to a beggar. He gave everything of himself, as if there were no tomorrow. (There wasn't, but not even Hitler was sure of that yet.) As an art teacher, Schulz would enthral his pupils with his chalk-talk stories, caring for them far beyond the demands of the job, and consuming the time he might have spent on his own art. He was consumed by the moment in the same way that his attention was consumed by an object. It was a miracle that he got anything at all drawn or written. He always needed someone to discover him because he had no energy left over with which to discover himself. *Cinnamon Shops* began in his letters to a woman friend, Debora Vogel. Without her, the book might never have happened. Women looked after him because he so obviously needed to be mothered. In his graphic work the dominatrix was omnipresent, and the figure most like him was usually on its knees. (All the women were real: when he drew them nude, their husbands recognized them, and raised a ruckus.) His life was like that. The trap was in his mind. To call him a Jewish historic victim is to diminish him, the Jews and history itself, which shrinks to a cartoon when read through hindsight, thereby encouraging the hopeless notion that the Jews of Europe were born only in order to die. But they were born in order to live: hence the tragedy.

Even with his tremendous powers of hesitation, Schulz managed to become a member of the Polish Academy of Letters. By the time of his real entrapment, he was famous enough for other literary notables to attempt a rescue. He might have got away, but typically he was unable to face the choice. The choice might have come down to the impossible decisions involved in packing a bag: socks first, or a spare sweater? He was like that. By giving us the man in all his frailty, Ficowski has helped to explain the artist in all his strength, but for the full measure of that strength we need to see those brilliant little books.

Theodosia Robertson promises us a new translation of them, done by herself: apparently the full etymological depth of the prose will be brought out. Some excerpts from her work in progress can be read in this volume. Since too much incorporated scholarship could only put the text further out of reach, one is glad to note that the extracts do not look very different from the same passages in Celina Wienewska's established renditions, most attractively available in *The Collected Works of Bruno Schulz* that was published in London by Picador in 1998. Recklessly lavish in its production standards, the book cost a whopping £50 sterling at the time and it was a commercial flop. I got my copy in a remainder shop for a pittance, and no doubt it can be picked up reasonably cheaply on the web. Edited by Ficowski and prefaced by David Grossman at his most eloquent, it is a truly beautiful book, appropriate to its subject in everything but its physical dimensions. Essentially a miniaturist writer, Schulz looks a bit lost in so monumental a volume, but there is an upside: there is room to reproduce his marvellous graphic work at its full value, and the book would be worth having if only for its colour reproduction of the single easel painting we know exists. Painted in 1920, it is called 'Encounter: a young Jew and two women in an alley'. From that one page alone, you can see that Schulz had absorbed the whole tradition of European painting, and would undoubtedly have added to it if his pictures had survived. Luckily the wave of history that rolled over images found it harder to wipe out words, and Bruno Schulz the writer is always with us. He is just a bit hard to get at. This biography helps.

Los Angeles Times Book Review, 3 November 2002

Postscript

The story of Bruno Schulz is the necessary corrective to the story of *The Pianist*. In telling the story of a single talented person being saved by chance, Polanski was being as bleak as he could be and still make a movie. A movie about Bruno Schulz would have to end with the star being shot through the head. Nobody would finance such a project. Schulz's story offers no consolation except that he at least lived long enough to prove that he was a genius. But at this point Michael Burleigh would step in to remind us that when we tell stories of great talents being arbitrarily murdered, we are once again courting sentimentality. As Primo Levi saw so clearly, the real story is about the extinction meted out to whole populations of ordinary people, not just to a few extraordinary ones. By that measure, every famous example misleads. Somewhere in the centre of this question is the point where the critic of the arts finds himself involved in modern politics whether he likes the idea or not. Artistic creativity is not the only thing in life. There are, or were, millions of lives that created nothing to last except the memory of a considerable existence, a moral continuity far more precious than all the beautiful things that have ever been made. A critic who can't see how artistic creativity is only a part of a much larger creation is trivializing his subject by the way he concentrates on it. When he does so incorrigibly, we call him an aesthete. It isn't that the aesthete is too serious about the artistic: he isn't serious enough about what gives rise to it.

CRITICISM À LA KERMODE

Frank Kermode's latest collection of essays, *Pleasing Myself*, should please a lot of other people too, but strictly on the quiet. In real life, Frank Kermode is softly spoken. An interlocutor does best to get as close as possible, so as not to miss a word. Many of the words are not Kermode's: they are quoted from writers he admires, and most of those are poets. The poets, could they be present, would be pleased to hear their lines pronounced with such a fine regard for rhythm, balance, sense and nuance. *Shakespeare's Language*, Kermode's last book before this, was justly hailed by its reviewers as the ideal critical tribute to the way the greatest of all poets actually wrote. It wasn't hard to imagine Shakespeare hailing it too. After all, the book brought him alive.

This new collection of essays works the same revivifying trick for poets of the twentieth century: Yeats, Eliot, Auden, Empson, Marianne Moore, Henry Reed and Roy Fuller are among them. Most of the essays are book reviews, and most of the books reviewed are books on: writing about writing. So this is writing about writing about writing. But Kermode is a practised hand at getting back through the layers of commentary to the ignition point of the gaseous expansion. In the beginning, somebody said something inspired, and this artist among critics already has it in his memory. For Kermode, language comes first. If a writer can actually write, here is a critic who can tell. The guarantee is that he writes so well himself.

Some reviewers were surprised that Kermode showed such a talent for narrative in his memoir *Not Entitled*. They shouldn't have been: he has always shown it. Some of his earlier books had grand, over-arching themes, but a knack for vividly recounting the events was always in plain sight. The first thing he looks for in art is a quality he possesses, and although he is too modest to think it sufficient in his own case, he is confident enough to call it a necessity in others. If they've got that, there is much else they can safely lack. Reviewing Roy Foster's first volume of the Yeats biography, Kermode ought to be two steps away from the poetry, but he is instantly in the poet's mind, which he knows to be a jumble sale. Foster is given credit for annotating the detritus: sooner or later we have to know about the Order of the Golden Dawn. But later is better.

First we have to know what Kermode knows: 'he had the ability to make all his interests coalesce . . .' In other words, you don't need the bric-a-brac to get at the talent: it is because of the talent that you might want to get at the bric-a-brac. If we want to know who Maud Gonne was, and whether or not Yeats ever managed to get her into bed, it should be because of 'The Cold Heaven'. Calling it 'his finest lyric' of the early period, Kermode speaks with authority, and not as the scribes. Recently, at a black-tie dinner in King's College, Cambridge, I heard him recite it by heart. 'Suddenly I saw the cold and rook-delighting heaven . . .' It was very easy to imagine Yeats there, pleased that his articulated sweet sounds were being so well respected. If he could have heard a performance like that on his All Souls' Night, he might have thought that a living man can drink from the whole wine after all.

On Eliot's 'missing' Clark lectures, Kermode makes an apparently peripheral remark about what Eliot did, or did not do, for Donne: 'there are a few, but too few, instances of close literary criticism, nose to text, brisk, arguable and fun'. Kermode is personally qualified to say that on all counts, but he is on his way to making a central point: Eliot's reasons for getting away from close literary criticism are the wrong ones. Eliot says the Brunetto Latini episode in the *Inferno* has a 'rational necessity' that Shakespeare's Octavius doesn't command when he talks about Cleopatra's corpse. Kermode quotes both passages and sees a difference: one is by Dante and the other by Shakespeare. 'But it would be hard to agree that the difference is about "rational necessity"'. And indeed it would. Eliot's big idea about rational necessity was part of his even bigger idea about the dissociation of sensibility. Kermode, by staying with the poetry, has taken Eliot's big ideas apart. The implication is that 'close literary criticism, nose to the text' is a big idea in itself, and the only one that counts, because it alone can bring everything in, including the irreducible fact of the individual voice.

Kermode once wrote a book about Wallace Stevens. Now an essay on Marianne Moore shows that he remains as pleased as ever about the American moderns. They had 'this dispersity': they were individuals, not a movement. Marianne Moore's poems are an extension of the principle she had been taught at Bryn Mawr: to find a disciplined way of doing as she pleased. 'Anything can get into them, including all the chosen pleasures of her life, the ball games and prize fights, the paintings and the exotic animals. To an extraordinary degree she did, though with great labour, exactly as she liked.' The way he makes the pleasures 'chosen' is an instance of how Kermode can switch on a single extra light bulb and show you a new corridor. To serve the purpose, poets can choose even their passions. The crunch comes only when the choice wrecks the work.

Empson chose to be difficult. He made things difficult for himself with Continental rhyme-schemes fiercely demanding in a rhyme-poor language like English; and he made things difficult for the reader by deploying a range of reference beyond any imaginable single encyclopaedia. Kermode is well equipped to follow up the references, but he makes sure always to follow them in a circle, so that you end up at what really matters about Empson: the compulsively memorable, singing lines whose simplicity the complication is there to protect. The protection was against himself. An appeal for sympathy would have cheapened his feelings, so he put the feelings almost beyond appreciation, as a beggar selling matches might paint a miniature on every box and price them at a thousand pounds each.

Once again, Kermode is the ideal appreciator because he is the ideal reciter. Empson had a way with a pentameter that made even the unstressed syllables prominent, and he would be glad to know that at least one of his readers, having got the lines by heart, doesn't miss a beat. 'Slowly the poison the whole blood stream fills'. I heard that line while our wine glasses were being refilled, and its companion while we were contemplating an overly challenging modern dessert of frozen oxtail soup arranged to look like hazelnut sorbet. 'The waste remains, the waste remains and kills.' Kermode knows exactly why 'Missing Dates' is a great poem even with its faults, although he himself, for once, can be faulted here. With typical generosity he borrows and acknowledges John Wain's tribute to

Empson's 'great reverberating lines', but follows Wain too readily in supposing that the dog's 'exchange rills' are dragged in. The rhyme might very well seem strained, but there is no guarantee that the poem didn't start from there. It takes a more than usually complete set of worksheets to tell us which rhyme-word triggered the chain reaction. Empson might have seen 'rills' first and come up with 'fills' and 'kills' later. (That would be an explanation for why the key line is written backwards: 'Slowly the poison fills the whole blood stream' would have been just as Empsonian, especially with its clinching spondee.) With a mind like Empson's, you never know. But it remains true that you can't begin to know what his mind is unless you hear the sonorities first, as he did.

Did you know that Kermode and Henry Reed once tooled around Seattle in a Ford Thunderbird and drank away the afternoon in the revolving restaurant at the top of the Space Needle? Neither did I. From the essay on Reed, the author of 'Lessons of the War' and 'Chard Whitlow' emerges as a misfit, a talent largely wasted, and a forlorn punster. But the talent was there, and one of the puns proves it. Puns rarely prove anything except an absence of wit, but it must have been fun to share the revolving sky-lounge with a man who could respond to the label of the next bottle of Mumm's Extra Dry by saying 'Poor baby!' Kermode is very good on poetic careers that were not fulfilled. He himself began as a poet – I think we could guess it, even if we had not been told – but his manuscripts were lost on their way home from the war. A cruel circumstance, offset by something else we could guess: he knows that a poet with a true vocation can't be stopped by anything short of gunfire.

There is an affectionate essay on Roy Fuller, a recognized war poet who came home to write poetry for the rest of his life. Kermode admires the way Fuller, like Wallace Stevens, could make a decent fist of an office job while serving his muse, to the tune of about 1,500 lyrics, give or take a hundred. Kermode can say, and make it stick, that part of Fuller's luck was to have no university. Kermode approves of everything about Fuller except, one suspects, the way he writes. 'Yet for all his various skills there is often in his writing, prose and verse, a certain ungainliness.' This is not exactly as damning as to say 'Wagner's music isn't as bad as it sounds' but it is getting close, because we know that for Kermode the gainliness is the *sine qua non*. Still, Hazlitt's unstinting praise of Milton makes you want to read Milton, even if it doesn't quite persuade you that Hazlitt wanted to read Milton.

Essays about prose writers are just as attentive to the style that tells all. Bertrand Russell's mountain of love-letters might have been written solely to inspire a single sentence from Kermode: 'He hated his women to be unhappy, because it upset *him*.' The piece on William Golding will send me back to *Pincher Martin*, which 'could hardly have been written by somebody who had not been a watch-keeping officer on a warship on North Atlantic convoy duty.' Kermode can say this with authority because he once kept the watch himself. Take it from one who knows. Philip Roth's *Sabbath's Theatre* is reviewed at the level of its writing, with blazing energy, as a matter of life and death. The whispering professor can turn the heat on when he wants to. Sometimes you wish he would do it more often. For devoting prodigious efforts of casuistry to calling Shakespeare an establishment propagandist, Professor Richard Helgerson of Santa Barbara is gently dismantled. Demolition would have been more appropriate. Seamus Heaney is duly praised for his Beowulf, but a duff translator from the French is let off with a slapped wrist, instead of a tanned hide. Even Jesus, if there was a temple to be cleansed, knew when to get the whip out.

But there is no point in whipping Kermode for his excess of Christian charity. It is one of the mainsprings of his receptivity, which has made him, in the long run, the opposite of a soft touch. There was a time when he thought the theorists had something. When it became evident that what they had was a tin ear for language, he gave up on them. Talent refuses to be trivialized, even by itself. My favourite piece in the book is a reminiscence of Australia's most volcanic literary event, the Ern Malley hoax. About sixty years ago, the young Kermode was on the scene when the hoax erupted. To embarrass the avant garde editor Max Harris, two young poets, James McAuley and Harold Stewart, invented Ern Malley and his complete works: a suite of poems comprising any nonsense that came into their heads. Harris fell for it, and for the rest of his life the laugh was on him. But Herbert Read said the right thing at the time, and Kermode repeats it now. A talented poet can't be entirely meaningless even when he tries. The creative spark is a hugely complex natural event which even those who possess it are only partly qualified to explore, and the less so because their attention is on themselves. Enter the great critic, whose attention is on them all, and who proves it with his marvellous memory.

TLS, 10 August 2001

Postscript

In 1974, when I published *The Metropolitan Critic*, the first of what are by now seven collections of pieces, it was fun to pretend that we toilers in Grub Street were bravely embattled against the safely tenured professors of the academy. It wasn't quite true even then – some of the best pieces in the newspapers and periodicals were written by academics – and today it is scarcely true at all. Only the occasional prodigy among the current bunch of penny-a-line men could hope to turn anything as good, or even as lively, as the pieces written by the professors. Fresh from victory over the arid theorists within their own ranks, they have brought their schooled humanism to a much wider forum than the quadrangle. Though very few of the academic hats can demonstrate quite the omnivorous range of John Bayley, it is necessary to remember that Bayley did time as a professor himself. If Grub Street's mission was to give the academy lessons in readability, the academy's mission was to give Grub Street lessons in scholarship. When the academics proved that they were readable too, it became obvious that an armed truce was more desirable than a war. Professor Kermode took the lead in giving the proof; and professors Ricks and Carey, to name only the most glamorous among several, have followed his example. After forty years, a picture that looked to the hasty eye as if it were hanging upside down is hanging the right way up. Young arrivals in Grub Street can now be told to look to the professors for instruction not just in reading, but in writing. Some of the more slapdash tyros need quite a lot of instruction in that, but only because the educational system is failing them in quite another way: it certainly isn't because the university professors have made themselves unavailable.

FAST-TALKING DAMES

A bit of a fast-talking dame herself, Maria DiBattista, in her valuable new book *Fast-Talking Dames*, is justifiably excited by the characteristic flip lip of her pre-war and wartime Hollywood heroines. One guesses that in her mind she is of their number: Jean Harlow, Rosalind Russell, Irene Dunne, Barbara Stanwyck, Carole Lombard, Katharine Hepburn, Maria DiBattista. A professor of English and comparative literature at Princeton, and published by Yale, she is heaped with Ivy League credentials but laudably determined not to be stifled by them. Especially in its wide-ranging and sometimes over-informative notes (Charles Baudelaire? Oh, *that* Baudelaire) the book occasionally lapses into the tenure-seeking stodge of an academic thesis, as if its governing spirit emanated from the assembled professors in *Ball of Fire*. But mostly she keeps in mind how Barbara Stanwyck, in that same movie, perched on the edge of the desk and talked rings around the fuddy-duddies. She would rather sound like that. The bright students who attend her seminars are in luck. It must sound like lunch at the wits' table in the studio commissary. This is the way feminism ought to be. Maria DiBattista's suggestion – potentially a revolutionary one – is that this is the way it once actually was. The whole of what we have come to know and value as female equality in recent times was prefigured on the popular screen before the end of World War II. If our author had followed up on some of the implications of this suggestion, she would have written an important book. Alas, she was talking too fast to hear herself think. Even so, *Fast-Talking Dames* could be the start of something big.

If her judgement had not been so good on the fine detail, she might have had a better chance of applying it to the big picture. But the fine detail was too fascinating to leave alone. Those perfect mouths with the epigrams coming out as neatly as the lipstick went on: how to step back from all that? Best not to try. The author does not do very much quoting from the scripts, perhaps for copyright reasons. She is no better than anybody else at paraphrasing a funny exchange of dialogue: a funny exchange of dialogue is already a paraphrase, and never benefits from being retailed at second hand. But she can tell which of the dames could really talk the talk. Myrna Loy gets high marks, and not just for the *Thin Man* movies. There are no prizes for spotting that she was good in those. But DiBattista can see that Loy was already good in her supporting role as the narcoleptic maneater in Rouben Mamoulian's *Love Me Tonight* in 1932. Ginger Rogers is rightly praised for *Roxie Hart*, Carole Lombard for *Twentieth Century*, Irene Dunne for *The Awful Truth*, Rosalind Russell for *His Girl Friday*. Apart from these recognized talents, which even a dullard can assess correctly just by agreeing with everybody else, there are unrecognized talents whose worth our author is able to weigh at a glance. With Marion Davies a glance is all you get. Nowadays her movies are hard to find, but DiBattista has seen enough of William Randolph Hearst's mistress working at her other job to reach the proper conclusion: she had a disarming gift for delivering a line. Just the gift, in fact, that Marilyn Monroe didn't have. All the blah about Monroe's lighting up the screen is well enough justified, but she never lit it up with her handling of dialogue. Words made her nervous and she still makes us nervous for her by the way she says them. DiBattista can tell what Monroe couldn't do because DiBattista can tell what Judy Holliday could do. When the movies sexed up and dumbed down in the fifties, it was a nice question which was the bigger victim: Monroe, who had exactly what the studio bosses wanted, or Holliday, who had more. When the camera dollied in for Monroe's butt-shot in *Niagara*, it was all over for Holliday, who also had a cute behind – cuter than Monroe's, as it happened – but fatally persisted with the belief that her mouth, and its closely attendant brain, should be the centre of interest. You could say that the star of *Born Yesterday* was born before her time, but it is equally true, and much more interesting, to say that she was born after it.

The post-war transition from smart Hollywood to stupid Hollywood gets us into the area of all the socio-political implications DiBattista doesn't deal with, or at any rate hasn't yet dealt with for publication. The sooner she does, the better. Film history can do without a treatise on the subject: it is fun to see a heavily accredited scholar like DiBattista getting carried away when she talks about screen comedy, but nowadays, to make your mark as a media critic, you have to write at least as well as they do in the medium you criticize, and whoever wrote *Wag the Dog* knows that 'credence' does not mean 'credibility', whereas DiBattista thinks it does. Feminism, however, has a missing chapter in its history, a glaring lacuna that distorts the whole account from the fifties onwards. Within arm's reach, our author has the material to fill the gap. Most of the sixties feminist advocates grew up when Doris Day was the fastest-talking dame on the screen. DiBattista has a refreshing admiration for Day's technical accomplishments, which were indeed considerable, but there is no disguising the fact that the declension from *His Girl Friday* to *Pillow Talk* was precipitous on every scale except the financial. You can mine a whole seam of post-modernist irony in the consideration that Cary Grant and Rock Hudson were both faced with at least as tortuous a journey towards usurping the standard masculine gender pattern as their female opposite numbers, but what matters is that for the Doris Day character in *Pillow Talk* the ideal lay in domesticity, not in her job. She wanted to be part of a couple. In *His Girl Friday* Rosalind Russell wanted to be part of the action. And *Pillow Talk* was meant to be the height of sophistication. A more typical female role model of the period was June Allyson, pouting loyally at home while James Stewart, camped out in the Mojave Desert, manfully concerned himself with the creation of the Strategic Air Command – a theme that took advantage of the B-36's capacity to fill the Cinemascope screen. The letterbox format was less suited to June Allyson's face, but she did her best. She not only pouted in Cinemascope, she lisped in four-track stereophonic sound, flooding the auditorium with an audiovisual guarantee that a woman's kiss was a susurrating highway back to the womb. It wasn't her fault, poor dear. Twenty years earlier she might have been trading poisoned darts with John Barrymore. But she and her sorority sisters were condemned to representing a girdled, uplifted world whose only edges were in the bones and stitching of their foundation garments. Faced with so much overwhelmingly off-putting evidence, the feminists, and especially the American ones, took it for granted that Hollywood was designedly engaged in proselytizing for the stereotype of the aggressively submissive home-maker, all petticoats fully starched. What DiBattista now needs to tell us is why they never pointed out that in an earlier period Hollywood had been engaged in doing precisely the opposite.

One of the reasons might turn out to be that in the crucial post-war period the classic movies weren't all that freely available, even on the swathe of late-night television re-runs that the Americans call the Late Show. Some of the classic movies were in danger of extinction. Reluctant as his post-modern worshippers might be to credit it, Howard Hawks, for example, was regarded during his busy heyday as only one step up from a Poverty Row director, like Don Siegel in the next generation. Though I hardly realized it at the time – and I was there for every showing – the Howard Hawks retrospective season at London's NFT in the early sixties was a feat of rediscovery as well as of organization. The Cinematheque in Paris played an important role, but the Museum of Modern Art in New York was the key venue for the preservation of Hollywood's greatest period of achievement. Hollywood itself never was, and Peter Bogdanovich's originality as a curator lay in his awareness that it never would be. (Until the prospect of sales to television saved the day, Hollywood's instinctive homage to a great original film was not only to remake it, but to burn its negative.) The preservation of the American film industry's richest stretch of poetry is a copybook example of how criticism and scholarship are at their best when they serve creativity through the power of appreciation. The whole era had to be dug up again, like Troy from beneath a sea of sand and the ruins of many lesser cities with the same name. But if a conspiracy theory is preferred, there is always the chance that the feminist cheer-leaders, instead of being unaware of how Hollywood had once projected female equality, were aware of it but didn't want to emphasize it, lest they kick a hole in their own case, which depended on the supposed axiom that every man's hand was raised against them. The pre-war, wartime and immediate post-war films that promoted the ideal of female equality were male initiatives. Females participated, often gloriously: but the films that featured Maria DiBattista's beloved fast-talking dames were designed, manufactured and marketed by men.

How did *that* happen? Well, tell us, Maria. But let there be no doubt that it was so. Apart from Mae West, who sometimes owned a share of her film properties and always took pride in writing the lines she spoke (DiBattista is correct to observe that she spoke them too slowly, but that was because the drawling diva never quite grasped that the same audience is quicker on the uptake in a cinema than in a theatre), the fast-talking dames spoke the lines that were set down for them. On this point, DiBattista inadvertently proves that time given to Charles Baudelaire is time taken away from finding out how movies are made. There is no reason to be ashamed of that, and it is not necessarily a disqualifying fault even for a film critic. Pauline Kael developed a tremendous reputation without having very many clues about how films got put together. But even Kael was aware that actors don't usually write their own dialogue. Sometimes they are so good at delivering it that you would swear they are making it up, but they aren't. (As Lord Bragg once found to his discomfort, it is very dangerous to assume that Gene Hackman can be interviewed for an hour of airtime on the assumption that the actual chap is the same fluent character we see on the big screen.) When talking about the films of Joseph Manciewicz and Preston Sturges, both of whom she admires – two more testaments to her acumen – DiBattista is obliged to concede in each case that the writer-director is the shaping spirit. But in most other cases you would swear she believed that the actress was thinking the stuff up.

She can't *really* believe that, but she carries on as if to submit to the reality would be less fun: as, indeed, it is. There are actors who are deadly bores when not given lines written by someone else: we would rather think of them as being brilliant, or at any rate interesting. I myself, who have been hanging around show business for most of my life, am apt to talk of how tough Steve McQueen was in *Bullitt*. Reality says that Steve McQueen never did anything tough in *Bullitt* beyond working his usual shit-heel trick of stealing sixteen pairs of new trousers from the wardrobe budget. Movies mythologize their stars, and the best reason for wading through the stellar autobiographies, no matter how crudely ghosted, is to remind ourselves occasionally that the person up there on the screen was born in a bed, not in a bath of light. This admonition particularly applies to our author, who has put herself in the dangerous case of appearing to suppose that her heroines not only believed what they so fluently said, but might actually have thought of it just before they said it. When dealing with the great tradition of screen comedy in the thirties, there could be no surer method of reducing a complex cultural event to an uninformative cartoon. In *Ninotchka*, for example, Greta Garbo jokes incandescently with actors who are refugees from Hitler pretending to be refugees from Stalin. The incarnation of a graceful, all-comprehending vision, a nymph poised between two converging armies of thugs, she bewitchingly articulates a liberal view of contemporary politics so sophisticated that it amounts to the prophetic. But she didn't think of any of it. The screenwriter Billy Wilder was remembering pre-Hitler Europe and the director Ernst Lubitsch was remembering his visits to Moscow. Garbo could barely remember the boat from Sweden, and her idea of a threatening mass movement was too much fan mail.

But when it comes to the movie stars, keeping your wits about you is hard work, because scrambling your wits is what they are in business to do. It is easier and more fun to talk about the fictional personae as if they were real, and it is hard not to be grateful when the real personality goes even a short way towards matching up with the fictional one. Carole Lombard was a scatological delight in real life. Clark Gable adored her foul tongue, and when we dote on one of her studio portraits and imagine that lush mouth saying a dirty word we would need to be saints not to get excited. But if she had actually been capable of making up the lines she said in front of the film camera she would have been more than a beautiful wildcat, she would have been a genius. Anita Loos wrote a couple of films for Jean Harlow early in her career. Since the real-life Harlow was revered for her smart talk, this was a rare case of a writer writing what the actress might have said anyway. Later on, there were very few instances of a woman star speaking even another woman's mind, let alone her own. What she was speaking was the combined and distilled wisdom of a male committee, up to and including the head of production.

Occasionally there was a female writer on the writing teams of the screwball comedies, but none of them had a female director. At the time it never happened even once, and with the qualified exception of Elaine May it would never happen at all until the advent of Nora Ephron, several decades in the future. The fast-talking dames were chosen for the part by men. Among the major film properties as the war approached, only *The Philadelphia Story* had a female participant in its command structure. Katharine Hepburn had stood beside Philip Barry while he was writing the play for

Broadway; she bought a controlling interest in the finished product; and she would not allow it to be made in Hollywood without herself in the starring role. Without her financial leverage, she would not have been given the part. (I interviewed her once, and that's what she told me.) The studios ensured that no woman ever acquired that kind of power over a major property again, and the same determination still applies even today. Barbra Streisand was an isolated case of a woman calling the shots. Goldie Hawn and Jodie Foster can get small movies made on their terms occasionally, but big movies never. The stakes are too high. As Meryl Streep proved in *Postcards From the Edge*, she can sing almost as well as she can act. She had all the qualifications for playing the title role in the film of *Evita* and spent years trying to land it. But the role went to Madonna because the movie needed the audience who bought her records, and if that audience really cared about singing it would never have bought them.

For the feminist who takes the standard line on male exploitation of the female, the best answer to the thirties film comedy conundrum is probably right there. It was a question of money. The fast-talking dames were allowed to strut their stuff because the product sold. Give the women what they want, especially if what they want is what they can't have: give them a dream. As a conspiracy theory, it checks out, with the usual proviso that conspiracy theories always do, and that's what's wrong with them. (There is also the consideration that if the pre-war ideal of female independence was only a sop to lull the women in the audience rather than a model to inspire them, then the post-war ideal of domesticity might have been similarly devoid of a reliably measurable effect. If it didn't convince Susan Sontag, why did it convince all those other women? Because they were helpless?) But this is where it helps to have been around for a while. I can remember my mother's memories of Myrna Loy in the *Thin Man* movies: I can remember her memories when they were fresh. In Sydney before the war, my mother and father had nothing except each other. The Depression forced both of them out of school in their early teens. Their working life was spent on the production lines if they were lucky. But they knew the way they wanted to sound to each other. They wanted to sound like Nick and Nora Charles, as played on screen by William Powell and Myrna Loy. An industrial product had come all the way across the Pacific to raise their hopes with its images of freedom, justice and egalitarian elegance. It was cultural imperialism if you like, but to say that the cultural imperialism was without a spiritual component is to make a very large assumption. You would have to assume that the fast-talking dames said all those witty things without anyone concerned believing any of it for a minute. It seems unlikely. Not even Goebbels could run a film industry based entirely on cynicism. He tried, but it didn't work.

The liberal Hollywood that produced the fast-talking dames was closed down after the war, by the red scare and by television. The second threat was as effective as the first. A film studio system possessing the monopoly of an outlet could afford to test its audience. Fighting for a share, the outlet suddenly found itself in the contrary position: the audience was testing it. No more high-speed dialogue to flatter those who were bright enough to get it, and flatter them doubly because there were those who didn't. Everybody had to get everything. It was democracy: or rather, it was an ideological component within democracy, an egalitarian emphasis made dictatorial. Pre-war film feminism had never been ideological in that sense: it had been concerned with equality – brilliantly concerned – but not with sameness. The feminine appeal of the fast-talking dames had been multiplied by their brain power, not eroded by it. That might have been the surest sign that men were dominant in the creative effort: the surest sign and the greatest weakness. When Maria and her students start to brainstorm the subject, they might quickly decide that the whole dazzling upsurge was a male chauvinist fantasy after all. Sensuality had not been sidelined, just sharpened up so as to race the motors of a smoother class of guy.

Much can be said to negate the achievement, but nothing to undo it. The films got made, and by a miracle they are still there, to remind us that there was once a continuous, sophisticated cultural effort to ameliorate common experience, week in and week out, all over the world. The comedies were chapters in a book that was all the more instructive for being so delightful. No doubt their collective message about female independence would have been more pure if Irene Dunne had physically resembled Kate Millett and Carole Lombard had been a ringer for Andrea Dworkin, but the box-office would have suffered, as it would suffer today if every movie were cast by the Coen brothers. What we need now from

Maria DiBattista and her beavering sophomores is an explanation of how an industry in the grip of market forces could have been a force for humanism. Inevitably our intrepid explorers will have to deal with questions arising, some of them potent with embarrassment. What if there never could have been any successful feminism in the first place without friendly men to further it? Logic always suggested that this might be so – if men naturally command the physical power to repress women, it is hard to see how they could give it up except voluntarily – but the films of Hollywood's first age of eloquence provide something more persuasive than logic: they provide evidence. What if an advanced industrial society is the only kind in which female equality can even be conceived of? The more we learn from ethnography about the true state of nature, the more it sounds as if it were designed to kill women, and the more we hear about forms of society putatively commendable for their authenticity, the more the authenticity sounds like a state of nature. And what if liberal democracy is the only political system by which an advanced industrial society can sustain itself?

It is very hard to convince the proponents of any modern progressive ideology that it would be tolerated only within the context it presumes to oppose. Perhaps, in the case of feminism, the best way to start would be by trying to argue that it is not an ideology at all, but something better: a demand for justice. Nor were the great film comedies a strict case of cultural imperialism, if imperialism necessarily entails an imposition by force. An imposition by influence is far more likely to be irreversible. Professor DiBattista could usefully do a whole book just on *The Philadephia Story*, right through to its latterday transmogrification into *High Society*, a vehicle for the future Princess of Monaco and her two-note singing voice. (The alert reader will detect that my jealous bile springs from loving admiration: not only would Grace Kelly have been perfect for the thirties, she played her roles in the fifties as if the thirties had never gone away. No lisping pout for her.) About *The Philadephia Story*, there is a salient fact which the diligent DiBattista is bound to unearth, so let me get in first, with hopes of being credited in a footnote. When the victorious Japanese paraded through the streets of Singapore, they were right to suppose it meant the end of the British Empire, but wrong to suppose it meant the beginning of theirs. Above the rows of flashing bayonets there were eloquent billboards to announce that the most luxurious cinema in town had a new American film showing. Guess which one.

Postscript

Even with the deadly interposition of post-war wholesomeness, the tradition of the fast-talking dames was never quite lost. Grace Kelly did plenty of fast talking in *To Catch a Thief*. What happened was that the heritage was absorbed to the point where it lost its definition. Doris Day's pillow talk was delivered at high speed, but it was the language of surrender. The problem now is not that the ideal of female eloquence has been entirely abandoned, but that it has been reduced to a component: something for a *Working Girl* like Melanie Griffith to do in between bouts of swooning at her own incompetence. Rarely is the woman's brightness the whole subject. I have already mentioned Anne Heche's performance in *Wag the Dog*, but let me mention it again, just to underline the lesson. The lesson is that if the scripts aren't there, the fast-talking dames won't be there either. Like Aaron Sorkin with *The West Wing*, David Mamet in his movie scripts has distilled the whole tradition of screwball comedy, giving the women, in particular, a chance to shine that they have not had for half a century. There is a radiant demonstration in *State and Main*, when Rebecca Pigeon and Philip Seymour Hoffman very believably fall in love with each other's wit. (His injured finger is joined to Cary Grant's in *Bringing Up Baby*, like Adam's to God's in the Sistine ceiling.) But really a television series, all other things being equal, is bound to leave even the most uncompromising movie for dead. In *The West Wing*, Stockard Channing gets the lines that her powers of delivery have always given her a right to. If the movies could have done that for her, she would have made a couple of unforgettable appearances every year since her Ida Lupino routine in *The Big Bus*. And the movies could never have done anything at all with Janel Maloney. Those of us who like the comediennes more than the comedians had better realize that television is where it's at. The movies are a vast conspiracy for ensuring that we will never get enough of Annette Bening.

ROUGH GUIDES TO SHAKESPEARE

Alan Yentob says that Leonardo da Vinci is a great artist. Michael Wood says that Shakespeare is a great playwright. There is nothing remarkable about saying these things, even on BBC1. All depends on how they are said. Long ago impressed by how much meaning remains packed into one of Wood's sentences even while he pounds it with emphasis from all directions, I have been living with his *In Search of Shakespeare* for some weeks, after securing a set of preview tapes well ahead of the launch date. The week that Barry Manilow broke his nose was a good time to start watching them. Weight-wise, Wood bears a sharp resemblance to Manilow: men like them are thin forever. Also the historian's nose is as salient as the singer's. Though more pointed than preponderant, it courts a similar danger as its owner lopes searchingly forward. The risk is increased by this presenter's habit of talking sideways while the camera tracks him. A potentially impacting object might get into range without his seeing it, so that when his head suddenly resumes a normal alignment it could be too late to take evasive action. In that event, of course, the footage would end up on the cutting room floor, but not before the abruptly rebuffed presenter ended up in the hospital. Wood's blithe courage as a walking talker is part of his boyishness.

Another part is an urge to update his frame of reference in keeping with the current buzz. In the context of lust and love in Shakespeare, *Sex and the City* gets a mention. 'The Elizabethans were very up-front about sex.' Well, it's true: they were. When Hamlet made his crack about country matters, the groundlings were prob-ably elbowing each other's ribs in the same way those dreadful lads on *Big Brother* do at the hint of a double meaning. That's why the gag is there: it's one for the punters. Shakespeare's language is not pure. Even at its most exalted, it declines to be exclusive. It switches between one level of decorum and another as an electron shifts orbits without crossing the space between. Wood is right to shuffle his frames of reference, the better to cover the individual case, and to match the general fact of his hero's gargantuan appetite for synthesis. The Victorian commentators, who were not up-front about sex, were at a loss properly to discuss one of the crudest, and therefore one of the most important, of the elements that contributed to Shakespeare's richness – a richness that was not refined, like gold, but complex, like the world. Wood has a nose for that complexity. All the more reason to hold one's breath as he steers the nose around trees, along tow-paths and through forests.

Actually one should not be too strict even about the excessive walk-talking that eats up time in the broadcast version of his essay. As in his previous shows, he is always walking through exactly the right landscape. When in search of Alexander, he and his crew slogged up all the appropriate escarpments to reveal Alexander's knack for positioning the enemy so that a sudden charge into the centre would do the business. To match his feeling for words and rhythms, Wood has a feeling for terrain. (The connection is not rare in literature – it helped motivate the Augustans as well as the Romantics – but among today's TV presenters it is almost unknown, partly because for them the whole world has turned into what Americans call the Flyover.) Was Shakespeare, during his Lost Years, ever in Lancashire? Asking the question sideways while both hands weigh invisible melons, Wood strides through the Lancashire mud. If Shakespeare had ever been in Lancashire he would have probably strode, or stridden, through mud like this.

There is usually a point to Wood's talking walk. He strides beside the Thames. Well, so did Shakespeare. Canary Wharf was less in evidence at the time, but beside the Thames must still have been an exciting place to stride if you were a country boy just starting off in the big smoke. Mercifully, in Wood's style as a programme maker, there is none of the sort of visual evocation known in the trade as Mickey Mouse. He and his crew can be a bit literal – we saw quite a lot of today's wool trade while the possibility was considered that Shakespeare's father once had the same sort of connection to fleece distribution as Tony Soprano has to waste disposal – but the tendency is kept well this side of the absurd. If Wood were to say that the young, on-the-make Shakespeare wolfed down the teeming experience of the London stews, we might be shown the presenter's speed of stride along the smooth macadam now covering the area where the stews once were, but we would not be shown footage of a wolf.

When Simon Schama says that Henry V was reputed in his day to have the personality of a leopard, we are shown footage of a leopard. We are also asked to believe that two intermittently intersecting tin swords represent the battle of Agincourt; but that is bearable even if feeble. The leopard is unbearable, and Schama must know it. At the same time as Michael Wood was establishing himself as one of the most promising young historians in Oxford, Schama was establishing himself as one of the most promising young historians in Cambridge, and I saw enough of him to know that he would rather be caught in a thunderstorm than in a cliché. Some students of the close relationship between Simon Schama and Mickey Mouse call such effects schamanic, but really they just mean that Schama is less in control of the producer than the producer is in control of him. He might consider trading off some of his enviable salary against more clout. Either Wood has done just that, or else he is luckier. Though often obliged to do his expounding on the move when he might have preferred to stand still, at least he can be sure that if he mentions Shakespeare's talent reaching a peak the screen will not be occupied by footage of Sir Edmund Hillary doing the same. Merely through word and gesture, he boyishly finds means to convey the thrill of the search. But inevitably gesture crowds out word.

When pointing something out, it takes time for a presenter to instruct us, through the window of the lens, that something worth looking at lies nearby, and then for him to go over there and point a finger at it to help us look at it, while generating repetitive emphases with the voice in order to convey how very much worth looking at it is. The voice-over is much more economical in this regard than any piece to camera. Producers and directors, however, love the piece to camera, and beyond a certain point they can't be fought, even by a presenter with Wood's prestige. In his book there is much more room for words and all they can evoke without needing to show. In his book, as a consequence, the references to our current media world look less trendy. Some critics complained that the screen-time devoted to Shakespeare's school days was too short, almost as if somebody was afraid that younger viewers might be scared off by the very mention of a school day lasting longer than a few minutes, and of lessons that had to be got by rote lest corporal punishment ensue. But on the page, Wood goes into Shakespeare's education at length. 'Shakespeare was the product of a memorizing culture in which huge chunks of literature were learned off by heart.' So, to a certain extent, were you and I, but we must forgive him for insisting on the obvious, because he is well aware that the audience he is after has never memorized anything. The reader is not allowed to suppose that the most effortless-seeming progenitor of the English language did it all by natural warbling. Ben Jonson, who said that Shakespeare had 'little Latin', could say so only because he had a lot of Latin: Shakespeare had enough.

Though denied a university education – the denial might have been his biggest blessing, because it forced him to operate in a context other than purely literary – Shakespeare was a great reader before he was a great writer. Ovid's *Metamorphoses*, for example, he knew by heart, and in the Latin, although he used a translation for speed. Leaving us in no doubt of what learned times the playwrights lived in, Wood earns his right to the apparent flippancy of saying that Marlowe's mighty line was 'the sound everybody wanted'. The rock and roll frame of reference fits well. The playwrights were young, hungry and competitive, and the first blank verse, when they heard it, must have hit them in the head in the same way that the first rock stars who are now old or dead were hit in the knees by rhythm and blues records and suddenly realized that here was a musical language in which anything could be expressed without the listener ceasing to yell for more. Wood isn't lowering the tone by drawing such analogies. He is raising it. He is talking about language as a marketable thrill, and that was the first thing Shakespeare's language was. It wasn't the last, but he would have had no theatrical career without that. He would have been just a poet.

Whether being 'just a poet' means being less of a poet is a nice question. On *Newsnight Review*, Germaine Greer said she would make up her mind about Wood's series when she had heard him on the subject of Shakespeare's poems. She wasn't pressed on the point: a pity, because I would have liked to hear more. She has formidable scholarly credentials – Wood must be waiting for her verdict with thighs atremble, and thus with gratitude that his jeans still fit so loosely – but I would have thought her best credential was that she knows an awful lot about the theatre, and is therefore proof against any notion that Shakespeare's poems are the acme of his poetry. An accomplished actress herself (there are those of us who think that her show of considering the opinions of some of her fellow *Newsnight Review* panellists merits a BAFTA award of its own) she is well aware that a line which has to be understood the first time it is heard can achieve the status of the poetic only by a far bigger miracle than a line written to be figured out on the page. Frank Kermode, in his fine book *Shakespeare's Language*, dares to suggest that some of the dense imagery of the later plays might have been as hard to follow for its contemporary audience as it is for us. He is almost certainly right. But equally there can be little doubt that Shakespeare had created a climate of trust in which his audience was ready to let some of the meaning go as long as they could follow the drift.

There was always a drift, and for a long time, until near the end, the drift was a flood. To assess the composition and dynamics of this torrent of meaning is where the student of language comes in, if come in he must. Wood's qualifications to do so are of a respectable order. 'Like the paintings in the guild chapel with which this story began,' he writes near the end, 'humanity's encoded memories are being erased everywhere across the planet.' The word 'encoded' sounds a bit Matrix-conscious, but the proposition is sadly true. In his screen performance I noticed only one solecism ('Apart from being a country bumpkin' means the opposite of 'far from being a country bumpkin', and he obviously meant to say the second thing rather than the first) but in the text there are none. He is a clean writer so it is no surprise that he is a clean reader. Germaine Greer might pounce on his apparent assumption that the line in the sonnets about the dun breasts is further evidence of the lady's darkness, whereas the argument insists only that she is not perfectly white, which no one but a freshly made snowman is. On the whole, however, Wood reads the dramatic poetry at the level on which it was written, with the proper sensitivity for both the theatrical requirements that shaped it and the theatrical opportunities to which its protean flexibility gave rise. There have been critics who could do that – Shaw could do it better than Coleridge and Hazlitt put together – but none of them has been a television presenter who could talk about the structure of the iambic pentameter while striding blind through Stratford upon Avon.

Wood has all the dubious skills, and all the undoubted publicity value, of a television presenter. He can thus call attention to his book, so we are lucky that it is excellent. It would be less so, however, if he knew less about showbiz, so there is no conflict. Making television documentaries, you either make compromises or you don't get the job done. You either learn to work with other people or you don't work. Veteran of many a weary argument in which he saved the project by appearing to yield a point, and then saved the point the next day by an adroit psychological manoeuvre – almost always it entails confirming a director in his opinion that he is Federico Fellini, but sometimes you have to convince the company catering manager that he is Marco Pierre White – Wood is unusually well placed to make plausible deductions about the man behind the name, the man we know so little about. Faceless and yet forceful, Shakespeare emerges from the book as the master general he must have been. From that fact alone, one further deduction might have been made: a deeper reason for Greene's flaring envy in the 'Shakescene' diatribe. Greene might have been annoyed by more than Shakespeare's unfair knack for a phrase and his energizing effect on the theatre: an effect which did, after all, boost the market for his fellow practitioners. Greene might also have been annoyed by Shakespeare's ability to bank the earnings. Greene might have spotted that Shakespeare had no plans for living from hand to mouth, and was on his way to good clothes, a coat of arms, and New Place. Greene couldn't have guessed that it would be called New Place. (Who could have guessed that the greatest poet who ever lived, after buying a new place called New Place, would go on calling it New Place?) But Greene, as he sucked on the last of his pickled herrings, could probably see New Place looming in the distance. Hence the bile. As a general rule, poets can stand it if one of their number shows an exceptional lyrical gift. But if he also shows a gift for worldly success, the knives come out.

Even Greene's knife, though, only pricked like a pin. Ben Jonson would have been a frightful enemy if he had so wished, but something about his 'gentle Shakespeare' soothed incipient ire. We can assume it was the gentleness. If Shakespeare, like Dr Johnson or Oscar Wilde, had talked for victory, we would have heard about it. How little we have heard about him tells us a lot about him. Part of his gift was to blend in, so that people would tell him things

– diplomatic aides, receivers of stolen goods, sailors who had been washed ashore on the coast of where was it? Illyria? We can infer that his face was not striking. Wood shows us a portrait painted in 1588, the year of the Armada. But we can tell by the way Wood fails to walk past the portrait, walk back, and lean over it while emphatically pointing out its features, that he doesn't care whether it is a portrait of Shakespeare, Marlowe or the current Earl of Wessex dressed for a costume ball.

Those who don't already think that such an indifference to the perennial topic of Shakespeare's appearance is exactly right should take a quick look at *Shakespeare's Face*, a compendium of essays dedicated to the questions supposedly raised by the 'Sanders portrait'. A judicious essay by Stanley Wells might slow the quick look down by about thirty minutes. Wells talks nothing but sense about Shakespeare. As a result he has almost nothing to say about the portrait. The other contributors, among whom the editor Stephanie Nolan is the most prominent, have a lot to say about it. The portrait came to light in Canada, where it was big news. 'Is this the face of genius?' asked the *Toronto Globe and Mail*. Art experts confirm that it is indeed a contemporary portrait. What nobody can confirm is that it is a portrait of Shakespeare. The scientific dating was a bit of a blow to my own theory that it is a portrait of John Malkovich, but I have whistled in a scientist of my own who suggests that the prankish and well-funded Malkovich could have engineered the whole deal with the aid of artificially aged carbon. Marjorie Garber, a Professor of English and Director of Visual Arts at Harvard, assures us that 'the male minx in the Sanders image, with his knowing eyes and flirtatious, up-curved mouth, seems about to burst into words – words as witty and perhaps as improper as our current taste will permit.'

How witty would that be, I wonder? We can better imagine how improper. The flirtatious, up-curved mouth, however, certainly looks as if it once adorned an actor – an actor of a particular kind, the kind some of us call a lip-licker. Shakespeare was an actor, but he was probably not a lip-licker. The lip-licker finds the fountain of his expressiveness in the pool of Narcissus. In my forthcoming thesis on the mannerisms of actors (it's called *Ah, Bogie!* Spot the reference) I address the question of whether lip-licking is the cause or the consequence of a career gone haywire. David Caruso was already licking his lips in the first series of *NYPD Blue*. Keen observers didn't have to wait for *CSI: Miami* – in which he not only licks his lips but keeps putting on and taking off his dark glasses – to decide that he was out of his head with self-regard. Mickey Rourke had a suitcase-full of collagen injected into his lips in order to give himself bigger lips to lick. As for Malkovich . . . but I don't want to give too much of my book away. Back to *Shakespeare's Face*, a book which has so little to give away that one feels compelled to toss it a bone. Here is the bone.

The book does have one merit. It assumes, surely correctly, that Shakespeare had ambitions beyond the lonely garret. The sumptuary laws specified plain cloth for anyone not noble. Shakespeare was out for the velvet. Contending with his energy for the right to exalted goods, he was a precursor of the bourgeois world we live in now. The grand total of 480 pictures that have at one time or another been supposed to be of him probably don't include even a single authentic case, but if there were ten times as many they would scarcely reflect his determination to take his place as a man of the world. Holding to the notion that an artist should be above such things, we can frown on that determination if we wish, but it is very doubtful if he did. So *Shakespeare's Face* is not quite as useless as it appears to be at first glance.

Nor, even, is Harold Bloom's scholarly new super-squib *Hamlet: Poem Unlimited*. Less than 150 pages long but somehow weighing like 1,500 pages of pulped railway timetables, Bloom's booklet engages itself in the doomed task of convincing us that Shakespeare was a great writer, and that *Hamlet* is a great play. The task is doomed because nobody in his right mind doubts these things. There are even people in their wrong minds who know them to be true. People who think Shakespeare was Queen Elizabeth know *Hamlet* is a great play: that is why they think Queen Elizabeth wrote it. But Bloom thinks we do not understand. He talks to us as if we were wilfully failing to take in an intractable fact. He is a British Airways stewardess trying to tell Liam Gallagher that the bar is closed. He tells us that *Hamlet* is up there with the *Iliad*, the *Aeneid*, the *Divine Comedy* and *Leaves of Grass*.

But is *Leaves of Grass* really up there with *Hamlet*? If Bloom can't tell the difference between chalk and cheese, or anyway between cheese and lesser cheese, the deficiency in taste can scarcely be

irrelevant to his pretended historical sweep, which means little if it
fails to detect points of quality and join them up. From that angle,
Bloom ought to be safe with *Hamlet*: it is, after all, pretty good. But
it is less certain that *Hamlet* is safe with Bloom, or that Shakespeare
himself is safe either. Possibly there is a professional deformation
that we ought to consider. 'You cannot get beyond Hamlet, which
established the limits of theatricality.' When F.R. Leavis decided that
there could be no completely serious English writing after Lawrence,
he allowed it to be inferred that there might be one exception:
Leavis. If Bloom is saying that only he fully appreciates Shakespeare,
he might also be saying that only he inherits Shakespeare's capacity
to view the world. This is a view of the world in itself, and one that
could be hatched only in the dark.

A star academic can get away with it. Anyone who worked on
the outside would be thought to have looped the loop. But really
not even Bloom is wholly isolated, because Shakespeare won't allow
it. In front of his class, and even in his study, Bloom is a Shakespear-
ean character, and in his deepest heart he knows which one. He is
Falstaff, talking up a storm, pinning Hal to the wall before the world
intrudes. His histrionic urge gets him to the party after all. Picking
your character is a good place to start with Shakespeare. You can
imagine yourself in tights, which helps you to remember that once
they had to be paid for, washed and ironed, and that the expense
came out of the profits that Shakespeare and his fellow partners
were keen to retain intact. In the world of art they created, it was
the practical and the physical that made the spiritual so intense.
The year after he graduated, Michael Wood played Oberon in a
combined Oxford–Cambridge production of *A Midsummer Night's
Dream*. All the women in the cast, and several of the men, were
enchanted by his elegance of leg. I can remember him now, striding
across the stage with his nose pointing at the audience, the boyish
portent of a shimmering career.

TLS, 11 July 2003

Postscript

This piece was written too early to catch Stephen Greenblatt's
Will in the World. Though so strong on the background that its hero

pales in the foreground, the book survives its cute title. Few critical works on the subject contribute as much. But a good many of them contribute at least something: if not a fact, then a slant of interpretation that looks not utterly invalid in the light of recent history. The question is about what exactly is being contributed to. How much of all this commentary should we have time for? When Greenblatt and I were graduate students in Cambridge in the late 1960s, some of our contemporaries risked failing grades in English by spending too much time acting for the dramatic societies. But quite often they were acting in Shakespeare, and wasn't every speech they learned by heart worth a hundred pages that had been written about it? The question haunts me still. (I think it still haunts Greenblatt: one of his best qualities.) At gunpoint I would have to say that the study of Shakespeare shouldn't end with merely memorizing what he wrote: after all, even the question of what he wrote is a subject for scholarship. But it should certainly begin there. J. Dover Wilson's *What Happens in Hamlet* is a classic of scholarship that every student should read, so as to have an inkling of what being a scholar takes. But the student should know *Hamlet* first, and preferably by heart. It is a matter of priorities. Armed with the memory of a few lines spoken by Cassius and Brutus on the night before the battle of Philippi, for example, I have an answer ready for Harold Bloom's deafening contention that *Hamlet* is the greatest play in the world. Yes, keep your voice down, nobody disagrees; but if *Hamlet* didn't exist, wouldn't you have to say the same thing about *Julius Caesar*? Or, failing that, about *King Lear*? About *Macbeth*? About *Antony and Cleopatra*? There is a special kind of academic madness that wants to get in amongst the great works of art and make itself indispensable by sorting them into some plausible order of importance. In the behavioural paradigm usefully supplied to us by Nick Hornby's *High Fidelity*, that specific breed of nutter can be hired as a part-time sales assistant, but he must never be left alone to run the store.

GENERAL ELECTION SEQUENCE
2001

1. The New Labour Machiavelli

'Yes,' said Peter Mandelson, 'but you're a wizened old media hack.' He said that to me, and I was flattered out of my wits. The trick of painless teasing is the height of charm, and Mandelson has so much charm that he pays the inevitable penalty: he makes an enemy of anybody from whom he withholds it. For those on whom he confers it, however, only one inference is possible: here is a fine mind. The question of what the fine mind is up to suddenly becomes subsidiary. It was on Tuesday that he called me a grizzled old media hack, and even though our close friendship was scarcely into its fifteenth minute, I had already decided that I had met the political genius I was waiting for – the one who could see that I, deep down, was a political genius too. Since, in all practical matters, I had previously been regarded as a joke figure even by my local residents' association, this was a late but welcome endorsement of my hidden qualities. But before I draw further conclusions about this historic one-on-one confrontation across Mandelson's kitchen table in Hartlepool, let us go back to the long-gone day – more than a week ago now – when Tony Blair announced a General Election clearly fated to confirm him in the post which he could well hold until the next arrival of the Messiah, who will almost certainly be wearing a Labour rosette.

As you may remember if you are the sort of person who relishes the shower scene in *Psycho*, the Prime Minister launched his campaign at St Olave's school in South London. Blair is a man who has a special voice for everything. At the funeral of the Princess of Wales he had a special voice for reading the Bible, as if the measure of its prose needed assistance from himself, with extra pauses, swoops and emphases to eke out its poverty of cadence. At St Olave's he had a special voice for speaking to children, as if children were a category of human being limited by delayed comprehension. The girl who pulled the sweater over her head was not a political dissident: she was a theatre critic. Two elections from now she might well vote for him, but she will never go to see him playing Hamlet, because she already knows that he will take his doublet off in the opening scene, thus to prove, in his shirtsleeves, that he is a pretty straight sort of Prince. Even the friendliest newspapers thought that Blair's performance at St Olave's reeked of stage management. Really this should have been old news. The Labour party has been controlling its leader's image for years: it's the Mandelson emphasis, as interpreted in recent times by Alastair Campbell. What made it news in the opening hours of the campaign was a creeping sense that the puppeteers were getting their wires crossed.

The creeping sense broke into a gallop a couple of days later, when a staged event in a Warwickshire tea room went so smoothly as to defy belief. Fated to go down in the annals of salesmanship as Blair's Spontaneous Encounter with 'the ordinary couple in Leamington Spa', the event featured such ecstasies of spontaneity from Blair, and such paroxysms of ordinariness from the ordinary couple, that any cat in the area would have died laughing. But there were no cats in the area. They had all had their accreditation withdrawn, lest they be caught on camera, rolling around with their paws up in the throes of hilarious death.

*

Unlike the Millennium Dome, which achieved incredibility through everything going wrong, the Leamington Spa Spontaneous Encounter Experience achieved incredibility through everything going right. The ordinary couple didn't turn up drunk and Blair didn't deliver the script meant to inspire two rehabilitated burglars in Stevenage the following week. But nothing was accomplished except a hefty reinforcement to the growing impression that, for Blair's management team, efficiency came first, even if reality had to be adjusted to suit the message. The downside to such an attitude is that the manipulation becomes another message. Blair's protean multiplicity of special voices lends weight to the view that this all-pervading bogusness comes from the top down. When Rory Bremner was thrown off the Labour Battle Bus, it occurred to me that Blair had realized Bremner was really in politics, and had realized it as a consequence of Bremner's having realized that Blair was really in show business.

By Friday the media had concluded that Blair's politics of the fixed smile had lost Labour the first week. The polls didn't shift, but the perception did. Hague and Kennedy had mixed it with the hecklers. Blair's minders had allowed him to face nothing more dangerous than a baby. Blair didn't stop smiling even when he kissed it. The baby could have been scarred for life with the imprint of ivory: the shadow of your smile. 'He'll look back on it in years to come,' said the baby's on-message mother. Over the weekend, the media consensus was that Millbank's management of their man was sclerotic in its finesse. The machine Peter Mandelson had helped to create was in a shallow dive on automatic pilot. Already there were whispers that the man who built it might be the only man who knew how to fix it.

On Monday, Mandelson seemed to agree. He published an article in this paper crying up New Labour's new emphasis on 'articulating core values and beliefs', but he left the way open for his readers to infer that the old emphasis on presentation was still in existence, and perhaps counter-productive. Anyone who recalled that Mandelson himself was largely responsible for the old emphasis might have found this pretty steep, but what mattered was how they might read it at Millbank, where Labour's campaign was being masterminded by the Chancellor of the Exchequer, Gordon Brown.

There were visions of the New Machiavelli driving a wedge between Blair and Brown, as once the old Machiavelli might have warned his Prince against a factotum grown too mighty. At King's Cross I caught the train to Hartlepool. Or, rather, I caught the first of three trains to Hartlepool. The first train accumulated only twenty minutes of delay on the way to York, and I'm bound to say that under New Labour the quality of public address system announcements has improved out of sight, although unfortunately not out of earshot. The best announcement was when the train was standing just outside Doncaster. 'We apologize for the slight delay outside Doncaster Station. This is because the driver is on the tracks talking to the signalman about the new speed restrictions. As soon as . . .'

Ready to vote for Mussolini, I caught the train to Middlesbrough that would qualify me for the train to Hartlepool, but after Middlesbrough my mood changed along with the look of the country. At the Ann Summers sex shop in Middlesbrough's glossy main drag the sales assistants had told me that the whole area had come up a long way in the last five years, and now I could see they were right. Between Billington and Seaton Carew the industries filled the horizon. There were still fields of allotments in among the villages, but the housing looked either refurbished or spanking new, and Hartlepool sparkled. The new Marina looked like a chunk of San Francisco's glass and pipe waterfront on a darker sea, or Sydney's Darling Harbour under a darker sky. The franchises were stacked sideways one after the other like an updated Monopoly board. Stand-alone edifices had been helicoptered in from global America: Pizza Hut, Kentucky Fried Chicken, the Warner multiplex. There were whole streets of discos with percussive names like Passion and Pow!. Hypermarkets hugely occupied the spaces left by the pit-prop yards that died with the pits.

One of the penalties a town pays for modern-day modernization is that it joins a homogenized world, but Hartlepool has kept a lot of its distinguished old buildings and buffed them up: the refurbs look even snazzier than the new stuff, and the general effect is of a civilized prosperity. Everyone you meet says that five years ago things were far otherwise, and the history books make that easy to believe. In the Depression, unemployment in the area ran at a steady 40 per cent. In May 1941, *Luftflotte 3* was overhead for three nights at a time, clobbering the docks. But the really devastating raid was ordered in by Mrs Thatcher, whose government finally laid the old industries waste. It could be said that she made regeneration possible, in the same way that an Australian bushfire benefits a forest. She certainly handed New Labour the opportunity to prove itself. It undoubtedly has. Where graving docks and the smokestack industries once cranked out the wherewithal for owners and workers to lead unequal lives, now the new industries are moving in to chase the government aid, benefit from the cheap rents and the freed-up workforce, and gush the cash-flow for a fair civic order. After more than half a day on the trains I bluffed my way into the students' café in the College of Further Education and heard a lot about the upcoming Summerhill complex, a council project to provide a recreational facility that will have everything: rock-climbing, BMX tracks, waterslides, something for everyone. Ann Summers didn't get a mention but Peter Mandelson did. It wasn't a Labour-controlled council any more, but it had been until last year, during the rebuilding period, and Mandelson was still what he had always been, a terrific constituency MP. When I asked what they thought of his leading the high life in London, they said that's the way it had to be. 'He's here for the surgeries.'

Next morning I turned up at his house in Sutton Avenue, where the prices run to about 50 or 60 thou. In London, as Mandelson learned too well, it costs ten times as much to live this neatly. The air of snug safety is somewhat offset by his police escort, but that's got nothing to do with Hartlepool, or even with the prospect of an incoming egg of the calibre that took out John Prescott. Northern Ireland will follow Mandelson for a long time. The only car he's allowed to ride in weighs three and a half tons more than it looks. Paranoia would be understandable, but he answered his own door and emanated a convincing air of cool. Fine drawn in slacks and loose woolly, he moved to match his easy murmur. On his own immediate confession, or insistence, it's only the press that makes him jumpy. Everything else – including, by implication, a rocket grenade with an Irish accent through his front window – is part of the game, but the press is something wicked. He recited from bitter memory a list of commentators who were on his case. Ten years ago, he said, it had been different, but by now the press had injected 'quantities of cynicism into the political bloodstream'.

Part of the press myself, if only on a part-time basis, I stuck up for our side by pointing out that using the press had been the basis of the presentational politics which he himself had done a lot to invent, and that the policy had reached its questionable apotheosis with Blair's Pied Piper routine at St Olave's. It was at this early point that he called me a wizened old media hack. We were in his kitchen, the coffee was still brewing, and already he had me reeling at how unguarded he could be. In conversation, the man determined not to bore himself is the one least likely to bore anybody else. Mandelson treats any topic to his own high standards of exposition and will continue talking unless interrupted. On the other hand, he listens carefully to the interruption and takes off again from what you said, instead of merely continuing with what he was saying before. When pressed in rapid exchange, he can cover any given topic in three or four nuanced sentences, any one of which could be used to murder him without even being misquoted.

He talks as if sound-bite land didn't exist, as if a wizened old media hack would never jot down a phrase and use it to frame him. If flattery were his intention, it would be an immensely flattering technique. But I think it's just him. He simply wasn't born for the game whose harsh rules he has done so much to make binding. On only two topics did he press the on-message replay button: Blair and Millbank. To take them in reverse, Millbank was wonderful, doing a great job, practically infallible. Blair had 'intelligence, integrity, selflessness' and many other qualities in common with Solomon, Einstein and Albert Schweitzer. But even here – in fact especially here – the beamed dogma suddenly expanded into genuine eloquence. Spotting that the tendency of my own argument was to suggest that Blair had been managed into existence by his back-up team, Mandelson took several minutes to explain that the opposite was true. New Labour's new direction, new deal and new society: it was all Blair's idea. Blair was a unique combination of vision and practicality. The job of his managers had been to hold the wall while he got on with it. I interrupted the flow to contend that they had also managed the media in order to project him. 'Protect him?' Mandelson asked, misinterpreting my mumble. 'No,' I said, 'project.' Mandelson said that for better or worse, 'we live in a personality-driven media age'.

Clearly, in his own case, he thinks it is for the worse. One day it might be known as the Mandelson Paradox: he accepted and mastered, on behalf of his party and the two men who led it to transformation – Neil Kinnock and Tony Blair – a set of atmospheric conditions in which he himself could hardly breathe. To pursue the cause in which he believes, he rated reality above his own tastes. There is a sacrificial element, which in his more vulnerable moments he might be tempted to admire in a mirror: that face out of a Renaissance painting could easily take on the pained resignation of St Sebastian shot full of arrows. Those of us whose bloodstreams have been tainted by cynicism might say he asked for it. There is certainly at least one man-trap question that not even he will find it easy to talk his way out of, even if his memoirs run to the full two volumes. If Blair is so great, and you did nothing wrong, why did he accept your resignation? Surely the truth is that he was done in by the silent borrowing, and not the supposed leg-up for the Hinduja Brothers. When it came to the crunch, Mandelson was in the position of the small boy who gets away with burning down the school and then gets busted for riding his bicycle on the footpath. But here again, I think, the weakness comes from the strength. For a man like him, elegant conviviality and conversational brilliance amount to a talent which is death to hide. He could no more be expected to lead the simple life of Arthur Scargill than Metternich could have been expected to live like a peasant. The civilized dinner table was not his aspiration: he felt it to be his natural entitlement. But in the modern, media-sensitive politics of the Mandelson age, what seems natural to you is the very thing you have to examine in advance for its possible effects. It seemed natural to John Prescott that an egg-thrower should be thumped in the face.

What Mandelson lost will be seen only in the long run. What Blair lost in the short run was dramatically on view that same afternoon, when Mandelson visited High Tunstall School. It's an ordinary school that anyone local can send their children to, but even by the exalted standards of St Olave's it looks like Arcadia. The children had organized themselves into a miniature House of Commons, complete with canopy for the Speaker, played by National Best Speaker Stuart Bevell (13) who can do a stunning impersonation of Betty Boothroyd. The Prime Minister had a bother-boy haircut but turned in a notably more fleet-footed Question Time performance than his model, and the Leader of the Opposition, son of a doctor from the subcontinent, had Hague's every needling technique well covered. What was astonishing, however, was the high standard of argument. Mandelson listened in unfeigned delight, and when he rose to commend them he paid the participants the compliment of being delightful on his own account. 'Do you feel you were unpleasant and aggressive enough?'

But the tease play was only the start. He gave them a run-down on what the House of Commons is like to be in, and how the close confinement encourages verbal aggression. 'It's not that they're nasty people. But you forget yourself, and before you know where you are you're shouting with the rest of them.' He gave the kids everything he had, and didn't patronize them for a second. The son of a prominent local Tory was given exceptional respect for his views. If Millbank had filmed the whole event, they could have had a PPB for the future: Labour education policies for the primary schools have worked, they could say, and the secondary schools are next. But whether Mandelson could have done all that with the camera on him is another question. Essentially it was a private performance.

Onward to a regeneration committee meeting at the Council chambers, where a *Newsnight* team was on hand. Immediately Mandelson tightened up. By arrangement, *Newsnight* filmed him only in the corridors and for the first few minutes of the meeting. When they backed out of the door he was himself again. Once again he was impressive, and this time for doing more listening than talking. As chairman of the cross-party committtee he got the best out of everybody. For a gifted talker there is always a temptation to crush the less eloquent by summarizing their long arguments with a single phrase, but Mandelson did not succumb. What he said was either usefully supplementary or else neatly summarized the points of contention. Though he would probably rather die than say so, a Labour-dominated meeting would have been less interesting. He told me afterwards what a joy it was to be able to draw on the experience of the Lib Dem old hand: 'good, solid, civic stock'.

For Mandelson, 'civic' is a big word. His fondness for the idea is one of the things that make him remarkable, because those who help to paint and frame the big picture are often impatient with local detail. In the eye of history, Mandelson will be seen to have helped alter the course of British politics from one millennium to the next, but the view of his influence will be impoverished if it does not include his respect for what should not alter: the unglamorous but necessary work in the constituency, the long meetings where every-one gets a say, the depressing moment when you recommend a skateboard ramp for the local layabout youths and find out the hard way that the vicar doesn't know what a skateboard is. I saw it happen, and wondered if it ever happened to Machiavelli. But Mandelson managed the moment well, as he can manage everything except the fundamental contradiction of his life. He is a master artist of politics, but politics is not an art. Machiavelli, who thought it was, found out it wasn't when the very people he had sought to advise put him to the rack. That evening Mandelson went out canvassing. I thought he was quite good at that too, but I suppose they all are, or they would never get elected. I left him there, and thus missed the episode when he was monstered by Jeremy Vine in the *Newsnight* minivan.

2. Incredible Shrinking Tories

In any democracy, there is never a more fascinating election than when only one party can win no matter how repellent its campaign. The fascination comes from the unblinkable fact that the future of the opposition is on the line. In 1983 I followed Michael Foot's campaign on its way to catastrophe. Clinging with the rest of the Keystone Kops to the running-board of his Model T as it swerved zanily between the trolley cars, I had only one thing on my mind: this is an accident that had to happen. Out of the wreckage, they might build something. Today the same goes double for the Tories. At least the crash of Foot's doomed vehicle left his party divided merely in two, even as the Kops took parabolic flight in all directions to wind up demolishing pie-stalls or disappearing into the windows of shops selling lingerie. But after this election the Tories might be left with hardly any party at all.

On Tuesday the spectre the Tories are facing was in plain sight at Clapham Junction station, in the constituency of Battersea. Like Gaul in the time of Julius Caesar (Conservative), the borough of Wandsworth is divided into three parts: Putney, Tooting and Battersea. Wandsworth is a Tory fiefdom, and if a fiefdom can have a flagship, Battersea is it. Unfortunately for the local Tory stalwarts, in 1997 it was lost to Labour by 5,300 votes. Not a hell of a lot, but except in the conditions of the then-prevailing apocalypse it would never have happened. On the questionable assumption that an apocalypse can't happen twice, a plumply pretty and terribly nice woman called Lucy Shersby has been deputed to get the votes back. If a Nigella-sweet voice and a cuddly deportment could do it, she would do it, even with the assistance of her local young Tory troops. Their amiably clueless arrangements reminded me vividly of the Labourite dogsbodies on the Foot campaign trail who couldn't assemble water, jug and glass into the same position before the visiting orator was on the point of expiring from thirst.

The Battersea junior task force had, however, managed to organize a cardboard sign: INCOME TAX UP TO 50P ADMITS BROWN. This powerful device was held up to face the prosperous crowds of homecoming evening commuters as they poured down the Shopstop chute from the station to the street. The young men in chinos, poplin summer jackets and Timberland footwear had stepped out of a Ralph Lauren advertisement, the slit-skirted young women out of a re-run of *This Life*. There was the usual London admixture of delinquents, fast-food mutants and deadbeats of all ages, but on the whole you would have said that this was the middle class at the throbbing peak of its reproductive cycle. Forty years ago – thirty, twenty, even ten – I would have been able to tell how they voted just by the way they dressed: Conservative. But now you can't tell, and that's the Tory nightmare.

The young Tory helpfuls seemed not to realize it was a nightmare, which meant that here was the nightmare compounded. They thrust leaflets into the well-groomed hands of the hurrying horde and showed no signs of surprise when the leaflets were returned to them as if tainted with botulism. But Lucy was due to receive a visitor, and *he* realized it. Unfolding from a needlessly small car came the radiant presence of Michael Portillo. Whether he was here to share Lucy's evident belief that his blessing might swing the vote, or whether he was here in the same spirit of posthumous defiance that sent El Cid (Loyalist Royalist) riding out dead in the saddle to meet the enemy, was not apparent from his demeanour. Nothing was apparent from that except gentle manners. A camera can easily make his features look brutal, but seen in real air they look sensitive even in their chunkiness, rather in the way that Michelangelo (Gay Rights) turned Brutus (Republican Revolutionary) into a pugilist with a taste for Stoic philosophy. Unlike Tony Blair's smile, which would remain fixed even if perforated by the bullets of a firing squad, Portillo's smile comes and goes; but when it is there, it is the smile of a man who has known indecision and suffering, and has overcome both while forgetting neither.

As the commuters continued surging towards us like Labour MPs into the division lobby, Portillo got going with a smoothly practised double-handed meet-and-greet routine, his eyes reassuringly suggesting that although there might possibly have been some fleeting reason for voting Labour last time, normal service had now been resumed. Portillo can get a lot into his eyes, including everything happening around him. He spotted me edging up and gave me the tolerant smile for media pests. I pointed to the sign about Brown's alleged admission. '*Did* he admit it?' Portillo's answer was already tried and tested, but he threw in a conspiratorial twinkle. 'Well, he's not denied it.' Instant buddies: that knack of bringing you in on a secret is one of the most valuable a politician can have. Con men, of course, have it too: but they have nothing else. Portillo's geniality is real.

Attracted by the splash and swirl of a big fish, a television news crew showed up. Lucy's team got tremendously excited, and, being so well bred, tremendously shy. One of them – a tall, gorgeous young man with a circa 1964 James Fox haircut and a closely tailored Heseltine-style blue pin-stripe suit, his whole appearance out of a mould you would have thought was long since lying in pieces somewhere in a Surrey lane – was audibly puzzled as to the news crew's provenance. 'Is it the Beer Beer Sear?' It was ITN. Imagine the equivalent young New Labour operative not knowing.

Flushed with their media success, Lucy's Gamma Force hoplites ushered their guest into a car bound for what they assured him was an even hotter spot, Battersea Park station. Since nobody else had thought of it, Portillo kindly suggested to the troops that I be guided by one of them towards the rendezvous. The terribly nice young man who got the job managed to get thoroughly lost, and we saw a great deal of the district before we reached the target zone, where I thought the show was all over. But apparently it had never happened. Though Portillo, Lucy and her praetorians were all present, there were no commuters in sight. I had memories of Michael Foot being led by sweating local worthies into a Peterborough roller-skating rink populated by a mass meeting of twenty-six people, two of them holding balloons.

Portillo never even snarled. He told me that there was a more serious gig coming up on the forecourt of a local service station: an interview with ITN about the National Insurance thing. Perhaps mischievously, he left it to the Battersea bunch to get me there. My two young guides, a male and female who were clearly meant for each other, pooled their knowledge of the area and took me off on a circumnavigation of the constituency that eventually got us to the destination, which was just around the corner from the departure point. Half an hour having elapsed, Portillo had already wrapped up the interview. With his apparently infallible courtesy he congratulated the Battersea Young Tory Commandos as if the future of the party lay in their hands: a daunting prospect. He might have thought he owed me one for putting me at their mercy, because he offered me a trip back to Smith Square, and yes, if I really thought it might be useful I could grill him when we got there. Shortly he would have to disappear into the depths of Central Office for a strategy meeting, but meanwhile how could he help? With just such grace and style, Thomas More (Christian Conservative) once bade the executioner to do his work well, but Thomas More knew that he was going to a better life. Portillo has less reason to believe that bliss is imminent, so his faith in humanity must be deep indeed.

As we settled into the leather chairs, he was already fielding my first question, and what other first question could there be? Yes, he admitted, in 1997 Labour ate into what should have been the natural Tory vote. After eighteen years the crucial centre of the electorate was fed up, and besides, Labour had done the necessary job of reforming itself in order to take over the Conservatives' economic views. 'In those terms it was an epic political victory for us.' Since Portillo himself lost his seat in 1997 and must have felt the deprivation keenly, this was a large gesture of respect. It was also a clever way of glossing the disaster to make it sound like a triumph. As to that, there is some truth to it, although it should be remembered that Labour was not reformed by Mrs Thatcher's example, but by the long influence of its own social democrats.

But Portillo was only bantering. He got down to cases when he admitted, if only by implication, that there was no automatically certain base in the landed and business interests to which the Conservatives could return. Everything would depend on an inclusive view of society that would compete with Labour by offering a real answer to the problems they would never solve by goal-setting management from the top down. Only 'the devolution of power and authority' could give the schools and the hospitals what they were crying out for: motivation. Pay was important, but motivation was everything. And if every critical issue in every institution had to go all the way up to state level and back down again before it could be dealt with, no amount of tax money would meet the case, because the people in charge of other people's destinies would never take effective responsibility if they did not feel that they were in charge of their own. Portillo expounded these arguments with passion, but even more striking was his lucidity. It might not seem much to say that he is the best mind on the Tory front bench, when he, Hague and Ann Widdecombe possess the only three faces most of us can put a name to. But even if Kenneth Clarke and Chris Patten were not in purdah or exile, Portillo would still count as a political intellect on a scale above tactics and even above strategy: a sectional interest can be given up for a national plan only on the basis of an historic view.

The stipulated few minutes had turned into many more and history was what we were now talking about. Flatteringly he asked for an addition to his reading list, and I suggested Alan Moorehead's *Gallipoli*, a book that brings out how right Churchill was about the Dardanelles, and how completely the War Council – a Millennium Dome committee *avant la lettre* – converted a vision for shortening the war into a sure-fire formula for lengthening it. Portillo countered by recommending John Lukacs's *Five Days in London*, in which it is stated that Chamberlain had the casting vote in the matter of a possible capitulation to Hitler in 1940, and sided with Churchill for two reasons – because Chamberlain had learned that Hitler was a bad man, and because Churchill had treated Chamberlain with decency after his ejection from power. So the time to say goodbye was the time to trail my coat. 'Will you and Hague have to rebuild the party together after the defeat?' The smile went off like a light: no irony, no complicity. 'We contemplate nothing except victory.'

He knows better than that, but he said the right thing, which is the political thing. Out there being led by her eager young troops in the wrong direction around Battersea, Lucy Shersby might drop in her tracks if Portillo spoke the truth. And anyway, the truth is that you never know. It's an election for the House of Commons, not the Politburo, and the fact that not even the most predictable outcome is ever a sure thing is the best reason for voting. And even if you had the power of Nostradamus (Liberal Democrat) to foresee the event, your vote could still affect the aftermath. If the Conservatives lose in a big enough way, Hague will probably get the push, and there is nobody except Portillo to take his place. But supposing that the Lib Dems do not expand into the vacuum, and the Tories do well enough for Hague to keep his credibility, it would not necessarily be a bad thing for Portillo, and could be good for the country.

Hague is a born fighter who will do a better job than Portillo of hazing Blair at the dispatch box for the next Parliament, and Portillo as Shadow Chancellor will have the opportunity to work on the plans that could rebuild the party in the only way it can be rebuilt: by proposing, in detail and without appeal to atavistic prejudice, an inclusive yet demonstrably workable order of social justice, thus to compete in the centre for voters who are no longer either the prisoners of their background or its privileged darlings. And to those who proclaim that there is nothing interesting about a centralized politics in which two similar parties are divided only by their proposed methods of achieving the same ends, there is a sharp answer. Those are the only politics worthy of the name, and we are very lucky to live in an epoch where they prevail.

Just how lucky was revealed to me all over again next day in Sloane Square, where I met one of Portillo's challengers for the Kensington and Chelsea constituency. If not the most formidable of his opponents, Julia Stephenson of the Green party is certainly the most unmanningly pretty. In a party whose candidates consist almost exclusively of pin-ups, she stands out for seeming to incarnate the thesis that being environmentally friendly is good for the skin. In her canvassing outfit of white plimsolls, clinging white pedal pushers and environmentally friendly velvety green top – it might well have *been* a piece of some environment, perhaps a swamp in Sri Lanka – she sprang along the King's Road handing out Green leaflets, which were readily accepted, especially by the men. From her they would have accepted a subpoena. Here was clear case of a born Tory who had gone missing. Her moment of revelation had occurred 'beside a Friends of the Earth skip in Haslemere. I was looking at the champagne-fuelled haze and I thought *there is more to life*.' She was right; there is. That's how the Tories lost her. Labour hasn't got her yet, but there is only one way for the Tories to get her back. An appeal to grassroots loyalty won't do. For her, that grass was never green enough. She wants a better world for everyone. Michael

Portillo will beat her, but the best thing about him is that he has already joined her. She threw her class instincts into the skip, and so did he.

3. Spontaneous Pint of Beer

For any ageing correspondent whose feet were giving out, the second weekend of the General Election carnival was a time for contemplation, stocktaking and summary. To put it another way, it was a chance to watch television. Out there on the road you pick up a lot of resonant detail, but the big picture is still on the small screen, because that's where the campaign teams are aiming their efforts if they've got any sense. Charles Kennedy's team actually admits it: their man doesn't tour the regions, he tours the television regions. Wherever there is a studio, no matter how far flung – Dartmoor, the Lizard, Scapa Flow – he will get to it. And that's the way he gets to you.

If he stuck to the national stuff, even Kennedy would be defined by how he stood up to getting worked over by Kirsty Wark on *Newsnight*. Though a Wark work-over must feel like being walked over by a water buffalo in stiletto heels, Kennedy handles it well. But he doesn't have to care, because he's already got the telly thing sewn up out there in the hinterland. If his points go up, you can bet that's where it comes from.

After years under the aegis of Peter Mandelson, Alastair Campbell and their emulous oppos, it remains extraordinary how mediawise some of the leading politicians aren't. Blair should have had a quotable paragraph ready for the woman at the hospital, and it wouldn't have taken a tactical genius to figure out that John Prescott was eventually going to get hit with an egg. At Labour's media training camp they should have rehearsed him with a few dozen cartons of Free Range hen-fruit, drumming it into him that when the inevitable albuminous missile made impact he should turn to the nearest camera, give it a wink, and say, 'Labour prosperity means eggs to spare.'

A campaign that tries to airbrush out the awkward moments in advance looks mechanical, and its works are always vulnerable to a mislaid spanner. But to be ready for the awkward moments isn't mechanical, it's common sense. Admittedly not all eventualities can be anticipated. The first President Bush, after he vomited into the Japanese Prime Minister Kiichi Miyazawa's lap at a formal dinner in Tokyo, would have done well to say, 'That sashimi was so good I couldn't keep it to myself.' But Bush's scriptwriters didn't see it coming. Neither, presumably, did Mr Miyazawa, or he would have had a towel ready on top of his napkin.

The random stuff that happens on a walkabout would be a gift to the leaders if they had the sense of humour to enjoy the uncertainty, but only Kennedy has much of that. Faced with the unanticipated, Blair imitates the action of the goldfish, and Hague, for all his quickness of reflex, can only make debating points: he doesn't engage with the punter, he disengages himself from the danger. But really it is an awful lot to ask of a politician that he should wing it like an improv actor. Even the best performers on *Whose Line Is It Anyway?* had a card-index of possibilities in their heads so that they couldn't be stopped cold. You can't blame the leadership back-up teams when they try to set the scene, vet the extras and repaint the décor. In their ideal world, a Party Election Broadcast would be the only kind of telly their blokes did.

Here again, Kennedy has come over best, perhaps because, in an art-form whose whole impulse is to eliminate contingencies, nothing can eliminate the contingencies of his fundamentally merry face. The only way to do that would be to eliminate him altogether, as the Tories, in the first two weeks at any rate, pretty well did with Hague: their Party Election Broadcasts, shot and lit like *Escape from New York* or *Assault on Precinct 13*, projected Britain as a Blackboard Jungle in which Willie Horton sat behind every desk. No doubt, in the original scripts, Hague was flying the rescue helicopter to lift you out, but he ended up on the cutting room floor. In the Labour PEB that started screening on Sunday night, everything ended up on the cutting room floor except Blair. The action was shot to advertising standards: if there had been a fly on the wall, it would have been a member of Equity. Blair's spontaneous pint of beer was lifted at exactly the right speed and angle. We have since been given Alastair Campbell's assurance that hoisting a pint was just something Tony happened to do when the camera was around. Cue footage of flying pigs.

On the scale leading down from calculation to chaos, the next rung under the PEB is the set speech to the faithful at which cameras happen to be present. The back-up team is in control of the setting and the leader is in control of what he says. Contingency, however, enters at the point where the evening networks decide which bits of the speech they will use. You can see a complete speech only on the fringe channels, where it usually turns out to be as boring as hell – a fair reason for the main channels not to run it *holus bolus*. But even if a leader's oration is a heap of feldspar, it can sometimes be a gold mine of implication. On Friday evening, *Sky News* went live to Hague speaking in Manchester. 'You know what I know, make no mistake about it, the Conservatives can win this General Election.' A little of that went a long way, and a lot of it glazed the eyes like a Ming vase – not just your eyes but Hague's too.

Further down the script, however, a bell rang. Hague mentioned the great unmentionable, the Millennium Dome! He said that the present government was 'too embarrassed to knock it down'. He forgot to add that the last Conservative government hadn't been too embarrassed about the idea of putting it up. Nevertheless, here was a hint of what Hague's campaign might conceivably be doing instead of trying to reassure the dwindling Tory faithful that their leadership elite still shares their prejudices: it could have been attacking Blair's administration on the mess it had made out of actually running things. It would need boldness from the Hague squad to attack foul-ups whose origin can be traced to their own party, but boldness Hague has, if it could only be used. Instead, with a target like transport wide open to be bombed, all the Tories can say about John Prescott is that he has the wrong instincts about incoming eggs.

As any Labour voter who rides the London tube is painfully aware, Prescott has a lot more to answer for than that. The transport snafu amounts to a national emergency, and few of the other public services are in much better shape. Yet the new all-Blair PEB is inviting an attack that never comes. 'Work that we've started,' burbles Blair, 'and that we need to finish.' You can say *that* again. And indeed he does say it again. 'We've made a start, but haven't finished it.' How good a start? And how can you ever finish, if everything you have so far done compounds the shambles? The

Tories never ask, and even the Lib Dems don't go far beyond suggesting that more tax money is the solution. Although Portillo has given the occasional polite hint, there is nobody to say outright, and say often, that the public services are a question of organization. Labour is proposing a new way of organizing the health service, but Labour ought to look incredible about proposing a new way of organizing anything. Britain isn't producing enough teachers to teach its own language. Britain can't lay a railway line that doesn't warp in the remorseless heat of its equatorial climate. Britain can't get rid of a Dome that it didn't know how to open for crowds that never came to see the marvels it did not contain. It's Blair's Britain that can't do these things. So let's get the bastard.

That last sentiment is not one I share, finding as I do that Blair's repertoire of special voices arouses sympathy, rather in the way that a chameleon crossing a tartan kilt might make you want to pick it up and give it a rest. But why the other parties aren't beating the crap out of his reputation for competence is one of the great mysteries of this greatly fascinating election. On the whole they are proposing to do what he does but either use less money (Tories) or more (Lib Dems). That there might be different and less shambolic means to achieve the same ends seldom comes up. The level of debate between the parties has never been lower.

The level of debate is higher on television, but not necessarily because the hard-arse interviewers have confirmed themselves in their new role as Her Majesty's Loyal Opposition. The best you can say for them is that they are even-handed: they grill everyone at the same high temperature, taking the smell of charred flesh as a sign of success. If John Humphreys has his way, Keith Vaz will be deported as an illegal asylum-seeker. Jeremy Vine of *Newsnight* continues morphing himself into the new Paxo. The aforementioned Kirsty is a dominatrix out of the collective imagination of men whose idea of fulfilment is to be lashed around the parlour on all fours by a schoolmistress in leather underwear. But the torture is mainly about major money and minor detail. Eight billion, twenty billion, thirty-six billion. You didn't deny that, does that mean you meant this?

The inquisitors are keeping the politicians honest, but at the price of keeping them running backwards with their gloves up. Here again, Kennedy does best of the top men. Jonathan Dimbleby is as tough as any of the hard-arses and has a far more developed historic memory, but Kennedy came out well from a gruelling one-on-one. He has the art of getting his message out along with a defensive jab. Hague, though the quickest-witted of them all, is hampered by the fact that his atavistic messages have to be defended anyway, so he is already running backwards on his way from the dressing room to the ring. As for Blair, all he can do with a needling question is look stung, as if his tormentors were ignorant of Blair's Britain's towering achievements. But the achievements are what is in question. Do they tower, or are they Dome-shaped?

It is hard for even the most choleric interviewer to inflict any real damage face-to-face, although he might enhance his own reputation by asking the same question umpteen times – the television equivalent of a ballerina's thirty-two *fouettés*. Up-country, trailing Hague's solitary school visit for *Channel 4 News*, Jon Snow capitalized niftily on the Tories' Blackboard Jungle PEB by grabbing soundbites from the kids in the playground. 'You haven't been burning any cars have you?' The selected urchin had the perfect reply. 'Not recently, no.' At Smith Square they must have spat tacks when they saw that, but they ought to get their man ready for when he next meets Jon Snow on the road. Hague could ask, 'You haven't been burgled recently, have you?' It is statistically almost certain that Snow's reply will have to be 'Quite recently, yes.' But Snow is an old hand who can still outshine the new blood, like his namesake Peter, now equipped with a vampire-bait open-necked lemon shirt as he dodges emphatically among the virtual columns that show Labour right up *here* and everybody else right down *there*.

The fringe channels are way ahead on election debates, a fact that would be generally acknowledged if more people were watching. Channel 5's *5 Talk* on Friday at 6 p.m. was exemplary, although you have to be aware that one of the things that the show is exemplary of is Blair's Britain, where classless young people look and dress like Frank Skinner and Gail Porter when she is dressed at all. *5 Talk* is fronted by two fledglings called James and Lucy (they don't seem to have any second names) whose costive tones might lead you to expect strident vacuity. On the contrary, they are fast-thinking and well informed. James, in particular, is a pink-shirted walking encyclopaedia of political savvy. The programme costs fourpence – Sir David Steel came in from Scotland on the phone, not in vision –

but gets high-quality results, thereby reversing the trend of Millennium Dome culture.

The twin subjects on Friday were devolution and Europe. George from Norfolk had taught philosophy in Sweden for twenty-five years but still felt too British to join the euro. James asked: 'Why would an economic policy wipe out a cultural heritage?' Nobody in the Labour party has yet managed to put that thought into a single line. The discrepancy between yoof-struck format and adult argument was astonishing. The show looked like a mixture of *The Big Breakfast* and *Never Mind the Buzzcocks*, but it sounded like Plato's *Symposium*. Plumbing the depths of their tiny budget, its creators sent out a leg-man billed as The Man in the White Suit to do cod scientific research in the street. He smuggled a taxi driver into a Lib Dem press conference on the economy and measured the cabbie's pulse as it dropped to five beats a minute. People watching paint dry were proved to have the same level of cardiac excitement. (A few punters roped in off the street, a piece of chipboard, a tin of white paint, and one camera: cost, negligible. Joke, fabulous. Why can't the big channels be that funny? Because they can't think any way but big.) Michael Portillo missed a trick here. The Man in the White Suit caught up with him while he was canvassing. 'I'm sorry,' said Portillo, 'I've got voters to meet.' He was polite as always, but if he had submitted to the pulse test and said 'Conservative politicians have the hearts of lions' he would have met a lot more voters and made his party look cheerful and creative, instead of like the *Bismarck* steaming in a circle with its rudder jammed.

But the election show with most fun for grown-ups is *The Boulton Factor*, an annexe of *Sky News*. If you're still looking for the women in this election, this is where they are. On the main channels you will see only Ann Widdecombe and the savagely divine Kirsty, who, you will have gathered by now, I have got on the brain. (In my dreams she interrogates me at the Ivy: 'Why have you brought me here? What are your motives? What are these oysters for? Why won't you answer the question?') On *The Boulton Factor* you get the press babes as guests, and they are wonderful. Ann Leslie of the *Mail* dissects the candidates with the edge of a polished fingernail, and Julia Hartley-Brewer of the *Mirror* echoes the same unanswerable point she made in print: that the Tories have thrown their grappling hooks into their own ship. Terrific traffic, which the suavely thuggish Adam Boulton marshals like a master. He is never called Adam, by the way: he is just the Boulton Factor. This is the James Factor, saying watch out for Kennedy: if the big parties are dumb enough to go on playing follow-my-leader, the man in the middle could develop a column that will jolt Peter Snow out of his lemon shirt.

4. Follow That Bus

At the foot of the Millbank tower on Tuesday morning, we of the media gathered like a punishment battalion of termites briefed to attack a steel traffic bollard. We knew in advance that there wouldn't be much to chew on. Soon Tony Blair's bus would be heading out for an undisclosed destination. We would follow. When we got there, nothing much would happen, except in our dreams. We could dream of Blair being attacked with rocket launchers by half a dozen female OAPs screaming 'Seventy-five p was a bloody insult, you grinning berk!' There were shadowy figures within Millbank who believed that we might stop dreaming of something like that and start arranging it: that we might hire the Nolan Sisters, fit them out with a few lengths of plastic drainpipe, and let them loose at a photo op.

In the Millbank mind, where media control was invented, the media out of control is the demon that never sleeps. Unless you had signed on the dotted line for a seat on one of the two press buses, you weren't supposed to go. I linked up with ace freelance photographer Brian Harris, who was covering the day for the *Indy* along with me. His handsome features weathered from years of room service, Harris is the breed of smudger who gets the shot if has to wade through a swamp, surface through pack ice, dance with the seventh wife of the mad revolutionary general. But he wasn't too keen to get on a press bus that charges £540 for a day trip, and neither was I. Why not just hire a car and follow the buses? After all, it was a free country.

Patiently awaiting its precious cargo, the Blair bus was surrounded by demonstrators with signs saying KEEP CLAUSE 28. The kind of enthusiast who can surround you all on his own had a sign saying SEEK THE LORD WHILE HE MAY BE FOUND. Here was an argument for the prudence of keeping Blair's various destinations a close secret: otherwise he would face torrents of this stuff when he got there, and perhaps worse. If Millbank overdid the caution vis-à-vis the press, Special Branch was merely being wise when it came to the loving public. In large letters, the back of the Blair bus was marked LEADERS TOUR. It was heading for the land where the possessive case has been abolished, and apostrophes are never used except incorrectly, to mark the plural. If I knew where Blair was going every day, I would be waiting there myself, holding my sign that says SO MUCH FOR YOUR EMPHASIS ON EDUCATION, DIMWIT.

To the drooping disappointment of the sign-holders, the Blair bus pulled away with no Blair in it. Maybe the Blair bus would pick Blair up at Downing Street. We piled into the car and headed off in that direction, but at Downing Street there was no Blair bus. Back at Millbank there were no press buses either: they had left without us, we knew not whither. Luckily, Harris had a contact on the second press bus who owed him one after a hairy moment in Beirut. Ducking beneath the surveillance of the on-board Millbank commissar, the contact whispered into his mobile that the bus convoy was proceeding through Notting Hill Gate, perhaps on the way to the West Midlands via Shepherd's Bush roundabout.

We caught up with the second press bus on the M40 and sat behind it while Harris communed again with his contact. Newport had been mentioned as one of the day's locations. It couldn't be Newport Pagnell, and probably wasn't Newport, Rhode Island: but there might be a Newport in or near Staffordshire. Harris signed off on the moby and studied the map, on which Staffordshire occupied about a thousand square miles. So there was no point trying to run up there ahead of them and lie in wait. Meanwhile I was calculating the total revenue per bus from forty or fifty media personnel all coughing up the full whack: somewhere north of 25,000 quid. 'Almost enough to pay for the petrol,' said Harris. It would have been a good line for Hague, who had run out of good lines the previous night while being trampled by Paxman.

The great Australian philosopher Rod Laver once said, 'When you've got your man down, rub him out.' Strategically, the idea makes sense, but not when extended to the spectators. By now Millbank had dealt with Hague: he had been rubbed out with such thoroughness that the only way you could tell where he had lain was by a man-shaped area cleaner than the surrounding pavement. But Millbank still had many enemies, and two of them turned out to be me and Harris. Whispered word came through from the bus that we had been spotted.

Somewhere in the command centre of the bus, Millbank operatives were processing the information that a mystery car had been observed trailing close behind the tinted back window. The face in the car's front passenger seat checked out against the hostile media list. James, Clive, 61, Australian origin. Used to be on television, now active on the Internet. Thinks he's funny. Back-seat passenger could be Harris, Brian, freelance photographer. Paying for divorce, ready for anything. Once got a shot of Blair in pyjamas with Mandelson picking his nose: not his own nose, Blair's nose. High possibility of upcoming satirical attack at arrival point.

The easy course of action for Millbank would have been to buzz Special Branch and suggest that we be removed from the bus's tail. It would have worked, too: Harris has so many points on his driver's licence that he isn't even allowed to be a passenger. But someone higher up the chain of command must have been given pause by two further considerations. The first consideration was that people are still legally free to travel on the open road, unlike on the railways, where they can travel only under tight restrictions. The second consideration was that the Bremner Battlebus Ban (instigated when it was assumed, perhaps correctly, that to give Rory Bremner a ride on the bus might result in his imitating everyone on board including the driver) had gained negative publicity. The current potential satirical attack was headed up by comparatively minor players but there could be a nasty media backlash if Special Branch took them out. Better use the charm weapon and suck them in.

Although we were getting our information from on board the bus, we had to deduce that last part. Until the bus arrived in Stafford we were still expecting to be stopped any time by a fast car full of heavy bluebottles saying 'Breathe into this bag.' But suddenly, strangely, the both of us were *persona grata* as the two press buses disgorged their cargo at a complex called THE STAFFORDSHIRE AMBULANCE SERVICE NATIONAL HEALTH SERVICE TRUST HEAD-

QUARTERS. The Blair bus, which Blair had joined *en route* after a quick flight, was circling the district in a holding pattern while the media took up position to cover the forthcoming spontaneity. The smudgers toted their trademark aluminium stepladders for seeing over the heads of the public, although these locations are so secret that it usually means seeing over the heads of nobody except reporters. I grabbed a spot on the ropes where I could clock the scene.

It looked like a military base. I counted at least thirty ambulance personnel in green overalls, most of them marked PARAMEDIC on the right breast, while the left breast bore the name: ALAN, PETER, GEORGE. (In the empire of New Labour, the valley of the lost apostrophe leads to the plateau of the missing surname.) The ambulances were all inside the hangar, where the main action would take place. A bomb-squad copper was towed past by his sniffer dog. The dog had that particularly hang-dog look that dogs get when their biggest thrill of the week is snorting a practice wodge of Semtex, but every other life-form on the concourse was polished and alert.

Abruptly I found myself being loomed over by an upright man in green overalls called Roger. He turned out to be the guy in charge of the whole outfit: Roger Thayne OBE, an ex-lieutenant colonel whose background in medical service includes the Falklands and Lockerbie. We had a point in common. Roger's son-in-law commands the 4th Royal Australian Rifles, currently active in East Timor, where they had been in a skirmish only yesterday. After telling him how I approved of the Australian government's action with regard to East Timor, I discovered that Roger didn't necessarily approve of the British government's action with regard to the Health Service. 'What you've got in the Department of Health are people who have never seen a patient, and they are advising people who do see a patient.' I asked him if more money would fix things and the answer was: not without a re-think. 'It's a question of morale. Doctors, nurses, want to look after patients, not paperwork.'

I was busily writing that down when the Blair bus pulled in and gave forth the power couple – Blair and Cherie, both in full smile mode, a grand total of sixty-four scintillating teeth exposed to scrutiny from a satellite. Blair had his jacket off already: ever since Peter Mandelson noted with horror that one of the smudgers had nabbed an under-arm sweat shot, Blair has been pre-cooled for all occasions. Bad news for jacket manufacturers, but it makes media sense. So do Cherie's long-top pants suits with the long-toed shoes. During many a chat-stop on the way to the hangar, she proved her grace. She has a way of standing with one foot in front of the other, like a figure on an Egyptian frieze, although she does so with her legs crossed, as if Nefertiti were dancing the tango.

Soon they were inside being shown how the ambulance unit could electronically monitor patients at home, with the aim of cutting down the number of death-defying sprints to the hospital. A handsome South African doctor name-tagged ANTON VAN DELLEN (doctors still have surnames) proudly informed me that this was a cutting-edge set-up, but I wondered if, inside, anyone was telling Blair (a) that the secret of its success lay in the determination of its commander to fight his own war with no bullshit from upstairs, and (b) that the doctor was an import.

Dr Van Dellen strode handsomely away on his mission of mercy, to be replaced in my view by the celebrated Blairite apparatchik Anji Hunter. Access-starved journos tell me that Anji is a hard case, but she didn't seem that way today. At my age I am immune to sexual desire, but there is a lingering aesthetic sense that appreciates a tall, slim female form draped in a black linen pants suit underpinned with strappy high-heeled sandals for the shapely feet, the toenails painted with the blood of slain lovers. This was one chic apparatchik. Getting as tough as I ever can when drowning in a woman's eyes, I asked her why the Labour poster campaign was still screaming at the punters to get out there and vote in case Hague got in. She said, 'Why don't you have a word with Alastair?' She meant Alastair Campbell, so she might as well have recommended having a word with Napoleon Bonaparte: nice idea, but it would depend on the availability.

Anji drifted elegantly back into the Blair bus and Alastair Campbell came hulking out of it. He was very nice. You could fill the Millennium Dome with media people eager to testify that he is not nice at all, but he was nice today. I don't think he was turning it on, although clearly it can be murder when he turns it off. He wasn't guarded in the least. When I suggested that New Labour no longer had any challenge from the left, he guilelessly let slip that Charles Kennedy might fill the bill. I noted that one down: the whole potential realignment of British politics compressed into a moment. His answer to the question I had asked Anji was simple: a foregone conclusion meant that the voters might stay home. When I said that the Tories might vanish altogether, he said 'Good.' He said it with a smile, but he meant it. 'What about democracy?' I wailed. This time his smile said he didn't mean it. 'Ah, come on. Don't give me *that* stuff.' I could have quoted him cold and launched a thousand cartoons, but it wouldn't have been fair. His laughter said that what he was saying was preposterous. There is nothing preposterous, however, about the possibility.

Even with some of the polls adjusting the Labour lead downwards because of new rules for asking questions, we are looking at a one-party state for at least one parliament into the future. As Campbell went back into the bus to plug himself back into his information system that deals with millions of people all at once instead of one sweating hack at a time, I was pondering the implications. Tony and Cherie emerged from the hangar and proceeded down the concourse. Craning sideways, I could see Cherie dropping to a crouch, either to kiss babies or else to converse with children and very small adults. We were informed that at the next stop Blair would reassure Shropshire and the waiting world about New Labour's commitment to a Strong Society. Medical staff would be safe from attack by schoolteachers driven crazy by late trains.

But I could catch the speech on the fringe channels late at night. Harris had got his stuff. The great thing about photographers is that they bring the same expertise to baby-kissing as they do to a Palestinian kid bouncing rocks off an Israeli tank: they do what they must, and when it's done it's done. But for a scribbler, the story rarely fits the frame unless he lies. Integrity means you can't stop taking things in, and on the road back to London I took in the thing that mattered. It was buried on page 17 of a stapled clump of bumf handed to me by the indefatigable Roger. At the request of the NHS board, his ambulance unit was being studied by Sheffield University 'to identify the transferability of the Staffordshire performance throughout the National Health Service'.

Eureka! If Roger's irascible voice was going to be heard at government level, the implications were enormous. It meant that Labour would not just be bringing the private sector into the Health Service, it would be dumping its cherished top-down, target-setting management system. This was the very thing that Portillo was saying the Tories would do. The Tories wouldn't be doing anything for the next hundred years, but if Labour moves in that direction it will be clear confession that from the health angle the whole of the last parliament was a waste. Tony's campaign slogans for the public services boil down to 'I've started, so I'll finish.' If he really means 'I got it wrong last time but this time I'll get it right' he is open to an objection that uses the words 'piss-up' and 'brewery' in the same sentence. But New Labour certainly can organize a bus-trip.

5. Lunging for the Tape

On Monday afternoon William Hague was in the Wirral, where he said, 'It's a campaign that's going very well.' No doubt King Harold said the same thing at Hastings, while his troops kindly pretended not to notice the arrow sticking out of his eye. Scholars have yet to agree about which of the two Roman consuls, Aemillius Paullus or Terentius Varro, said the same thing at the battle of Cannae. To escape being massacred by 7,000 of Hannibal's Libyan heavy troops, the depleted legions turned around just in time to be charged by 10,000 of Hasdrubal's cavalry. At this point either Aemillius or Terentius said, 'It's a campaign that's going very well.' It probably sounded better in Latin.

There was comparatively little media coverage in ancient times: a concept difficult to explain to some of our young people today. Even for us adults it is sometimes hard to believe that there were no *Big Brother* cameras in the Garden of Eden to get the pictures of Adam and Eve being ejected naked. Nobody was watching. If *Survivor* had been there nobody would have been watching either, but *Big Brother* could have done a lot for Eve's subsequent career as a lap-dancer. We are so accustomed by now to seeing people in toe-curling circumstances right there on television that we think it normal. But in the pre-electronic world, Hague would have been able to say 'It's a campaign that's going very well' and nobody would have caught the moment except the flabbergasted inhabitants of the

Wirral. Today we can all watch and wonder. We can even wonder if he might be right.

For Hague to snatch a victory, the Queensland gambit would have to work. On the weekend, the press told us a lot about the Queensland gambit, a stratagem which can be outlined in a single sentence if you don't mind doing without the graphs and pie-charts. The side sure to lose warns against the dictatorial ambitions of the side sure to win, whereupon everyone votes for the side sure to lose, which then wins. It worked in Queensland, but you have to remember that Australia's most fun-filled state is also the place where the responsible authorities took a long look at the first cane toad and decided it was environmentally friendly. By the time they found out that it could poison a moving car and couldn't be killed with a flame-thrower, it had spawned a million children and learned to vote.

For the Queensland gambit to work this week, Hague would have to distract our attention from a blatant contradiction in logic. If he means anything by saying that his campaign has gone very well, he must mean that the Tory faithful at which it was aimed have come back to the fold. If he simultaneously paints the picture of a triumphalist Labour government taking its overwhelming majority as a mandate to extinguish liberty, he must mean that there are no longer enough Tory faithful to vote their beloved party in. The second part of the anomaly concedes that the natural constituency of the Tories has shrunk to a rump, and thus concedes that he was wrong to aim his campaign at its traditional hopes and fears. Therefore the campaign was ill conceived and could never have gone well.

The Tories had made the capital strategic mistake of falling back to reinforce their base camp when it was already overrun, instead of staying out in the field, living off the land, and maintaining contact with the enemy. By late last week the Smith Square general staff had realized this, but they still hadn't persuaded their field marshal, whose ebullience aroused memories of Montgomery during the Arnhem operation. Montgomery was still claiming a masterstroke after it turned out that he had dropped his paratroopers on top of a Panzer division. On Friday night Hague started lacing his speeches with some stuff about the public services, but was still banging on about asylum and the euro. By Sunday night, using God knows what combination of drugs and threats, his frantic lieutenants had persuaded him.

It must have been his toughest weekend: he has the guts to fight a losing battle forever, but to admit to your friends that you've been wrong takes character. Anyway, he did it, and on Monday he switched his themes to the central ground on which some of us had been expecting him to fight from the beginning. The new Tory PEB backed him on both strands: there was new stuff about the public services, emphasizing the undoubted fact that Labour's claims to having made a good start were open to question. There was also some old stuff about undeserving interlopers and the threat to the pound, thus to reassure the diehards that their saviour was not repudiating his earlier stand. So the PEB was trying to attract the central vote without abandoning the faithful. Unfortunately the Queensland gambit tacitly admitted that not even both groups put together would be enough to swing it unless some of the central voters switched. It went without saying that if they did switch, they would switch to the Conservatives.

This was a big thing to go without saying, because there was always the chance that they would switch to the Lib Dems. Over in Labour's Fortress Millbank, the anti-apathy scare campaign had the same drawback. If the sleeping voters piled out of their cots to stop the Tories by voting Labour, that would be OK. But what if they decided to stop the Tories by voting Lib Dem? Both main parties were thus running the risk of reinforcing the Lib Dems in the marginal seats. All Monday afternoon on *Sky News* you could watch the three leaders preaching to the nation through stump speeches in the marginals. *Sky News* has had a good election. As a lean operation it likes nothing better than free talent, and here were the three top performers each doing their full cabaret act live to camera for no fee. It was like getting the Three Tenors to sing at your daughter's wedding under the delusion that it was a charity appearance.

Hague, as we have seen, was in the Wirral, warning the country against the dreadful consequences of the Labour landslide that wouldn't happen because his campaign was going very well. Blair was at Enfield Southgate in London, the seat Portillo lost in 1997. Blair was talking to schoolchildren again: as it was in the beginning, so shall it be in the end. 'We've still got a massive amount to do, but we've made a start.' It was the same vulnerable message, but the man delivering it was at his best yet. He talked to the kids without talking down. 'When I was young, anyone who owned a house voted Conservative.' It would have been too complicated to explain to them that Margaret Thatcher had inadvertently created the new house-owning constituency that was now voting Labour, but there was not much he shirked.

You could see why Alastair Campbell loathes the idea of uncontrolled access. A big kid said that the local hospital had beds but no nurses. 'We are recruiting,' said Blair. If Jeremy Paxman had been standing there in short pants he would have pointed out that the nurses, doctors and teachers were being recruited anywhere in the world except Britain, whose education system had ceased to produce them. This kind of off-the-cuff stump confab can be lethally dangerous when the cameras are watching, but you can't help feeling it ought to be the real stuff of politics, especially when even Blair was being forced to talk turkey. Another big kid – a black girl facing the daunting prospect of university tuition fees – was given a masterly answer that left none of the difficulties out. For once Blair had got it right: talking to the punter and letting the news crew overhear it, instead of talking past the punter into the camera. At last his campaign was going very well. But there was someone else whose campaign was going even better.

Charles Kennedy was at Cheddar Gorge in Wells, where the Lib Dem majority over the Tories is a mere 528. This was incubus territory for the two main parties, because if the dozy swing voters they are trying to motivate should make their mark for the Lib Dems instead, the Tories will have worked to their own ruin and Labour will reinforce a new opposition. But a nightmare for them was dreamland for Kennedy. It was easy to predict, when the Lib Dem manifesto proposed raising taxes, that Kennedy was running for second spot. With the Lib Dem poll figures in the low teens the idea looked romantic. Now their poll figures were in the high teens and it looked classical: a flanking run on the wing with a smile of pity for the opposing forwards as they moved across too late. 'They need sensible and worthwhile opposition,' he said, meaning Labour. 'They're not going to get it from the Conservatives.' He said the Tories were heading for civil war. Meanwhile the media were heading for him. By this time he didn't need Honor Blackman to help him hog the screen-time. Up there in Hartlepool, Peter Mandelson must have been shaking his elegant head in admiration, like one of the Wright Brothers watching newsreel footage of Baron von Richthofen. Look what the new boys were doing with his invention.

Monday was probably the crucial day of the election. In the evening, Blair went up against Paxman on *Newsnight*. The previous week, Paxman had pounded Hague into the floor of a setting that looked like *Pebble Mill At One* in the days when the local punters pressed their noses against the window to watch an alderman being interviewed about the exciting prospects in store for Birmingham. The Prime Minister was in a position to stipulate a more dignified ambience, but he must have been well aware that the one-on-one with a career hard-arse like Paxman is his most perilous gig. Up-country on Friday afternoon, Jon Snow had hammered Blair on the transport issue: the issue the Tories had had to lay off because they invented the mess. Snow was less hampered by guilt. When Blair recounted what Labour had set out to do, Snow said, 'You didn't do it.' Blair had had no answer ready, but he was ready for Paxman.

Diving at you with a screaming snarl, Paxman carries all kinds of ordnance under his wings – smart bombs, rockets, napalm canisters – but the weapon to watch out for is the toffee apple. Blair dodged everything except the sticky question about why he let Mandelson resign if Mandelson had done nothing wrong. But otherwise the triumph of his defence was the way he turned to the attack. Paxo was out to lunch about the gap between rich and poor. Blair was needlessly windy in his answer. He could have just said that if the poor get richer it doesn't matter how rich the rich get: it's the only way to tax them progressively, because if you hike the rate they dodge it or decamp. (The same message worked for Ronald Reagan: it multiplied the deficit, but it kept him in office.) Blair couldn't get that idea into a snappy line, but at least he had an answer. Paxo was out to lunch, dinner and the next breakfast when he asked Blair to feel sympathy for Hague, and this time Blair said exactly the right thing. 'I sympathize with anybody who leads the Conservative party.' Across the lower half of Paxman's features, a smile of acknowledgment appeared: fleeting but with a hint of warmth, like summer in England.

As they settled down for the run to the judge – such was the catchphrase of the great Australian race commentator Ken 'Magic Eye' Howard – there was time for speculation about the future. Back at the start of all this I made the large prediction that it would be the most fascinating election of modern times, because although almost nothing would happen beforehand, almost everything would happen afterwards. It was an easy sooth to say: clearly the Tories will have to start again. You can have a lot of fun fiddling with the chess pieces. The longer Hague stays, the better for Portillo, especially if a euro referendum comes up: if Portillo has to lead against that, his hands are tied by what he has already said while backing Hague. Kenneth Clarke would be free to argue on terms instead of attacking the principle, but he can't be brought back until Central Office gives up altogether on the Little England thing, which means saying goodbye to home base for keeps. They should have drafted Chris Patten any way they could: he is bound to be their Grey Eminence, but with an official post he could have done something to shut up the Black Widow, whose 'Never' speech left Hague's ankles tied with his own trousers.

But the realignment might go far beyond that. If the Tories are wrecked, it is because they have been replaced by Labour as the wealth party. If Labour can be opposed only from the left, it won't be by its own left, which is irrevocably wedded to a chimera: an unaspiring working class that had to be fobbed off with social justice because it could never get preferment. Now that the whole country is either middle class or on benefits, the natural New Left are the Lib Dems. Kennedy has everything to play for, including the delicious possibility of offering the Tories an alliance instead of asking for one. He went into this election as Prince Hal, a joker of the panel games who stayed too long in the hospitality rooms afterwards because the girls were pretty and the talk was good. He will come out of it as Henry V, with Labour as the French army: overconfident, overmanned, and above all overmanaged.

Too thoroughly convinced by its own success in managing its bid for supremacy, Labour is still under the illusion that the public service departments can be managed the same way. Labour is already talking of a new, supreme management layer to manage the management layers. The Millennium Dome not only hasn't gone away: it's expanding. Unless Professor Quatermass can find a way to stop it, the damned thing will cover the entire country. As the grisly envelope eats its way outwards, its quisling minions will be open to ridicule from anywhere except the old right wing that wants to cut the public sector back. The public doesn't want the public sector cut back. The public wants the public sector fixed, and by now everyone belongs to the public. There are no leafy enclaves: there is no house, be it ever so grand and well protected, that can't be reached by *Big Brother*, a cold call, a dope dealer or a thief. The British are all in it together at long last.

Speaking as an Australian by birth and upbringing, I can promise you that equality won't be as bad as you think. It just means giving up on the idea that there is a class born to rule. The idea had some attractive aspects: the born rulers were often cultivated and public-spirited, and their women gracious and well-spoken. Goodbye to all that. What you have to watch out for is the new rulers: getting there took fanatical application, and now they find it hard to stop being fanatical. Last week I tailed one of the Blair press buses up to Stafford. Now Millbank wants to charge the *Independent* £540 for a bus ride I wasn't even on. It would appear that my name is on a list. Free men don't like lists, and confident rulers don't keep them.

6. Standing on a Landslide

On Thursday morning there was finally time to think. Media people who had spent weeks on the press buses awoke to the strange spectacle of a view through the window that did not move. It would be a long day before the polls closed, and the mind was free to ponder the paradoxes of democracy, the sweep of history, the vanity of human wishes and the startling beauty of David Beckham.

In Athens on Wednesday night, Beckham was a poetic thing to see. He didn't have to be scoring a goal to look poetic. He looked poetic just trapping a lobbed ball with his chest, as if rising to sacrifice himself by intercepting a meteorite. He looked poetic just standing there, while the missiles sportingly thrown by the Greek fans bounced around him. He looked too poetic to be the incarnation of a socio-political trend, but he was.

So was Jesse Owens at the Berlin Olympics in 1936, but Hitler didn't get the point. Blinded by racial science, Hitler stuck to his conviction that America was decadent. He couldn't see that a nation able to produce so beautiful and accomplished a human being out of its own underclass had a lot better chance of dominating the world than he did. If Owens had been white, Hitler might have seen the truth.

If David Beckham talked and dressed like Edward Fox, we might see it too. But the self-mutilating haircuts, the hunger for tattoos, the marriage to one fifth of a pop act and the lifestyle out of Graceland by way of Playboy Mansion West all combine to delude us that he is a prisoner of vulgarity, a clumsy aspirant to the standards of his betters. Forget about it. This is a man who knows his place in a new sense: that there is no place above his he would care to reach. Half a century ago, he would been been six inches shorter, worn shorts as long as his little legs, earned a fixed wage, saved up for a bungalow and counted it a great day if he shook hands with royalty. Now he *is* royalty. He is a king, and Victoria is his queen: he's got a better deal than Prince Albert. There is scarcely a man in the land who would not like to be him, up to and including the Duke of York, who would love to shine on the golf course as Beckham does on the football field, but has been held back by his birth.

Rewind the tape sixty years, to a conversation between Churchill and Lord Halifax. Churchill was no social radical, and Halifax was so reactionary he would have handed the country to the Nazis if they had guaranteed to preserve his privileges. But the two true-blue Tories were agreed that 'the boys from the state schools' had done well in the Battle of Britain, and that when the day came they should have their chance to rule.

Since they were presaging nothing less than doom for the Old Establishment of which they were parts of the furniture, their colloquy was a pretty generous gesture, perhaps made easier by the likelihood that it would take a long time to come true. And such, indeed, was to be the case. The Prime Minister of today is still one of the boys from the private schools. But Tony Blair presides over a country that has changed on just the lines those Old-Boy old boys predicted, although it took every contentious minute of the elapsed time for Britain to get to where it is now.

The welfare state was an Establishment invention: Lord Beveridge was an Old Boy par excellence. The retreat from Empire was managed by the Conservatives, not by Labour: Iain MacLeod, although sulphurously branded with the sign of the intellectual, was a Tory grandee in all other respects. Over-impressed less by Marxism than by the planning that won the war, the Labour party wedded itself to a command economy. Hugh Gaitskell joined his name to Rab Butler's, but Butskellism could fly only so far from Labour's traditional expectations before the chain on its leg brought it back. Harold Wilson, the only Labour Prime Minister before this one who ever got used to winning, did so because he was a juggler who could placate the union block votes by allowing them to think that some day their dream would come true.

But their dream could never come true, and the Labour party's best minds knew it. Finally Roy Jenkins, the key man in the whole reforming process that has led Labour to its present command of the centre instead of an unenviable domination of the left edge, headed the breakaway. He is still often condemned for being a would-be Establishment figure himself, a sucker for the hallowed ploy by which the landed ascendancy absorbed its enemies on the left, gagging them with ermine. Certainly the present Chancellor of Oxford University has had a lifelong interest in filling his place at high tables. But he was a true rebel.

Both Gordon Brown and Michael Portillo have no doubt studied Jenkins's use of the chancellorship as a training ground and a launching pad. Whether or not Jenkins guessed that his Social Democratic Party would have only a limited life is a nice question. But he certainly knew that his personally created *fronde* would force Labour to think again about the command economy. Labour's switch to the centre was already under way when Thatcher's victory in the Falklands gave her the boldness to launch free market economics. Michael Foot was thrown as a sacrifice on to the guttering pyre of Old Labour's incinerated delusions. Clause 4, the sacred text of universal nationalization, was kept on the party card only as a talisman: not as an article of faith, but as a gesture to past legitimacy. Kinnock got stuck with the gesture.

Kinnock didn't win the country, but he won the party that rules it now. Labour was set free from its dragging links to the industrial proletariat, which Thatcherism had atomized: the lower orders had divided into the prosperous and the unemployed, and the only answer to unemployment was expansion. John Major was the Tories' first overt answer to Labour's drive into the centre: ever since the cautionary tale of Sir Alec Douglas-Home the Tories had fielded leaders of relatively humble origins – the boys and girls from the state schools – but they had all behaved as if their eventual place in the Establishment was the destiny that had shaped them from the start. Major looked shaped by the humble origins. His fate was to be lampooned by the new media ascendancy that likes its politics drawn as a cartoon, with the grandees in their great houses and the representatives of the common people sullen at the gates. But reality was no longer like that. By countenancing Major's leadership at all, the Tories were already saying goodbye to their perennial snobberies.

*

They just didn't say goodbye fast enough, and Labour got in. But goodbye – a long goodbye, admittedly – is what the more enlightened Tories had been saying ever since the war. It was in giving up their empire, their privileges and their prejudices that they had been at their best. If they had studied their own history better, they would be doing better now. The dumbest of them needed total disaster as a teaching aid. But the cleverest, and the best, have provided for decades an example that Cool Britannia would do well to study. The Tories who believed in public service were cultivated enough to want a cultivated country. Their civilized enclave was not enough for them. I can remember a time when Tory peers vied with Labour peers for the honour of raising the taste of the people: which was, after all, the same ideal that the red radical Gramsci died cherishing.

The New Britain is philistine to the core. It is one of the cruellest paradoxes of my time in Britain that its once fruitful broadcasting system now reinforces the stupidities it was brought into being to ameliorate. To compound the paradox, a woman who thinks of herself as a Conservative started the rot: when Margaret Thatcher removed the quality requirement from the ITV franchise bids, she blew the whistle for the rush to triviality. It was a crime bred from the capital error of thinking that an ideology can be a view of life. The free market has an unrivalled capacity to harness brains. But the free market does not have a mind, and its bastard child, managerialism, is not a thing of the spirit: just a toy for the untalented.

Such aberrations would matter less if Britain, at governmental level, had any real management tradition to draw upon. But since the war Britain has had an almost flawless record of being unable to assemble its technologists under a competent technocrat. Instead it has assembled them under incompetent committees, and the results lie rotting and rusting in a crowded chronological line: the ground-nut scheme, the Brabazon, Blue Streak, Skybolt, the TSR2, the tilting train, Nimrod. So many and huge have been the fiascos that they would scarcely fit into the Millennium Dome – the supreme fiasco, and the true symbol of the Blair government's first term of office. Labour's only excuse for the Dome is that the Tories planned it. In that respect as in so many others, the two great parties are squeezed together by intimate historic bonds. It will be interesting to see if a third great party, if there is to be one, will know how to detach itself from the Dome culture, which can be defined as the unfortunate tendency to engage in gigantically superfluous schemes when the essential matters of public welfare are smothered in paperwork.

The broadcasting system showed a hint of its old glory on Thursday night, when the election programmes took over the studios of the main channels and managed to include some actual human beings along with the virtual technology. The lesson that the viewing public does not give a shit about virtual technology will probably never be learned: it runs counter to every channel controller's unshakeable belief that the small screen must be made large by the flash of gadgets, or else the fatally distractable punters will switch off to watch something else – a pin-ball machine, say, or their washing machine on its second rinse.

Sky News had done well throughout the campaign season, but on the big night even they decided that the droll Adam Boulton needed assistance from tables that lit up, walls that swivelled, and hovering gizmos that represented the state of the parties with creep-ily contracting and expanding suppositories: a visual pain in the arse. I wanted to see Boulton shooting the bull with Ann Leslie and the press babes, but no chance. Nobody can compete with the Beeb when it comes to doodads, so there is no point trying. At BBC1, David Dimbleby, born under the old Establishment in the days when it knew what it was doing, presided over a studio gone bananas.

Peter Snow's tomato sauce shirt was the closest touch with reality. Everything else was virtual. There were neon staircases in the sky with robotic simulacra of the party leaders climbing up them or threatening to fall off the edge. A staircase that was presumably real

– unless Snow himself was virtual, a distinct possibility – was wheeled on so that he could run up and down it, shrieking and choking simultaneously while his artificial paradise swirled and swam with images utterly stunning in their irrelevance. There was also a new laser version of the Swingometer. In the long-gone reign of Bob Mackenzie, the Swingometer was a piece of cardboard and it told you something. Now it can shoot down a flying saucer but it tells you nothing.

In keeping with the election's strange mood of misogyny, the whole demented Beeb scene was all but babe-free. Boys' toys it had in plenty, but you looked in vain for the swell of a breast. Unfortunately for the cause of the banished women, David Dimbleby's one and only female aidette completely missed the point about the return from Oldham West, which revealed the sudden and shocking electoral presence of more than 5,000 potential Nazis. David wanted to talk to her about that, but she wanted to talk about something else.

Elsewhere in the asylum, Jeremy Paxman was in charge of a mezzanine area called The Café. No refreshments were served, perhaps as a gesture to Paxo's satiated state. (He was still digesting William Hague.) But the human conviviality was a welcome relief from the dingbat electronics. One of Paxo's guests was Neil Kinnock. In a moment of brain-fade, Paxo drew Kinnock's attention to the beamed-in image of Blair's car arriving at the count in Sedgfield. Paxo said that the car contained Neil Kinnock. The delighted Kinnock said, 'I should be so lucky.' You could see what Kinnock has that Blair hasn't: an unstudied amiability. You could also see what Blair has that Kinnock hasn't: the Prime Ministership.

Over on ITV, David Dimbleby's brother Jonathan had an out-of-body experience to match Paxo's. Jonathan screwed up his commentary on the Torbay declaration by mixing up the parties. He owned up like a man. 'I'm a complete nana.' In all other respects he was running the superior studio. John Sergeant, all on his own, did the work of six people in the Beeb studio, and did it better. Losing Sergeant can be counted as one of those little triumphs that are steadily lobotomizing the Corporation. ITV had plenty of Beeb-style virtual hoo-hah but Sergeant's presence made up for it. He is not beautiful, but he is bright. Mary Nightingale was there too, and she is both. Good looks ought not to matter in female television presenters, but at three o'clock in the morning I couldn't see the harm.

The studios turned red as the night wore on, with proportionately less blue and a startling amount of yellow. As with the election campaign, there was much pizzazz but little tension. Speculation on the aftermath was already rife. At BBC1, Paddy Ashdown used a startling word about the Tory future. The word was 'split'. He wasn't pursued on the point, but he ought to have been. Surely the Europhile and Europhobe wings of the Conservative party can't be reconciled: they spring not from two opinions, but from two separate views of the modern world. Here was a topic begging, nay barking, to be discussed. It was decided that the topic of when Hague would be dumped was more interesting.

The new era dawned with Blair's arrival at Millbank. At 7 a.m. Blair was hailing Gordon Brown as 'a brilliant chancellor' but their warm embrace lasted 0.006 seconds on my laser chronometer. If they have made a secret deal about the succession, God help them both. A secret deal between Bob Hawke and Paul Keating bedevilled Australian politics for a decade. At Smith Square, Hague was closeted with his advisers. What were they advising now? Perhaps he was advising them. 'Call to me all my sad captains,' said Mark Antony at the moment when he, the saddest captain of them all, realized what he had to do. Hague came out, addressed the cameras, and fell on his sword. He went the way he fought, with bravery. What Sven Goran Eriksson said about David Beckham in victory applied to Hague in his defeat. 'He behaved like a captain.'

Postscript

From 19 May 2001 onwards, the above six pieces appeared in the *Independent* at various times during the two weeks of the General Election. Originally only three pieces were commissioned, but I got carried away, and the editor, Simon Kelner, generously went with the flow as my dispatches came pouring in. Later on, during the invasion of Iraq, the perfect word popped up: 'embedded'. Following one party's bus in an election campaign, even if that party is the likely winner, you are as effectively blocked off from a general picture of the action as a journalist embedded in an armed formation. The journalist tries to tell himself that the smell of a sweaty flak jacket and the nearby crunch of a mortar bomb are bringing him and his readers into an unprecedented intimacy with the action, but the prosaic truth is that neither he nor they would have a clue what was going on even if all the embedded reports could be combined into one. I really thought I was on to something when I chanced on the bumf about the ambulance unit: hence my gung-ho tone. The facts alas said that the Labour strategists had no intention of following up that particular lead: it was strictly a photo opportunity. On the other hand, I made the right guess when I suggested that the Conservative party was about to disappear. But I didn't need to be at a tube station with Michael Portillo to figure that out. What was useful, about slogging along with the foot soldiers, was the reminder that politics is grinding work, best done by proper grown-up people who can survive without immediate applause. It really isn't a bit like show business. Anthony Howard and several other qualified commentators said nice things in private about my potted analysis of recent British history, but once again I didn't need to be out there meeting the people to get all that. I got most of it from books. For the politician to get out there, however, can be very handy, especially if he has the knack of taking in what he sees. Four years later, John Howard won his third Federal Election in Australia largely because he was a lot better than his opponent at telling what the average home owner was thinking. The Australian intelligentsia, stuck inside its jacuzzi of constantly recycled opinion, was convinced that the average home owner was motivated by nothing except the deadly fear of a hike in the mortgage rate. Howard knew better than to call 50 per cent of the population cowards. A stint on the bus or the zoo plane is still the best way to be reminded that human beings are not statistics, even when they vote.

PRIMO LEVI AND THE PAINTED VEIL

What do we need to be told about Primo Levi that he doesn't tell us himself? In his middle twenties he spent a year in Auschwitz. Later on he wrote a book about it, the book we know as *If This Is a Man*: one of the great books of the twentieth century, and possibly the greatest among its sad category of great books we wish had never needed to be written at all. The book is beyond anybody else's power to summarize, since it is already a summary. The same might be said of his other writings, which were published intermittently during the remainder of his life and cumulatively suggested that one of the best reasons to continue living, after one had seen the world at its worst, was to get things written that would establish a place for the introspective self even in a context of overwhelmingly destructive historic forces.

But a commercial exploitation of his personal history was the last thing on his mind. Slow to commit himself as a full-time professional writer even after he was famous, he went on earning a salary as an industrial chemist. Though his waxing fortunes would have permitted a move up, he never left the flat in Turin where he had spent his whole life except for those fateful two years away when he was young: one year in Milan, the other in Poland. Everyone who knew him knew that his home life was hard. Having assigned to his wife the duty of looking after his ailing mother, and having thus made sure that they would spend a claustrophobic day with each other before he came home to them in the evening, he had created conditions for himself that might have been considered too obvious a stress-inducing mechanism even by Goldoni. And it all went on for years, whereas a Goldoni play only seems to.

But Levi never complained in public. Though Turin is a tight-lipped town, there were friends of friends who said that he complained to certain women, some of whom in turn complained that he was never allowed out for long. It seemed a fair inference that his reasons to stay were better than his reasons to leave, always granted that his wife was not herself struggling with the question of whether to keep him or kick him out. In his creative work there were hints at personal unhappiness, but the obliquity served only to bolster the impression that to preserve a decent reticence was a condition for creating at all. He must have struck some kind of workable balance, because he never stopped writing for long. In Italy, where there is a Booker committee around every corner, literary prizes count. He won them all. In the wider world, he was on his way to the Nobel Prize. It was only a matter of time. His life was a testament to the virtues of getting the past in proportion. All over the world, his admirers took solace from his true success, which was to grow old gracefully in spite of everything: think of what had happened to Primo Levi, and yet he still wanted to create, to live a life of order, to stick with it to the end.

Thus it was doubly, shockingly unexpected when, at the age of sixty-seven, at the apartment block in Turin, he killed himself by throwing himself down the stairwell. Though the possibility should not too soon be ruled out that he told us quite a lot about this before he did it, there is certainly no denying that he couldn't tell us much about it afterwards. Previously, he had left little room for other commentators to be more profound about his life than he could. Now they had space to operate. They also had what looked like an open invitation. There was a mystery to be investigated. Why, exactly, did he kill himself? Auschwitz had been ages ago. Could it have something to do with that other mystery, the mystery of his private life? For modern biographers, who increasingly feel less inhibited about writing to a journalistic brief, the prospect was hard to turn down. Two of them moved into the Turin area and got on the case. We must try to be grateful that they proved so diligent. They interviewed everybody except each other. The diligence, however, has produced two books which, arriving at the same moment, weigh on the spirit almost as much as they do on the muscles. You can just about hold one of them in each hand, but not for long.

Called simply *Primo Levi*, Ian Thomson's effort is already heavier than a housebrick. More mysteriously entitled *The Double Bond*, Carole Angier's is heavier than Ian Thomson's, partly owing to the abundance of material yielded by her talents as a mind-reader. To

increasingly comic effect, women pining for the allegedly maladroit
Levi ('like a child in matters of the heart', even though – perhaps
because? – 'a Colossus of thought') show up under sobriquets to
protest that nothing will make them speak, little knowing that Angier
has access to their brainwaves by telepathy. Unvoiced appetencies,
normally resistant to verbal notation, are transcribed at length. Even
on the level of ascertainable fact, rarely can she make a point in less
than a page. She turns subtlety into a blunt instrument. She refuses,
for example, to be fooled by the seemingly obvious connection
between Levi's direct experience of Auschwitz and his suicide forty
years later. She is confident on the subject. 'Not Auschwitz, but his
own private depression, killed him in the end.' If she means that
the memory of Auschwitz might not have been enough to kill him
without his private depression, there could be some sense to what
she says, and thus reason for the confidence. But if she means that
the private depression would have killed him even without Auschwitz, she is being confident about what she can't possibly know. She
could be in a position of certainty only if Levi had killed himself
before he got to Auschwitz. But he killed himself afterwards. It was
long afterwards, and in the interim he had accumulated plenty more
experience to be depressed about; but to assert that his most terrible
memory played no crucial part in the decision that sent him over
the balustrade is to make a far larger claim to knowledge about the
way his mind worked than he ever did.

*

Ian Thomson is less given to speculation, which is the main reason
why his book is considerably shorter than Carole Angier's. Since life,
too, is short, and time reading about Primo Levi will probably be
time taken away from reading Primo Levi unless the reader is
devoted to no other subject, it should logically follow that if either
book is to be recommended, Thomson's should be the one. Apart
from his harder head, another reason for Thomson's comparative
conciseness is that he simply writes with more snap than his rival
can command, although like many another in the new generation of
serious literati he somehow dodged the remedial English course on
the way to his honours degree. At school Levi had a friend called
Giorgio. 'Phlegmatic, lazy, sensitive and generous, Levi called him
"Giorgione" . . .' Surrounding evidence suggests that all those adjec-

tives apply to Giorgio, not Levi, but the word order suggests the opposite. 'To brutalise' does not mean to treat like a brute; 'exult' does not mean 'exalt'; 'refute' does not mean 'rebut'; 'contend' does not mean 'oppose'; and participles, if they are meant to dangle occasionally, ought not to dangle so far that that they confuse the sense. Of Natalia Ginzburg: 'Born to an exemplary anti-Fascist family, her father was arrested in Turin in 1934 . . .' But unless there were exemplary anti-Fascist families before the advent of Fascism, it was she, and not her father, who was born to the exemplary anti-Fascist family. These blemishes in written English would be less striking if Levi himself had not been a fastidious master of Italian prose, which he learned to write at a time when a mistake was a mistake and not a sign of free expression.

Luckily Thomson's brio and sense of relevance are proof against his solecisms. Into his smaller space he packs with reasonable neatness most of the pertinent facts adduced by Angier, plus a few more that she somehow missed, perhaps because she was busy dreaming up code-names for the ever increasing crowd of women whose lips were sealed. She didn't find out, for example, that in 1939 Levi's parents enrolled him for English lessons with a woman called Gladys Melrose, a Londoner scratching an existence in Turin as a teacher for Berlitz. Gladys Melrose ignited Levi's admiration for Aldous Huxley: an admiration which was to have large consequences later, when Levi formed the Huxleyan aim of studying the extermination camp as a laboratory of behaviour. Thomson also notes, as Angier does not, Levi's fondness for Louis Armstrong. A taste for good-time jazz is not necessarily a sure sign of a sunny nature (Mussolini's passion for Fats Waller was of no help to the Ethiopians) but it does suggest at least the capacity for lightness of spirit. It's the kind of detail that adds to our picture of Levi's character by making room for a quality he must have had but which is not often enough mentioned: a charming openness, on the mental level at any rate, to those easy pleasures from which, he was inclined to believe, his nature had shut him out. Did he snap his fingers as he listened to 'Sugar Foot Stomp'? Did he hum along with 'Savoy Blues'? Nobody ever asked, and at this rate nobody ever will, because not even Ian Thomson seems to realize that those little concrete details outrank any amount of abstract speculation.

His publisher, alas, shares the same obtuseness. Louis Armstrong, though present on page 118 of Thomson's book, is missing from its index. So are Fred Astaire and Ginger Rogers. They are in the text, but they don't make it to the status of a fact that a scholar might want to look up later on. Yet there is a danger of depopulating Levi's imagination if we automatically assume that his principal mental symbols for two lovers swept away by passion were Paolo and Francesca from Canto V of the *Inferno*. The Fascist regime had banned Hollywood movies by 1941, but in Milan there were bootleg screenings. At one of those screenings, Levi marvelled at Fred and Ginger dancing in *Top Hat*. It was one of the last things he did before he went off and joined the doomed little group of young *resistenti* who behaved as if they had been trained for nothing else except to get arrested. He fell in love with one of them. Her name was Vanda. What did he see in his mind's eye, in the last hour they ever spent together? Was it Paolo and Francesca riding on the storm, or was it Fred and Ginger floating a magic millimetre above a white floor, touching each other with the lyrical chasteness that reduces the soul of a shy young man to a sob of longing? Because Levi is a classic, there is a bad tendency to think that he was raised on a strictly classic diet. But he took everything in: probably the main reason why he was able to take in even Auschwitz. Dreadful grist, but a brilliant mill.

You know you are getting old when the biographers scramble the most elementary facts about World War II, as if it all happened before their time: which, of course, it did. Thomson gives us a picture of Levi, in the Lager infirmary, finding out from German and Polish newspapers that the Allies were 'moving towards Normandy'. No newspaper of any nationality could possibly have carried such information. The newspapers might have said that the Allies were moving further into Normandy, or else were moving out of it as they expanded their bridgehead south and east; but if the newspapers had said that the Allies were moving *towards* Normandy they would have been privy to the biggest Allied secret of the war. On the other hand, Thomson has a sure sense of what Jewish bourgeois society was like in Turin before Mussolini made the unforced error of copying the Nuremberg laws.

Thomson paints a picture of assimilation rather than persecution. In Germany and Austria, it was the very success of the assimilation that got the anti-Semitic intellectuals so excited, with disastrous consequences: but for Italy this had never been true. Anti-Semitic theorizing had never been powerful enough to infect even the Church, whose rank and file were later to behave very well during the Nazi round-up, with the result that the Italian branch of the Final Solution was a relative flop. The theory being lacking, there had never been much practice. Thomson's version is young Primo is bullied because he is a shrimp, not because he is a Jew: is bullied, in fact, even by other Jews. Angier can't resist wheeling the anti-Semites on early, as if Fascism had always been bound to bring them to power. But not even the Fascists, some of whom were Jews, had harboured any such expectation until Mussolini fell prey to the brainstorm that did as much as anything else to demoralize the country. (Most of the more intelligent Fascist hierarchs realized that their dream was on its way downhill from the moment that Mussolini issued the Manifesto of Racial Scientists in 1938, but they were counting on the usual gap being maintained between rhetoric and actuality.) In Angier's book, the Holocaust is practically waiting to grab Levi in the school playground. Levi told his Italian biographer, Fiora Vincenti, a story about his being given a hard time at school by a pair of athletic boys. Making it clear that a more powerfully equipped biographer is now on the scene, Angier goes on interpreting the story until the athletic boys end up as Jew-baiters. The interpretation is longer than the story; and anyway, if that was what Levi meant, why wouldn't he have said it? She puts herself continually in the untenable position of knowing more than he does about the one subject he knew more about than anybody, and of wanting to get more said when saying everything he could was his principal object.

Admittedly, 'everything he could' did not always mean everything he knew. There is such a thing as a decorum that goes out of date. As Thomson notes, Levi held back from evoking the pitiable scene at Fossoli when the SS gleefully photographed the prisoners as they squatted defecating in the railway siding before the train departed. Typically, the SS got a particular charge out of photographing the women. Luciana Nissim, who was there, recorded the moment in her *Memoir from the House of the Dead*, which was published before Levi had finished writing *If This Is a Man*. Thomson plausibly conjectures that Levi was held back by 'some strange puritan stringency', but to a man of his generation – and, indeed, of mine –

it is the word 'strange' that would seem strange. Why add insult to injury by speaking of the unspeakable? That the SS could visit such barbarism on women was the proof that the Devil was loose. For all his determination to tell the whole truth, Levi thought he could not do it unless the Devil within himself was kept on a short leash: vengeance and hatred were his enemies, not his friends. And decorum: well, that *was* his friend. Look what had happened when it had been outlawed, in that militarized bedlam where anything went and only luck could save you.

'Only luck could save you' was a favourite admonition of Nadezhda Mandelstam's to anyone cherishing the illusion that in Stalinist times there might have been a strategy for dodging the scythe. Solzhenitsyn knew that it was only the accident of his being a mathematician that saved his life. Levi knew that it was his qualification in chemistry that kept him in the work camp and out of the gas chamber. But a lot of other lucky breaks were necessary as well. He had a few words of German; he fluked a double soup ration; and, at the end, the scarlet fever he almost died of saved him from the forced march on which he would have died for certain. One of the many great things about him was that he never attributed all these strokes of fortune to a benevolent fate. When, after the war, someone in Italy said that Providence had intervened so that Levi might bear witness, Levi got uncontrollably angry for one of the few times in his life. Here lies the full meaning of the 'Kuhn's prayer' sequence in *If This Is a Man*: a full meaning which Angier goes on worrying at in an unnecessary attempt to make it fuller still.

Kuhn thanked God for sparing him. When Levi said that if he had been God he would have spat at Kuhn's prayer, Levi was saying that there was no such thing as divine intercession for an individual case. The point isn't really all that hard to understand. Levi, after all, devoted the best of his magnificent literary powers to driving it home. Levi also made the uncomfortable point that when it came to surviving the initial selections, high qualities of character were more likely to be a drawback than an advantage. Angier, when praising the 'bold' personality of one of Levi's female contemporaries, does so by imagining her being caught up in the Holocaust: 'I think she might have survived.' But Levi spent a good part of his last book, *The Drowned and the Saved*, pointing out that the Lager system punished any signs of fighting back with certain death. So unless her boldness had been accompanied by a prophetic capacity to keep it concealed, Levi's friend wouldn't have lasted five minutes. Angier's intuitive grasp of survival potential is the very kind of sophisticated incomprehension of his message which added to Levi's despair in the later part of his life.

The question remains of how desperate he was already. It will always remain, because it is unanswerable. For all we know, suicide is the mandatory escape route for anyone with clear sight, and the rest of us get to die in bed only because we have the gift of regrowing our cataracts from day to day. Seen steadily and seen whole, life is hard to bear even in conditions of civilized normality. In Levi's case, there was the Holocaust. Later on there were all the forms of its denial: forms that he tirelessly analysed, but with a growing sense that he was trying to mop up the incoming tide. It could be argued that these later disappointments would have been enough to tip him over the edge even if he had never had direct experience of the Holocaust in the first place. But since he did have such experience, it seems perverse to subtract it from the equation, especially when Levi himself made a famous statement on the subject as long after the event as 1978, the year in which his fellow survivor Jean Améry drank poison. Levi had always been impressed by Améry's contention that the man who has been tortured once stays tortured. Writing about Améry's suicide, he returned to the same idea. Thomson quotes what Levi said:

> Suicides are generally mysterious: Améry's was not. Faced by the hopeless clarity of his mind, faced by his death, I have felt how fortunate *I* have been, not only in recovering my family and my country, but also in succeeding to weave around me a 'painted veil' made of family affections, friendships, travel, writing and even chemistry.

Carole Angier is very bold to leave this crucial passage out, although one can see that it might have interfered with the main thrust of her original research, in which it is established, to her satisfaction at any rate, that Levi, if he recovered his family, certainly did not succeed in weaving around himself any kind of veil whether painted or otherwise when it came to family affections. Not only was the young Primo Levi 'pathologically shy' (not just shy) but the older, post-Auschwitz Primo Levi stayed that way, torn between the wife he was unable to leave and the women he could not allow himself to love. There is no notion that Levi might have been honouring his wife for her loyalty, love and sacrifice, and that the other women, in declining to twist his arm, might have been honouring him through respecting his real wishes. Early or late, he was the victim of a sex problem – a view Angier sticks to even while, on her own evidence, the ageing hero looks to be grappling with the same sex problem as Warren Beatty. The child was the father of the man, and the man was a child in matters of the heart. Why? Because he was depressed all his life. What depressed him? Depression. Thus Angier reduces a moral genius to a helpless plaything of his own childhood and adolescence, a message we might find comforting. But we should watch out for that kind of reassurance. In the democratic component of liberal democracy, there is a sore point called egalitarianism, and the craze for biography might be one of its products. The craze for biography puts the reader on a level with superior people. Part of the effect of Thomson's book, and the whole effect of Angier's, is to suggest that Primo Levi was a bit like us; which is only a step away from suggesting that we are a bit like him. *Magari*, as the Italians say: if only it were true.

TLS, 21 June 2002

Postscript

In a book review there is room to say only so much, but perhaps I should have found room to say that Levi himself didn't approve of the term 'Holocaust'. Unfortunately, to open a question of terminology would have imposed the obligation of following it up, and in this case to no clear end, because a preferable term has been slow to present itself. When we tell people that they don't know enough about the Holocaust, at least they have some idea of what it is we are saying they don't know enough about. If we tell them that they don't know enough about the Shoah, they aren't even aware of what subject it is that we suppose them to be ignorant of. On this point it is important to remember that Levi, while never less than scrupulous in his personal use of language, was generously prepared to accept that other people could feel keenly even if they spoke clumsily. The American TV mini-series *Holocaust* was much derided by experts when it was first screened, but it was not derided by Levi. He thought its heart was in the right place. As he grew older, Levi found out the hard way that the precious truth he was trying to guard had more to fear from misplaced fastidiousness than from vulgarity. Were there such a thing as life after death, he would have found out from his biographies that the truth itself can be put to inhuman use, and not only by tabloid journalists. Reputable scholars can persuade themselves that duty requires a full disclosure of any truffle unearthed. Very few among even the more serious reviewers of these two books raised the question of what Levi would have thought about the prospect of the women in his life having their privacy intruded upon while they still breathed. Until the day he died, he did his best to protect all concerned from the consequences of having loved him. The day after, all bets were off. It is offensive to pretend that we have a right to behave this way simply because Levi was a great man who gave us our best account of what it was like to share the fate of the anonymous millions, and that his life, therefore, is a proper object of study in all details, no matter how embarrassing they might happen to be for his family and intimate friends. Now that his protesting voice is supposedly silent (and how truly vulgar his biographers are to suppose that) his dearest wish – to restore and preserve the concept of a private life – is trampled upon simply and solely because he was famous. His loved ones are maltreated because he shared the fate of Elvis Presley. Thus the celebrity culture soaks upwards, like wet rot in a wall.

A BIG BOUTIQUE OF AUSTRALIAN ESSAYS

After only four annual volumes, *The Best Australian Essays* has reached the point where the law of increasing expectations begins to kick in. By now the series has done so much that we want it to do everything. Speaking as an Australian who lives offshore, I would be well pleased if each volume could contain, on every major issue, a pair of essays best presenting the two most prominent opposing views. This would give me some assurance that I was hearing both sides of the national discussion on each point, despite my being deprived of access to many of the publications in which essays, under one disguise or another, nowadays originate. (I leave aside the probability that most Australians living in Australia are deprived of access too, the time having long passed when any one person could take in all the relevant print.) But the editor, Peter Craven, could easily point out that my wish is a pipe-dream.

Even in the United States, where the First Amendment theoretically rules, nobody now believes that everyone should be heard: that awkward ideal has now been replaced by a more realistic one, the town meeting at which the moderator merely ensures that everything worth hearing is said – an object which dictates that not everyone gets a say. Craven could add that he is not running a town meeting either. He is selecting for quality, and a criterion of quality automatically limits variety. There might be some views worth hearing but nobody has written them down with sufficient skill for the essay to rank as literature. At the risk of putting words into Craven's mouth, I would suggest that *he* would suggest that the compiling of an annual literary anthology – a showcase for the essay as an art form in which Australians excel – is his first object, and that if I want to plug into the complete national discussion I should keep googling until I attain omniscience. He's running a boutique, not a shopping mall. It's a big boutique, but selectivity is still the selling feature.

That being accepted, what wealth is here: so much that there is little point in complaining about what is absent. In the 2001 volume I thoroughly enjoyed Richard Hall's assault on Keith Windschuttle's view of Aboriginal history, but I was still at the stage of thinking that an essay by Windschuttle should have been in there too. Windschuttle, however, best advances his arguments in book form, rather than through the essay. His *The Killing of History* is an important book about the disastrous effect of Cultural Studies on the proper study of history, and his *The Fabrication of Aboriginal History* is at the very least considerable, or so many people would not have rushed to consider it. For my own comfort, I would like to believe that his argument against the use of the genocide concept when it comes to the crimes committed against the Aboriginals is a necessary correction to a vocal but slipshod consensus. On the other hand, Richard Hall the hard-nosed foot-slogger was undoubtedly right to point out the dangers of a scholar's trusting the reliability of official reports. As well as being right about that, he could *write*. 'The revisionist historians have dug themselves into their trenches and want to stay there.' Launched with the economical accuracy of an old-time brawler, Hall's sentences hit home. If you had only his essay to go on, you would think there was a good case for regarding the behaviour of modern Australia towards its Aboriginals as being in grim parallel to the behaviour of modern Turkey towards its Armenians. Make way for the Pilger vision of the irredeemably racist land in the South. But now, in this year's volume, we have Noel Pearson's essay 'The Need for Intolerance'. After duly praising Paul Keating's legacy on Aboriginal policy, Pearson enters his caveat.

> Federal Labor is dominated by what I call the progressivist intellectual middle stratum. They have played a role in achieving recognition of Aboriginal people's property rights, but I contend that the prejudice, social theories and thinking habits of left-leaning, liberal-minded people make them unable to do anything further for Aboriginal people by attacking our real disadvantage factors. The only answer to the epidemics of substance abuse that devastate our communities is organised intolerance of abusive behaviour.

This is not impeccable prose. Pearson was never trained in the punchy, unadorned directness of Hall's hot-metal hinterland. Those 'disadvantage factors' sound like sociology, and academic sociology at that. But taken as a whole, the piece is a powerful example of how a book review (in this case, of Don Watson's monograph on Paul Keating) can be a good way for an essay to begin its life. The piece gets you right into the true centre of the national debate, by reminding you that on this point the national debate is a local branch of an international debate, the one about whether, beyond a certain point of restitution, welfare can ameliorate injustice without furthering it. And just because it is Pearson talking, the argument against the genocide concept is given useful reinforcement. It is unlikely that any Armenian has ever addressed a Turkish audience in the same way, *per media* an annual collection called *Best Turkish Essays*. So however bad the past was, the present must be in better shape, must it not? I put the point as a rhetorical question because I have been mentally fighting a court case ever since *The Rabbit-proof Fence* was premiered in London. After the screening I tried to reassure a hovering television news camera that things had come on a bit in recent years. An Australian woman overheard me. 'How can you *say* such things after seeing a film like that?' She proved impervious to the argument that the film was set in the past, and could scarcely have been made if the present were not different. The concept was too subtle for her to grasp. It turned out that she was a lawyer. She can attack me as often as she likes, but I hope to God that she never defends me.

John Button's fond reminiscence of John Gorton, 'A Knockabout Bloke', continues the good work of adding nuance to Australia's political past. After Paul Hasluck and Diamond Jim McClelland, we are no longer surprised that there should be politicians who know how to write for the page as well as they shout from the stump or characterize the Right Honourable Member for Woopwoop as a galah. But once again subsequent riches make it hard to imagine the initial poverty. Donald Horne, when he personally inaugurated the modern tradition of wide-ranging political commentary with his book *The Lucky Country* in 1964, took it for granted that Australia's politicians had always been a second-rate, semi-articulate bunch at best. There was reason even at the time to think that he had misstated the case. Whatever Menzies' prose style lacked, it wasn't a literate background, and right back at the beginning of the federated nation stood Deakin, one of the most learned public men of his time. But Horne was pretty much correct about the confinement of the political mind to politics itself, as if the practical business of running for office and keeping it could have no general resonance in the surrounding culture. Written in a fruitful retirement, the example of McClelland's newspaper column was enough to show that things needn't be that way, and now here we have Button bringing out Gorton's complexity – and by extension the complexity of the interchange between the parties and the factions – in a book review of Ian Hancock's book on Gorton that adds a lot to the book. In calling such a book review by its right name, an essay, and in placing it where we can all see it, this collection is doing exactly the kind of work that it should be doing. Whether it should be doing more is reduced to a side issue.

Apart from the politicians and activists, the political commentators are present and, where appropriate, incorrect. Mungo Mac-Callum celebrates Gorton too, with an enchantingly tasteless account of his funeral. 'For sensitive organisations such as the Mafia, or even the Labor Party, it might have seemed a bit uncouth.' Just how couth MacCallum is might seem to be in question, but in fact he operates in a tradition that stretches back to Alfred Kerr in Berlin in the 1890s. On a bad night in the theatre Kerr would review the audience. Showing a similar gift for facing the wrong way at the illuminating moment, Mungo, louche bearer of a laurelled surname, brings out the all too human in the all too political. If only there were room, we could probably stand a bit more of that approach. After four annual volumes Patrick Cooke has not yet turned up, yet I can think of at least a dozen of his *Bulletin* columns that went through a current political contretemps like an angle grinder through balsa. I suppose there are better reasons for shutting out Bob Ellis. It could be said that his elephantine compendia of bits and pieces, far from subverting the conventions of reasoned discourse, are intent on their final destruction. But all his books are in my shelves beside me as I write this, and I have followed his personal saga with guilty fascination. The guilt comes from the way he has never been tempted to clean up his act, whereas the rest of us who started off with him at Sydney University in the late 1950s have been glad enough to be gazetted as official Establishment figures. Somehow he saw a cold future on the way, and refused to join it. It was instructive, however, that when politicians in Canberra suffered from aching conscience in the night, they would join him.

Craven might say that his time for the no-hopers is limited by the abundance of the distinguished. Ably representing the big-name commentators on the wing of what Pearson would like to call the progressivist intellectual middle stratum – I wish he would call it something snappier, but I can't think of a better name either – Robert Manne is here to spell out the blatant iniquity of the Howard government's policy towards asylum seekers. Those of us who were puzzled at the time that the iniquity was not quite blatant enough to inspire the Beazley opposition to notably different policies might still be puzzled now, but there can be no doubt about the forceful-ness with which Manne puts the case. The bloggers might pounce on his position for what they think to be its reflexive assumptions, but they find it less easy to mock his style. Margo Kingston, not here this time, has always been a softer target in that regard. In the 2000 volume her essay 'Hansonism Then and Now' yielded a paragraph that sharply pointed up the dangers she runs by letting her notions of the self-evident rule her syntax. I marked its first two sentences with an exclamation mark in the margin.

> Howard's downgrading of our commitment to United Nations human rights treaties feeds off the widespread feeling in the bush that one-world government is the ruin of us all. It is intellectually dishonest and destructive of our established identity as a tolerant nation and a world leader on promoting international human rights standards.

On first reading, the 'It' at the start of the second sentence seems to refer to the one-world government. On second reading, it seems more likely to be connected with Howard's downgrading of our commitment. But a second reading is a big thing for a writer to ask for, and it should never be asked for on grounds of sense alone. Making sense straight away should be the first aim, and the more so the more your argument aspires to nuance. Paul Sheehan is probably our best example of how to do it properly. Before the Referendum, I thought the best-seller status of his book *Among the Barbarians* was an important checking move in the rush to republicanism of the progressivist intellectual middle stratum. (What the hell are we going to call it, us on the old social-democratic left who don't want to be forcibly enlisted on the Darwinian right? And what are we going to call ourselves?) By bringing out in detail Australia's rich debt to the colonial past, Sheehan made the visions of those who repudiated it look crass. He did this so well that I thought he was against the republican programme himself, and I was quite surprised, when I met him during the Sydney Olympics, to discover that he was for it. Discovering that, I realized on the spot that a republic might indeed be on the way, because when a line of thought achieves the capacity to generate and contain criticism of its own weaknesses, it begins to be strong. In sharp contrast to Margo Kingston's piece, Sheehan's 'The Parties are Over' in the 2000 volume remains an enduringly effective example of the constructively subversive essay, buttressing a position by taking account of its attendant difficulties. In the latest volume Sheehan is talking about something other than politics: 'Miracle at Bert's' deals with a magic water that sounds as if it might confer eternal life. I would be in the market for a crate of it, if only to buy more time in which to read Sheehan. I don't agree with him about the course that Australia's future will necessarily take, but I wouldn't want an Australian future without writers like him in it. Luckily that prospect is no longer in view.

I have confined this notice to politics because it is the field in which I have most needed instruction, and the *Best Australian Essays* series has done a lot to provide it. When my generation of expatriates went sailing to adventure, most of us believed that what we were leaving behind was a political backwater. In fact it was one of the most highly developed liberal democracies on earth, a fitting framework for the cultural expansion that has since made it the envy of nations many times its size. Part of the cultural expansion has been the discursive writing devoted to an explanation of how the liberal democracy developed in the first place. The landmark books made an obvious difference. Paul Kelly, for example, wrote a shelf of them, and although I have never been able to agree with the general drift of his opinions, I would have to admit that a good part of the detail in my own contrary opinions I got from him. Behind the books, however, lurks a less obvious determining factor: the proliferation of the essay. Up until World War II, the Australian essay was best exemplified by Walter Murdoch, whose belletrist treatment of a set theme would have been no surprise to Sir Roger de Coverley. The war correspondents, with the omnivorously curious Alan Moorehead to the fore, made the breakthrough that adapted journalism to complex subjects. Post-war, and in a multiplicity of genres, the essay made its exponential advance to the wealth of commentary we enjoy now, and enjoy all the more because the commentators are often commentating on each other. I didn't have to wait for Watson's book on Keating before I realized that I had made a bad mistake in belittling Keating's capacity to improve his mind, if not his language. Essays from various hands convinced me that his sensitivity to culture went far beyond his covetous admiration for an ormolu clock or a teak table. I still think it a pity – and a pity for his beloved country, not just for himself – that he got his vision of Australia's modern history from people who got theirs from Manning Clarke. But I won't be guilty again of abetting a view of Keating that leaves out an essential nuance.

The word 'nuance' is worth repeating because it is not just an attribute of the essay, it is the essay's reason for being: the essential characteristic that separates a mere performance from a real contribution. In this volume, the essays on culture *tout court* are mostly as subtle and illuminating as we have come to expect, spoiled for choice as we now are. To take one for the many, Helen Garner's piece on journal-writing, called simply '*I*', demonstrates all over again why her presence among the essayists so precisely echoes the presence of the late Gwen Harwood among the poets: the responsible intellectual instrument of a feminist who has loved men, her scrupulous reasoning is always looking for the weak point in her own position and accepting it as a further opportunity. Peter Porter's memories of his reading when young in Queensland add up to a valuable example of what is becoming a characteristic expatriate theme: the mental journey home into the old Australian school system that taught its pupils to parse a sentence. That prescriptive training was the real secret behind the Australian expatriate wave of world conquest, and is the real secret behind Peter Conrad's inclusion in this volume, even though he is only writing about Britney Spears, and dwells on the subject of the pop diva's all-American boobs without a single mention of Kylie's all-Aussie behind. Craven wasn't going to miss out on a piece as well written as that.

*

The same poser will probably emerge in the next volume, when the editor will have to choose between a home-grown piece about Charles Conder – there was a fine one, by Angus Trumble, in the March issue of this magazine – and the stunning *tour de force* Barry Humphries turned in for the *TLS*. As a *prosateur*, it should hardly need saying, Humphries is talented to the point of genius, but he would be less able to prove it if he had not once, long ago, been obliged to sit still at a scarred desk and prove that he knew how a relative clause worked before he was given an early mark. Just as a living culture will attach itself only to a functional democratic structure, so the nuances will attach themselves only to a grammatical framework. There can be no real freedom without its underlying discipline. These volumes – and what an elegantly hefty set they make, all lined up – are encouraging evidence that the real freedom has somehow been preserved, despite the enthusiastically misdirected egalitarianism of the (wait for it) progressivist intellectual middle stratum. Strangely dedicated to assaulting the very idea of elitism in a nation of which to be a citizen is already to be a member of an elite, it is a stratum whose members, as I have already grown sick of saying, need a more portable name. In his book *L'Imparfait du présent*, Alain Finkielkraut thought of one. He called them the negligent vigilantes. I might pinch that for my next essay, if Noel Pearson doesn't pinch it first.

Australian Book Review, May 2003

Postscript

Patriotically thrilled, I permitted myself to go overboard – not about the book, which really was full of good things, but in my tacit suggestion that there was a wealth of other good things that had been left out. The truth about the Australian essay as a form of expression is that the general standard could go a lot higher yet and still be unremarkable. Apart from a widely shared inability to detect a counterfeit phrase before it is committed to paper, the main fault is conformity, especially among non-conformists. There is a massed choir of lone voices who draw inspiration from, instead of being put on the alert by, their ability to sing in unison. The result is a confident reliance on orthodoxy, as if it were a body of proven fact.

Sadly, this is more likely to happen on the Left than on the Right, because the Right can still be relied on to produce the greater number of dedicated cranks willing to spoil one another's party, whereas the Left regards its shared opinions as simply the normal configuration of rational thought. In newspaper think-pieces about grand politics, this normalization of ideological opinion is carried to such a degree that no authorities need be referred to except phantoms. Writing in the weekend edition of the *Sydney Morning Herald* for 8–9 September 2001, the respected political analyst Louise Williams wrote the following paragraph.

> While local opinion polls show the Prime Minister's tough posturing over the *Tampa* played fabulously at home, the same is not true overseas. Instead, the stand-off has raised serious questions about Australia's place in the world and the immediate and future pitfalls of a Howard-led foreign policy that has turned Australia inwards.

In the less symmetrical world of recalcitrant fact, Howard's handling of the *Tampa* incident raised no serious questions 'overseas' except among people who shared the views of Louise Williams. The only serious question raised anywhere was why Kim Beazley, at that time leading the Federal opposition, had no policies about illegal immigration that were notably different from Howard's. But here comes another paragraph, leading on from the phantom overseas scrutineers of serious questions to another set of ghosts, the 'experts' and 'insiders' who seem to have no precise location, but are evenly distributed throughout the universe, connected through time and space by a strangely intense telepathic concern with Australian politics.

> Under the two Howard governments, experts say, Australia's international prestige has declined, in terms of Canberra's capacity to influence international events and of our ability to win international support. 'You could say that Australia currently does not have much coin,' one insider said.

But after the *Tampa* incident Australia had enough coin among people-smugglers to make their trade look a lot less profitable, which could be said to have been the first and most important international event that an Australian government at the time should have been interested in. There is charm however in Ms Williams's confidence that she can cite the opinion of 'one insider' without making us wonder what all the other insiders might be saying to the contrary. The 'one insider' kept on cropping up in different contexts throughout her piece. Presumably he or she was not always the same person, but invariably the same central view was propagated, namely that Howard was ruling the country by a confidence trick aimed at the gullible population, who either didn't know or didn't care that their once proud nation was sinking into disrepute overseas. Finally the views of the protean 'one insider' were summed up by Ms Williams's most imposingly qualified consultant, the 'one expert'.

> The biggest folly, however, may be taking foreign affairs leads from opinion polls conducted in Australia's suburbs, said one expert, noting that international issues are inherently complex and do not lend themselves to popular political solutions.

Three years later, this cherished central tenet of the 'one expert' helped lead the Australian Labor Party to clamorous defeat, after which – but not, disastrously, before which – it was at last realized by some of those in charge of the party machine that an opinion poll conducted in Australia's suburbs is exactly what a Federal election is. Those of us who would like to see the ALP restored to some of its former glory and fighting strength had better realize that a recovery will be slow to happen if the progressive intelligentsia goes on writing bad essays. They are often written from genuine compassion – some of the immediate consequences of the *Tampa* incident were hard to be proud of – but high feelings turn loose expression into low comedy, and the result is a growing sub-literature of personal statements that express nothing substantial except the author's impatience. There could have been a book of them ten times as big as the one I reviewed. I would have had a lot of fun reviewing it, but beyond a certain point there is no reward in blasting away at a sitting duck.

SLOUCHING TOWARDS YEATS

Yeats was a great poet who was also the industrious adept of a batso mystical philosophy. Do we have to absorb the philosophy before we can appreciate the poetry? If we are lucky enough to be in a state of ignorance, the question won't come up. The poetry will get to us first. Suppose you've heard this much: that Yeats's best stuff came late. So you pick up the 1950 edition of the *Collected Poems* and start from the back. The last few lines in the book are the first you see.

> And now my utmost mystery is out:
> A woman's beauty is a storm-tossed banner:
> Under it wisdom stands, and I alone –
> Of all Arabia's lovers I alone –
> Nor dazzled by the embroidery, nor lost
> In the confusion of its night-dark folds,
> Can hear the armed man speak.

Forty years ago, when I first read those lines, I had to remind myself to start breathing again. They still hit me with the same force, and I still can't fully understand them. But I began to understand them when I realized that putting together a phrase like 'dazzled by the embroidery' was something hardly anybody could do. 'A woman's beauty is a storm-tossed banner' is something an averagely gifted poet might fluke, although not often. To write 'dazzled by the embroidery', however, you have to possess the means to put ordinary-sounding words together in an extraordinarily resonant way.

That was what Yeats really meant by his seemingly twee talk of 'articulating sweet sounds together'. In his earlier poetry, that richly combinative capacity was always operating, if only intermittently condensing to full force, and in his later poetry – say from *Responsibilities* onwards – it attained incandescent fusion more and more often, until, with *The Tower* and all the poetry that followed, far into his old age, he was tremendous all the time. Except for Professor Ricks, who finds the later Yeats less a poet than a rhetorician, nobody sensitive to poetry doubts the magnificence of Yeats's steadily maturing achievement, his wresting of complexity out of mere fluency; and the otherwise acute professor could have reached his contrary opinion only after a small asteroid had passed through his brain, perhaps while he was listening to Bob Dylan.

Apart from such cosmic interference, nothing can get between Yeats's mature poetry and the reader except the magnitude of the attendant scholarship. Unfortunately that magnitude has now received a massive augmentation. The second and final volume of R.F. Foster's whopping biography of Yeats is Pelion, just as the first volume was Ossa, and now both mountains are piled on top of what was already a great dividing range, with Yeats's unassisted voice squeaking thinly on the other side of it, hard to hear even in its valleys. Many learned reviewers will be grateful for Foster's thoroughness. Let's try not being grateful.

The defiant lines spoken by the Arabian lover (ah, how I did, how I do now more than ever, fancy myself as that Arabian lover, poised on a racing dromedary) put a rousing end to 'The Gift of Harun Al-Rashid', which was pinned to the tail of the 1950 *Collected Poems* only as a result of a posthumous round-up, and is actually not a very late poem at all. Barely latish, it was first published in 1923. Alas, it was not published in *The Tower*, Yeats's mightily confident 1928 book of poems that contained 'Sailing to Byzantium', 'Nineteen Hundred and Nineteen', 'Leda and the Swan', 'Among School Children', 'All Souls' Night' and other knockouts in such profusion that even Professor Ricks must sometimes wonder whether *Blonde on Blonde* quite survives the comparison. But 'Desert Geometry, or The Gift of Harun Al-Rashid', to give it its full title, made its debut as the introduction to Book II in the first, 1923 edition of *A Vision*, Yeats's prose *summa* of all things mystically deep. This gives Foster the chance – nay, the mandate – to explain a living poem in terms of a stone-dead rigmarole. Here is a sample of Foster:

> The alternative title, 'Desert Geometry', hints that against the phases of astrologically determined personality a diagrammatic version of historical process is to be sketched out. This replicates

a spiral movement, for which WBY found authority in philosophers back to Heraclitus, and which also expresses the form of
each person's journey into consciousness, in constant tension
with his 'daimon'.

Clearer now? Foster himself follows up with a sample from
A Vision. Risking our sanity, let us do the same.

As man's intellect, say, expands, the emotional nature contracts
in equal degree and vice versa; when, however, a narrowing and
widening gyre reach their limit, the one the utmost contraction
the other the utmost expansion, they change places, point to
circle, circle to point, for this system conceives the world as
catastrophic, and continue as before, one always narrowing, one
always expanding, and yet bound for ever to one another.

Keeping that up for hundreds of pages, Yeats may or may not
have added to the discoveries of 'philosophers back to Heraclitus',
but he certainly added more than his share to the flimflam cranked
out by every tent-show seer from Madame Blavatsky through
Ouspensky and Gurdjieff to L. Ron Hubbard. It would be good to
think that having codified his vision he got it out of the way and
left himself room to synthesize experience in the only mode that
mattered: the poetic. In fact, however, he was still tinkering with his
revelations to the very end, and published a reworked edition of the
book not long before he died. So we are stuck with the connection
between the high art of his poetry and the low comedy of a self-
deceiving boondoggle. The question that matters is whether the
connection is important. Surely Joyce was merely being polite
when he regretted that Yeats didn't put the 'colossal conception'
of *A Vision* into 'a creative work'. There is nothing colossal about
A Vision except its waste of time. Except, of course, that Yeats didn't
think so. Genius has to be forgiven its foolishness. Newton was just
as interested in his wacko chronology as in his celestial mechanics.
But about Yeats's rickety paranormal hobbyhorse, his secretary Ezra
Pound spoke the cruel truth early on. He said Yeats's ideas about
the phases of the moon were 'bug-house'.

Startlingly, Yeats's otherwise patient wife George thought the
same. This is where Foster's book comes good, although it takes
a long time doing so. Upon the publication of *A Vision*, she told a

friend that there was 'nothing in his verse worth preserving but the personal. All the pseudo-mystico-intellecto-nationalistico stuff of the last fifteen years isn't worth a trouser-button.' George emerges from this book as a model of good sense. Foster would have done the same if he had taken a tip from her at the start, and viewed the spiritualist clap-trap with a more dismissive eye. Admittedly George was up to her neck in it. At the long sessions of automatic writing, George was the channel, or control, or whatever you care to call it. But on the evidence of the wearisomely cited transcripts, George was serving her own ends. Having seen off the poisonous Maud Gonne and her even more dangerous daughter Iseult, both of whom Yeats had proposed to in rapid succession, George wanted to make sure that the Gonnes stayed gone. Magically, voices from the Beyond instructed Yeats that he should spend more time in bed with his wife. This could have been funny if humour were among Foster's tools.

To regret its absence is not necessarily frivolous. For a critic, humour is primarily a means of compression, and compression is what a book like this needs most. At least a third of it is junk because it analyses junk, and junk analysed is still junk. That being said, it is gratifying to have all the details that prove Yeats's stature as a practical politician. After he recorded the birth of the terrible beauty, Yeats had a right to think that the literary revival of which he had been such a prominent member had ushered in the new Ireland. But in the Free State there was no automatic welcome for his Protestantism, for his Ascendancy background, and above all for his liberal, tolerant outlook. (Although he had some noxious views about hierarchy and due deference, to paint Yeats as a fascist is a waste of breath: he believed in free speech, for example, which no fascist does.) As a Senator who vocally insisted that Ulster could be won for a united Ireland only by an example of enlightened domestic policy, he was in danger.

Worse, so was George, whom he loved despite her devotion. Bullets punctured the windows of their grand house in Dublin. George played it cool, just as she did in his last phase when monkey-gland injections helped harden – if that's the word we want – his perennial conviction that wisdom was to be found under the storm-tossed banner of a woman's beauty. He was already in his dotage when he found himself between the sheets with a twenty-seven-year-old stunner called Margaret Ruddock. He cast her horoscope, which failed to tell him that she was not only giftless but psycho. She ended up in the bin. Other mistresses gathered around his death-bed, where George kindly marshalled the traffic. She forgave both them and him that he had written immortal poems so often to them, and so seldom to her. But that was what they were for: to be wild swans, to flood the everyday with the unknown, to ready him for Byzantium. This book will be essential to Yeats scholarship. but ever since Professor Donoghue, following Dr Leavis, decided that Yeats's poetry needed too much explanation, the burning question has been about how essential the scholarship is. If it keeps young students from some of the greatest poetry ever written, then the answer is easy: about as essential as a suit of armour to Ian Thorpe.

Postscript

For a significant cultural figure, there is always room for a biography. But I don't believe there is room for the Indispensable Biography, the one encouraging the seductive notion that its subject can't otherwise be understood or even appreciated. If the cultural figure isn't already alive in our minds before he is explained, no biography, however huge, can do anything except kill him off. We might, of course, have got from his work the wrong impression of his actual character; and to have the facts supplied might rescue us from being gulled on the level of practicality; but if his art is real, it has already made the best sense of his life. Without the biographical facts, we might assume from his work that Brecht, for example, was a tireless campaigner for human betterment. He wasn't, but if we get from a biography the idea that he wasn't a great poet either, we have allowed his life story to get in the way of his true life. Ditto for Pablo Neruda and Nicolàs Guillèn. The same obfuscation is particularly likely to happen in the case of Yeats, who could be such a fool that even those drawn to the magnetism of his poetry can be repelled again when they find out exactly how foolish he was. Something like this must be going on when academic critics as finely tuned to poetry as Professors Donoghue and Ricks turn against Yeats. It can't be that they have belatedly contracted a case of tin ear. When Dr Leavis announced that only a grand total of three Yeats poems were the 'fully achieved thing', nobody could doubt that his limiting judgement was fully achieved nonsense, because he had no real sensitivity to poetry anyway, a failing proved by his prose, which was colourless even when it was still vigorous. But the younger men could hear Yeats's music. One can only conclude that they ceased to approve of the man who made it. Scholarship got in the way of criticism.

With all that said, however, there is undoubtedly a case for being told in advance that the magnificent detachment of E. E. Cummings from the workaday business world was made possible by a trust fund, and that the apparent anti-Semitism of one of his poems was indeed the expression of a prejudice, although he was nothing like as bigoted as his wife. If I had known those things before I wrote my first article about him, I would have been slower to praise him as an example of the unfettered intelligence. I found them out from a poorly written but awkwardly accurate biography. But I read it only because I had always loved the best of his poetry, and I still do. I really don't think there is all that much of substance in Foster's two volumes about Yeats that is not already there in Jeffares' single volume, but undoubtedly the Foster behemoth is more up to date, and deserves to become the standard work. Heaven help us all, however, if a generation of students should feel compelled to wade through it before they have submitted themselves to the full impact of the poetry to which Yeats gave his life, and in which, and nowhere else, he is truly alive.

CYRANO ON THE SCAFFOLD

His nose preceding him by a quarter of an hour, the hero of *Cyrano de Bergerac* is a reminder that there were once things plastic surgery couldn't do. Today it can turn Michael Jackson into his own sister. But the original Cyrano, furiously active as poet, swordsman and celestial fantasist in seventeenth-century France, was stuck with his deformity. If he had been born in the late 1890s, when the play that bears his name was written, he still would have been stuck with it. The playwright, Edmond Rostand, could count on that fact, and use it to bring the sophisticated theatre-goers of Paris to their feet after reducing them to helpless weeping. Appearance was destiny. If a man's appearance ruled him out in the eyes of the woman he loved, there was nothing he could do about it. Except, perhaps, one thing. What if he could rule himself back in through her ears?

Armed with a tragically inflexible law and a comically rich possibility for how it might be broken, Rostand was inspired to a poetic narrative that conquered the world. The eloquent but very ugly man, Cyrano, loves the beautiful young woman, Roxane. She favours the beautiful young man, Christian. He lacks the words to thrill her. The heartbroken Cyrano, wanting her to be happy, lends him some. Thus supplied, Christian wins her hand, but he is killed in battle. In the end, with the mortally wounded Cyrano dying in her arms among the fallen autumn leaves of the convent courtyard, Roxane finally realizes that it was his words, and therefore him, that she had loved all along. Alas, it is too late. And yet hooray, for true love has won through. *Sacre bleu, quelle histoire!*

There are reasons, which we will get to, for thinking that this seemingly unbreakable dramatic arc works best in the original French, but it would still provide a good night out in Esperanto, and at the great classical theatre on the Ginza a kabuki version would not be inconceivable. In his own country alone, there were more than a thousand performances of the play while Rostand was still alive. Many of the productions he supervised personally. Their accumulated box office receipts ensured that he would die rich. His magnificent house at the foot of the Pyrenees is still there to inform visiting writers that if they envy the domestic arrangements of Pinter, Frayn and Stoppard then they haven't seen anything yet. Rostand's chuckling ghost lives well. There may be plastic surgeons in California who live better, but not even they have yet managed to take the sweet sting out of an immortal story.

A brilliantly successful bullion raid from the start, the plot-line of *Cyrano de Bergerac* will probably never cease to make money until every male baby born on Earth is a clone of Orlando Bloom. Men who can't wow a woman with the fearful symmetry of their faces will always have to talk for victory. Cyrano will go on showing them how, in a coruscating tragicomical pastiche that almost no amount of miscalculation can make dull. It must be said, however, that the new production at the National Theatre might have been designed to prove otherwise. A critic, in my view, should always report the reaction of the audience before he delivers his own opinion. Well, the first-night audience clapped dutifully at the end, and there were cheers for Cyrano himself, as incarnated by the film star Stephen Rea. But the Germans have a phrase that fits: *der Beifall war endenwollend.* The applause wanted to be over.

Things never looked promising to begin with. In the Olivier Theatre there is no curtain to go up, so the audience, as it came in, was already faced with the huge and deadly suggestion that the sets would consist mainly of scaffolding. This turned out to be true, although the space-station centrifugal stage machinery was occasionally put into operation so that the scaffolding could be seen from a different angle. On its first appearance, the vast metallic structure was dotted with supernumeraries whose weary attitudes suggested that they might have expired from boredom while bolting it together. Ever since the first post-war translations of Brecht spread their pervasive influence, student productions of any play at all have characteristically established their dedication to the alienation effect with precisely those two elements: scaffolding, and an opening tableau of underemployed walk-ons. This was going to be a student production. The premonition did not necessarily spell disaster: last month in Wellington I saw a student production – admittedly buttressed by the participation of a few semi-pro actors – which cleverly adapted Gogol's *The Government Inspector* to local New Zealand small-town politics. Seated on each side of a tin shed, the audience had a wonderful time. Gogol had a big nose: so big that he made it the disembodied hero of its own story. These were desperate things to be thinking of in the million-dollar arena of the Olivier while waiting for the main actors to join the scaffolding, but without trust there is no life.

The trust paid off, but only in small change. The big notes had already been thrown on the fire long before a misconceived production reached its opening night. The scaffolding had already told us that we would not be seeing seventeenth-century Paris. The attire of the actors soon told us that we would not be seeing many seventeenth-century costumes either. There were a few of them dotted about, but only because they had been preserved in the same skip as all the other clobber, which dated variously from any time up to the day before yesterday. Rostand gives some warrant for this, because he himself, writing more than two centuries after his reported events, didn't care very much about strict adherence to temporality. But he cared like mad about theatricality. He wanted the full romantic tackle, and he wanted it to swash until it buckled. Cloak, plumed hat and proper sword: he specified them all for his dynamic hero. It was thus three times a bad sign when Cyrano made his entrance minus any of them. The plume sprouting from Cyrano's hat is meant to be the mark of his panache. In French it is actually called a *panache*, and provides the once inexhaustibly prolix Cyrano with his dying word, the last word of the play. The plume on Stephen Rea's hat was a mere shy puff instead of a proudly flying banner. The sword was a sword-stick: a different thing, and not appropriate for holding Cyrano's cloak extended at the back, as one of his friends describes.

But he had no cloak. Instead, he had an overcoat, of a type worn by students all over the world to indicate that they are in rebellion against bourgeois values. No sooner had I seen this overcoat than I was thinking once again of Gogol, who wrote a play called *The Overcoat*, and had a big nose. I would have been thinking of catching the next plane back to New Zealand if Cyrano, along with everything else he had been deprived of, had been deprived of a big nose. Mercifully he had one, and the quality of its putty looked sufficiently durable to last the night. Perhaps it had been provided by the same construction firm that won the contract for the scaffolding, which clearly would last forever.

Except for the nose, Mr Rea had been comprehensively sabotaged before he left the dressing room, but he generously agreed to remain on stage even when the choreography was taking place. The choreography – the supposed necessity for which would have been news to Rostand – was fit to drive the audience out of the theatre and into the Thames, but it wasn't going to do that to Mr Rea, who staunchly defied several kinds of doom simultaneously, like a boy on a burning deck with his finger in a dyke. His close-ups on screen prove him to possess a winning charm of facial expression, and his voice on the soundtrack is blessed with a melodious Irish burr fit to render any Roxane breathless. On stage, to which he is no stranger, both these attributes were still in evidence, but the large nose necessarily worked against the first, and the larger distances it had to cross unnecessarily worked against the second. The Olivier only *looks* as if it could swallow the sound of a Boeing 747 revving at full throttle against the brakes. In actuality, a quite small mortar bomb could go off on stage and most of the audience would still notice. Even in those cavernous expanses, an actor's voice can ring if it has power. Mr Rea's voice hadn't. Unfortunately Cyrano is lost if he can't shout the place down. It is not enough for him to be audible. He must be able to dominate the stage and everyone on it with a single bark of anger, and send a sigh of regret winging to the gallery. For Cyrano, vocal confidence is a handy attribute even in the movies. Steve Martin, playing Cyrano as a small-town fireman in the excellent *Roxanne*, talks with a fluency that makes his mouth, and not his nose, the centre of all eyes. In Jean-Paul Rappeneau's movie of 1990, Gerard Depardieu commands silence from everyone else each time he speaks. Most memorably of all, in the Stanley Kramer movie of 1950, José Ferrer raged with the effortless verbal authority that makes Cyrano's tenderness mean so much when he succumbs to it.

For a stage Cyrano, verbal authority is not just a nice plus, it's the whole game. For all I know, Stephen Rea in real life has the verbal authority to hail a taxi in a whisper. But as Cyrano he showed little confidence in what he had to say. He should be excused for that, because what he had to say was a brand-new English translation that achieved the difficult feat of making Cyrano no more thrilling as a speaker than a police commissioner at a press conference. Derek Mahon, who claims responsibility, is an accomplished poet in normal circumstances. His poem about mushrooms in a garden shed is a justly celebrated anthology piece. He is even an accomplished poet when translating from the French: his version of Valery's *Le cimetière marin* miraculously conveys almost all the pastel nuances of the original. But Rostand, although he has pastel nuances of his own, employs them only as grace-notes to his vaulting exuberance of invention, which depends for much of its effect on being compressed and energized within strictly rhyming couplets. Disastrously, Derek Mahon was persuaded to keep the couplets but throw away the compression, by making the rhymes so approximate that they were usually undetectable, and piffling when they were not.

I prefer not to believe that the persuasion was done by himself. The fee should pay his bills while he hides out in a foreign country until all this blows over, but when he gets back he will probably be too polite to point the finger. Those less bashful will be inclined to detect the same genius for miscalculation that placed the order for a thousand tons of scaffolding. Here again, the director, Howard Davies, might not have been solely responsible. There is a school of thought, to which I subscribe, which holds that some kind of interstellar virus has taken over the separate brains of prominent theatrical people and united them into a single autistic personality dedicated to the unremitting gestation of bad ideas. The virus was already active when Tyrone Guthrie invented the thrust stage, the awful precursor of theatre in the round. In his memoirs, Sir Alec Guinness said all that needed to be said about the thrust stage: in the absence of a proscenium, the actor could never make a clean entrance or exit, and most of his moves would be dictated by the requirement of giving every sector of the audience a fair share of looking at his back. But Guinness was only an actor, and the directors were already in control, with every dullard dreaming that he was the new Meyerhold or Piscator. The virus struck again with an even more debilitating notion, the raked stage, down which no broken king can stumble without the audience fearing that he will join them in the stalls. The virus decreed that a raked stage could be dispensed with only on the understanding that a flat floor would provide the base for a sufficiency of scaffolding, which would be mandatory if the text made reference to trees and balconies.

In the last scene of this triumphantly viral production, the dying Cyrano asked that his chair be placed against 'this tree'. This tree was a tower of metal tubes. But by then we were used to the anomaly. Towers of metal tubes had been pretending to be trees all night. The tops of the towers had been pretending to be balconies. High on her tubular balcony, Roxane, persuaded by Cyrano's ventriloqual ardour, gave Christian her permission to climb the jasmine tree. The climb up the jasmine tree took him long enough for me to concoct a brace of appropriate couplets to which he is welcome, if the production can do a deal with my agent.

> Bless me, Roxane, and let your heart take wing
> To lift me as I climb this scaffolding:
> Send down a kiss from your lips red and ripe
> As my hands, bloody from these lengths of pipe.

As played by Claire Price, Roxane was worth climbing the Chrysler Building to reach. If she looked a bit less like Kate Winslet, Miss Price would probably be a film star by now. As things are, she is well on the way to being a first-choice theatrical leading lady for any company still harbouring the politically unreconstructed belief that a female object of love should actually be beautiful. Her performance in the National's *The Relapse* established her as a house favourite, and during her excursion to Sheffield it was noticed that Kenneth Branagh's Richard III – another and more swinish swain with a deformity problem – had believable reasons for throwing himself upon Lady Anne. She managed to look equally fetching in *Cyrano de Bergerac*, even if the Olivier's lack of footlights – another viral breakthrough – ensured that the full glory of her face was only intermittently visible. But she had very little that was fetching to say. When Christian made the mistake of trying to woo her in his own words instead of Cyrano's, she reproved him thus.

> You'd better smarten up and quickly, brother:
> go home and get your stupid head together
> or we can drop the idea of real relations.

As dialogue, this was worse than updated, it was dysfunctional. Updatings disfigured almost every page of the text, but most of them were merely dreary. The phrase 'chatting up the chicks' rang out. 'Space cadets' were referred to. 'Stereo' was rhymed with 'brio', even though the two words do not rhyme anyway. Most of this could be ignored, and Mr Rea even had the sense to ignore one of his own lines. To chime with Cyrano's interest in outer space, he had been given an echo of Captain Kirk: 'to boldly go . . .' In the printed text Cyrano continues the line, but on stage the three dots were as far as Mr Rea took it, having sensibly decided that he had enough to deal with. Contemporary references, as a means of jazzing a period text, made their first appearance in the opera house, where it has long been supposed that the libretto of a piece by Offenbach or Lehar can be brought back from the dead if given a sprinkling of commentary based on current affairs. Since audiences for music will laugh at anything labelled as a joke, the case seemed proved, and the virus ensured that the same assumption was transferred to the spoken theatre, where we are now regularly assailed with crassly updated scripts whose directors, unburdened with any sense of humour of their own, are under the illusion that they can call in any catchpenny comic writer and get results that would have amazed Nestroy. They are right about that, but not in the way they think. Derek Mahon is not among the gag-writing journeymen. He knows even less than they do about comedy, as his jokes prove, but he knows much more about the texture of language. He should have known enough not to make Roxane sexually aware. 'Real relations' means sex, and Roxane is supposed to be thinking about love.

In the long run there might not be a lot of difference, but Rostand was writing about the short run, in which Roxane wants to be loved before she is touched, and Cyrano wants her to love him, even though unromanticized sex is something he knows all about. The original Cyrano certainly did: syphilis was probably what he died of. Rostand himself was one of the great boudoir operators of his time: among the actresses he conquered was Sarah Bernhardt, and among the illustrious women of the *beau monde* was the legendary Anna de Noailles. There is thus some warrant for supposing that the thing sticking out of Cyrano's face might be a phallic symbol, and one of Derek Mahon's inspired updates – Cyrano's claim that his nose is a popular addition to his powers of cunnilingus – might not be without merit, although the way of putting it was sadly without grace. If Cyrano had rolled a condom onto his nose as a gesture towards safe sex, it would have been no more anachronistic than a jasmine tree assembled with a spanner, and might even have made a point; but only if modern points are the kind you want to make; and there is not much point in making those if they ruin the ones that are already there, and are essential to the plot.

One of the essential plot points is that Roxane, a woman young enough to be still thinking the way men think always, attributes all the virtues to Christian just because he is beautiful, even though he is as dumb as they come. Some of the most beautiful actors in the world are of exotic origin, but Zubin Varla is not among them. He is more beautiful than I am, but at the rate his temples are retreating he will soon have my hairstyle, and it is hard to avoid the conclusion that a knockout like Roxane would not fall for him at first meeting unless he spoke like Cyrano, whereas the whole point is that she falls for him *before* he starts speaking like Cyrano. I am sorry to labour the obvious, but the virus has driven me to it. One thing you should be able to count on with any theatre company, no matter how dedicated it might be to social engineering, is that if it wants to cast the role of a handsome, not very bright young man, there are plenty of candidates available. Worse than not looking especially gorgeous, Mr Varla looked as smart as a whip. Miscasting is never an actor's fault, so we should confine ourselves to observing that here was a Christian with all the disqualifications, plus one more that Rostand would never have dreamed possible.

Christian turned out to be deaf. In the published text, wooing Roxane from below her scaffolding, he is merely hesitant when the hidden Cyrano prompts him. But during rehearsals somebody had a better idea, and so we were forced to listen when Christian turned Cyrano's every suggested line into a string of off-colour puns. The audience did not laugh much, but kindly decided not to lynch him. Remarkably, Roxane decided not to either, and carried on listening as per the unjollified text, instead of parachuting off the back of the scaffolding and booking into the convent early. Luckily that was the low point for Christian. Later on, at the Thirty Years War, he got the chance to die an heroic death in defence of the scaffolding, which the enemy was attacking with machine guns. Those of us who had been hoping that it would be attacked with a Tomahawk cruise missile might have been disappointed, but for Christian, weak with hunger, it was time to climb the pipes, as men weak with hunger so often do. Thus elevated, he was shot in the chest and dived to an early death. The less fortunate Cyrano was obliged to keep breathing until his belated demise among the falling leaves. Luckily these were not represented by falling clamps and bolts. They were just words. In theory, words were all he had ever needed. Unfortunately he was never given the right ones.

Lying there in the arms of Claire Price – not normally the worst fate a man can imagine – Mr Rea must have felt his false nose weighing like a lead balloon. He is all too aware that in the 1983 Anthony Burgess version Derek Jacobi finished the evening with the audience pulling the walls in: men signed up for fencing class while women sobbed into each other's handkerchiefs. As Antony Sher reveals in his memoir *Beside Myself*, Jacobi's performance convinced him that he had no chance to play it handsome plus false nose, but should follow the lead set by his own looks, which he had never liked. He would observe the difference Burgess had drawn between 'the visible soul' and 'the casual dress of flesh'. The Burgess version had enough zing to set the actors and the audience on fire. Burgess kept the exactness of the couplets even when he opened the rhyme scheme into quatrains. Before him, Christopher Fry had deftly done the whole thing in couplets. But for some reason we still think that strict rhymes mean restriction, and that to throw them away means freedom. Why?

Because it is true. In the English theatre, the norm of fluent speech was set by Shakespeare, who had all the technical skill to turn Chaucer's narrative couplets into a viable dramatic form, but chose to do otherwise. He went for blank verse instead, thus establishing an expectation beside which a latticework of spoken rhymes will always sound artificial. Not even Dryden was powerful enough to put the expectation into reverse. For the French, the normal expectation has always been rhyming couplets. Corneille, Racine and Molière set a rhythm which rebellion could never break, but only work within. The first riot on the opening night of Victor Hugo's *Hernani* took place when he broke the rule of always putting the adjective and noun inside the same hemistitch. The audience knew exactly what he was up to because they had been hearing classical couplets all their lives. Rostand could count on that universal expectation when he gave Cyrano the energy of a wild animal. The wild animal is in a cage, and what a French audience hears is its repeated assault on the bars. (You could even call them scaffolding if you like, but in French you would have to say *échafaudage*.) For

Cyrano, however, his confinement does not mean prison. Without the fierce requirements of rhyme, his wit would never have been driven to its dizzy height, just as, without the burden of his nose, he would never have been compelled to the nobility of his sacrifice. The great truth at the heart of the play emerges even from this production: if we love someone we can't have, but love them so much that we want them to be happy with someone else, it might not be as good as we'll ever feel, but it's probably as good as we'll ever be.

TLS, 30 April 2004

A NIGHTCLUB IN BALI

The shock wave from the car-bomb outside the nightclub on Kuta Beach in Bali went all the way to Australia in a matter of minutes. As soon as the young Australian survivors stopped trembling long enough to touch one button at a time, they were calling home to say they were all right. But there were some young Australians who did not call home, because they were not all right. The Australian casualty list is lengthening even as I compose this opening paragraph, and by the time I reach a conclusion the casualty list will be longer still. I owe it to my dead, wounded and bereaved countrymen to say straight away that I have no clear idea of what that conclusion will be. This is no time to preach, and least of all from a prepared text.

Some of Australia's commentators on politics might already be realizing that. Now they, too, must feel their way forward: the bomb has done to their certainties what it did to the revellers in the nightclub. Before the bomb went off, the pundits had all the answers about the attack on the World Trade Center in New York. In the year and a bit between September 11th 2001 and October 12th 2002 they had, from the professional viewpoint, a relatively easy time. One didn't question their capacity for sympathy: Australian journalists pride themselves on being a hard-bitten crew, but most of them could imagine that being trapped hundreds of feet up in a burning building was no fit way to die. What one did sometimes question was their capacity for analysis. A prepared text was rolled out, and went on unrolling.

According to the prepared text, the attack was really America's fault, because of its bad behaviour elsewhere in the world. For insular Americans, the attack was a salutary illustration of what the Australian pundit Janet McCalman called their 'lowly place in the affections of the poor and struggling'. Australia, unashamedly America's ally, was effectively an oppressor too. If you took into account the behaviour of the Australian government when faced with the crisis engendered by the arrival, or non-arrival, of a Norwegian container ship full of Afghan refugees, Australia was even more guilty than America. Australia (perennially a racist country, as John Pilger's historical researches had incontrovertibly proved) was a flagrant provocation to the wretched of the earth. Imperialist America was not only treating the helpless Middle East as its personal property, America had racist Australia for its lackey. No wonder al-Qa'ida was angry. On Christmas Eve, in the Melbourne *Age*, another pundit, Michael Leunig, called for a national prayer for Osama bin Laden on Christmas Day. 'It's a family day,' Leunig explained, 'and Osama's our relative.' It is not recorded whether the aforesaid Osama, sitting cross-legged beside his Christmas tree somewhere under Afghanistan, offered up a prayer for Michael. He might have done: after all, they were on a first-name basis.

The prepared text kept on unrolling. Bob Ellis, with whom I was once at university in Sydney, is famous in Australia as an engagingly erratic commentator still carrying a torch for the old Australian Labor Party, the one that cared about the welfare of the workers until Bob Hawke re-educated it to care about the welfare of Rupert Murdoch and Kerry Packer. Though Ellis's torch is a jam-tin nailed to a broomstick and fuelled with household kerosene, he carries it with a certain shambolic panache. The Australian descriptive term 'rat-bag' is often used of him even by his friends, but nobody doubts that his heart is in the right place. Certainly he doesn't. He was easily able to discredit President Bush's 'war on terrorism' by pointing out that terrorism is everywhere, and is especially prevalent in the allegedly civilized Western democracies. A letter from a creditor, explained Ellis, can be a terrorist act. (Considering what it must be like for a creditor trying to get Ellis's attention, this might even be true.) A concept basic to the prepared text was that there could be no end to all this deplorable but understandable Islamist outrage until the Palestinian matter was settled: a settlement which was in America's power to bring about just by picking up a telephone and instructing Sharon to back off. There was one conspicuous reason, however, why America would never do this: John Howard was Prime Minister of Australia. John Howard, sustained in his post by nothing except a majority of the Australian electorate, was a fascist in all but name. The mere presence of John Howard in

Canberra, instead of in his local gaol, was overwhelming evidence of America's global power to crush the hopes of the poor and struggling.

Such was the consensus before the nightclub in Bali turned into a nightmare. Consensus might be too large a word. There are publications in Australia that dissent from the standard view: the magazine *Quadrant* is only one example, and so prominent a newspaper as the *Sydney Morning Herald* carries the opinion of several commentators who sing a different tune. Though they might enjoy promoting themselves as lone voices, the lone voices add up to a considerable choir. But they must get used to wearing a sticky label: Right Wing. The consensus considers itself to be left wing in the best sense. The appellation is one that an old stager like me is reluctant to grant, because the consequence of granting it, and then expressing dissent, is to be classified as conservative. In my own case, the main thing I want to conserve is the welfare of the common people: in that regard I am plodding in Bob Ellis's zig-zag slipstream as he carries his ramshackle torch.

But let us allow for the moment that the mass outcry against American hegemony is the voice of the true, the eternal and the compassionate left. Allowing that, we can put the best possible construction on its pervasiveness. Not just the majority of the intellectuals, academics and schoolteachers, but most of the face-workers in the media, share the view that international terrorism is to be explained by the vices of the liberal democracies. Or at any rate they shared it until a few days ago. It will be interesting, in the shattering light of an explosive event, to see if that easy view continues now to be quite so widespread, and how much room is made for the more awkward view that the true instigation for terrorism might not be the vices of the liberal democracies, but their virtues.

The consensus will die hard in Australia, just as it is dying hard here in Britain. On Monday morning the *Independent* carried an editorial headed: 'Unless there is more justice in the world, Bali will be repeated'. Towards the end of the editorial, it was explained that the chief injustice was 'the failure of the US to use its influence to secure a fair settlement between Israelis and Palestinians'. I count the editor of the *Independent*, Simon Kelner, as a friend, so the main reason I hesitate to say that he is out to lunch on this issue is that I was out to dinner with him last night. But after hesitating, say it I must, and add a sharper criticism: that his editorial writer sounds like an unreconstructed Australian intellectual, one who can still believe, even after his prepared text was charred in the nightclub, that the militant fundamentalists are students of history.

But surely the reverse is true: they are students of the opposite of history, which is theocratic fanaticism. Especially they are dedicated to knowing as little as possible about the history of the conflict between the Israelis and the Palestinians. A typical terrorist expert on the subject believes that Hitler had the right idea, that *The Protocols of the Elders of Zion* is a true story, and that the obliteration of the state of Israel is a religious requirement. In furthering that end, the sufferings of the Palestinians are instrumental, and thus better exacerbated than diminished. To the extent that they are concerned with the matter at all, the terrorists epitomize the extremist pressure that had been so sadly effective in ensuring the continued efforts of the Arab states to persuade the Palestinians against accepting any settlement, no matter how good, that recognizes Israel's right to exist. But one is free to doubt by now – forced to doubt by now – that Palestine is the main concern.

The main concern of fundamentalist Islam is with moderate Islam, and especially with those Islamic states which, if they have not precisely embraced democracy, have nevertheless tried to banish theocracy from the business of government. That fundamentalism loathes the Western democracies goes without saying: or rather, it goes with a lot of saying, at the top of the voice. But the real horror, for the diehard theocrats, is the country with a large number of Muslims that has been infiltrated by the liberal ideas of the West. As a rule of thumb, you can say that the terrorists would like to wreak edifying vengeance on any predominantly Islamic country where you can see even a small part of a woman's face. Starting with Pakistan, you can see more and more of a woman's face as you move East. It was therefore predictable, after September 11th, that the terrorists would bend their efforts in the same direction. I only wish that I had predicted it straight away: we would all like to be blessed with as much foresight as hindsight. As things happened, it took me a few days.

A few days after the towers collapsed in New York, I flew East myself, from London to Sydney, thence to keep a speaking engagement in Adelaide. I flew by Malaysia Air, on a flight in which the crew outnumbered the passengers. The transit lounge in Kuala Lumpur was where I had my revelation. There was a prayer room for the faithful and an open bar for the rest of us. The two schools of thought were getting along fine, but it wasn't hard to imagine another breed of traveller who wouldn't stand for it. Here was an obvious target, and there were plenty more on the way to Australia, including the whole of Indonesia, where the fundamentalists were getting a lot better hearing than they were in Malaysia, but only because the Indonesian government was even more scared of what they might do.

My speech in Adelaide was supposed to entertain several hundred Australian businessmen, but I threw in a few sentences designed to register on a different kind of laugh meter. Making jokes about the Australian intellectuals is a dangerous business when your audience is anti-intellectual anyway, which, I think it fair to say, my audience was: there is too good a chance of flattering a prejudice. I had to make it clear that I was joking about my fellow professionals, not my enemies. But compelled by the memory of my revelation in Kuala Lumpur, I couldn't resist caning the Australian *gauchiste* commentators for their persistence in representing Australia as racist, exclusionist, illiberal and immature. I did my best to make my message funny, but I also tried hard to make it clear. Australia, though it certainly had the tragedy of the Aboriginals to haunt its conscience, was one of the most mature, generous and genuinely multicultural democracies on earth. For that reason alone, Australia would be in the firing line.

Well, now it is, and sadly our best hope will be that some of our neighbouring countries to the North and West will draw most of the fire. Next month I have to be in Australia again, to deliver a speech in Sydney and Melbourne: a speech about libraries. In the speech, which I am composing now and have put aside to write this, I will propose, among other things, the founding in Australia of an Islamic library to which all the world's genuine Islamic scholars who are free to travel might come, there to continue the work of bringing a critical scrutiny to the sacred texts – the very work that was forcibly interrupted by the theocrats in the nineteenth century, an interruption that led directly to the disasters of today. But to get there in time I will have to fly there, and I can't say I'm looking forward to the trip. I will be an old man soon, and the fact that I will be flying home through a long war-zone will bother me less than it would once have done, because I have had a life. But nobody wants his certainty of death pre-empted by a bunch of maniacs impelled by their certainty of Heaven, and the thought of all those slain or maimed young Australians, so full of life because they were too young even to realize what it means to be born and raised in a free country, will bring me home in despair.

Guardian, 16 November 2002

Postscript

The above words were not easy to find at the time, but something needed to be said. Later on, at the ceremony in St Paul's Cathedral, I had only to read out the short lesson set down for me, and that should have been easier. But some of the bereaved parents were present. It was hard to look them in the eye. The *Guardian* gave my article a title I would not have chosen myself: 'The Day My Country Lost its Innocence'. I didn't believe that modern Australia had ever been innocent in the sense that was obviously meant. In that sense, Australia hadn't been innocent since Gallipoli; and there were plenty of bereaved loved ones after World War II who were well aware of what had been at stake; and the European immigrants who helped to enrich Australian culture post-war brought hard knowledge with them. But in the legal sense Australia was certainly innocent of the Bali bombing, although the attempt to pronounce it guilty began almost straight away. Australia was an ally of the United States; and the United States backed Israel; and Israel oppressed the Palestinians; and the terrorists were consequently doing their bit for justice. Thus went the line of reasoning. Perhaps there was something to it – a lot of intelligent people believed it – but it was notable that the terrorists themselves, when apprehended, said little in its support. They smiled a lot, as if they had even bigger things in mind.

OUR FIRST BOOK

This year we celebrate the two-hundredth anniversary of the first book to be printed and published in Australia. Though our first book was snappily entitled *New South Wales General Standing Orders Selected from the General Orders Issued by Former Governors*, it is unlikely that very many people were madly excited even at the time, and today the anniversary of its first appearance is scarcely front-page news, although the book contains at least one permanently newsworthy item of information, which I will get to later on. For now we need merely note that an all-Australian book is no longer a novelty. Today we are quite accustomed to buying books that were written, printed and published in Australia. If we wished to, we could build a personal library of Australian books and if we wanted to own them all we would need a house as big as all of Kerry Packer's houses put together. In my own personal library in London I started an Australian section about twenty years ago. Every time I make a visit home to Australia I bring an extra, empty holdall. By the end of the visit it is full of Australian books, some of them dating back to beyond the time I left for Europe in late 1961. They were the Australian books I wasn't reading when I was a student because I was too busy reading British and American ones. I didn't find Australian books so interesting then. Now I do. So back they go to London to be added to my Australian section, which by now is crowding out a whole wall of its own. My apartment is on the sixth floor of a warehouse conversion in the Butler's Wharf area south of Tower Bridge, and I have already been advised by the mortgage surveyors that if I add many more books to my library the day must inevitably come when the beams under the floor will give way and my whole apartment will collapse into the apartment below, which will in turn collapse into the apartment below that, and so on until about fifty people are wedged into the underground car-park with plenty to read while they await rescue.

The book that tips the balance could well be the *Collected Poems* of Les Murray, which our splendidly independent publisher Duffy and Snellgrove brought out this year. It is a big book, just as its author is a big man. I already have one copy that the publishers kindly sent to me, but I have bought another while I am here. I want to keep the first copy clean and use this second copy to make notes. This second copy, when I squeeze it into the Australian poetry shelves in my apartment, might be just enough to crack the creaking beams. It would be a fitting way to go. My dying thought as I descend, however, might well be the opposite. In the days when I was young and healthy, I never saw myself as a bookish person, just as Australia didn't see itself as a bookish nation. In fact it already was, but the fact had not yet become clear, and even today it has still not become as clear as it ought to be. If I have a single aim in this address, it is to try to bring that fact further into the light. But I would not have the aim if I had not begun in darkness, at a time when I saw myself as an athlete, in a nation of athletes.

There are good reasons for our being more immediately excited by physical prowess than by spiritual refinement. Our children want to play in the sun or run to the surf more than they want to sit down to study, and we want them to want that. When we say 'He's always got his nose in a book' we might say it proudly, but even today we are usually a bit worried about the 'always'. When I was young, 'He's always got his nose in a book' was a confession of desperation about one's own son's physical constitution and an accusation of weirdness about someone else's. 'She's always got her nose in a book' was less troublesome. Reading was, after all, women's business. Heroes were men and men did things. If occasionally they wrote things, it was because they had done them first. The excitement was in the doing: the excitement was in the action. There was, there always had been, and there still is, something to that emphasis. Finally it's the life of the mind that counts, and all other forms of life must lead to that: after all, the mind is the last thing we will have, if we are lucky. But I would be the last to deny that in the sentence *mens sana in corpore sano* it's the *corpore sano* that has the first appeal. Certainly it was the way I felt when I was still in fighting trim, and I want you to know, as I stand here before you –

you bursting with sun-drenched vigour and I visibly the wreck of a human being – that it was only by an accident of fate that I did not become an Australian sporting hero, a successor to Murray Rose or Lew Hoad, a precursor of Ian Thorpe or Lleyton Hewitt.

The accident of fate was lack of sporting talent, but it took a while for that to become manifest. Growing up in Kogarah, on Botany Bay, I was within easy cycling distance of Ramsgate baths. I would spend the whole weekend at the baths, telling my mother that I had no time to mow the lawn because I was training for the 110 yards freestyle. In those days the races were still measured in yards instead of metres, Australia not yet having separated itself from all the other English-speaking nations including America by converting its measurement system in order to make it easier for the Japanese and Germans to sell us cars. Unbeknownst to my mother, when I was at Ramsgate baths I rarely completed the full 110 yards freestyle. What I completed was the ten yards freestyle. I was among the first of my generation to perfect the tumble turn. I mean among the first of my generation of amphibian dabblers, the boys who hung around the pool and occasionally dived in, but didn't do much of all that swimming from one end to the other over and over for hours at a stretch that the serious swimmers did. But my tumble turn was almost as convincing as theirs. Unfortunately, instead of employing my tumble turn to increase my speed over a given number of laps, I employed it to impress girls. For this, ten yards of freestyle was all that I deemed necessary. Starting five yards from the end of the pool, I would execute a tumble turn, swim another five yards in the opposite direction, and stop, trying to look as if I had been engaged in polishing a minor technical point in my otherwise impeccable tumble turn.

One of the girls actually was impressed. Her name was Alison and she looked very beautiful in a Speedo. Eventually I found that it was easier to go on impressing Alison by escorting her to the sandpit for a long discussion of my future as a swimming star, a discussion in which, you will not be surprised to hear, I did most of the talking. But her eyes shone, and that was all that counted, even if they shone with the porcelain glaze of boredom. The full story of what happened in the sandpit can be read in my book *Unreliable Memoirs* and I won't bother you with a précis of it now. The book is still available in most good bookshops and some bad ones, and if you want to consult the original manuscript you can find it in the archives of my kind host for this address, the State Library of New South Wales. Turn to the paragraph about what happened in the sandpit and you can see that the page is stained with tears of happiness. Sufficient to say now that almost nothing happened in the water, and that the results of my intensive training were finally revealed to my mother at the Boys' Brigade swimming carnival at Drummoyne in which I did indeed complete the 110 yards freestyle, but only after all the other competitors had left the pool. Let me assure you however that, hard though it might be to believe, I had the physique, I had the strength, and I even had the ambition. What I did not have was the true desire, except the desire for Alison, which was a different matter. Sitting beside my mother, Alison was at the Boys' Brigade swimming carnival too and I never saw her again.

It was a similar story with my tennis. In the private schools of Australia, and the so-called public schools of England, there has always been a certain type of boy who, when he says 'my cricket' or 'my rugby', really means it. He is in possession of his manly sport: you can tell by the thickness of his neck and the cinema credits embroidered on his blazer pocket. When I referred to 'my tennis' it was with less justification, but it can't be denied that until the age of about eleven I was a hot prospect. My ability to sustain a long rally was already attracting attention. Every day of the school holidays I sustained the rally against the back wall of our house, my only available opponent, and the attention I attracted was that of Mrs Thorpe, who lived next door. Of delicate sensibility, she had been advised by her physicians to get plenty of sleep during the day. While I was sustaining a long rally, her head would appear suddenly over the back fence, teeth bared in a snarl and her eyeballs resembling little pink windmills. When she pointed out to my mother that sleep was made impossible by my ability to sustain a long rally, I was forbidden to practise. But when my mother was out, the lure of Wimbledon was too strong, and once again I was out in the yard hitting my tennis ball against the back wall a few thousand times while I dreamed of beating Pancho Gonzalez and Mrs Thorpe dreamed of beating me to death. I knew I was behaving badly but I couldn't stop. Fame beckoned. I had seen Lew Hoad in the newsreels and I wanted to be him.

Incidentally, when Thomas Mann was writing his last book in

California, the expanded version of that marvellous novel *The Confessions of Felix Krull*, he had a photograph on his desk to provide inspiration for the portrait he was creating of an irresistibly attractive young adolescent male. Remember you heard this here first, because no reputable scholar or commentator has yet spotted it: that photograph was of Lew Hoad. I offer this item of information for any PhD student who might be contemplating a thesis about the influence of Australian tennis-players on the modern German novel. Anyway, I knew how Thomas Mann must have felt, although in my case the longings aroused by Lew Hoad's freckled, jug-eared and shyly smiling dial were rather different. I merely wanted to be an Aussie tennis player victorious at Wimbledon. The back wall was my gateway to glory. But I later found that the skills acquired did not necessarily transfer to an actual tennis court, where the opponent was more mobile than a brick wall. The dream, however, has never died, and even today I can't resist giving Lleyton Hewitt my advice. Since the advice is delivered to the television set, he probably doesn't hear it directly, but thought-waves can be powerful. I'm fairly sure that my advice was the reason he eventually abandoned his habit of wearing his peaked cap backwards at all times, even in bed. As science has now established, wearing a peaked cap backwards is the universal sign of the international idiot. No matter how handsome, no young male tennis player looks good that way and Lleyton looked worse than most, especially when seen in close-up with his fist in the air pulling the intestines out of an imaginary opponent while he yelled silent abuse at his girlfriend in the grandstand, a tirade which apparently meant that he was doing well instead of badly. More recently he has still been yelling the silent abuse but the cap is no longer always in evidence. When it is, it still tends to go on backwards, and I still tend to shout at the television set, my face contorted in a way, I am told, that bears a disturbing resemblance to the way Lleyton looks while disputing a line call. The best way of putting it is that he and I have a problem and we are both working on it. But the problem would not be there if I were not still, in my secret heart, an Australian sporting hero and man of action.

The dream of being a man of action can be a fruitful dream for a man of letters to have. Hemingway had it, and among the results were 'The Snows of Kilimanjaro' and *Death in the Afternoon*. Hemingway in real life was a great reader but he played his bookishness down, because he wanted to be thought of as a great hunter. The far less physical Aldous Huxley, in an essay called 'Foreheads Villainous Low', tried to point out that Hemingway had overdone the he-man effect, and that the strain of pretending not to be an intellectual was doing Hemingway's prose no good. In response, Hemingway tried to point out that Aldous Huxley was a wimp. Hemingway's side of the argument got more support from the intellectuals than you might expect. Even among intellectuals, in fact especially among intellectuals, the idea is apt to linger that action comes first. Hamlet was an intellectual, and traced the roots of his fatal inaction to too much thinking. He pronounced the verdict upon himself: by pondering too closely on the event, he was sicklied o'er with the pale cast of thought. Fortinbras, who would assume the throne that Hamlet forfeited by dithering too long, prided himself on not being similarly afflicted. The idea that too many ideas will bind the muscles is an idea that comes with the capacity to have any ideas at all. Creativity is filtered through the intellect but it has its wellspring in the primary drives that made us chase and kill wild animals long before we thought of writing anything on their cured skins.

Hence the tendency of any revolutionary movement in thought or the arts to declare war on museums, libraries, and books themselves. The Futurists were only one of the twentieth-century avant-garde movements who proclaimed the desirability of smashing up the museums and burning down the libraries. This intoxicating notion wasn't even new with them. George Bernard Shaw, in the preface to his play *Caesar and Cleopatra*, had already said that he thought it a blessing for human history that the library of Alexandria had been burned down. Actually there were two main libraries in Alexandria, but he conflated them for dramatic purposes, principally to provide indirect lighting. When the leaping flames lit the faces of Caesar and Cleopatra it spelled the end of the old Egyptian civilization, but Shaw quite liked the idea of old civilizations ending because he thought that their accumulated fustian wisdom got in the way of founding a new one, the socialist civilization that would bring justice to all. And though our historical imaginations don't usually go back much beyond the burning of the library in Alexandria, it was by no means the first time that a civilization had died with its books.

The first libraries were palace archives, and they had all vanished with the palaces. Three thousand years before Christ, Syria and Babylon stored their records on clay tablets and catalogued them for reference. Thirteen hundred years before Christ, in the Kingdom of Hattusas, tablets were catalogued by title and author. Ozymandias founded a library, but Shelley doesn't mention it in his poem: the library was under the sand that stretched far way, and we know that now because a few of the tablets were dug up again. In Assyria, Ashurbanipal had his own library of 1,500 books, but presumably other people were allowed to consult them, because many of the tablets that still survive carry warnings against late return. Nowadays if we bring a library book back late we get fined. We have to imagine what the penalties were like then, because a tablet spelling out the punishments for bringing a book back late has never been found. We can presume that the penalties were drastic, especially in Babylon, which is nowadays called Iraq. We can assume that some distant ancestor of Saddam Hussein was sitting at the front desk, wielding his date-stamp like a weapon of mass destruction. But despite the care put into preserving the books against depredation, all those libraries vanished with the civilizations that gave rise to them. And already you can hear a warning bell to presage a heavy theme: that they had libraries was what made them civilizations. No library, no civilization. No civilization, no library.

The library as we know it now came in with the Greeks, mainly because the stone or clay tablet had given way to a technological advance: papyrus. A papyrus roll could be reproduced with some ease. It still took time, because it still had to be done by hand, but the rolls could be copied, and therefore bought and sold. Because they could be bought and sold, the papyrus rolls were available for private collection. The private library, as opposed to the palace library, took over as the model, and one of the things I want to propose is that the private library and the palace library, or call it the state library, have, or should have, an indissoluble connection. Aristotle's enormous personal library was the model for the library of Alexandria. Somewhere around 300 BC the Greek king of Egypt, Ptolemy Philadelphus, built the complex of libraries we call the Alexandria library, which copied every book in the world it could get its hands on and stole the originals if necessary. Any ship docking in Alexandria had its books confiscated as the price of tying up to a bollard. The Library of Alexandria had almost half a million rolls in it at the time Caesar watched it burn. He preferred to occupy himself with Cleopatra than fight the fire: roughly similar activities, as Mark Antony later testified. But Caesar had got the idea, and he commissioned a great library of Greek and Latin books to be built in Rome. He didn't live to see it open and beget its children.

Augustus built two libraries, the Octavian and the Palatine. They both burned, but the one on the Palatine was replaced by, of all people, Tiberius, otherwise a legend for destructive tyranny: an anomaly we might have to examine. As late as the fourth century AD, the Roman Empire, by then far into its decline, held at least twenty-eight libraries in the capital city alone, most of them attached to that popular gathering point for the leisured class: the baths. If Ramsgate baths had had a library next door I might have got the right idea much earlier, but let that pass for the moment, because we should consider what Shaw was saying. He was saying that no library had ever guaranteed the continuity of a civilization. What was more, the very impulse to accumulate scholarship might have got in the way of the necessary political action that would have kept that civilization fresh. It's a seductive notion. Not even Shaw was the first to have it. He was only echoing Schopenhauer's attractive idea that knowledge is better gained from life than from books. Who can doubt it?

Well, in fact they all did. Deep down under the image-breaking rhetoric, they all knew that their bright idea was merely an emphasis. Schopenhauer was a learned man who wanted his books published. If Shaw had really been certain that too many books got in the way of true learning, he would not have wanted his own books published. In real life, he was so keen on their being published that he insisted on supervising their production, taking fanatical care over their appearance, specifying everything from the type-face to the width of the margins. Nor were the Futurists, Dadaists, and all those other furiously doodling advocates of starting again with a clean slate, fundamentally averse to getting their books into circulation. Their books looked like nobody else's books, but they were still books. All the early-twentieth-century cultural revolutionaries who sounded off against the stifling weight of a public library were at heart unfailingly keen to get their own books into it. They just thought it was a pity that all those other books were there already, silting up the shelves. The writers who thought libraries were choking them with the past but still wanted their own books to be part of the future were like the painters and graphic artists who thought, or said they thought, that museums were a dead weight. Translating thought to deed, Apollinaire swiped some small, portable *objets d'art* from the Louvre and Picasso kept them for a while at the back of his studio. But Picasso wasn't quite as confident as Apollinaire that the museums should be dispersed. Born as a canny operator as well as a great artist, perhaps Picasso already had a suspicion that some of his own pictures were heading for that very destination, and that their presence in an official collection would help to raise the price he could charge private owners for whatever he turned out next. There is also evidence that Picasso feared the cops might come and ask him awkward questions about some of his ornaments.

Apollinaire, of course, feared the cops wouldn't come: he wanted to breathe defiance, to enjoy the thrill of his fine idea brought to life. Far into the twentieth century, the fine idea kept cropping up that the most equitable way for museums and libraries to serve the common people would be to distribute their contents at random while turning the buildings into meeting halls. As late as the 1960s, in the flush of student activism, the young rhetoricians of the Western universities – most of whom gave living proof that they were barely capable of organizing toilet facilities for the mass meetings they addressed – loudly proposed that freedom would be furthered if established institutions were to be dismantled. But the large part of what they said had already been discredited. Indeed if further proof was necessary, their programme was being discredited at that very time, because their proposed Cultural Revolution of the West was taking for its model the Cultural Revolution in the East, the one in China. As Jung Chang's magnificent and terrifying book *Wild Swans* was eventually to make clear, China's Cultural Revolution was an obscenely vindictive bloodbath, just one more hideous instalment of Mao's war against his own people.

*

To be fair to our young freedom fighters in the 1960s, information on the tragedy in China was hard to come by at the time, especially if your ears were stopped because your mouth was permanently wide open. But the truth wasn't hard to guess. The evidence was already in, from previous totalitarian adventures in the twentieth century, that the future dreamed of by the Futurists, should it actually arrive, would have an awful resemblance to historical house-cleanings going back at least as far as Tamburlaine and his famous wall of skulls, lime and living men. In the first twelve years of the Soviet Union the Russian avant-garde artists were allowed to live and even to flourish. But they were already realizing that there was a price to be paid for a state endorsement of their new start. Suddenly feeling not quite so young as they once had, they found themselves confronted by screaming adolescent Komsomols who had been sent to visit the art schools in order to impose an official programme called Proletkult, which seemed to be based on the preposterous notion that the avant-garde was itself part of the stifling past, and should be swept away in the name of an even newer new art dedicated to nothing except furthering the aims of social revolution as defined by the Party. The result was a forecast of an all-too-typical twentieth-century picture. Highly experienced artists and intellectuals who had merely advocated the virtues of destruction were horrified to find themselves taken literally by vociferous but clueless post-pubescent junior agitators all wearing the same mass-produced peaked cap. Their only virtue was that they rarely wore the cap backwards. In 1929 the commissar for education, Lunacharsky, having been reprogrammed by Stalin, cracked down on the avant-garde artists he had previously encouraged, and their dream officially became a nightmare. Most of them realized that it already had. For some of them the crack-down might even have come as a relief: at least they were merely going to be interrogated, tortured and shot, instead of harangued by a posse of confident teenage dolts. Forty years later, in the Chinese Cultural Revolution, some of the survivors found that to be the worst thing: being surrounded by dogmatic young thugs shaking their fists as they screamed excerpts from the aesthetic wisdom of Madame Mao.

What had happened to Russia happened to Germany when the Nazis came in, and this time the world found out straight away, because the Nazis took pictures: moving pictures. The burning of the books in the Operplatz in Berlin is one of the abiding images of the twentieth century. The sole virtue of the Nazis was that they infallibly discredited their own ideas from the moment they put them into action, and made sure the world realized it by boasting about their atrocities as if they were accomplishments. Immediately it became obvious that Heinrich Heine had been right when he predicted that any regime that burned books would soon burn people. Some of the people scheduled to be burned managed to leave early and take their books with them, thus removing many of the best private libraries from the purview of the Gestapo, who were great readers in their way, although they were always great hunters first. As Victor Klemperer tells us in his marvellous two-volume diary, the Gestapo were always very interested in what books you had on your shelves. The result was a house-cleaning, but here already the anomaly comes in that we noticed in the case of Tiberius. Not even the Nazis succeeded in destroying everything. Admittedly they were short of time. The Thousand-Year Reich was fated to last only twelve years. But they didn't realize that. And we are forced to conclude that the main reason they didn't obliterate every book that they hadn't written themselves was because they had a weird urge to preserve the printed evidence that the culture they were busy annihilating had once existed. In Poland in 1942, in the ghetto of the town called Drohobycz, the great writer Bruno Schulz met his death when a Gestapo officer called Karl Günther shot him in the head. But until that moment Schulz had been employed in the category of Necessary Jew, because he knew something about books, and the Nazis were busy cataloguing their literary loot before sending it back to Germany to be incorporated into some weird and wonderful library of superseded, decadent cultures. Adolf Eichmann himself, who took pride in his expertise on the Jewish culture whose living representatives he had been deputed to annihilate, was some kind of collector of Jewish manuscripts, which he enjoyed pottering about with almost as much as he enjoyed rewriting the timetables so that all the trains ran to Auschwitz.

Goebbels, who had a literary background and some pretensions as a novelist, kept an important private library. After the war, Goebbels's personal assistant, an ex-journalist called Wilfred von Oven, got away safely to Argentina, where he published, in two volumes, an unintentionally comic masterpiece called *Mit Goebbels bis zum Ende* – With Goebbels to the End. In the year 2000 I found a copy in Henschel's great second-hand bookshop in Buenos Aires. When I sat down in a café in the Avenida Corrientes to begin reading my new treasure, fascinating facts leaped from the yellowed pages. Did you know that Goebbels gave up smoking the day after

D-Day? Neither did I. Apparently he had figured out that the time to give up smoking is when you are on a psychological high, and he was feeling good because he sincerely thought that with the Allied armies actually present in Europe it would be easier to reach a political arrangement with them, presumably because they were closer to hand. Whatever the wisdom of that, he took up smoking again twelve days later. But another fact is even more fascinating. He also, says von Oven, started reordering his library. As the end approached and the Russians were almost within shelling distance of the Operplatz where his sinister team of student myrmidons had once scornfully read passages aloud from the books he had ordered to be burned, the Reichsminister decided that his library of classic German literature should be cleansed of Nazi texts. The book-burner started burning his own stuff, but only so that the stuff he had secretly known to be better all along could keep its own company undisturbed by ideological junk. And even the Great Helmsman Chairman Mao, the biggest enemy of Chinese written culture since the mad First Emperor of the Ch'in burned the classical texts; even Chairman Mao, who encouraged the notion that his own Little Red Book of platitudes was the only book that a Red Guard in a peaked cap need ever read; even Chairman Mao kept a personal collection of classic poetry in his library in Beijing.

Mao's personal library was called the Library of Chrysanthemum Fragrance and I often think of it while sitting in my own library, the Library of Cheap Cigar Fragrance. I think of it because of the supreme evidence it provides that even a beast can have a feeling for books, and that the feeling must come from somewhere very deep in the psyche. The apparently self-contradictory phenomenon of the barbarian bookworm had a precedent not just in Tiberius but in the long history of the Christian theocracies, whose virulence we ought to remember, now that we are worried about another kind of theocracy, and wondering what to do about it. Not just the Catholic church but the Protestant churches that later competed against it had a solid tradition of burning both books and people. You can't fault either wing on that one: Calvin was as lethal as Torquemada, a fact I once got into trouble for pointing out to the minister of Kogarah Presbyterian church when he carpeted me for giving my Sunday School class a lecture on free love. But there was something about our theocracies – let us call them ours out of an acknowledgment of the past, if not out of pride – that demanded a special library be kept of the books on the *index expurgatorium*, even if only the most thoroughly accredited theological adepts were issued with a library card. Tamburlaine, Attila the Hun and Genghis Khan, all of whom simply destroyed everything, were not running theocracies. They didn't think they were creating anything except destruction. They had their descendants in the twentieth century, and especially in the late twentieth century. Pol Pot wanted everything to do with the mind destroyed. At the peak of his cold-blooded dementia he required the persecution, torture and death of anyone who wore glasses. But he was not an ideologist in the sense that Stalin and Hitler were. Though both godless men, they were also theocrats: they had ideas in their heads. The ideas were totalitarian ideas, but one of them was the idea that some sort of memory should be maintained of the liberal ideas that had been superseded.

This quirk on the part of the great hunters, the man hunters, can only be explained with reference to a deep instinct in which some sort of scholarly pretension is bound up with the urge to pure action. One important consequence, in the case of the Soviet Union, was that the KGB kept a copy of its number-one enemy book, George Orwell's *Nineteen Eighty-Four*. When Yuri Andropov was head of the KGB he had the copy copied and circulated to his top echelon of staff, and the results were part of what seems unlikely even in retrospect: the elite of the oppressors somehow allowed the transformation of the regime that they had previously preserved by exterminating, without hesitation, everyone who showed signs of opposing it. The oppressors retained the power to go on doing so, but they had lost the desire; and that deep instinct to become informed about actions, instead of merely to perform them, had somehow helped them to lose it.

With these considerations in mind, it is time to go back fifty years again to the young would-be swimming champion and tennis ace, and talk about *his* deep instincts. Another of my athletic ambitions was for running. Heavily under the influence of a classic photograph of the great Australian sprinter Hector Hogan leaving the starting blocks in Helsinki, I would practise my start on the strip of lawn in front of our house. One of the secrets of Hogan's electrifying speed out of the blocks was the way he kept his head down until he was upright. I would practise keeping my head down.

It was probably the main reason I ran at full speed into the lower branch of our box-gum tree. The branch caught me across the forehead and practically ended my future literary career right there. The impact was probably the main reason why some of my metaphors still come out mixed. It didn't do my sprinting career much good either, but that would have been threatened anyway by my attendance at Sydney Technical High School, where quite a few of the boys could run faster than I could. One of them, the future international rugby star Reg Gasnier, could run twice as fast as I could while he was carrying a football, and probably could have done so while carrying a refrigerator. But I was fast enough on my feet to get to Kogarah's little lending library in a matter of minutes so that I could take out yet another armful of detective novels by Ellery Queen and Erle Stanley Gardner.

Once a week in the early evening I scooted up the hill to the library to change my maximum allowed number of books for the same number of new ones, or sometimes the same ones if I wanted to read them again. Walking slowly home in the reverse trajectory, I would already be deep into the first book of the batch before I got to the front gate, which I would open without looking, sometimes surprising myself when I encountered Mrs Thorpe setting out the empty milk bottles. I had no method for surreptitiously marking the books I had already read, so there was always a chance of getting the same book again anyway, and not realizing until I had started to read it. Later on in London I worked briefly and disastrously at the front desk of one of the Lambeth lending libraries and I encountered little old ladies who solved this problem by making a personal mark in each book they had read. There were always a few little old ladies who tremulously asked the classic question 'Have I read this one?' but the rest of them had skills of encipherment that they might previously have employed at Bletchley Park. One woman drew a little square at the bottom of page 98 of any book she had finished reading. Another drew a little circle in the right-hand margin of page 123. I was a bit worried about the woman who made her mark on the back right-hand endpaper. Her mark was a swastika. But on the whole the little old ladies were smarter than I had been back in Kogarah. I just took pot luck.

I was more careful about the books I bought rather than borrowed. Each of them, I believed, was an individual work of art in every aspect, and especially in regard to its cover. I collected every book by Leslie Charteris featuring his greatest creation, the Saint. I preferred the Pan paperbacks to those published by Hodder and Stoughton, because the Pan cover paintings were glossier, often showing the Saint in black tie supported on either side by a glamorous female with a shrink-wrapped décolletage: a foretaste of the James Bond film posters in later times. On the floor of my room I would arrange side by side my complete set of Biggles books in the green dustcovers that showed the aeronautical hero posed in his flying suit against a green sky. The effect, I now realize, presaged the methods of Andy Warhol by twenty years, although my mother was less impressed on the aesthetic level than I was. Nevertheless I am sure it was not deliberately that she trod on my precious copy of *Biggles Flies East*, irreparably coarsening the hero's fine-drawn features. She just forgot to look down when she came in to make my bed, a task I had excused myself from on the grounds of my intellectual commitments. Previously I had excused myself on the grounds of my sporting commitments: swimming training, etc. One instinct had transcended another. Books had started to become my life: not out of a reasonable assessment of what life should be, but out of an unquestioned impulse. It was just another kind of love: I doted on a book as if it were the contents of a girl's Speedo. As I brushed a linen spine with my fingertips, there was undoubtedly a libidinous element, and Freud would not be surprised to hear that it still haunts me. Even today I find a woman reading a book an arousing spectacle, especially if I wrote it. At my age there isn't much left to be aroused by, but there it is: or rather, there it isn't. Alison, by the way, was a bit of a reader. Admittedly it took her all summer to read a single issue of *Women's Weekly*, but that made her all the more satisfactory to look at, because her lips moved when she read. I accumulated books with the assiduity of Don Giovanni accumulating conquests, with the difference that I did not discard them. My room turned into the germ of the personal library I own today, the one preparing itself for the descent into the car-park.

*

At any size, however, the personal library has a drawback inseparable from its advantage. What goes into it is all to your taste, and there is a tendency to be disdainful of what stays out. For this reason, all the personal libraries in the world can provide no adequate substitute for a public library that takes everything. But I didn't know that at the time, and I conceived early on a suspicion of big public libraries that in some respects lingers to this day. At Sydney University I would visit Fisher Library only because my girlfriend was a librarian working in the basement, and when my second-year History essay on the first Lord Halifax necessitated research in the Mitchell Library downtown, I took one look at the thousands of books on display in the reading room and retreated immediately to the Botanical Gardens for a smoke. Rothman's king size in a flip-top box had just arrived in Australia and I developed an elaborately casual way of flipping the top to extract the contents one by one. My bronchial cough deepened on every visit to the Mitchell. When I consulted the catalogue, there was something about the Dewey Decimal system that scared me into paralysis, and in the rare case when I had an actual book by or about Lord Halifax in my hands the absence of a dustcover somehow sealed it shut. No picture of Biggles or the Saint, just a standard binding disfigured by numbers on the spine. Glumly I would enter the title in my bibliography, as if noting the title were somehow the same as having read the book. It was presumptuous of me to be disappointed when I read the marker's comment written at the end of my essay. 'You express yourself quite well, but your trouble in this case is that you have nothing to express, a deficiency you might have repaired if you had actually consulted the books listed in your surprisingly full bibliography. The three marks I am giving you out of the possible ten are for your style.' I quote the marker's comment from memory, but I am pretty sure I've got it right. My three out of ten for a history essay stuck with me like a scar.

It should have been two out of ten. In the year before I sailed for Europe I spent a lot of time with Sydney's notorious Downtown Push. The Push was a hotbed of libertarian ideology, centred on the principle that the best way to rebel against bourgeois society was to crash its parties and seduce its young women, the more respectable the better. One of the parties the Push crashed was in Bellevue Hill, at that time the very pinnacle of genteel luxury. The parents of the house were away in Europe, whence they had come as refugees before the war. The daughter of the house was still resisting the attentions of the Push leaders but she was naively keen to prove to them that she understood their anger at the spectacle of a house that had been paid for with money that had actually been earned. The Push operated on the assumption that money was legitimate only if borrowed or won at the racecourse. The Push also believed that the best place to stub out a cigarette was on the carpet, grinding it well in with the heel. As the daughter of the house frantically circulated amongst the hubbub trying to pick up the butts before they set the stippled Wilton on fire, I wandered drunkenly into a room identifiable as a library by the number of books present, although only their shape and size told me for certain what they were. They were all in European languages, none of which I could read. All I got was an impression of beauty and complexity, of a mystery speaking in tongues. I took one of the books down. The author was Thomas Mann's brother Heinrich. The date on the title page was 1932, the year before Hell broke loose: that much, at least, I knew. But the date was all I could read, so I put it back. What I was looking at, as I backed slowly out of the room, was a monument to what I didn't know. Perhaps one out of ten would have been a more appropriate mark.

And so, almost perfectly clueless about what the world outside Australia had recently been like, I sailed away to see it. In the course of forty years I have learned to read some of those languages, just for the books. Journalists sometimes kindly call me a linguist but the harsh fact is that I have barely mastered English. Of any other language I can read, I can speak barely enough to stay out of gaol. But reading I can do. Reading, it turned out, would be my adventure, my only field as a man of action. I would never win at Wimbledon, take out the Gold Medal for the Olympics 100-metres freestyle, cover prodigious distances in training for the mile like John Landy. But I have covered prodigious distances in my own mind, and all the more prodigious because I was starting from zero, and there was nothing special about my mind. If I had been as clever as Les Murray, I might have done it all without leaving Kogarah, and might have been there to help stop the local council turning its pretty railway station into a neo-brutalist combination of a flak tower and a U-boat pen. But I was dense, with the impervious density which youth often has when it grows up surrounded by blessings. Having grown up in Australia, I had failed to understand it. I had thought the whole world was like that: safe, sure, fair. What I read in the other languages showed me that the world was far otherwise. And finally what I read about Australia, in my own language, showed me that Australia, too, was an historical event far more complicated than I had allowed myself to believe. The nation that Donald Horne called the lucky country wasn't just lucky. I have a lasting admiration for Donald Horne's books – I own them all – but in one way he was too successful. His central tenet, that his homeland was a lucky strike consistently mismanaged by second-rate politicians, caught on as a dogmatic aid to national self-doubt. As I read on through our recent and gratifyingly rich heritage of commentary and memoir, it became clearer to me all the time that we hadn't become a prosperous and reasonably equitable democracy by the accidental dispensation of benevolent nature and a favourable geographical position. The country had been built, by clever people. Our constitution itself was the work of people who had studied history. They were readers of newspapers and periodicals, they were eternal students in the best sense, they were bookish people. They had built a bookish nation. But as so often has been the case with Australia's consciousness of itself, the problem was to realize it.

When I covered the Sydney Olympics for the London newspaper the *Independent*, I tried to point out that Australia's alleged lack of national self-confidence had never been anything more serious than a lack of self-awareness, and that the supposed need to take the final step towards political maturity was an insult to the countless victims in those purportedly mature nations which had somehow succeeded in going mad. Some of the victims who survived had come to Australia and helped to diversify and expand its culture – and that undoubtedly was a move towards maturity – but they would not have been able to help with our cultural maturity if the political maturity had not been there to welcome them. The result has been a nation which, even while some of its commentators were eloquently worried about its identity crisis, already had an identity unmatched in the world's eyes; a nation which has by now become, in my view, uniquely placed to exercise an international influence in a world where influence is becoming steadily more important than power. What I would like to suggest now is that we might mark our position in the world by building a new and potentially resonant symbol: and at this point you might decide that I have gone mad myself.

I never went back to the house in Bellevue Hill. I doubt I could have found it, and if I had, the man of the house might have asked me awkward questions about the cigarette burns in his carpet. I imagine his beautiful library was broken up when he died and the dealers sent the pearls of his collection back to Europe to be sold on. But over the years I have built a personal library something like his, collecting the books in all the world's cities where the refugees went, and where I later went to make films. I have one of my pearls here, and I'm sure he had a copy of it too. It's the book that the nineteenth-century Prussian scholar Ferdinand Gregorovius wrote about his travels in Italy. I bought the book from a dealer in Staten Island, New York, in 1983. An inscription on the title page says it once belonged to Anna Liebmann. Either she or one of her children must have got away to safety, and probably the next generation sold her books because they wanted nothing to do with the old language. You can't blame them, because the language is German. *Wanderjahre in Italien*. It's a book of astonishing elegance, and all the more astonishing because it was produced to be sold at a low price to a large public. There is no publication date, but from my other books in the same series I would guess that it was printed in about 1922. The publishing house was Wolfgang Jess Verlag, of Dresden. Apart from its books, scattered throughout the world, no trace of that house now exists. It was already gone before the fire-storm. The Gestapo, remember, were great readers.

I wish my library were all treasures, but it isn't. After it crashes into the car-park, only a part of it will be worth keeping. But I can think of other Australian collectors whose personal libraries are so selective, and yet so comprehensive in particular fields of interest, that they are cultural treasure-houses in themselves. Barry Humphries is only one example. He is a man of great learning, and one day, when he is studied as an Australian genius, the students would benefit by having access to his books. The Americans were first to act on this principle. All students of Evelyn Waugh must eventually travel to Austin, Texas, because that is where his library is, preserved intact. We could copy the Americans in this even if we don't want to copy them in anything else. We don't want the McDonald's University of Hamburger Science, although we might conceivably want McDonald's if we want to feed the kids in a hurry. We might also want the libraries of some of our most learned cultural and scientific figures all gathered into one place, each individual library in its own house. I see it as a kind of library city, dedicated to the study of books as artefacts as well as for their contents. What you would be getting would be all the best books not just of Australia, but of the world entire, because our best creative minds have always ranged widely in their reading: if they ever called Australia insular, it was because they themselves were not. To keep the books beautiful, to preserve them from the defacement that comes with preservation, some way might be devised of numbering them invisibly, the numbers to be scanned with a pair of special glasses issued by the graduate student at the front desk, who would be performing his curatorial duties as part of his PhD. To work, study and live for a time in the library city would be a prize for the new intellectual elite, an elite not to be feared in a country which, after all, consists entirely of elites. The expense would be large, but probably not as large as the total amount expended already on the task of transferring the contents of books to microfilm in the name of preservation, a preservation that not only seems to entail the destruction of the actual books, but is also based on a misconception. Despite the huge publicity campaign that warns us of the contrary, the paper of modern books does not deteriorate, a fact explored by Nicholson Baker in his witty treatise *The Double Fold*, although really we don't need him to tell us when we have beside us a copy of *Mit Goebbels bis zum Ende*. It was printed on the lowest quality of paper ever made, but its every ludicrous sentence is still legible even as the margins crumble. And if we look at the thin but creamy paper of *Wanderjahre in Italien*, we can see immediately that it will spontaneously disintegrate at about the same time as Kogarah railway station in its modern form.

It wouldn't matter where this library city was actually situated. I suppose there would be the usual fight between Sydney and Melbourne so that it would end up in Canberra. In my own daydreams it is somewhere near the ocean, so that the lucky student who had qualified to read there could take a break to go swimming in the way I once took a break to go smoking. Perhaps part of the library city could be an Islamic library, so that Muslim scholars from all over the world who are brave enough to go on building a secular body of commentary and criticism to set beside the sacred texts could congregate there in relative safety from the pressure that will inevitably be brought to bear against them by zealots who share their faith but think it can be protected only by remaining unquestioned. There would be dangers, but there is always danger in learning. Pursued far enough, it shakes every faith except its faith in itself. I think personal libraries can contribute to a greater library, just as the State Library of New South Wales has always been nourished by the nearby example of Mitchell's library; but I think so only because the greater library is a collectivity that supersedes the individual; almost the only kind of collectivity that does. Somewhere in the book that we shut out of our own collection might be the fact that would alter our own orthodoxy, and it is part of a nation's true maturity to make sure that the awkward book is available somewhere. Which brings me back, at long last, to our first book.

One of the orthodoxies many of us share is that the Europeans came to this country in order to commit robbery with violence against the native population. Well, let's look at page four of the Governor's standing orders. 'It is His Excellency's positive injunction to the settlers and others who have fire-arms, that they do not wantonly fire at, or take the lives of any of the Natives; as such an act would be considered a deliberate Murder, and subject the offender to such punishment, as, if proved, the Law might direct to be inflicted.' The robbery happened, alas, and so did the violence; but it wasn't the first intention. We blundered into it, and on that issue it might be said that we have been blundering ever since. But something got built, and it was something wonderful; and we would be playing false to our young people who died in Bali if we were to go on saying that Australia is a selfish provocation to the less fortunate world. Australia is the hope of the less fortunate world, and principally because of the example we provide that thoughtfulness and justice and tolerance don't just fall out of the air like the sunlight, but are the fruit of a continuous critical interchange, which could never have been had without the books. It was always true, and now it's time to say so.

IN MEMORIAM SARAH RAPHAEL

One day it will be part of British art history that Sarah Raphael died young. Today, on the day of her funeral, everyone who knew her must cope with the first loss – the loss of her physical presence. Perhaps the cruel law of chance that took her so soon was trying to make up for its early prodigality in giving her everything. She was brilliant, she was beautiful, and she had the generous, unstudied charm that does not always go with those gifts: being down-to-earth when you are so favoured can't be easy, but she could always manage it. Once, when I first knew her, I was looking through a stack of dauntingly authoritative paintings leaning against the wall of her studio and I ventured to suggest that 'Sarah Raphael' wouldn't quite do as a name: 'Sarah Michelangelo' might be more appropriate, or even 'Sarah L. da Vinci'. The gag got a laugh – she looked more than usually lovely when she was laughing, which she usually was, even while she worked – but there was a thoughtful addendum. 'You really think I'm quite *good*, don't you?' I really did, and nobody who had seen any of her work thought anything else.

Which brings us to the second loss, the one that will affect many people who never met her, and eventually whole generations to come, because rarely since Rex Whistler was killed in Normandy in 1944 has there been a deprivation so calculated by fate to impoverish the future. Right from her first phase, she looked destined to put into reverse the dire expectations for the next round of young British art: she could draw, her canvasses had more in them the longer you looked, and there wasn't a dead shark in sight. At Camberwell School of Art (where she went after Bedales) she was a star student, but there was no surprise in that. She had been born into a cultivated household – her father is the writer Frederic Raphael, two of whose books she illustrated – which is always a help towards an apparent precocity, although later on things tend to even out. The real surprise was in her thematic range. Precocious wasn't the word for it. An historical synthesis is usually something that artists attempt only later on, as the final prelude to their achieved individuality. In the initial stages they work through one influence at a time. Young Sarah seemed to have been influenced by the whole European tradition all at once, and to have absorbed the lot.

The first thing of hers I ever saw was a postcard reproduction of one of her big oil paintings. The postcard was a magic window on the past. On the other side of the window were Cossa's frescoes in the Schifanoia palace in Ferrara, and Paolo Uccello's Green Cloister in Santa Maria Novella in Florence. All the colours and characters of the Quattrocento were there. But when I went to her first big solo exhibition I found that she was already out of that phase and into something less crowded, rather in the way that the young Picasso, having proved that he could paint a whole nightclub full of people, switched his attention to individuals. The first picture of hers I bought was a huge oil with almost nothing in it except a centrally placed oval mirror framing her self-portrait in the act of painting: the one and only time, as far as I know, that she used her own good looks as a subject. It was the opposite of conceit, because the other thing in the picture, down in the foreground, was a grotesque homunculus that she had borrowed from Velasquez, just as she had borrowed the idea of the painter painting himself from Rembrandt. The picture was a set of quotations, but the arrangement and the execution were all hers, and typically luscious even in their austerity. It was a picture about chance, about beauty being a fluke. But there was no fluke in the technique, and the picture was also about that: about an abundant young talent discovering how spareness, too, could be a means of expression. It was a bravura piece: look what I can do. It was also a renunciation: look what I can leave out, see how I can discipline myself to serve the purpose. Barely managing to fit my wrapped trophy into a taxi, I already knew that it would be the last of her big pictures that I would ever be able to afford. The millionaires were already moving in. New York's Metropolitan Museum had made a purchase. Every possible prize, except of course the Turner, was getting set to drop into her lap. If you do the rounds, you run into a lot of young artists who are going to be something. But she was already something.

Like all her admirers I wanted her first flush of enchantment to go on for ever, but she was too serious to stay with a winning streak. On the face of it, her next phase looked like a total abnegation. Suddenly her pictures were drained of colour. Nothing remained except greys, dark greens and chilly blues, and the paint itself was acrylic, almost military in its determination to be non-seductive. But you didn't have to look long to see why. The subject matter was terror. There was no overt violence: many of the pictures just showed people walking in the park. But something was going to happen to them, or they were going to do something to someone else. Like those interrogations in Harold Pinter's early plays that lead you to nothing except a realization of what it feels like to be helpless, these pictures summed up the anxieties of modern history without having to mention it. They were so mature that there seemed no way forward, and no need to seek it. She had discovered something uniquely hers. Regrettable for its bleakness, admirable for its truth, it was a personal manner so powerful that it would have served most artists for a lifetime.

Then she transformed herself yet again. A working visit to the Australian desert brought all the colours back with a rush. But this time the colour was without form, except for the way that a new and ravishing *pointilliste* technique (it was as if a re-born Seurat had met Clifford Possum Tjapaltjari over cocktails) arranged individual grains of red dust and molecules of stone into a resplendent Mandelbrot set, a polychromatic map for chaos. Some of the paintings were enormous and all of them were tremendous. The buyers went at them like a lynch mob. At Agnew's I walked slowly so that someone with a lot more loose change would beat me to the one I wanted most. It was fabulous, with a price-tag to match. While painting my portrait she had given me a frightening lecture on how little of the money a painter gets to keep after the gallery takes its cut, but by now she was such a hit that freedom beckoned. She could have – she always could have – just painted away in a style the well-heeled public had learned to like, while exploiting her glamour in the glossies to boost the market. But she wasn't like that.

There was another metamorphosis, into a kind of neo-pop *summa* that looked as if the sixties were getting a re-run on a bigger screen, in a better theatre. Miniature motifs were repeated and counterpointed endlessly: Philip Glass had taken up embroidery. (In 1998 she moved to Marlborough Fine Art for 'Strip', an exhibition that put her pop phase riotously into one room. Her last exhibition, 'Small Objects in Transit' – etchings and monotypes – closed there last month.) She was having fun, but it was easy to predict that she was getting ready for whatever would happen next.

Until now, there was always something that was going to happen next. My own bet is that it would have been the real synthesis – the majestic one, not that merely sensational one she started off with. We will have to guess what it would have looked like, and at the moment guessing hurts too much. One thing we can be sure of: it would have included human figures painted to a standard seldom seen in British art since the eighteenth century. Throughout her short but lavishly fruitful career, whatever phase she was currently caught up in she never ceased to paint portraits, and her lasting reputation would be assured by them alone. They are monumental even when small, and universal even in their solitude. The National Portrait Gallery already has two of them. In the future, when Tate Modern comes to its senses and begins to concern itself with artists instead of trends, there will be a room full of Sarah Raphael portraits so that the new young artists may flock, marvel, and resolve to do likewise. They will learn, from an artist born for greatness, that it takes more than a concept to reflect life. No matter how far she strayed into the abstract, humanity was always her subject, and all the grief that went with it. Human grief gave the coherence to her exuberance, the chest-voice to her joy. For all her conspicuous blessings, it was part of her genius that tragedy was not strange to her: but to lose her so abruptly is a hard way to have it proved.

Independent, 17 January 2001

ALDOUS HUXLEY THEN AND NOW

When we were young, clueless and longing to be profound, what a thrill it was to open a novel weirdly entitled *Eyeless in Gaza*. The thrill was doubled when the author turned out to be quoting *Samson Agonistes*. 'Eyeless in Gaza at the mill with slaves.' At one point in the text a pair of lovers are lying on the patio when a dog falls out of an airplane and explodes right beside them. A quotation from Milton and a canine kaplooey: sophisticated, or what? That, kids, was the kind of multilevel blast that Aldous Huxley used to give us when he was current. Nowadays, the titles of his books are more alive than his books, but still he won't lie down. The legend lingers. God-like in his height, aquiline features and omnidirectional intelligence, Huxley was a living myth. He was the myth of the man who knew everything. Inevitably he attracted contrary myths designed to shrivel his looming outline. To borrow the haunting rhythm of another celebrated Huxleyan title, *Point Counter Point*, it was a case of Myth Counter Myth. Among the counter-myths was the one about his holding forth on a string of topics at the dinner table. On every topic, he knew all there was to know. But a fellow guest noticed that all the topics began with the same letter. Suspicious, the fellow guest retired to the library and checked up. Huxley had been quoting verbatim from the *Encyclopaedia Britannica*.

That particular counter-myth had an element of possibility. Huxley did indeed know his way around the *Encyclopaedia Britannica*, from A ('This letter has stood at the heart of the alphabet during the whole period that can be traced historically') to Zygote ('the biological term for the fertilised egg ovum'). From one of his early essays we find that he owned a half-sized edition on thin paper and when travelling always had a volume of it with him. But from the same essay we learn that Huxley carried the volume only because he could not concentrate properly while on the move.

From all his other writings we must deduce that when at his desk and undistracted he read everything, and not just in the humanities but in science, history, politics, sociology, psychology and religion. You name it and he'd read it. Especially he'd read it when you couldn't name it. He made people who were merely quite bright feel worse than stupid: he made them feel narrow. In Britain, his land of origin, critical disparagement became common after his relocation to America in 1937. Even when set in Europe, hadn't those brittle young novels – *Crome Yellow, Antic Hay, Those Barren Leaves, Point Counter Point* – been flashily yearning for a wider world? So let him have it. But any British feelings that their star had deserted them were only an adornment to a more basic British feeling, expressed in an everyday motto you can still hear in the school playground, even from a teacher: 'Nobody likes a clever-dick.' Good riddance to scintillating rubbish.

When living in Britain, Huxley was already a presence in the American slick magazines: he was an adopted figure of fashion, showing up in *Vanity Fair* like Noel Coward or Cecil Beaton. When living in America, he was given space in *Esquire* for his views and photo-spreads in *Life* for his beautiful face, plausibly represented as the icon of higher thought: he was up there with Einstein. Fame in America, as usual, meant fame everywhere. While he was alive, Aldous Huxley was one of the most famous people in the world. After his death, his enormous reputation rapidly shrank, until finally he was known mainly for having written a single dystopian novel about compulsory promiscuity and babies in bottles, *Brave New World*. For that, and for having been some kind of pioneer hippie who took mescalin to find out what would happen. Where did he go? A glib answer could be drawn from the title of his first book of madly clever short stories: *Limbo*. A better answer might be that he vanished into the comfort zone where names are referred to with some confidence but not for the detail of what they did. People of a certain age might still say that so-and-so is like someone out of *Point Counter Point* but they will probably not have read it recently or at all. Only a specialist in post Great War literature could quote from *Crome Yellow* or *Antic Hay* the way we can all quote from *The Great Gatsby* or *Decline and Fall*. In the comfort zone, a reputation is fragmented into the sort of quiz questions finely calculated to ensure that beyond a certain stage you will not go on doubling your money. Which of these books was written by Aldous Huxley? Was it (a) *In Our Time,* (b) *Time and the River,* (c) *Time Regained,* or (d) *Time Must Have a Stop*? Would you like to phone a friend?

But the time might have arrived for Huxley's return to the discomfort zone, where we have to deal with what he said as a permanently disturbing intellectual position (point of view, counter point of view) rather than dismissing it as an obsolete set of fads and quirks. How should we live? Can nothing harmonize the turbulence of our existence? How can we stop development from destroying the human race? The questions that racked his brain are still with us. They drove him to mysticism in the end. If we don't want them to do the same to us, we had better find out how so clever a man should come to believe in the All, the Good, the Transcendental and a lot of other loftily capitalized words that look like panic disguised as tranquillity. Unless we are smarter than he was, which for most of us is a remote possibility, then our chances of escaping his decline into what sounds awfully like flapdoodle are remoter still. We need him back so that we can examine him. We need to know what happened in that clever head.

Shining a light in his eyes is a good way to start, because his eyesight, or lack of it, ruled his life more than he was willing to let on. He could talk about a wall-sized Paolo Veronese as if he could see it at a single glance. Actually he had to look at it a few square inches at a time. Chief among the many merits of Nicholas Murray's new biography of Huxley is that it appreciates the full weight of his early tragedies without overdoing the retroactive prediction of his future behaviour. But underdoing it would have been a grievous fault. One of the tragedies was the early loss of his beloved mother, another was the loss of a beloved brother, but those were merely devastating. What happened to his eyes changed the way he saw the world. Later on, as a grown man, he had to read about the discovery of antibiotics by holding his face very close to the page. Had they arrived earlier, his disease would have been cured instantly. As things were, he was left at the age of sixteen with only one eye functioning, and that only partly. He was still one of Eton's star pupils, but from then on nothing was effortless.

Nor should we conclude from the famous names of his school and family that he had been issued with a free pass by his background. His parents belonged to the working upper middle class, not the landed gentry. Most of the wealth in the house was the wealth of the mind, and he would have led no cushy life even had he been able to see properly. But his ruined eyes made the life of a writer into hard labour: right to the end, he was always hoping to score the hit in the theatre that would free him from the treadmill of piece-work, the forcing house of the multi-book contract, the debilitating chanciness of writing film-scripts. At the start, he showed heroic tenacity in continuing to prepare himself. At Balliol he went on reading at his usual rate of eight hours a day even if he had to do it with a magnifying glass. Sometimes not even the magnifying glass would work the trick. From his fluent prose style – it always loped along, even when its feet were no longer in contact with the earth – we could probably guess that he read Macaulay, but it is useful to be told that he read him in Braille. English was still a new subject at Oxford. Determined not to waste what was left of his eyesight on trash, Huxley read everything in English literature that mattered. He had already started to do the same in French literature while he was still at school. The result of his literary studies, formal and informal, was the solid foundation of what Murray calls his 'wide and easy allusiveness'. We are bound to acknowledge the wide, but should put a question mark over the easy. A macaronic tendency to drag in an untranslated quotation, whether in French, German, Italian or Spanish, would be a mark of his prose for the rest of his life, and could have been a tacit claim that there was really not very much wrong with his eyes at all, if he could take in all that print. In any audience for the ballet there is someone with a bad leg who knows an awful lot about dancing.

Against the odds posed by his comparative indigence and absolute injury, Huxley had managed to give himself a magnificent preliminary education. But somehow it had to be turned to account, or he would have lived out his life as a schoolteacher whose pupils could guy him behind his back to his face. The option of enlisting as an officer and joining the bulk of his generation in the graveyards of the Great War had been providentially removed by his affliction. Instead, his front line was Garsington, the country house where Lady Ottoline Morrell assembled around her the most glittering cenacle of the time: Bertrand Russell met T. S. Eliot's wife there, with the usual results, and D. H. Lawrence was present to study the hyper-cultivated *haute bourgeoisie* that he would later despise in print for having presumed to tolerate his rebellious nature. Eyeless in Garsington, Huxley orated to the gathering because he was unable to read faces well enough to pursue an ordinary conversation. Erratically enthusiastic even in her first youth, Ottoline was often made fun of in retrospect, and especially by the writers she fed for free. Huxley was not guiltless in that regard. Though his adult life was marked by his personal kindness, he made a cruel caricature of her as Priscilla Wimbush in *Crome Yellow*.

In its form a throwback to the novels of Thomas Love Peacock, *Crome Yellow* teems with bright people making speeches, which often clog the action. When they make speeches, they tend to quote other speeches. Even the few dullards, wheeled in for purposes of contrast, are weighed down with learning. Take the journalist Mr Barbecue-Smith, allegedly the author of platitudinous bestsellers peddling spiritual uplift. Huxley introduces him thus:

> Mr Barbecue-Smith arrived in time for tea on Saturday afternoon. He was a short and corpulent man, with a very large head and no neck. In his earlier middle age he had been distressed by this absence of neck, but was comforted by reading in Balzac's *Louis Lambert* that all the world's great men have been marked by the same peculiarity, and for a simple and obvious reason: Greatness is nothing more nor less than the harmonious functioning of the faculties of the head and the heart; the shorter the neck, the more closely these two organs approach one another . . .

Mr Barbecue-Smith should have been a perfect oaf, but Huxley could not resist making him an oaf who had read Balzac. So the range of reference deployed by Mr Scogan, the accredited philosopher, can be imagined. Or rather it can't. One of his speeches goes on almost uninterrupted for two and a half pages, bringing in a large part of the history of civilization since the Renaissance as he forecasts the rationally ordered future. ('In the upbringing of the Herd, humanity's almost boundless suggestibility will be scientifically exploited . . .') Pursuing an idea, the characters come to a standstill and spout, like the fountains in the garden. From our viewpoint they would do better to pursue their passions. Luckily Priscilla pursues hers: the New Thought, the Occult – for her these things are objects of desire, tantalizingly retreating before her down the corridors of her own house, out of the French windows and into the ha-ha. Weirdly got up and tireless in her extravagance, she made the book a hit. Everybody loved it except Ottoline. Murray points out that Huxley apologized when she bridled, but goes light on the sad fact that he betrayed her all over again when he sent Lilian Aldwinkle heavily emoting through the pages of *Those Barren Leaves*. As the chatelaine of the Cybo Malaspina, a Garsington transferred to Italy, Lilian has all of Priscilla's mad passions plus one: she is a menopausal maneater aching to blend with just one more genius. Ottoline's loopy but boundless enthusiasm for the arts was too much fun to go unspoofed. Huxley couldn't leave it alone. In politeness, he should have. Luckily inspiration won the day. If all the other characters had been given the free rein he gave Lilian, *Those Barren Leaves* would never have ceased to be required reading. Alas, the book's leading man is a typical Huxley hero: effortlessly knowledge-able and seductive, he tires of all that and retreats to a hill-top to make long speeches about his quest for a higher form of Being. The speeches leave you longing for Lilian, who has Ottoline's lust for life along with her batso thirst for a fad. Ottoline might have been a bit much when bedtime loomed, but as a dinner-table hostess she was a genuine spotter of talent, and Huxley's talent was hard to miss anyway. The only question was about the form in which it would express itself. Those orations to the mesmerized company were the spoken rehearsals for his written act. Professionally, he began as an essayist, and it could be said that forty years later he ended the same way. It was his natural form, and Garsington was an important stage in its first flowering. He talked himself into it.

But the crucial event at Garsington came in the bewitching form of his future wife, Maria. Belgian, art-struck and delicately lovely, she had a crush on Ottoline but transferred it to Huxley. He was a lucky man. His mother reborn, Maria became the key to his existence. Maria took care of everything. She typed his manuscripts, set up the houses, fended off the pests and vetted his mistresses, generously employing her own charms to help him pull in the best qualified candidates. This biography features, for the first time in print, the story of the *ménage à trois* between Huxley, Maria and the Bloomsbury siren who went to bed with both of them, Mary Hutchinson. (Make way for the movie that will do for Huxley's back catalogue what *The Hours* has done for Virginia Woolf's.) Consid-ering that Huxley spent so much time in later years talking about the necessity to civilize the sexual impulse, it is instructive to find out that he himself civilized it by indulging it up to the hilt. In *Brave New World*, it will be remembered, the Alpha males of the ruling elite get their fill of the designated babes. It turns out that Huxley wasn't just dreaming.

The old, integrated European culture is generally thought to have been atomized by the Great War. But it had fallen apart only politically. Still the stamping ground of the artistically minded elite, Europe had entered on yet another civilized phase. For English people with the means and tastes to get themselves to a villa and stay there, France and Italy were homes from home. Effectively there were no borders for the enlightened. With Maria smoothing the way at the wheel of the new Bugatti, the successful young novelist Huxley was one of the star turns and recorders of a movable feast: Garsington on wheels. It is easy to see how he was confirmed in the insidious idea that the cultivated elite should cherish its separation from the mass of humanity. Though later on he softened the proclivity, he never quite lost his readiness to blame the *mobile vulgus* for multiplying at an indecent rate and thus threatening to queer the pitch for the patrician order. (He even had the percentages worked out: 0.05 per cent were in the club, 99.5 per cent were outside the rope. Hands up if you know where you fit.) The best we can say for him is that he did not fall for Fascism.

There were Fascists all around his Italian villas. Though he initially saw them as not much worse than a bad comic opera whose chorus was prone to fisticuffs, he finally concluded, and long before the Nazis established their full grip on Germany, that a totalitarian solution to the anomalies of mass society was worse than the problem. Commendably, he spotted most of the horrors of the Soviet regime straight away, even if he had no idea as yet that its own experiments in population-reduction would raise legitimate doubts about the supposedly ameliorative effects of that end. On the subject of ends and means – *Ends and Means*, among his best collections of essays, was another of his resonant titles – he was always capable of questioning the means. His weak point, however, was his failure to see that some of his favoured ends would inevitably bring questionable means into existence, and that the ends were themselves questionable for that reason.

But the weak point was yet to become obvious. For the time, he looked good. He wasn't the only one who thought that industrial society was turning out too many idiots (most of us still think it when we are caught in a traffic jam) and he was on the side of the angels, or seemed so, in proclaiming that one of the greatest dangers the idiots posed was that they might elect dictators. Not liking dictators qualified him as a progressive in a period when George Bernard Shaw saluted Hitler as an exemplar of creative energy and H. G. Wells nose-dived to the foot of Stalin's throne. As soon as 1928, in *Point Counter Point*, the crowning novel of his early success, Huxley had created a British proto-Fascist called Edward Webley. With a strident rhetoric that would later be echoed by Sir Oswald Mosley (moving in the same high social circle, Huxley had spotted Mosley on the way up), Webley makes long speeches about planning. The long speeches help to wreck what might have been a classic novel. An obvious victim of Huxley's multi-book contract, *Point Counter Point* has at least two different false starts folded into it (why leave them out when you can bodge them in to make up the bulk?) and many a promising conversation is padded out with the unlikely erudition that the author could shovel in so much more speedily than he could invent plausible action and follow where it led. Most of the characters do more orating than real talking. In other words, they speak essays. But the essayist who speaks for Huxley is not Webley. It is the brilliant (of course) writer Philip Quarles. 'The problem for me is to transform detached intellectual scepticism into a way of harmonious all-round living.' Quarles is after the All. Webley is after power, and Huxley knew there was a difference.

Nevertheless Huxley followed prevalent fashion in assuming that the mass industrial societies would have to be organized somehow, and some form of elite would do the organizing. Beneath the supposed satire of *Brave New World* there is a deep acceptance of this putative necessity. *Brave New World* was a sensation in 1932 and for long afterwards. When I first read it in Sydney in the late 1950s, all the male students of my generation were running around calling themselves Alpha plus and deciding which of our female contemporaries was the most 'pneumatic', the book's word for bedworthy. The book remains famous today, although it is probably now more referred to than read. When referred to, it is often supposed to be the book that did a better job of forecasting the future – i.e. our present – than Orwell did when he published *Nineteen Eighty-Four* in 1948. When read, *Brave New World* rules that supposition out. Orwell wasn't trying to forecast the future: he was trying, for the benefit of the West's gullible progressive intellectuals, to demonstrate what the Soviet Union was actually like to live in. Orwell's vision never came true for the West: a turn of events, or non-events, for which we partly have him to thank. After Orwell's book came out, Huxley was fond of saying – he said it to Orwell himself – that he, Huxley, had come nearer to projecting the probable future. But *Brave New World* hasn't happened either, and there are good reasons for thinking that it never can.

*

In the book, the Alpha ruling elite controls the supply of sex and drugs, the reward by which they themselves are consoled in their task, and all the lower orders down to the Epsilon semi-morons are kept in line. It hasn't turned out that way. Bill Clinton, nominally the top man of the ruling elite, never controlled the supply of sex: indeed the supply of sex came very near to controlling him. Drugs remain the enemy of the state, and not its friend. It might very well be true that a liberal democratic state would do better to make drugs legal, thus to pacify the inevitable dissatisfactions in a society where glamour and success are free to exalt themselves. But the same society which allows the freedom for such anomalies would be unlikely to apply the restrictions that would confine reproduction to approved genetic programming. Only a totalitarian society could line up the bottles. If Huxley was warning the world that even a free society might be tempted into totalitarianism, he was doing something useful. The society of *Brave New World* includes an outcast reservation of Savages – they can be visited in their theme park by helicopter – who suffer from love, pain and poetry as the human race once did before science came to its aid. Thus Huxley pays lip service to his humanist belief that creativity is too important a hostage to be given over to an ideal of improvement. But he was scarcely likely to aid his humanist cause by assuming that the alternative to planning wrong was to plan right. Deep under the book is the idea he had nursed from childhood and would never lose: one way or another an elite would have to be in charge. *Brave New World* doesn't attack that idea. It reinforces it, by leaving open the possibility that there might be a less flagrantly manipulative way for an authoritarian intelligentsia to determine the lives of the common people.

Huxley's fondness for the idea of 'intelligent and active oligarchies' (the term popped up in an article for *Harper's Magazine* called 'The Outlook for American Culture') might have sprung from his shortage of sympathy for the 99.5 per cent. No doubt he backed Eugenics for the same reason. But his pacifism was something else: it indicated a shortage of political nous. As a leading light of the Peace Pledge Union in the 1930s, he went public with his private notion that war would happen less often if more people could be persuaded to dislike it. The persuasion would be done by the enlightened. Somewhere in the glowing bowl of this pipe-dream bubbled the notion that human mentality, or at any rate the elite's share of it, would need to be transformed by some kind of collective access to a higher form of existence. Just as he could never accept that a decent system of ethics would be more likely to arise in a school for mentally handicapped children than amongst any intellectual elite no matter how attuned to the Transcendental, he could never accept that peace is not a principle, merely a desirable state of affairs.

Huxley, however, was not the only genius talking poppycock about politics, and few of the others had his cachet as a novelist. His success in Europe was complete but his need to earn would never let him rest. Financially, he was walking a tightrope no stronger than a shoe-string. His reasons for resettling in California were excellent, and there was not even any need to lower his exalted standards of smart company. Garbo and Chaplin greeted the Huxleys as fellow lions. The stars bowed to the sage. With America's share of the next war drawing ever nearer, Los Angeles became one of the intellectual centres of the modern world as the European refugees flocked in. Thomas Mann had been on the *Normandie* with the Huxleys on the trip over (characteristically the modern Goethe had travelled first class but uncharacteristically he condescended to visit them in steerage) and now he was sharing the same sunlight. With Thomas Mann at the other end of the dinner table, Huxley had no need to think that he was casting his pearls before swine. And even Mann was only *primus inter pares*. The intellectual level was stratospheric. Above all, it was European, and in the best sense. Huxley heard all the news from the old world. America didn't isolate him. But it did insulate him.

Those who think that Huxley's fine brain turned to mush in California are apt to ascribe his declension to the mind-bending stuff he took in: the Wisdom of the East, hallucinogenic drugs, ESP. They tend to ignore the significance of what he left out. He never really grasped that the war was bound to be something much bigger than a conflict between nationalisms; that it would leave, when the smoke cleared, no alternative to accepting liberal democracy as the only guarantee of liberty; and that in liberty there could be no such thing as a universally shared Perennial Philosophy. (*The Perennial Philosophy*, his book compounding all the positive thoughts of West and East into a tutti-frutti of moral uplift, was the equivalent for its day of *It Takes a Village*: there was nothing in it to object to, which was, of course, the objection.) As even Solzhenitsyn would fail to realize, the one thing a free society can never be is spiritually united. It was a conclusion Huxley might have been forced to if he had been in the middle of the action. But he was fatally well placed to go on believing that mankind could and should aspire to a higher state than the one it was stuck in.

There was nothing perverse about his interest in Eastern philosophy. Millions of people, after all, had always believed that there was something to it, and he can be forgiven for assuming that swamis who could tie their legs in knots or inhale mercury through the penis might have commerce with the Transcendental. Nor was there necessarily anything preposterous about his conviction that mind-expanding drugs might be worth looking into. If we ourselves are contemptuous of materialism, people who appear to have everything must be excused for bombing their own brains in the hope that there might be something more. Huxley's interest in ESP, however, showed a serious anomaly. At Duke University, Professor J. B. Rhine had made extra-sensory perception a laboratory study. Huxley was not just keen to believe that Rhine had discovered something substantial, he was keen to believe that statistical analysis had proved Rhine correct. If Rhine had been correct, research into telekinesis would now be funded by General Motors. Huxley knew next to nothing about statistical analysis, or any other form of mathematics beyond arithmetic and school-level algebra. He was right to be interested in all forms of science. His sympathy for the sciences made him a permanently valuable advocate for their creative connection to the humanities. (In 1962, the second last year of his life, when the Two Cultures controversy between C. P. Snow and F. R. Leavis shook the intellectual world, Huxley's intervention was a welcome note of sense.) But he was debarred from the language that connected the sciences themselves. His admired and admiring friend, the great astronomer Edwin Hubble, could understand everything Huxley meant when he talked about music. But Huxley had to take the mathematics for granted when Hubble talked about the expanding universe. About science, the best Huxley could do was talk an extraordinarily good game.

Damagingly, his fluent talk about science mesmerized even him: the biggest trap lying in wait for eloquence, no matter how self-deprecating. He tried to sound scientific about the world's political crises, and trying to sound scientific made him insufficiently critical. He went on advocating solutions to problems he had misstated. He kept on wondering how an economy could be rationally planned, without ever wondering whether it should be. As if Malthus had been right instead of wrong, Huxley still thought that if the world's population increased beyond a certain point all those people would run out of food. Never having placed sufficient weight on the fact that it was the advance of technology that had increased the birth-rate, he placed still less weight on the capacity of technology to solve the problem. He also failed to notice that all the famines took place in countries that were not democracies. With ideological extermination reducing the world's population almost as fast it might otherwise have increased, he still thought that the world's bugbear was nationalism, as if, for totalitarianism, nationalism were not merely a tool, and as if totalitarian states would not go on killing people whether at war or not.

Safely domiciled in the part of the world that suffered least from deprivation and political instability, he took his surroundings for granted as a set of conditions from which Mankind could aspire to higher things, instead of as the higher thing that the rest of the world could only aspire to, and with increasing desperation. Had he been less cushioned, the war and its aftermath might have made more impact on his thought. Exiled to New Zealand, Karl Popper was forced by the memory of his experience in Europe to reach a minimum definition of democracy. It was the system in which the government could be replaced at the people's whim, so that no oligarchy, intelligent or otherwise, could perpetuate itself in power. The implication was that the 99.5 per cent didn't need to be instructed. All they needed was to have a vote. Exiled to Britain, Friedrich von Hayek reached the conclusion that a liberal democracy could have a planned economy only to the point where government regulations protected the people against arbitrary injustice: but to restrict the free market beyond that point would always result in totalitarianism. In Paris when the war was over, Albert Camus, having seen both Nazis and Communists in action from close to, defined democracy as that regime created and sustained by those who know that they do not know everything.

Challenged only by orthodoxies that derive their notion of harmony from a supposed access to exalted knowledge, these were the conclusions that would dominate the world we have lived in ever since. Huxley missed out on every one of them. All the opportunities were there for Huxley in America, and he even, for a while, took one of them: the biggest one. Unfairly overshadowed by Evelyn Waugh's *The Loved One*, Huxley's own response to California, *After Many a Summer Dies the Swan*, was and remains his best novel by miles. (In Britain it is more catchily called just *After Many a Summer*: an American editor must have thought the allusion to Tennyson needed spelling out.) Though his earlier novels show far more inventiveness than is nowadays credited to them, they were indeed all silted up by the Nilotic flood of his compulsive erudition. Rather than pursue to a conclusion the promising situations he had set up for them, his characters quoted literature to each other at length, and he often neglected to tip off the reader about what literature they were quoting. But even without the learned bric-a-brac, every novel would still be weighed down by long speeches (essays, in fact) from guru figures preaching about the necessity of a higher state of Being than the one enjoyed around the dinner table.

In *After Many a Summer* there is less of that. For once there is a gusto for the vulgar. Every Los Angeles novel before or since quotes the billboards, but Huxley quotes them with enjoyment: possibly because the words were big enough for him to read. Sunbathing on the heights of her magic castle, Virginia Manciple the pure-minded sex-pot harks forward irresistibly to Candy Christian. Virginia knows nothing. She merely exists, while the men go mad around her. She had one antecedent: the raunchy, truth-telling servant girl Gladys in *Point Counter Point*. But Gladys got only a few paragraphs, whereas Virginia is there from first to last. The William Randolph Hearst figure, Mr Stoyt, was bound to be aced out by *Citizen Kane* (Huxley got there first, but Welles got there the most), because Stoyt doesn't even have any dignity to lose: but all the other characters are so alive that they speak their own individual dialogue, instead of getting it from the library that Huxley carried in his head. Even more unusual for Huxley, the import of the book is that the observable world is inexhaustible: i.e. is all there is. The shattering final scene when the immortal people turn out to be apes is there to tell us that wherever humanity might be heading, eternal life isn't it. But there is still one guru, and he is an indication that Huxley's quest for a more significant life is not dead yet. Huxley had always liked the idea of small, locally governed communities that would stave off the nefarious pressure of highly industrialized world states, thus to leave the minds of the elite free for the seeking of the All. This time the guru's name is Propter, and his little workshop is designed to supply his simple needs. But the workshop is equipped with machine tools. Now where did *they* come from?

Nevertheless that one marvellous novel pointed the way Huxley might have gone next. But finally it, too, is programmatic, and proves that Huxley was right to suppose that he was something less than an artist. Ever since Garsington, the Huxleys had been great friends with D. H. Lawrence, who died in Maria's arms. In homage to Lawrence, Huxley had always been generously ready to concede that feeling might rank above thinking. (F. R. Leavis, self-appointed guardian of Lawrence's posthumous reputation, loftily 'dismissed' Huxley in favour of Lawrence, while declining to notice that Huxley's written appreciations of Lawrence left his own in the cold.) But Huxley needed a humility beyond generosity: he needed a realization that there was indeed a harmony that would make a unity out of eternal conflict, and that art was it. He loved art: art of every kind. His essays prove it. Nobody in modern times has ever written better about poetry. When he talks about Chaucer, he beats even Chesterton, and sends you running to the nearest copy of *The Canterbury Tales*. From the arts angle, to read all the essays in sequence is like being enrolled at the college of your dreams. They have all recently been published again as *Complete Essays* in six scholarly volumes (not scholarly enough in places: too many of those foreign phrases still go untranslated) edited by Robert S. Baker and James Sexton. With due acknowledgment for their efforts, however, a less daunting way to read Huxley's essays is in the original collections. *Music at Night*, his collection of 1931, would be a good place to start, because it shows how wide-ranging and undogmatic he could be when writing about his proper field, the humanities. In saying goodbye to the avant-garde, Huxley wasn't embracing philistinism – he was just saying that popular art was more likely to stay in touch with ordinary human truths. It remains an important point, and made by so learned a man it carries extra force.

Despite the inevitable outbursts of bookishness, Huxley's essays are easy to read and always informative, even when all they now inform us of is how much of his scientific information has gone out of date. What they lack is the inventiveness he lavished on his novels but seldom followed up because he wanted to philosophize instead. If the novels were too much invaded by the essay, his essays were insufficiently invaded by the novel, which is a soul-searching instrument, a register of the mind's adventures, not of the memory's contents. If he had put everything into his expository prose, he might have lifted it to the extra level at which it would have been possible to question his own assumptions, and thus make a drama out of a monologue. An essay written in 1956, 'Hyperion to a Satyr', hints that he might have invented the New Journalism all on his own, had he realized the potential. Beat this for an opening sentence. 'A few months before the outbreak of the Second World War I took a walk with Thomas Mann on a beach some fifteen or twenty miles south-west of Los Angeles.' And it gets better. 'At our feet, and as far as the eye could reach in all directions, the sand was covered with small whitish objects, like dead caterpillars. Recognition dawned. The dead caterpillars were made of rubber . . .'

It turns out that the beach no longer has such visitations, thanks to the post-war construction of the gigantic Hyperion Activated Sludge Plant. Unfortunately for the reader, the intervention of the sludge plant is the point where Huxley's tactics as an essayist return to normal. He gives us a long, global and no doubt reliable history of sewage treatment since earliest times, but neglects the opportunity to argue with himself. For a writer who had spent his lifetime decrying the onward march of the Machine and rooting for the ideal of the small, self-sustaining community, an industrial development the size of the Hyperion Sludge Plant should have given him pause to reflect. No small community could make a thing like that. But his knowledge was doing all the talking, as it so often did. If he had dramatized the conflicts that were inherent in his concepts, he might have arrived at the higher reality that was already all around him: liberal democracy. He might have helped to defend its inexorably confusing multiplicity against the attack that would be a long time coming but is now here: the attack from the imposers of harmony, the adepts of the All. Alas, he was one of them, and all because of his ineradicable belief – his one and only stupidity – that the mass of mankind was too dense to see the inner light. But there is no mass of mankind. There are only individuals, and except in a society that is not free they will always refuse to be persuaded that their everyday lives are not worth living. You can tell from their faces, if you've got eyes.

New Yorker, 17 March 2003

FORMULA ZERO

If the wheels can come off an empire, they came off Bernie Ecclestone's Formula One empire in Austria on Sunday, when Rubens Barrichello, under team orders from Ferrari, slowed down to let Michael Schumacher take the win. A zillion petrol-heads all over the world were thus given an unmistakable television signal that they might as well have been reading the business section of their local newspaper. The fix was in.

The bottom line and the finishing line had revealed themselves as being identical. The chequered flag was a cheque book. As a writer by profession, I resorted naturally to word-associations for the expression of my outrage. Elsewhere in the audience, there was probably a circus performer in Singapore who threw knives at his wife, a removal man in Auckland who heaved a chest of drawers out of his attic window. How apt, I exclaimed to one of my study walls full of strangely noncommittal books, that the stitch-up should have taken place on a circuit called the Spielberg. Ideally, a racing circuit should be called the Hitchcock, to convey suspense. But when they're racing on the Spielberg, a tent-pole production devotes a mountainous investment to a predictable materialistic outcome with a spiritual quotient the size of a mouse. My metaphors became ever more mixed, the books ever more aloof, scared by the spectacle of homicidal fervour from a man who had previously confined his passion to fingering their spines. Far away in Vancouver or perhaps Valletta, a dog-breeder was filling a bucket of water in his bathroom.

For many years now, the circus performer, the removal man, the dog-breeder and I have all been united by our propensity to rearrange any schedule so that we can be seated before the television set to watch the latest Grand Prix. All of us might have been racing drivers in a different life. Circumstances having dictated otherwise, we are willing to let other men do the driving for us. Admittedly, they have unfair advantages, these others: they are younger than us, better-looking, and they combine a flat stomach, sensitive fingers, unflinching valour and an enormous salary into a sexual signal that few fashion models can resist. The injustice cries to Heaven, which gives no answer. But we are content to let it happen. Let these gifted children race for us: as long as they race.

Most of the time they do, and there is none of them who is not admirable for his bravery alone, quite apart from his skill. Mainly owing to the tireless efforts of Jackie Stewart, Grand Prix racing has become much safer than it was when I started following it, but it is still a lot more dangerous than writing. Takuma Sato could easily have been killed last Sunday when he was side-swiped, and Juan Pablo Montoya was only a split second from being decapitated in the same accident. The cars are very strong in the cockpit area nowadays, but a high-speed impact against the wall can still do to a driver what it would do to an egg in a steel box, no matter how tightly the box fitted. Ayrton Senna was killed that way, Mika Hakkinen almost was, and the carbon-fibre front end was only a partial protection for Schumacher's legs when he sailed across the gravel-trap and smacked the tyre-wall at Silverstone. It was probably the fresh memory of that incident which helped to persuade the Ferrari management they should stack up the championship points for him while they could, even at the expense of disappointing the watching world and painfully reminding Barrichello that his newly extended contract carried a price in enforced humility. Schumacher has a big say in what the Ferrari team does. He ought to: if they are on top now, it is because he put them there, and he did it with his practical wisdom as well as with his supernatural flair. If he shared in the Spielberg decision through patching into a conference call from the radio in his car, he, too, was probably remembering Silverstone. Brave by nature as they all are, he would have been more likely to recall what happened to his season than what happened to his leg. I would have remembered the leg. Johnny Herbert had his career ruined by smashed legs; Jacques Lafitte had his career ended by them; and Allesandro Zanardi, racing in the American version of the same sport, actually lost them. I, however, am not Michael Schumacher.

No, you're not, says the Devil in my ear, *and it's because you're a human being*. But the Devil is a casuist as always. Admittedly Michael

Schumacher is an easy man to dislike. It was especially unfortunate for him that the driver he stole the victory from on Sunday was the hardest man to dislike in Formula One. Rubens Barrichello, a cuddly toy already nicely padded under his padded suit, is the top half of Kelsey Grammer with a nervous smile to match. Nobody so quick was ever so cute. But Schumacher gives the air of having arrived at ordinary affability only by hard study, and the mask – modelled in rubberized plaster by Arno Breker as an archetype of Aryan manhood in a rare benevolent mood – is always apt to slip. He is a natural sporting hero, but sportsmanship is not his natural mode. Let us not, however, distract ourselves with a glib antipathy. Sportsmanship is not the natural mode of Formula One.

It might be, if it was just the drivers racing each other. But the manufacturers are racing each other too, and there's the rub. Whatever way the formula is readjusted, a few manufacturers will each produce a car decisively faster than the rest of the pack, even if their respective cars are only fractionally faster or slower than each other. But the cost of producing a competitive car is so enormous that none of the top manufacturers can protect their investment for long unless they have a champion, or at least a championship contender. The best drivers are attracted to the best teams. So instead of the contenders being spread evenly through the field – as they might be through an equivalent of the draft-pick system in American football – they are quite likely to end up two to a team. Theoretically the sharpest competitive edge in Formula One racing is between the two team-members; and indeed this might be so; but only if the team allows them to race each other. Unfortunately it is in the team's interest to allow only the opposite, so that the prospective champion is placed out of danger from his closest rival.

Effectively this has been true of modern Grand Prix racing since the beginning. When Mercedes-Benz made their post-war comeback, they had a car that nothing else could touch. Juan Manuel Fangio was signed to come first, Stirling Moss to come second; and that's the way the game played out, even if Fangio loftily ceded Moss the British Grand Prix as a consolation prize. (To prove it was a gesture, Fangio trailed Moss over the finish line by only a few inches. To prove he was accepting a poisoned chalice, Barrichello, poor mite, did the same at Spielberg.) If they had really been racing, Moss might have given Fangio a proper fight in every race on the calendar. But it never happened except in our dreams. Team orders prevailed. As Richard Williams pointed out in these pages yesterday, team orders prevailed again in 1958, when Phil Hill handed Mike Hawthorn the last race of the season and the championship along with it. When Mario Andretti and Ronnie Petersen were both driving for Lotus, the fix was blatant. Petersen was at least as fast as Andretti, and sometimes needed all his skill to come second: he was treading on the brakes while Andretti was treading on the accelerator. In a later period at Lotus, Ayrton Senna, then clearly on his way to supremacy, refused to have Derek Warwick as second driver because Warwick might have been a contender, and Senna thought the team lacked the wherewithal to support two contenders. Senna was probably right, but I remember the way Derek Warwick's wife pronounced Senna's name at a restaurant near Monza on the evening before Warwick went out to race in the slower car to which Senna's realism had condemned him.

Before his untimely death canonized him, Senna's realism was commonly called ruthlessness by everyone in the sport. To a certain extent it was: when he figured out that he would become champion if Prost could be removed from the track, he accomplished this by driving into Prost, thereby removing himself as well, but with the championship in the bag. He engineered the impact straight after doing the sums in his head, thus setting a bad precedent. Such behaviour brought Formula One close to being a Demolition Derby, but it was a natural consequence of a team's readiness to back up its top man, even if his conscience-free behaviour was at the expense of its second man. More recently, tighter rules have made the deliberate shunt harder to pull off, but as with the professional foul in football, the spirit of the thing is hard to quench.

This depressing *Realpolitik* comes with the financial commitment of the top marques: they can't afford anything less. Unfortunately we petrol-heads are on their side. We don't want an Americanized version of the sport. In American motor racing, all the cars are effectively the same, and thus run beside each other, to the delight of the American audience, which, although not as dumb as it is often painted, certainly likes things simple. But out here in the undeveloped world – i.e. everywhere except America – we like the complications of Formula One, and so do bright American refugees like Juan Pablo Montoya. Montoya follows in the tradition of

Mario Andretti and Jacques Villeneuve: charioteers in standardized cars who had fun racing wheel to wheel, but came over to Formula One because it was more interesting. And indeed the interest of Formula One is enormous: the leading manufacturers, interpreting the formula to its optimum, come up with machines so precisely attuned to the task that the full distance is as far as they can run before they fall apart while being measured by the scrutineers. Petrol-heads all over the planet bore their friends and families helpless with details of the technology before being left alone in front of the piece of technology that eventually generates the cash-flow for the whole adventure: the television set.

Rarely does it provide a thrilling spectacle. Apart from the occasional shunt, it mainly shows you a procession. But to the fan, the questions are endless, convoluted and enthralling. Can the driver of the car that is a second slower make up the difference? Montoya almost can, but Schumacher either knows how to get another second of supremacy out of the Ferrari engineers or else he is driving faster than ever. It is all, inherently, fascinating to think about. Unfortunately it is also as boring as hell to look at. Schumacher and Montoya won't be racing wheel to wheel unless their cars are identical in performance, and at the moment the Williams is a second down. The only people racing wheel to wheel will be the two drivers of the quickest marque, because their cars *are* identical in all respects. And if the championship is at stake, the fix will go in.

As things stand, Ferrari, Michael Schumacher and Barrichello will go before motor racing's governing body the FIA on 26 June, for the Spielberg production to be investigated and solemnly ruled upon. It will be a date in the annals of fatuity. First of all, there can be no doubt about what happened. Second, Formula One is ruled by Bernie Ecclestone. He invented it, and it's all his. On the whole he has done a brilliant job. He rules a community richer than most small countries; nobody gets hurt except volunteers, and he diverts hundreds of millions of people across the globe, thus fully justifying the hundreds of millions of pounds he diverts into his own pocket. There is nothing Bernie can't arrange. It was a wonder that he confined himself to slipping the Labour Party a mere million. Nobody who has ever met him would have been surprised if Cherie Blair had started smoking two packs of Silk Cut Extra Mild every day in public. But now he has to arrange something more challenging, and pronto. Formula One is in the toilet, and looks all the more obscene because the toilet is made of gold. The only cure is to outlaw team orders. The circus performer, the removal man, the dog-breeder and I can all just about stand watching two cars the same colour coming first and second. It's the reward for technical achievement. But if their drivers aren't racing each other, there is no reason to watch at all. For the next Grand Prix, the huge world-wide television audience will be down by at least one name I can vouch for. Anyone who feels like joining me can register his protest the same way I will. It can be done at the touch of a button. You can bet that the man in question will get the message. It's a boycott, Bernie: either the racers race, or I read my books instead of shouting at them.

Postscript

I had a record stretching back for decades of being interested in Formula One no matter how tedious it got, so if even I was protesting, the sport was in trouble. Not long afterwards, the boom was lowered on team orders, but nothing could stop the Ferraris dominating the events. Michael Schumacher and Rubens Barrichello were racing each other again, but they would have had to crash into one another if any other marque was going to have a chance. It's in the nature of the sport that a little difference makes all the difference. But the technical edge of a leading team would matter less if the cars could pass each other. It is downforce that makes the sport incurably uneventful. The Americans, in their various versions of open-wheel racing, equalize the technology to make sure that the cars can race beside each other. So the American versions are superficially more exciting for the TV audience than Formula One, just as baseball on TV is superficially more exciting than cricket. Actually there is a lot happening in a baseball match that can't be deduced from the image on the screen by anyone except an expert. Usually it takes the commentators on the spot to pick the difference between a slider and a knuckleball. But the overt struggle for supremacy is easy to follow, and even if the pitcher pitches a perfect game – no hits, no runs – the spectacle is not necessarily boring. Formula One is often a boring spectacle even to those who understand the details of its true fascination, the struggle behind the scenes for the decisive technical edge. As a result, there are always a few voices in favour of Americanizing the sport. But only a few. Like food, Formula One is something that the world does better than America, and it adds to the fun that the Yanks don't get the point. The fun needs a lot of adding to, but there is cause for pride even in that. My promise not to watch, incidentally, lasted for two whole races.

In the following season, elaborate new rules were introduced to even things out, and in the 2005 season the rules were made more Byzantine still, to the point where, near the end of a race, it could be won by the car whose tyres were in the best shape. The dominance of the Ferraris melted away in the technicalities, and there were several occasions when the final laps became almost as exciting as watching kittens fight. The downside, however, was that the television commentary became full of talk about tyres.

A MAN CALLED PETER PORTER

When I first read him more than forty years ago, I thought Peter Porter was the same age as he is now. Impressed by his evident conviction that the modern world was essentially a Technicolor version of one of those Dürer woodcuts in which the knightly rider was flanked by death and the devil in his journey through a landscape ravaged by war and plague, I pictured the agonized artist as a gaunt, white-bearded figure hunched under a velvet cap, knocking out his long-pondered apocalyptic visions by candlelight. Not that his poems creaked: indeed they hurtled. But however long their rhythmic breath and legato their line, they still sounded like the last gasps of a sage, and all the sages I had ever heard of had whiskers on them. It was a poem by him that first led me to look up the word 'eschatology'. The poem was called 'The Historians Call Up Pain' and 'eschatology' was the last word in it. Up until then I had thought I understood roughly what he was talking about in the poem, although I had to delve deep into my memory of Sydney University First Year History lectures on the Holy Roman Empire in order not to be stopped cold by the word 'chiliasm'. Deep down, as in a sunken cathedral, a bell rang: 'chiliasm' was something to do with the millennium. But what was 'eschatology', precisely? I didn't even know what it meant vaguely. I had seen it before, probably rendered phonetically in my own lecture notes, but I had put off finding out. Now it was time, although I couldn't tell then that it would be far from the last time that I would owe some of my education to Peter Porter. Whenever, today, I read 'The Historians Call Up Pain', its colloquial yet erudite sonorities bring back for me a place, a year and a state of mind in which I was ready for a new kind of mental thrill. The historians may call up pain, but the poets, when you remember your first encounters with them, call up the past: your past, the personal past, a stage of your life. Popular music works the same way, but no popular music ever had a vocabulary like this.

> We cannot know what John of Leyden felt
> Under the Bishop's tongs – we can only
> Walk in temperate London, our educated city,
> Wishing to cry as freely as they who died
> In the Age of Faith. We have our loneliness
> And our regret with which to build an eschatology.

I had very few books in those days. Luckily one of them was the Concise *Oxford English Dictionary*. 'Eschatology' turned out to mean the branch of theology concerned with the end of the world, the last things. Well, that fitted. He was talking about the last things as if he were one of them. It was death-bed stuff. In the absence of any biographical notes on the author, I judged his home address to be a veterans' hospital, possibly an iron lung. But I was in pretty bad shape myself. The year was 1962, I had just arrived in London, I was cold and broke, and it felt as if life on earth were coming to an end. Here was a poet who spoke to my condition. Suddenly I was less alone. I had become a walker in our educated city: a description that took redoubled force from the consideration that I could hardly afford to ride on a bus. In the winter of that year I was living in a large paper bag on the floor of a kind English acquaintance in Tufnell Park. His name was Geoffrey Hindley, he was working for Thames and Hudson at the beginning of what would be a distinguished career in publishing, and he had pressed upon me a slim volume called *The Less Deceived*, by some librarian called Philip Larkin. By Larkin I was suitably bowled over: was encouraged, even, to rise from my paper bag and write a few more poems of my own.

But Peter Porter I discovered by myself, and the impact, as a consequence, was even more to be cherished. Nobody had said: 'You must read this: it's good.' The poems themselves said that, especially when I didn't fully understand them. The first poems of his I read were in a little book called *Penguin Modern Poets 2*, published that year. There comes a time in your life when most of the places you go to you will never go back to, and nearly all the books in your shelves you will never read again. But this little book I go on and on picking out of its shelf. Until recently I bought every copy of it I found second-hand, until I realized, with a jolt of guilt, that I might be depriving some other young walkers in our educated city of an essential discovery. The volume featured three poets: Kingsley Amis, Dom Moraes and Peter Porter. I knew who Kingsley Amis was. There were whole passages of *Lucky Jim* that I could recite from memory, and very soon I felt the same way about his poetry, which would have ranked him unquestionably among the most celebrated modern poets if it had not been for the gravitational distraction of his celebrity as a novelist. Moraes I had somehow read about in a copy of *Isis* that had reached Sydney before I left. He was an *Isis* idol, and when I read his poetry I thought that 'idol' was a fair description, although in the not very long run he turned out to be one of those poets whose mature accomplishments come mainly at the beginning.

But of Peter Porter I knew nothing, and only realized that he might be of Australian origin from internal evidence in his work. Provocatively scattered among the copious European references there were weatherboard churches, Bunya pines, milk shakes, the Canberra Temperance Hotel – which was perhaps in Brisbane instead of Canberra but certainly wasn't in Salzburg or Vienna – and (the title of a poem, this) 'Phar Lap in the Melbourne Museum'. Phar Lap had been born in New Zealand but it sounded as if Australia might be the point of origin for the poet, a long way from John of Leyden and the bishop's tongs. You will guess correctly that I wasn't reading many literary magazines at the time, or the literary pages of the heavy newspapers. I couldn't afford to. Sometimes, today, I wonder heretically whether that kind of ignorance wasn't the best state to be in. I wasn't reading about books, I was reading the books themselves. I was in contact with the primal stuff, just as, when I slept, I was in contact with the floor. Sleeping without a mattress is not as dangerous as flying without a net, but it can be equally invigorating. So can reading and judging poetry without the pre-emptive commentary of professional intermediaries, or even the fervent introductions of an enthusiastic adept. If there is a line in the poem that gets through to your mind unannounced, like a cosmic particle appearing in a bubble chamber, then it must have been sent by real power. Phrases, lines and whole stanzas by Peter Porter had that kind of brain-drilling impact. Let me start with the phrases.

'Once bitten, twice bitten.' It was part of the title of one of his poems – later I found out that it was the actual title of one of his early collections – and I thought straight away that it was the ideal condensation of an attitude: a proclamation of innocence, and a protest against being saddled with it. By now, all of his friends have long known that he makes a point of presenting himself as the incorrigible gull; just as, less self-destructive in his personal habits than almost anybody else, he has always presented himself as someone about to disintegrate physically; and, more neatly dressed and better-looking than almost anybody else, as the werewolf in the cheap Daks suit that 'hugs me in its fire' with a classical overtone of the shirt of Nessus. I hope, before the busy scholarship of posterity gets a look in, that the accumulated ribbing from his delighted colleagues will help to establish that his tremulous stance as a victim of fate was always more persona than actuality. As the Italian scholars have taught us, there is a difference between Dante *personaggio* and Dante *poeta*, and it would need a very clueless student to believe that Porter *poeta*'s large and still steadily increasing achievement was not the product of a confident artist in majestic control of his output. But it should also be said that he has never pretended to be in control of events. From the beginning – and this is surely part of the reason why he never sounded young – he had an unusually honest capacity to register the terrifying indifference of circumstances to the individual, no matter how blessedly gifted that individual might be. The proper name for this is humility, but he was always ready to play the patsy in order to underline it. He made himself out as the man who, in everyday life, would not get what he wanted, and who was twice as culpable for wanting it. Once bitten, twice bitten: that whole idea in four words, or six syllables if you prefer. It was chastening to see him pack such a lot in. He was eloquent, but reading him made me feel garrulous, as it still does.

Another pregnant phrase: 'If only I had a car'. Porter *personaggio* was without wheels. It followed that he could not get the kind of girls he had already condemned himself for wanting, the 'girls in Jensens'. That was yet another phrase, and one I painfully remembered when I paid my first visit to the King's Road and saw what he meant. When London first began to swing in the early 1960s, it soon became horribly clear that the promised freedoms of swingingness would not include freedom from the fixed exchange rate between cash and sex. The most desirable young women seldom walked when they could ride, and what they were riding in was not only priced to be out of reach, it was shaped to look it. The sinuous apex of the bird-puller car market was reached by the Marcos sports two-seater, which was actually designed so that young women of a certain refinement would be obliged to lie down straight away when they got into it. But Porter had already seen this happening in the 1950s: 'Love goes as the MG goes' was another phrase potent with impotence. As the patter and rattle of bongo drums leaked from the coffee bars, the MG was usually going home to where the rich lived, and the girl was in it. Either in the passenger seat or behind the wheel, she – I loved this phrase – 'vanished on the road to Haslemere'. There was a longing in the cadence: the longing for what was teasingly available, except that you couldn't have it. I knew just how he felt. Moving up from phrases to lines, I can still quote from memory the line that made me realize I knew. 'The flesh-packed jeans, the car-stung appetite.' He was deriding himself for desiring what he was not supposed to desire. Here was poetry that said, in its every stanza, that art and history were what counted. Yet it was also poetry that admitted the full force of the advertised consumer world. Despite the consolations of high art, money mattered; possession mattered; even breeding mattered. Out there in Haslemere, he said, 'the inheritors are inheriting still'.

He could not bring himself to say they shouldn't, because he could not deny his hankering to share their privileges. That suave matinee idol Harold Macmillan, in his scarcely believable role as prime minister, extolled a way of life 'based on the glossy magazine'. Macmillan actually *said* that, and your political convictions did not have to start very far to the left of centre for you to find what he said absurd. But Porter did not find it absurd that anyone should *feel* that way. He said that it had always been that way. It had been that way in the time of the Jacobean playwrights. The MG girl on her way to Haslemere showed up in a poem called 'John Marston Advises Anger', from which came another compulsorily memorable line that I found myself mouthing glumly as I watched the high-born miniskirts swerve out of reach. 'It's a Condé Nast world and so Marston's was.' For the line to work, you didn't have to know exactly what John Marston wrote. At Sydney University I certainly hadn't known, although some of the examination questions suggested by their wording that it might be prudent to pretend I did.

But you did have to know what a Condé Nast world was. It was a world of advertised attractions that really did attract. It was useless to say they didn't. Not even Trotsky would have been able to get away with saying that. He might have said that they shouldn't, but that was a different thing.

Porter was saying that they shouldn't, but saying it from the position of strength – strength, not weakness – conferred by his admission that they did. By conceding his own lust, cupidity and frustration, he was reinforced in his bold determination to identify those same things as important strands in the coaxial central cable of history. Here was the fruitful paradox behind his eschatological manifesto: if, despite the threat of nuclear annihilation, there was to be a future after all, it would be made of the same stuff as now, because now was made from the same stuff as the past. There would be a future as long as there were humans. In the long run, even inhumanity was human. After all, sharks don't build concentration camps, and ants only look as if they do. Cruelty has always been a component of the human world; things had always been terrible for just that reason; and creative for the same reason. Life, although it had always seemed, to the sensitive and cultivated, as if it were coming to an end, was a continuity. This was a cold consolation to draw, but if you were living in a paper bag it had a charm all the more seductive for being ascetic. I found myself unable to stop learning his poems by heart.

Later on, when I wrote my first critical article about him, I fatuously chastised him for his obliquity, and said that his poetry fascinated me despite my not much liking it. In just such a way, men say of the woman they love, but who is giving them a hard time, that they love her but don't much like her. The truth always was that I loved his poetry, and in the matter of his obscurity I didn't even have the courage of my convictions. Scarcely able to read French prose in those days, I had nevertheless put in the hours memorizing the great modern French poems since Tristan Corbière and Laforgue – my recital of them would have made a comic performance excelling even the only intact speech in French by Edward Heath that we have on tape – and I had reached the correct conclusion that Rimbaud's 'Bâteau Ivre' was an inexhaustibly rich treasure house, a true masterpiece. But I still believed then, and partly believe today, that its magnificence comes at a high price to the reader, who sometimes can only feign to be abreast of its action. Rimbaud had once written a new poem on a cafe table, using his own fresh excrement for ink. If I had been the proprietor of the cafe, I would have charged the pungent little vandal double for the mess and triple for not making sense. But he did make a kind of sense, of course; and so, I gradually realized, did Porter. Not all that much later still, when I wrote about Porter again, my conclusions reflected my awareness that the way I had learned his poems without trying proved that they had a certain kind of intelligibility after all. In fact they were as understandable as could be while getting so much in.

In recent times I have had the privilege of collaborating and contending with him in several series of dialogues for ABC radio in Australia, and the subject of intelligibility in poetry has often come up. Though I still think he is too generous in finding Wallace Stevens valuable as a whole instead of in part, and in rating the later, deliberately opaque Ashbery as high as the earlier Ashbery whose thread I can follow, the Porter line on this point is hard to rebut. It is not, after all, as if he endorses holus bolus the idea of poetry written for poets, and he positively dislikes the idea of music composed for musicians. Loving music too much to put up with the music that has no inspiration beyond its own technique, he feels the same way about poetry. He would be no more likely to quote J. H. Prynne than to whistle anything by Schoenberg after *Verklaerter Nacht*. But he is right to think that there can be poetry that makes sense of itself beyond any argument paraphrasable in prose. The evidence has been in since the very earliest Eliot that tone and intensity can do the uniting in a poem, and the weight of its fragments can hold them together. Porter still writes that way, becoming clearer and clearer as he goes on only because he has always written that way, and his approach to a theme has become part of our repertoire of recognition. As now, so then, his characteristic tone was of a delphic bulletin you couldn't quite follow, illustrated with imagery you couldn't forget. If he had not been driven by a sense of structure, he would have been impossible to remember even by the phrase. But I found myself remembering him by the line, and then by lines that linked inseparably to each other: by stanzas, in other words, although he did not always write in stanza form. Indeed his signature form in those days was a one-piece oratorical extravaganza, welded together by the arc-light intensity of the paragraphs that had been drawn into it. Paragraphs like this:

> Outside by the river bank, the local doctor
> Gets out of his '47 Vauxhall, sucking today's
> Twentieth cigarette. He stops and throws it
> Down in the mud of the howling orchard.
> The orchard's crouching, half-back trees take the wind
> On a pass from the poplars of the other bank.
> Under the scooping wind, a conveyor-belt of wrinkles,
> The buckled river cuts the cramping fields.

The poem was called 'Death in the Pergola Tea-Rooms' and soon I knew it all, or anyway I could recognize any line from it, which is really the way we learn poems by heart unless we deliberately set out to memorize every word for performance on stage. Because I never put in the donkey work of rote learning, I never could recite the whole of 'Who Gets the Pope's Nose' without making a mistake. But it wasn't often in the next four decades that I failed to remember its last stanza, especially when I was suffering from the effects of too many cheap cigars in a hot foreign city: New York in August, for example, or Buenos Aires in January.

> And high above Rome in a room with a wireless
> The Pope also waits to die.
> God is the heat in July
> And the iron hand of pus tightening in the chest.
> Of all God's miracles, death is the greatest.

Here was an unmistakable music, but it wasn't the music of a bush ballad. It was a music that went back at least as far as the tough articulation of Metaphysical poetry: at least as far as Donne. The displaced and reinforced rhythms of St Lucy's Day were somewhere behind the way that line about the heat exploited the momentum of the line before it. 'The Pope also waits to die.' (Wait for it.) 'God is the heat in July'. Even remembering it under your breath, you had to observe the heart-seizure of delay as the first line turned over into the second: the staccato pause before a dying fall. But Porter didn't have to go to Rome to get the sense of Christendom winding up. He could get that in Harrods. There had been nothing

startling about that death knell since *The Waste Land*. What was startling was the energy: the snap and syncopation of the dirge, as if the
orchestra on the tilting deck of the Titanic, instead of playing 'Abide
With Me', had broken into 'I'll Be Glad When You're Dead, You
Rascal You'. Porter, like Amis and Larkin, might be delivering the
opinion that England was all but dead: but, again like them, he was
delivering it in an English language that was as exultantly alive as it
had ever been in its greatest flowering. This was what I liked best
about the best of the poetry that came out of what was journalisti-
cally known as the Movement: that it continued to be lyrical even as
it pushed on into the furthest reaches of resignation, whether
personal or political. (Porter is usually assigned membership in the
Group, which followed the Movement: but by now, I think, we can
afford to shuffle those tags, if we can't forget them altogether.) Those
two areas, the personal and political, were connected, of course: for
an artist they always are – one of the main reasons why artists aren't
to be trusted in their political opinions. But Porter, especially, could
scarcely conceal the impresario's delight he took in assembling the
last things and counting them off. If this was a *Totentanz* out of
Holbein, it had lyrical flourishes out of Charlie Parker. Perhaps
motivated by my personal circumstances at the time – there was a
Haslemere girl in a cashmere twin-set and tartan skirt ensemble who
didn't want me to touch any of it or even breathe out in the same
room – I especially admired the closing couplets of a dramatic
monologue called 'Made in Heaven'. Clearly the poem was taking its
heartfelt revenge on some unattainable young woman who had
married for advantage, and had lived to repent at leisure. But the
poem didn't take advantage of her: not, anyway, in the sense of
neglecting to admit the power of her initial attraction, which had
been a poetic power.

> As she watched her husband knot his tie for the city,
> She thought: I wanted to be a dancer once – it's a pity
>
> I've done none of the things I thought I wanted to,
> Found nothing more exacting than my own looks, got through
>
> half a dozen lovers whose faces I don't quite remember
> (I can still start the Rose Adagio, one foot on the fender)
>
> But at least I'm safe from everything but cancer –
> The apotheosis of the young wife and the mediocre dancer.

Cancer was much mentioned by Porter, and would go on being so. He wrote about it as if he had it. He didn't, but it was a useful marker for a theme. Written out more fully, the theme was that the body disintegrates. He wrote about his as if it already had, so for his younger friends it has been progressively more startling as the years go by to find him looking almost exactly the same as when we first met him. (Those of us who have lost our hair find it hard to suppress the suspicion that it has been stolen in the night by those who have kept theirs.) Written out more fully still, the theme would be *carpe diem*; and the same theme, elevated beyond the personal, would be that society disintegrates too. In this last aspect he fitted all too well into the frame already assigned to Larkin and Amis, both of whom seemed to thrive on the idea that it was all up with the England they loved. In Porter's poems about the First World War trenches – 'Somewhere ahead of them death's stopwatch ticks' – there was plangent evidence that he had the same sense of a tragic loss of social coherence, even though his sense of the injustice that had made the coherence possible was equally vivid. From all three poets, the sense of an accumulating historical disaster seemed to me irresistibly persuasive on the artistic level, even though I personally believed that history was getting better all the time. By and large I endorsed Sartre's joke on the subject. It was the only successful joke Sartre ever made, so we ought not to be shy about repeating it. Sartre said that he could have no real quarrel with history, because it led up to him. My three chosen poets had the opposite opinion: even Amis, superficially the most self-assured of men, showed signs to the keen eye that he felt disabled by the cultural wreckage piled up around him, and neither Larkin nor Porter made any secret of it. That they could treat this shared vision with an eloquence precluding sentimental indulgence was surely a sufficient claim to seriousness. In my own view of the way poetry in the English language was coping with post-war reality, their accumulating achievement was at least the equal of what was coming out of America. By picking on these three I don't mean to say that there weren't other Britain-based voices who impressed me just as much. I found much to memorize in the early collections of Thom Gunn, and David Holbrook, though he turned hopelessly chatty afterwards, had one poem, featuring the daunting line 'I do not want to have had my day', which for me permanently nailed down the feeling of falling apart that comes when you realize you have postponed your visit to the dentist for so long that he will call an ambulance if you finally turn up and open your mouth. Donald Davie, whose Olympian stance and *de haut en bas* critical attitude drove me high up the wall for the way they left Herbert von Karajan looking diffident, had one poem that I thought splendid: 'Remembering the Thirties'. And, of course, one good poem is enough to make you a poet. (One major poem is enough to make you a major poet, for that matter: another bogus classification crying out to be ignored.) But these three poets, Amis, Larkin and Porter, were clearly going to go on being excellent, no matter what the critical opposition.

Some of the critical opposition was home-grown, and from a powerfully influential source. Al Alvarez not only thought that Ted Hughes got in more of the *angst* of the modern world than Larkin, he thought that the American heavyweights got in more of it than any of the British English poets at all. Lowell and Berryman, according to Alvarez, were the grownups: the poets who flew in the face of danger using its hot wind for uplift. Sylvia Plath's suicidal commitment was a proof of seriousness. In comparison with the American effort, anything home-grown was threatened by the enervating heritage of the genteel. Only Hughes and a few others could hope to break out, to break through. Alvarez's presentation of this line was dramatic, obviously heartfelt, and, as always with him, argued with a command of rhetoric all the more persuasive for being tersely stated. I didn't like to disagree with him. Reverential by nature for anyone who can write an elegant sentence, I have never enjoyed disagreeing with the essayists I look up to. Lately, as an Australian who believes that the still-flourishing Japanese right wing should not be encouraged in the convenient fantasy that the United States tricked their country into World War II, I felt bound to disagree in print with Gore Vidal, from whose earlier prose I learned a lot about the assembled sweep of plain rhythms. But in condemning American imperialism he had neglected to examine the extent to which he himself carried American imperialist assumptions, and I thought he needed to be called out on it. Much earlier, and presuming hugely on my scarcely established position, I had felt obliged to call Alvarez out on what I saw as the dangerous extent to which he was praising as professional commitment the careerist presumption of the American poets in taking the whole world's suffering upon themselves, not just as if it were their responsibility – all artists feel responsible for everything – but as if it were somehow mirrored in their own interior drama, their unblushingly proclaimed psychic turmoil. It was the desire and pursuit of the whole: a potentially misleading desire, in my view, and a doomed pursuit. Convinced that Hannah Arendt had been right when she said that an artist is making a mistake when he views his own soul as the battlefield of history, I thought that the British poets, in restricting their historical and geographic scope, had a better chance of being true to the world beyond their set borders. None of them would have been capable of the blasphemous foolishness shown by Lowell when he described the dead Sylvia Plath as rising in her saddle to slash at Auschwitz. The British poets didn't even mention Auschwitz. They had their own worries closer to home, and universal resonance, I thought, was more likely to arise from the treatment of those than from self-consciously, and self-servingly, addressing a big theme.

But Porter did mention Auschwitz, as confidently as he mentioned the Battle of the Somme. One of my British poets was an Australian, and what separated him from Larkin and Amis was the overt, stated inclusiveness of his historical range. Neither Amis nor Larkin much liked the place they called 'abroad'. Porter loved it. Much more than theirs, his curiosity was at home everywhere, and in all times. He ranged further, and further back, than the *echt* British poets had chosen to find legitimate. Larkin deplored the very idea of writing poems about paintings. Porter wrote poems like that all the time. Amis, in one of his finest poems, harked as far back as a European princeling who had to bring his land to ruin before finding out the elementary truths about decent behaviour. But Amis rarely harked back as far as ancient Rome. Porter practically lived in ancient Rome: he was on quipping terms with Martial. I hadn't thought Alvarez right when he argued that provincialism was a disabling flaw in the home-grown poets. But there could be no doubt that he was right in thinking them provincial. They were proudly so; and effectively so; but being so, there was bound to be a great number of reference points that they left out, even when the reference points were in their heads. Porter used what was in his head. There was a lot in there, and, as we now know, there was to be a lot more.

In the best sense, the body of Porter's work, both in poetry and in prose, is an education: an education both for him and for us. From his published beginnings, he showed none of the mandatory Movement diffidence about a display of erudition, and he has gone on to build in print the university that he never attended, and which can't be attended by anyone in any other form but this. What the Germans call *Bildung* is made manifest as the work of a lifetime. His body of poetry, in particular – his enchantingly conversational prose serves, but as a subsidiary – reminds us of how Proust would bring into his great book anything that excited him about the humanities. A critical anthology as well as a novel, *A la recherche du temps perdu* is forever in search of understanding: the understanding depends on what has already been understood by others; and Porter's poetry works in the same way. In the field of classical music alone, his poetry could serve as the ideal introduction for the beginner, and the ideal reminder for the adept that the treasury of achievement belongs not to an individual nation, or even to the West, but to the world. And as with culture, so with history, the vivid pyramid built by this benevolent pharaoh marks a tomb asking to be plundered before it is even occupied. How does Porter escape Arendt's dictum that an artist should not pretend that his own soul is a measure of all the world's agonies? He escapes it by his selflessness. All who know him in real life are well aware that he is the most selfless of men. But there are seemingly humble people who are monuments of conceit in their public work. You would not need to know this artist personally, only to know his art, to realize that he is selfless even at the centre of his creative impulse. His famous poems written in honour of his first wife's tragic death are merely the most obvious example. It took a supremely self-effacing poet to make a subject of the awkward fact that he couldn't help seeing such an event as an opportunity for expression as well as a cause for grief. Milton never did that for Lycidas, or Tennyson for Hallam. You might say that it was a specifically modern possibility. But even in the framework of that modern ambition in which anything at all is grist to the mill, it was a specifically Porter possibility. Confessional poetry, of the type exemplified by Lowell when he printed his ex-wife's letters without permission, excuses itself from ordinary responsibility on the grounds of a higher calling. Porter excused himself nothing. He made a self-examining, and indeed self-flagellating, subject out of the poet's unstoppable urge to make poetry: the necessary shame of seeing inspiration in absolutely anything. You could call it reckless-ness if you liked, but surely a better word was courage. The hallmark, then as always in his work, was a sense of intellectual adventure.

Being Australian helped. Offended locals often remarked of the post-war Australian expatriates that they were treating the world as their oyster. Actually the first wave of Australian invaders into Britain were music-and-theatre people stretching from Melba through to Robert Helpmann. The second wave were the war correspondents: Chester Wilmot, and the commanding figure of Alan Moorehead, later to be the acknowledged mentor of Robert Hughes. Porter, Barry Humphries and Michael Blakemore were in the third wave, and the bunch to which I belonged were only the fourth. When my lot hit the beach, it was still not realized that these occasional incursions were adding up to a determined assault. No doubt I was unusually clueless, about that as about everything, but as I dug my foxhole below the dunes it took me some time to realize that Porter had already gone in miles ahead by parachute. As Baudelaire pointed out, writers who use military metaphors are laying claim to a belligerence whose physical consequences they would prefer to avoid. So I hasten to point out that there never was a battle, because there was never any real opposition. Except perhaps in Haslemere, Britain welcomed us with an open house. No criticism from the natives ever equalled the opprobrium from home, where for a long time the expatriates were thought of as having sold Australia short. But in fact they exemplified Australia's greatest strength, and carried it with them as a flag. They were confident that the whole heritage of the arts, learning and history was theirs to be possessed by right. If anything about the Australians appalled the resident intellectual, it wasn't their accents or their table manners, it was their world-eating propensity to loot the museum of history. Unplaceable by class, the Australians had no inhibiting expectations that they would be stopped at the door. The native assumptions of accreditation by background did not apply to them. They did not believe that they needed a double-barrelled surname to walk at large in Europe.

In the literary field, Porter was an early example of this freedom. Now nobody is astonished to find Germaine Greer helping herself to a naked young male body by Praxiteles, although she hopes that they will be astonished by what she says about it. The old Empire has turned upside down; Australia is a productive demonstration that the colonial investment didn't all end up in the debit column; and Australian voices help to project the English language, with a nasal shading to the vowels perhaps, but with all its resources fully and boldly deployed. Peter Porter is a big part of that Australian expatriate story, which even in Australia is now seen to be part of the total Australian story of an emergent, rapidly proliferating culture growing on the well-grounded trellis of political stability. Australian literature has become a thing of glamour. Inevitably, Australian poetry, as a highlight of the literary picture, is becoming a thing of glamour too. Already there is talk about which one is *the* Australian poet, Peter Porter or Les Murray. Actually both know that there are many other Australian poets who count. Murray writes about the late Philip Hodgins, and Porter about the late John Forbes. Both died too young; neither ever really left home for long; and they would have been enough to establish a national literature by themselves.

But really there is no such thing as a national literature. There is only literature, and a nation can participate in it only by ceasing to be nationalistic. Nor is there any competition between stars, although the illusion that there can be is the inevitable consequence of literature being granted journalistic attention. It could be said that Murray is to Porter as Heisenberg is to Einstein: Murray dealing with the subatomic world, and Porter with everything from the atomic to the celestial. It could be said that Porter is to Murray as Haydn is to Mozart, with the proviso that nobody can understand Mozart who does not love Haydn. These hyperbolic things could be said, and probably will be: but they should be said only as part of the inexorable buzz of commentary that swarms around a successful literature – a buzz it craves, so why protest? It's a Condé Nast world. But it's also a more serious world than that, and Porter has helped to make it so. In doing so, he exults, even as the last things gather to overwhelm him. One of his later collections is called *Fast Forward*. Perhaps I am especially fond of it because it is dedicated to me: one of the biggest honours I have ever been paid; an honour so big that I have never known how to thank him. The poems in *Fast Forward* are, as always, mainly flashbacks, but they do point to a future: a permanent future, built on the hope that is left when all disappointments have been faced. You can't say that of those who have suffered unjustly, and Porter is always careful not to say it. But he does say it about himself, even in the poem called 'Dejection, an Ode'. If this is dejection, listen to the vaulting music of its opening paragraph. I said earlier that in his first poems you could hear a sonority both colloquial and erudite. Well, here, in 1984, you still could, and even today you still can.

> The oven door being opened is the start of
> The last movement of Rachmaninov's Second Symphony –
> The bathroom window pushed up
> Is the orchestra in the recitative
> Of the Countess's big aria in *Figaro*, Act Three.
> Catch the conspiracy, when mundane action
> Borrows heart from happenings. We are surrounded
> By such leaking categories the only consequence
> Is melancholy. Hear the tramp of the trochees
> As the poet, filming his own university,
> Gets everything right since Plato.

But the strength of those lines depends on a poet who knows that he can't get everything right since Plato: he can only desire to, and be as true as he can to the desire. Everything is indeed connected to everything else, but suffering is still suffering; injustice is still injustice; and the four horsemen will always ride. Our consolation is that even our metaphors of destruction are human creations. The same horses once drew the sun out of the sea. They are there again above the portico of St Mark's in Venice, and one of them shakes its mane in Bernini's fountain in the Piazza Navona. Art, thought, the humanities, creativity itself: it really is a unity. Until it ends, it can't be started again; it can only be added to; and Peter Porter, by helping us to see, hear and think in his way, has added to it abundantly. What was it he said about the fifth horse, Phar Lap? It was his simple excellence to be best.

TLS, 13 February 2004. This essay was first presented as a keynote lecture for the Peter Porter symposium organized by the Graduate School of English Studies, University College London, and by the Robert Menzies Centre.

Postscript

At the Melbourne Festival in 2000 Peter Porter and I went on stage to do nothing for an hour except talk together about literature. The unscripted dialogue attracted a gratifying amount of approbation, much of it centred on the fact that we had done a lot of quoting from memory. To the blushing surprise of us both, to quote from memory was hailed as a rare and daunting display of skill from the exotic past, like scrimshaw, wampum and the ability to measure distance in miles instead of kilometres. The dialogue between literati was itself regarded as an unusual form – which, indeed, in the non-English-speaking countries it is, although in Germany and France it is common, and in a country like Argentina it is a staple (Borges and Sabato said some of their best things while talking to each other). In the age of the interview and the profile, two question-and-answer forms that have been worked to death, Porter and James found themselves in the delicious position of having started something new. The word of mouth got out from Melbourne and the media moved in. Radio really counts in Australia – the publishers would rather have their writers on radio than on television – so we had good reason to be pleased when the ABC invited us to try the same dialogue form from a radio studio. The distinguished arts producer Jill Kitson pressed the buttons in Melbourne when Porter and I went into the ABC's studio in London for our first series of six dialogues. The programmes went to air in Australia as soon as post-production had been completed in Melbourne (post-production consisted mainly of toning down my heavy breathing) and they worked well enough on the national network for Jill Kitson to commission another series, which was duly followed, in the course of time, by a couple more, to a grand total of twenty-four programmes, with, we hope, more to come. In the pub after each recording session we try to make it a rule not to talk away the material for the next one, but the rule is hard to keep. Most writers, when they talk to each other at all, talk about sex, money, physical ailments, and the unending perfidy of their literary enemies. Porter and I talk about those things too, but we have always enjoyed talking about the arts, and the chance to do so on the air has been very welcome. With an uncharacteristic stroke of acumen, I retained the webcasting rights, and all the dialogues can be heard in the audio section of www.clivejames.com, together with, in the video section, a television dialogue we recorded in my living room. (Viewers are free to decide whether faces add anything to voices: I think, in this case, on the whole, not.)

Like many of the best things in life, this broadcasting partnership happened by accident, and was followed up more through self-indulgence than through altruism. But every writer cherishes the dream of setting the young on fire, even if only by a cigarette butt tossed casually over the shoulder, and when we meet young people who say that they were inspired by what we said to rush off and read the books we were talking about, we can congratulate ourselves for all those guilty hours when, the last two left after a long lunch, we went on arguing about everything we knew. He knows more than I do, but if I live long enough I might catch up; and that's the way some of the young Australian writers feel about both of us, or so they say. Not that you can trust them 2.54 centimetres. We're agreed on that.

WEEPING FOR LONDON

Watching Sydney Harbour Bridge erupt in coloured flames to mark the end of a brilliantly organized Olympics, I wept for London, city of the dud Dome and the invisible River of Fire. Last week I was in Paris and wept for London again. When I first came to Europe forty years ago, the London Underground and the Paris Metro were much of a muchness, even if the Metro had the edge in style. Now the comparison draws tears of blood. I still travel on the Tube, but only when there is no appointment waiting for me at the other end, because it might have to wait forever. Also I am getting to the age when a long staircase starts to matter. The Metro has an unfair advantage there: dug shallow, it needs few escalators. But in all other respects the Metro's supremacy is a clear case of intelligent management. At St-Germain in the late afternoon there was still room down in the entrance hall for a Piaf-style singer good enough to pull a shower of coins. The train came hissing in on rubber tyres: wheels that don't wear out rails. In my carriage there was a live jazz band playing Hot Club standards. When I got off at Châtelet, there was a woman on the platform reciting Racine's *Phèdre* from memory at the top of her voice. Nobody mocked her and many listened in respect as the perfectly cadenced alexandrines resonated in the station's tiled vault. She was probably a nut, but might well have been a licensed busker like all the others. Look at the map and you will see that all I had done was cross the river, but the trip was nearly as rewarding as walking across the Pont Neuf, and anyway it was raining. Remember the last time you rode the Tube when it was raining outside? How far did you get? We apologize for the inconvenience caused. Or, to quote the new and even odder version: 'We apologize for the inconvenience caused to your journey.' Sir Kingsley: 'Yes, but it isn't my journey that's being inconvenienced, is it? It's me, you posturing sod.'

With John Prescott in charge of the finances, no doubt the London Undergound will soon be fixed. After all, he was the man who saved the Dome. Without him, it might never have happened, and we would have been deprived of the best long-running entertainment since Nimrod. I have always liked the cut of Prescott's jib: in this government he stands out like a good man in a bad advertising agency. But it is often a mistake to suppose that honesty precludes cunning. I bet it was his idea to stage the Dome jewel robbery, which would have been a PR masterstroke except for one crucial flaw. The fact that it was a *bungled* robbery was right in keeping: the spectacle of the blaggers bouncing their hammers off the armoured glass was pure Dome. But the actors playing the Sweeney mucked it up. They should have arrested those children for singing hymns without a licence. Instead they arrested the villains, thus transmitting a fatal air of competence. The essence of Dome culture is that nothing must go right.

A few years of weathering have done nothing for the Centre Pompidou, which still looks like the place where all the world's sewer pipes come together in conference, but you have only to go up to the fourth floor to see what it's got that the Tate Modern hasn't: paintings, properly arranged. Again, the French have a certain advantage. Most of the painters were either born in France or else lived there, so the State had ready access to so much good stuff that not even Goering could manage to take it all away. But as with the Metro, those in charge know how to capitalize on a lucky break. The paintings are grouped so that you can see who's who, what's what, and when's when. (The same applies on the top floor of the Musée d'Orsay: first the Impressionists, then the Post-Impressionists. Get it?) The present arrangement of the Tate Modern is meant to discount all that, purportedly so as to enlarge our comprehension, really so as to make the holes in the collection look less gaping. But the conceptual drivel written on the walls is a fearful price to pay, and the Domish impulse behind the whole effort is neatly symbolized by the glowing plastic cap placed on top of an otherwise impressive building in order to deconstruct its monumentality. Over and above the candy-tipped chimney, or rather below it and stretched out flagrantly ahead, is that unbeatable testament to architectural arrogance, the bridge that rewrites the rules of suspension with such virtuosity that it doesn't work. Paris has one just like it, but I doubt if its creator will get another commission for anything bigger than a funfair ticket booth. In London, the same genius responsible for our non-crossable bridge is currently erecting a new obovoid office block for the Mayor, who sensibly doesn't want to move into it. A country in which Ken Livingstone has become the voice of reason is facing an uphill struggle.

Sydney learned its lesson with the Opera House, which looks sensational from the outside, but whose revolutionary inside caused more trouble than it was worth. The architect, rethinking the conventions of theatrical design to fit a restricted lateral space, proposed to work all the major set-changes from the fly tower instead of the wings. It was expensively discovered that the conventions of theatrical design, like the conventions of bridge suspension, are not susceptible of being rethought. The remains of Utzon's innovatory fly-tower mechanism are now rusting in a paddock somewhere near Broken Hill. Eventually London's Dome will reach a similarly obscure destination, but not before all the wrong solutions have been explored. The free market has spoken: the Dome site is worth hundreds of millions more without the Dome. But in this instance the government, with its dwindling prestige on the line, can't afford to listen to the free market. And you never know, the government might be right for once. It was Mrs Thatcher who gave Blair's Britain the courage to be born. Believing that the State should get out of the economy, she never grasped that a government is either *dirigiste* or it is nothing. Apart from an utterly buggered broadcasting system, her lasting and festering bequest is the transport chaos for which Blair will have to take the rap. The Dome might not be enough to sink him – he can always blame Heseltine, dump Prescott or hand Simon Jenkins a poisoned peerage – but the trains could lose him the next election.

Postscript

Though the Dome went on costing three million pounds a month even to keep empty, its hollow thunder was eventually stolen by the Diana Memorial Fountain, a purpose-built safety hazard whose running expenses perpetually increase as new dangers are revealed. So far it has not bred sharks. In Edinburgh, the Holyrood parliament building was the most ludicrously overpriced folly of the lot, but you had to go north of the border to get its full impact: it was never a joke in England. It should be said that a building project can go a hundred times over budget and still be worth it. Australians justifiably proud of the Sydney Olympics should remember that their beloved Opera House cost its weight in lottery money. The question turns on whether something considerable has been created. It doesn't have to be admirable: just considerable. I don't especially like either the Centre Pompidou or the Mitterrand pyramid at the Louvre, but I would have to admit that there are many people who do. About the Dome, no conflict of opinion is possible. The number of people who find it even faintly interesting would be lost in one corner of it, if it had any corners. My invention of the Dome Culture was meant to be a joke in passing, but as time went on I started to wonder whether it might not be possible for a whole nation to contract a case of butter fingers. Christopher Booker put in some valuable work when he identified the virus of Neophilia, but Dome Culture goes far beyond that. Dome Culture is not just an urge to make it new, but to make it ridiculous. The disease may have started with the inexplicable decision of the Post Office, back in the 1970s, to paint a few pillar boxes yellow, to see if the public liked it. The public hated it. So the experimental pillar boxes were painted red again. But that was not true Dome Culture as we have now come to know it. If the Dome gnomes had been in charge, every pillar box in the country would have been painted yellow, and the response to the subsequent outcry would have been a vast multi-media publicity campaign to prove that red is bad for your eyes.

An extra note – This book was already at the stage of its first proofs when the London transport system was attacked on July 7th, 2005. For a while I thought of removing the above piece, because for once the London Underground was no source of mirth. But within a month people were making the same old jokes again, especially the one about the stupidity of any terrorist who thought that the tube needed to be bombed in order to be brought to a halt. I don't think it was a case of people revealing their essential callousness: they were merely revealing their sense of proportion. I, for one, had spent too much time earning my Freedom Pass to waste any more of it by not using public transport: a free ride is a free ride. The next bunch to attempt an outrage seemed to lack the secret for building bombs that went off, and one could look forward to the day when young people clever enough to succeed in such an enterprise would lose the urge to try it, having noticed, perhaps, that the older men who encouraged them to seek martyrdom were seldom keen to seek it themselves.

ATTACK OF THE KILLER CRITICS

The recently published ninth edition of the excellent *Chambers Dictionary*, which has always prided itself on keeping up with new words, gives only one meaning for the noun 'snark'. It's 'an imaginary animal created by Lewis Carroll'. The tenth edition might well carry a second meaning: 'an adverse book review written with malice aforethought'. If the dictionary were compiled on historical principles, like the *OED*, it might mention that the word 'snark' was first used in this sense by Heidi Julavits in a long and fascinating article about book-reviewing which she published in *The Believer*. Elsewhere in the literary forest, Dale Peck, writing in *The New Republic*, had attempted to bury Rick Moody's novel *The Black Veil* under an avalanche of abuse. Generating a small but widely reported kerfuffle, this event was one of the stimuli for Julavits's contention that the killingly personal review might be reaching such epidemic proportions that it needed its own monosyllabic name, like plague.

Plausibly claiming to have identified an industry-wide rise in the prevalence of a snide tone, she called such a review a 'snark'. Since the noun derives from the accepted slang adjective 'snarky', one would have thought it a rather understated label for an attack whose intent is often not merely snide but outright murderous. Better acquainted with the concept of gangsterism in public life, the Germans call a killer review a rip-up and the Italians a tear-to-pieces. But this new, English word – English tempered by an American determination to believe that serious people can lapse from high standards only in a temporary fit of civic irresponsibility – is probably violent enough, and it certainly captures the essential element of personally cherished malice.

The desire to do someone down, or indeed in, is the defining feature. Adverse book reviews there have always been, and probably always should be. At their best, they are written in defence of a value, and in the tacit hope that the author, having had his transgressions pointed out, might secretly agree that his book is indeed lousy. All they attack, or seem to attack, is the book. But a snark blatantly attacks the author. It isn't just meant to retard the author's career, it is meant to advance the reviewer's, either by proving how clever he is or simply by injuring a competitor. Since a good book can certainly be injured by a bad notice, especially if the critic is in a key position, the distinction between the snark and the legitimately destructive review is well worth having.

But there's a catch. Over the course of literary history some of the legitimately destructive reviews have been altogether too enjoyable for both writer and reader. Attacking bad books, they were useful acts in defence of civilization. They also left the authors of the books in the position of prisoners buried to the neck in a Roman arena as the champion charioteer, with swords mounted on his hubcaps, demonstrated his mastery of the giant slalom. How civilized is it to tee off on the exposed ineptitude of the helpless?

Back in the early nineteenth century, the great historian and mighty reviewer Lord Macaulay might have said that the ineptitude of the poet Robert Montgomery had not yet been exposed. And indeed the dim but industrious Montgomery had grown dangerously used to extravagant praise, until a new book of his poems was given for review to Macaulay. The results set all England laughing and Montgomery on the road to oblivion, where he still is, his fate at Macaulay's hands being his only remaining claim to fame. Montgomery's high style was asking to be brought low and Macaulay no doubt told himself that he was only doing his duty by putting in the boot. But Macaulay must also have given thanks that it asked quite so blatantly. Montgomery had a line about a river meandering level with its fount. Macaulay pointed out that a river level with its fount wouldn't even flow, let alone meander. Macaulay made it funny, but from Montgomery's viewpoint funny would surely have meant worse. He had been exposed for all to see as a writer who couldn't see what was in front of him.

Across the pond, Mark Twain later did the same to James Fenimore Cooper. Making hilarious game of the improbabilities in Cooper's tales of arcane woodcraft, Twain's essays about Cooper have been American classics ever since. So have Cooper's tales, but only in the category of enjoyable hokum. After Twain got through with him, Cooper's literary prestige was gone. Reading the reviews that did him in, it is impossible to avoid the impression that Twain would have enjoyed himself less if Cooper had been less of a klutz. Like Macaulay, Twain used someone else's mediocrity as an opportunity to be outstanding. This is getting pretty close to malice, for all its glittering disguise as selfless duty.

The same applied in the twentieth century to Dwight Macdonald's attack on *By Love Possessed*, a novel by James Gould Cozzens that was not only a bestseller but had a huge critical success. Think of the reception for *Captain Corelli's Mandolin*, switch it back to 1957, and you get the scale. Cozzens had his face on the cover of *Time*. Macdonald thought the face needed a custard pie, and wrote a review that convincingly exposed Cozzens's masterpiece as portentously arranged junk. Macdonald usefully did the same for the clumsy prose style of the New English Bible, but there he was attacking a committee. In the case of *By Love Possessed* he was attacking a man. When you say a man writes badly, you are trying to hurt him. When you say it in words better than his, you have hurt him. It would be better to admit this fact, and admit that all adverse reviews are snarks to some degree, than to indulge the sentimental wish that malice might be debarred from the literary world. The literary world is where it belongs. When Dr Johnson longed for his enemy to publish a book, it was because he wasn't allowed to hit him with an axe. Civilization tames human passions, but it can't eliminate them. Hunt the snark and you will find it everywhere.

New York Times, 10 September 2003

Postscript

Living in a brand-name economy, Americans like to see things clearly labelled even when it comes to matters of the mind. A literary controversy has to be marked CONTROVERSY so that the readers can prepare themselves for the unusual spectacle of people disagreeing with one another in print over a question that really has no simple answer. In America there must always be an answer or else there is something wrong with the question. Written at the kind invitation of the *New York Times* – whose cultural section has lately entered

on a welcome new phase of encouraging the unclassifiable voice –
the above piece will probably seem elementary to a British or
Australian reader, but I reprint it here as an example of what can
look like boldness in a context where consensus is held to be the
norm, rather than the aberration. Had I been bolder still, I could
have pointed out that the star critics of a dominant media outlet –
the *New York Times* for example – have far too much power, because
any common opinion on a given topic in the field of the arts is
largely imposed by them. Snarky reviews in minor publications do
little damage. They can easily be put down to personal ambition.
But the ponderously delivered verdict of a tenured critic in one of
the major publications can kill a play or a book overnight. The
verdict doesn't have to be hostile, merely 'negative', a word meaning
anything less than ecstatic. How these concentrations of influence
emerged in a democracy is no great mystery: Tocqueville foresaw
just such an outcome. The mystery is why so many intelligent people
should accept the resulting mediocrity of opinion as a fact of life.
It was, however, an American financial mogul who told me that he
thought that the literary culture of London left the New York
equivalent looking comatose. He told me this at a book-launch held
in his own apartment, where the crowd was dotted with extremely
beautiful women. When I confessed to one of them that I had found
Moby Dick a hard read, she reacted as if I had just revealed that I
earned my living as a roach exterminator. Perhaps I had egg on my
tie.

PHILIP ROTH'S ALTERNATIVE AMERICA

' "Portnoy, yes, it's an old French name, a corruption of *porte noir*, meaning back door or gate. Apparently in the Middle Ages in France the door to our family manor house . . ." ' Thus the young Alexander Portnoy dreams of convincing the pert shiksa ice-skater that he is not a Jew. But even in his dream she is not to be misled. ' "You seem a very nice person, Mr Porte-Noir, but why do you go around covering the middle of your face like that?" ' As the narrator goes on to explain, to us if not to her, it is because of his nose, which, unlike his penis, is now, with the onset of adolescence, so insistent on extending itself that it can't be persuaded to retract even temporarily. 'That ain't a nose,' shouts his interior voice, 'it's a hose! Screw off, Jewboy! Get off the ice and leave these girls alone!'

The Jewish notables who vilified Philip Roth after the publication of *Portnoy's Complaint* in 1969 were objecting to a lot more about its hero than his preoccupation with sex. They didn't like his preoccupation with his nose, either. They didn't like Roth's apparent suggestion that there was no level ground for a young American male Jew between the twin peaks of tormented insecurity and priapic self-assertion. As a goy who was born and raised in Australia, where the book was banned, and who first read it in England, where it wasn't, I couldn't see their point at the time. I was too busy rolling around fighting for breath. It was the funniest book in the world. What was there not to like, except perhaps the hilarious sexual frankness that had caused the distinctly non-Jewish puritans of my benighted homeland to wig out? Why should his own people attack him?

With his latest book, *The Plot Against America*, the answer becomes clear. It was because the very idea of 'his own people' was bad news to people who wanted their ethnicity to be a minor issue, not a major one. A re-reading of *Portnoy's Complaint* – and there could be no more delightful occupation – reveals that the rabbinical elders who convicted its author of *Judische Selbsthass*, Jewish self-hatred, had quite a lot to go on. Not without reason, they were even more shaken up by what was going on in Portnoy's mind than by what was going on in his pants. Compared with his throbbing self-consciousness as a Jew, Portnoy's throbbing crotch was a sideshow. But Roth's judges convicted him without trying him first. He was proud of his background: savagely proud. Along with all the other themes he has explored since, his exultant celebration of Jewish-American social cohesion is there in his first book to become world famous. The earlier books – *Goodbye Columbus*, *Letting Go* and *When She Was Good* – had each stated some of his future subjects, but *Portnoy's Complaint* stated the whole lot, packed together and painted like a circus act. *Portnoy's Complaint* is a trick car out of which, instead of a family of dwarves, novels climb one after the other, at an astonishing rate and seemingly without end. None of them is without its felicities, a round dozen of them are indispensable reading, a good handful of that dozen are among the best novels ever written in America, and all of them can be found tightly encoded into his original masterpiece. That lavish celebration of baseball in *The Great American Novel*, for example, is there in little, in the scenes where the grown men of Portnoy's Arcadian neighbourhood play seven-inning softball on a Sunday spring morning while the youngsters long to be so masculine, funny and sure of their place. But this new novel was in there too: a novel wholly, instead of partly, concerned with being unsure – with insecurity.

Insecurity saturates *The Plot Against America*. Unfortunately the saturation goes right to the level of its telling. For a writer blessed with the eyes and ears to find real life fantastic in every detail, fantasy is the wrong form. As a narrative idea, Roth's latest brainwave is down there with *The Breast*: perhaps even further down, because at least *The Breast* had Kafka's cockroach for a predecessor. The predecessor of *The Plot Against America* is Robert Harris's *Fatherland*: a considerable book in its own right, but one that exhausts the possibilities of its narrative trick, yielding Roth little room for manoeuvre. In *Fatherland*, America is unable to intervene decisively against Germany, leaving the Nazis a free hand in Europe. In *The Plot Against America*, America is unable to intervene decisively against Germany, leaving – what? Well, it leaves Roth a chance to speculate about what might have happened to America's Jews.

*

But first of all, and you might well ask, what happened to America? Charles Lindbergh became President. To make this plausible, Roth has to re-jig the 1940 Republican convention. The re-jigging entails quite a lot of jiggery-pokery, but he just about makes it stick. There is a persuasive swing to the way Lindbergh captures the electorate's imagination by flying from city to city. It would be more persuasive if he were doing it in Germany, where Hitler, in his first campaigns, actually did do that. He made a point of dropping from the clouds all over the place, and Leni Riefenstahl's orgasmic scenes of the smitten populace searching the sky for the arrival of his aircraft are a fair registration of the enthusiasm he actually aroused. You can just about imagine Lindbergh having the same effect on the American backwoods, and there is no strain at all in imagining the appeal of his message: 'Vote for Lindbergh or vote for War.' Voting against war with Germany was what almost everybody was keen on until Japan attacked, and they might well have remained keen on it afterwards. If Hitler had been less crazy he would never have declared war on the United States, which the terms of his treaty with Japan did not oblige him to do. If he hadn't, Roosevelt might still have had a hard job to get America into the war against him. That was the true fork in history, which Roth might have chosen to treat, but it would have meant leaving Lindbergh out. Roth, however, wanted Lindbergh in, because Lindbergh had anti-Semitic views.

Roth's preparation of an alternative history is just a rearrangement of the furniture. If it had really concerned him he might have done it more adroitly. But what really concerns him is the retroactive prospect of an America with its traditional anti-Semitic prejudices given official endorsement. 'Our homeland was America,' says the Roth-like narrator. 'Then the Republicans nominated Lindbergh and everything changed.' Roth's challenge is to show how it changed. The challenge is not easily met, because America was never Germany. Certainly America was no stranger to official brutality: in America's gaols and police stations between the wars, the third degree was common. There are plentiful records, some of them filmed, of Henry Ford's armed goons violently repressing protests from laid-off workers, of Bonus marchers being put to flight by the troops of that barely controllable authoritarian General Douglas MacArthur, and, of course, of racist atrocities in the South. But there was no case of a minority's being permanently threatened with violence backed by federal law. The Nazis did indeed come to power legally, after which they remade the laws in their favour, so that the hounding and eventual extermination of the Jews could be done on a legal basis. But none of that would have been possible if Hitler had not been granted dictatorial powers.

In the United States, where the separation of powers is a fundamental principle of the constitution, not even the most charismatic President – not even, say, Charles Lindbergh – could have instituted, in peace time, racially selective federal laws without the approval of Congress. Had Lindbergh set about gaining such approval, he would have had to sway the media, not to mention Hollywood. As every anti-Semite is eager to insist, the Jewish representation in those fields has always been large. Aware of these considerations, Roth knows that an American version of Nazi Germany's 1935 Nuremberg Laws framed against the Jews won't do even as a fantasy. So he introduces the idea of the Office of American Absorption. He isn't clear about how this apparently benign organization could have been set up without a debate in Washington about its possible malignancy, but he is disturbingly persuasive about how it might have operated had it come into existence. Bright young urban Jews of the Portnoy type are selected for temporary resettlement in the rural heartland, where they are encouraged to question the ethnic solidarity of their origins. The result is meant to be an erosion of their communal identity. This nightmare by Roth gains force from its closeness to the dream of every Jewish assimilationist. Not only calling themselves Americans first and foremost, but feeling it, the young Jews forget their heritage as a prelude to denying it.

Roth is dealing here with a continuing dilemma – individual acceptance is bound to be hindered by any cherishing of a collective uniqueness – and might have made more of it. He shows how the views of the Lindberghs, man and wife, might have made the anti-Semitism of the American upper orders even less shy about expressing itself. Jews not only can't get into the country club, they can't get into an ordinary hotel. He also shows that top-level anti-Semitism might have gained quite a lot of tacit support from top-level Jews. In Germany during the Weimar Republic, the influx of orthodox Jews from the East was frowned upon by assimilated Jews who were already there, on the grounds that it would inflame Nazi-style anti-Semitism further. (Actually the Nazis didn't need any inflaming, but the full possibilities of that fact were not yet apparent, even to them.) Even in America, and especially in uptown New York, there was a sad but understandable tradition by which the settled and successful *haute juiverie* frowned on the raw immigrants whose habits might fan *goyische* prejudice. If Roth, as well as seizing on the real-life character of Lindbergh, had seized on the real-life character of, say, Walter Lippmann, he might really have been on to something. When Britain was battling alone against the Nazis, the destroyers-for-bases idea that saved Britain's life was almost wholly Lippmann's. But he had come too far in downplaying his own Jewish origins to take up the collective fate of the Jews as his chief concern. During the war he wrote nothing about the extermination of the European Jews, and after it he wrote little. Lippmann was the living definition of the Jew who considered himself an American first, and he might have provided Roth with the ideal demonstration of just how divisive that attitude could have been if there had been a subtle but comprehensive campaign to destroy Jewish solidarity. It could be said that by declining to adopt the role of representative Jew, he had already been conducting one.

And *he* could have said, and been right, that the very idea of a collective Jewish identity – the idea that all Jews were connected in a conspiracy of blood – was a fantasy made real only by Hitler. Even in Germany, and especially among the Jewish intelligentsia, it took time to grasp the reality that the Nazis would make no exceptions. It just seemed too insane. As Hannah Arendt once argued, you had to be a madman to guess what was coming. In Roth's alternative America, the man who spots the implications of the insidious new official encouragement of anti-Semitism is a journalist unhindered by a sense of proportion. If Roth doesn't seize on the real-life character of Walter Lippmann, he does seize on the real-life character of Walter Winchell. This is the most daring stroke in the book, and leads to its most original single sentence, which Roth puts into the mouth of another force for good, Mayor Fiorello LaGuardia:

'Walter is too loud, Walter talks too fast, Walter says too much, and yet, by comparison, Walter's vulgarity is something great, and Lindbergh's decorum is hideous.'

Roth's Winchell fights the good fight, and pays for it with his life. After President Lindbergh mysteriously disappears, there is an ultra-right *coup d'état*, Winchell's own presidential candidacy is terminated by his assassination, and America temporarily goes openly pro-Nazi as a prelude to preparing war on Canada. Why did Lindbergh disappear? It would be spoiling the story to tell you. Roth does a pretty good job of spoiling the story himself, by dishing out the improbabilities with shameless haste: if it were not for the quality of the writing, you could be reading *The Da Vinci Code*. Luckily for the reader's mental health, Roth is no more capable of an uninteresting sentence than Dan Brown is capable of an interesting one. But you would wonder why Roth bothered, if it were not so obvious that his chief concern is not with official repression, but with social prejudice, as it was then and still is today. Here, once again, and as always, he is in a cleft stick. He knows that he was brought up in an artist's Arcadia, the ideal combination of domestic stability and psychic turmoil. ('Doctor,' Portnoy asks his analyst, 'what should I rid myself of, tell me, the hatred ... or the love?') Lest we doubt that, he gives it to us again: the Weequahic neighbourhood of Newark, New Jersey, in all its emotional uproar, gnawing neurosis, flagrant embarrassments, and career-forming linguistic vitality. (With the proviso that literature should never be thought of as a branch of sociology, the novels of Richard Price can be said to give us the bitter contemporary reality of the boroughs that once inspired Roth's sweetest memories.) But Roth also knows that another Arcadia patronizes the one he came from. To the blessed denizens of WASP Heaven, or Lindbergh Land, the noisy passions of his childhood will always look like a joke. The only possible defence mechanism of the Jewish comic writer is to get in with the joke first, and time it better: it was Woody Allen's idea to stick himself with a rabbi's beard in *Annie Hall*. But to the mind in which it is operating, the defence mechanism must inevitably seem a form of concession, and especially when the mind belongs to Roth – a man who has taken comic writing to the highest level of philosophy, politics and social analysis.

Roth emerged from his borough as a full-blown sophisticate, and it is hard for the sophisticate to look back on his origins without looking down. Porte-Noir can't lust after his button-nosed ice-skater without tacitly conceding that a standard marriage to a nice Jewish girl is beneath his ambitions. His irrepressible schlong is a rock drill to a higher stratum. The price of rising in the social world is an apparent alliance with the prejudiced; to prove that there is no alliance is a constant battle; and the result is a torn conscience. In Roth's case, the torn conscience has been the motor of a steadily accumulating literary achievement without parallel in his time – an achievement whose resonance reaches far into Europe and the Middle East, making even the most illustrious of his American contemporaries look comparatively provincial. He is aware to the point of self-laceration that he was born in the right spot: he was probably already aware of it when he put his childhood pennies into one of the Blue Tins that helped to build Israel. But he is stuck with the anguish of an insoluble paradox. As an individual, he rejects the role of being a representative: but he is bound to be a representative when he fights prejudice.

As a man of reason, Roth must have figured out early that it has always been even worse for blacks: any photograph of Duke Ellington taken late in his life shows the accumulated effect of what being cast as a representative can do to the face of a genius. Ellington was too polite to say that an invitation to the White House was no full consolation for all those times he would have liked to sleep in the kind of hotel that wouldn't have let him past the front desk. There was never a hotel that Roth couldn't get into, but he can be excused for inventing an alternative and worse American past in which his father would be told that the room he had been given was unavailable after all. It's an understandable bad dream. But it hasn't led to a good book, and couldn't have. The United States will never be free of racial prejudice for the same reason that it will never enshrine racial prejudice in anything like the Nuremberg Laws: it's a free country. Being that, it is bound to be full of things we don't like, but the federally sanctioned destruction of a racial minority isn't among them, and hasn't been since Wounded Knee. As Roth must have realized long before he finished writing it, the insuperable problem with *The Plot Against America* is that America is against the plot.

Postscript

Not long after completing the above piece I belatedly read Saul Bellow's *Ravelstein* and wondered whether I had been right in implying that Roth has the greater cosmopolitan scope. Trying to rate Bellow and Roth in order is an occupation for someone who shouldn't be reading either of them. But there can't be much question about their relative standing when it comes to international politics. Bellow's writings on the Middle East bring all his rhetorical power to the task of defending Israel against its external enemy. Roth deals with the internal enemy as well. In non-fiction at least, he has the full range of tragedy. In fiction, both of these majestic writers give us so much that it is often easy to forget how all they do depends on the shape of a sentence. Each is a bewitching example of the individual voice that starts, as Roth once put it, behind the knees. In the case of Roth, I am sometimes reduced to a childish longing that he would write books to order, so that I could telephone for a take-out. There are subjects that demand his voice, and only his. For instance, I would like him to write a book about how, in 2004, the Red Sox came back from nowhere to take the pennant from the Yankees, and went on to bury the Cardinals in the last game of the World Series. But he might not do it. Great writers write what they must, not what we would like. Their voices do not belong to us. We get that illusion only because they sound the way we do to ourselves, in those interior flights of eloquence that never reach the page.

THE MIRACULOUS VINEYARD
OF AUSTRALIAN POETRY

Poetry and glamour don't usually mix, but Australian poetry is starting to look like a special case. True, there is not yet much of a chance that Les Murray and Peter Porter will be asked to pose for photo spreads like Cate Blanchett and Nicole Kidman. But in the rest of the English-speaking world there is now a general agreement among the literary tipsters that poetry is something the Aussies do with an extra zing: the way they do food, wine, bush hats, satyromaniacal cricketers, telegenic crocodile-wrestlers and insatiable media tycoons. The general agreement, admittedly, is still a bit simple-minded, but it is steadily moving up-scale. If it ever catches up with the abundant reality, however, the word 'miracle' will have to come into play, and for once it will almost fit. Australian poetry is a thing for awe, for dropping to the knees and giving thanks. Pinch me if you see what I see. Whence came this abundance?

Before we trace the abundance to its historical origins, we should be aware of its true scope, which is even more extensive than we might think. Take a look at *Best Australian Poems 2003*, edited by Peter Craven. It's the first volume of a new series that from now on will come out annually. There are forty poets represented in it, nearly all of them with something substantial. ('Substantial' meaning that you can't ignore it, even when you don't like it.) If you already know something about the Australian literary world, you will recognize the names of David Malouf, Les Murray, John Tranter, Fay Zwicky, Chris Wallace-Crabbe, Peter Porter, Bruce Dawe, Alan Wearne, Peter Rose, Thomas Shapcott, Geoffrey Lehmann, Geoff Page, Dorothy Porter, John Kinsella, Bruce Beaver and probably several others. But then there are names that are only now making their first impact; and then, a long way back, trailing along with his

fractured Globite portmanteau spilling manuscripts, there is Clive
James, who is very glad to be included. For a long time I have
worked offshore, but now I have been brought home, and am
mighty proud to be included in this number, because the number is
select, even though it is dauntingly large. Mere quantity, of course,
is no proof of fertility. We must not forget the Soviet cultural
commissar who boasted that his district had 167 registered writers,
all members of the Writers' Union. 'A hundred years ago, there was
only one.' The one he meant was Tolstoy.

But the poets in Craven's anthology all have a claim to the title,
and you could make another anthology from the poets he has left
out. (They would probably like to make a rissole out of him. I
imagine the boiling fat has already started to fly.) Rivalry, and indeed
outright bitchery, has always been inseparable from the Australian
poetic scene, which, even as it booms like the Sydney Olympics,
continues to work rather like world championship ice-dancing:
agreement on technical merit is sometimes possible, but there is
rarely much agreement about artistic impression. Also the judges, to
go on with the metaphor, tend to do a bit of skating themselves.
Most of our best poets have been among our best critics, and vice
versa. Individualists who cling together only to get a fair share of the
blankets, the poets are a family in which incest is functional, even
when one of the results is casual murder. Poetry pays peanuts
even when on a government subsidy, but the stakes are high: higher
than ever, now that Australia no longer need look to overseas opinion for validation. For admiration, yes: but an extramural certificate
we no longer need. Glory begins at home, and glory is the pay-off.
(You've never really been flattered until you've been quoted.) Everyone would like a reputation. Speaking as the kind of poet who has
usually had to do without one, I have to say that I am childishly
pleased that a place has finally been found for me. My own
sustaining belief has always been that poems matter more than
poets; that no poet should write anything unless he feels an inner
need; and that a life's-work should be the accumulated moments of
necessary expression. In other words, it shouldn't be a career. My
recently published book of collected poems, called *The Book of
My Enemy*, has more than four hundred pages of work in it. They
were written at a rate of fewer than ten pages a year, and there is
not a line among them that I wrote to help keep up my reputation,

because I didn't have one. I'm glad to say that the book has already run through five printings in Britain alone, and been treated with respect by the critics even when they obviously thought it strange that a transplanted Aussie talk-show host should be driven to verse, instead of driven to the studio in the back of a large car with Margarita Pracatan at the wheel.

But having ploughed a lonely furrow, I am gratified to discover that it has led back to such a flourishing vineyard. Come to think of it, that might be the best metaphor of the lot. There is such a variety of wines, and not all of them are owned by Penfolds. You've got your Murray Hermitage, your Kinsella's Retreat, your Beaver Creek, your Shapcott's Landing ... It even works by areas. Down there in Hobart, beyond the sweep of Craven's purview, there is Stephen Edgar, for my money the most subtle vintage now on the market. I chanced upon my first bottle of Edgar Special Blend Grand Reserve only last year, and since then I've been drinking almost nothing else. Exquisite in the nose, and shattering in the follow-through.

Poetry, like the Internet, can make a connection from remote places. Stephen Edgar knew Gwen Harwood when she was alive and well in Hobart. Ever on the lookout for mother figures, I have always found it satisfactory that women should have been so important to Australian poetry. In the post-war boomlet before the boom, Harwood and Judith Wright were essential names, up there with A.D. Hope and James McAuley in the combined effort that prepared the way for the Poetic Nation. I thought Wright lapsed into the abstract in her later years, whereas Harwood always produced the full rich, considered, resonant artefact. If our rhythmic eloquence started with the Bush Balladeers, it smelled a lot less of horses after the women joined in. The days are over, thank God, when a full history of Australian poetry could be written. It has come too far: there is too much to it. But if there were such a thing as a full history, the housewife poets would have an assured place. They had time only to write what was essential. They never had one eye on their reputations: they always had both eyes on the Hill's Hoist. Harwood practically dug her own potatoes. Now that it's boom time, the danger is that every otherwise unemployable Australian youth will want a career as a poet, and produce unnecessary poems to stake his claim. But I started out as an otherwise unemployable

Australian youth myself, so I can't whinge, and a few other poets of my generation would be wise not to do so either. There's another focal point for glamour, of course: the Generation. I can already see the movie that will be made after our lot have moved on. Some Heath Ledger of the future will play Les Murray, striding towards the breakers with his surfboard under his arm . . . It will be nonsense, but the movie-makers will be looking back on an enchanted time, and they will be right.

Weekend Australian, 6–7 March 2004

Postscript

Beyond its obvious purpose of barking for my own act, the above piece had an ulterior motive, which was to help make a fashionable talking point of the Australian poetry boom. Joe McCarthy taught us a valuable lesson in PR. One day he would say there were 167 communists in Government service, and the next day he would say that there were 293. Thus he changed the question of whether there were any to a question of how many. By talking about whether the Australian poetry boom was international or merely national, I hoped to get the idea of an Australian poetry boom, of whatever kind, into the general cultural discussion. I hope my manoeuvre had some effect, but the awkward truth is that Australian poetry, regarded as a commercial proposition, still rates as a field in which the publishers take a loss, and even the best poets must wonder whether they wouldn't be better off chalking their work on a brick wall. The only independent Australian publishing house for poetry, the excellent Duffy & Snellgrove, has since gone out of business. The void will leave the serious poets trying to sell themselves to the major publishers, who are bound to be at least as impressed by media glamour as by real achievement. Australians are great book-buyers *per capita*, but the total market even for prose is small, and when you consider that the market for poetry is necessarily a lot smaller, you are looking at a very slim return on the dollar. What to do about that is an abiding question. Nor are there many outlets among the magazines and upmarket newspapers. As a result, the jostling for position among the poets is much more fierce than I dared to make out. In the long view of history, I am convinced, ours will look like a golden age, but for those of us actually there it looks more like the first week at Ballarat. Who stole my shovel? You're digging on my claim, you mongrel. And where did you get those canvas pants?

THE UNIVERSITY OF THE HOLOCAUST

For the Israelis, anti-Semitism is merely a nightmare. For the Palestinians, it's a catastrophe. If you believe, as I do, that the Palestinians' cause is just, nothing could be more depressing than to hear them spout the very stuff that guarantees they will never get an even break. The mad idea that the Jews have no right to exist is a potent intensifier of the almost equally mad idea that the State of Israel can somehow be eliminated. I say 'almost' because a friend of mine in Australia recently presented me with a plausible case that the Middle East would probably be a more peaceful area if the State of Israel had never been founded. Like her argument that the Aborigines would have been a lot happier if the Europeans had never shown up, this contention was hard to rebut, except by rudely pointing out that we were both sitting in an Italian restaurant in Melbourne, history having happened.

But history might have happened otherwise, although in the case of the Jewish presence in Palestine you would have to go back beyond the 1850s (when the Jews were already a majority in Jerusalem) to somewhere near the beginning of the Old Testament, and equip the Canaanites with grenade launchers. To the perfect madness of the first idea, however – the idea that the Jews are candidates for extermination – no concessions are possible. Anti-Semitism is so obviously insane that no refutation of it should be necessary, and indeed after the Holocaust the feeling was widespread throughout the world that the whole demented notion had at last become an historical back number, like phlogiston or the belief that mirrors could leak lightning. Throughout the world: but not, alas, throughout the Arab world.

Why this should have been so is hard to unscramble at this distance, but briefly, and without too much distortion, it can be said that the Arab nations never studied at the University of the

Holocaust. Their interests lay, not in Europe, but in the area containing the nagging presence which was already threatening to become a Jewish state. The Arab nations on the whole concurred with the British mandate's lethal reluctance to admit Jewish refugees into Palestine, and several of the Arab leaders saw nothing wrong with Hitler's determination that as many potential colonists as possible should be dealt with at source. One of the leaders, the Grand Mufti of Jerusalem, spent time in Berlin urging Hitler to get on with it. We should hasten to remember that another of the leaders, King Abdullah of Transjordan – grandfather of the future King Hussein – was always a model of far-sighted tolerance, and quite saw the possibility of fruitful coexistence with the infidel incursion. But we should also remember that Abdullah paid for his liberalism with his life, in an early version of the price exacted from Anwar Sadat for even entertaining the idea of peace. It was the choleric Grand Mufti who set the tone. He had been reading the same Koran as Abdullah, but had reached different conclusions. Our own best conclusion should be that the Koran was not the book to blame. There were other books, borrowed from abroad, and one of them was that putrid old Tsarist forgery *The Protocols of the Elders of Zion*.

Remember the name, because it goes on cropping up throughout the bloody history of the area. (In Egypt, supposedly the most enlightened of the Arab nations, the state television system recently dramatized it as a TV serial.) The historian Golo Mann once said that Nazi-style anti-Semitism was a crime encouraged by bad literature, and literature doesn't get any more bad than *The Protocols*. But before we get to the written word, we should look at more substantive phenomena that might account for intransigence among Israel's enemies. There are plenty to consider. A year before he declared the Israeli state, David Ben Gurion was ready to accept a partition of Palestine: even though his resulting portion would be tiny, at least it would be independent. But when he realized that the Arab states would not recognize a Jewish state even if it were the size of a tennis court, he was ready for what was bound to happen when he made his unilateral announcement. The State of Israel was declared, and the Arab nations immediately combined to attack it.

*

One of the consequences was the flight of the Palestinians. In fairness to them, we should not mince words: the flight was an expulsion. The instrument of expulsion was terror. The nascent Israeli state already had an unfortunate heritage of terror, much of it due to the initiatives of Menachem Begin, a University of the Holocaust alumnus armed with the inflexible conviction that the only answer to the threat of overwhelming violence was to get your retaliation in first. When the tiny new state was attacked from all sides, his brainchild, the Irgun, teamed up with the Stern Gang to massacre almost 300 Arabs at Deir Yassin, and the exodus of the Palestinians understandably ensued. Though their disappearance suited Ben Gurion's purposes – already embattled on half a dozen external fronts, he would probably have lost the war if he had been forced to fight on an internal front as well – the Jews were suitably sorry at the time. But the Palestinians were sorry forever. We should not forget their grief.

The Arab nations, alas, forgot it immediately. With the honourable exception of Jordan, every one of them turned the Palestinians away, and not even Jordan has ever given them much beyond citizenship. There is enough oil money in the Arab nations to give every refugee a hotel suite with twenty-four-hour room service. Instead, far too many of them have been obliged to remain in camps that are really display cases, so that they can testify with their desperation to Jewish inhumanity. The inhumanity was thought to be endemic in the Jewish race. Arab theorists believed that there was scientific literature to lend this contention weight. The Jewish leaders had already been startled to discover, as early as 1949, that *The Protocols* had been officially translated and printed in the Arab nations. With the rise to power of Egypt's Gamal Abdel Nasser, the bad literature became a driving force. As Amos Elon reveals in his invaluable book *A Blood-Dimmed Tide*, Nasser discovered in *The Protocols* a proof 'beyond all doubt that 300 Zionists, each knowing the others, control the fate of the European continent and elect their successors from among themselves'. He didn't say how successfully they had controlled the fate of the European continent when Adolf Eichmann was in charge of the train timetables, but what he did say is recorded in the official collection of *Nasser's Speeches and Press Interviews*. If Nasser was not precisely a madman, he was certainly no model of detached judgement when he sucked Hussein of Jordan into the 1967 war, thereby laying the West Bank open for occupation and the Palestinians to the second stage of their suffering.

The suffering might have been worse. If Israel, between 1967 and 1973, was fatally slow to realize that the Palestinians had fair nationalist aspirations, one of the reasons was that they seemed to be doing fairly well. Arabs in the Occupied Territories, as Arabs have always done within Israel itself, prospered economically to an extent that might have made the leaders of the Arab nations wonder why their own poor were quite so destitute. Luckily the anomaly could be put down to the continuing efficacy of the infinitely subtle international Zionist plot. Israel came so near to losing the 1973 war that Golda Meir and Moshe Dayan both had to resign in apology. It was the end of the old Labour Alignment's preponderance in government. Begin was at last allowed into the Knesset from which he had previously been excluded as if infected – which indeed he was – and the inexorable rise of the hardliners began. But even then, the settlement movement might have been slower to start if a bunch of PLO 'moderates' had not attacked a defenceless school containing nobody except twenty-two Jewish religious students and murdered them all.

It was a crime encouraged by bad literature. The crime has gone on until this day, and it will continue to be a crime even if the Jews prepare a counter-crime of their own. Some would say they already have. On one occasion, a single Jew walked into a mosque and killed thirty helpless Arabs before his weapons could be disentangled from his ultra-orthodox beard. But no Israeli government, however keen on reprisals against terror, has yet proclaimed the desirability of killing any Arab it can reach. Hezbollah and Hamas both proclaim the desirability of killing any Jew, and there is nothing novel in the proclamation. For a quarter of a century before 1988, when Yasser Arafat finally recognized the state of Israel, it was the founding objective of the PLO to 'liquidate' it. Losing people at a crippling rate for a country with such a small population, the Israelis had no reason to doubt that the word 'liquidate' was meant in the Stalinist sense. In the last five years of suicide attacks, Israel has lost almost half the number of people that died in the World Trade Center. To inflict proportionate damage, al-Qa'eda would have had to burn down Brooklyn. Nearly all of the dead Jews were noncombatants going about their everyday lives, and no doubt that was what made them targets. Any Jew, anywhere. Hezbollah has killed Jews in that well-known centre of the world Zionist conspiracy, Buenos Aires. Where next? Reykjavik?

A week ago, shortly after Hamas's spiritual leader Sheik Ahmed Yassin finally met his rocket, some of our media representatives were impressed when one of his supporters promised that the Gates of Hell would now be open. For the Jews, those same gates have been open for a long time. People who hold the understandable belief that Jewish reprisals will create more Arab terror should be equally prepared to consider whether more Arab terror might not produce an effect on the Jewish side that we have not previously had to contemplate because they have so far been able to keep their own maniacs chained up. Out on the extreme, far beyond Ariel Sharon and even beyond Benjamin Netenyahu, there are ultras who would like to see every Arab dead. Yitzhak Rabin, the lost hero of Israel, was murdered by the Jewish equivalent of the Arab fanatic who killed Sadat, the lost hero of Egypt. Rabin always believed that the loudly racist Gush Emunim settlers on the West Bank were a threat to democracy. Sharon couldn't see it. By now he can, and those who loathe his ruthlessness might come to bless it when the time arrives for Jews to shoot Jews – as well it might, on the inevitable day when the last settlers are ordered out of the Occupied Territories. It wouldn't be the first time Jews had shot Jews. In 1948, when Ben Gurion ordered the Irgun to disarm, their response was to run a fresh supply of guns into Tel Aviv. Ben Gurion ordered that the ship should be attacked. Twenty of the Irgun were killed, and Begin ended up swimming in the harbour. Some optimists believed he had learned his lesson.

*

The University of the Holocaust had as many dumb graduates as clever ones. Nazi anti-Semitism was so awful in its irrationality that any contrary force is likely to be irrational as well. The only rational contrary force is called liberal democracy, which conquers extremism by containing it. In answer to those who think Mel Gibson, lonely creator of *The Passion of the Christ*, might be Hitler reborn with a more photogenic hairstyle, it should be said that if he had wanted to produce a truly anti-Semitic film, he would have had the Jews on screen whispering in Hebrew about setting up a world conspiracy with money swindled from the Romans. Authentic Jew-baiters don't equivocate. In its classic form, anti-Semitism did indeed emerge as a by-product of Christianity. None of the abuse recently heaped on world Jewry by the ex-Prime Minister of Malaysia and the top Imam of Australia was not first heaped by Martin Luther. But Christianity finally got over it, mainly because the democratic states deprived Christianity of political power. In a democratic state, the passion of the Mel, whatever it might happen to be, must be tempered for rational ears if it is to open big on the first weekend.

The Mel's passion aside, however, we really do have fanatics of our own, preaching versions of *The Protocols* that differ from it only by substituting America as the source of all the world's evil – including, of course, the depredations of the Israeli state, which generate such universal anger that a bunch of young head-cases in Bali are moved to blow up a nightclub. In reality, they blew up the nightclub because they didn't like the way young Australians dance. I don't much like it either, but I don't think blowing their legs off is an appropriate cure. My opinion, which I assume most of the readers of this newspaper share, was not transmitted to me by a sacred text, although I suppose the teachings of Jesus were in on the start of it. In the world of today, any reasonable and widely shared opinion is the result of a long and complicated history of enlightenment culminating in liberal institutions, which we should be proud of and teach our children to revere, instead of favouring the fantastic theory that a regard for civilized values somehow exacerbates a conspiracy against the wretched of the earth.

It shouldn't need pointing out that the Bali bombers knew no more about the history of the Middle East than I know about quantum mechanics. But it does need pointing out, because so many Western intellectuals are incapable of reasoning their way to any conclusion that does not suit their prejudices. There are limits, however, to what they can say unopposed, and very definite limits to what they can do without legal sanction. With Islamic fanaticism as we now face it, no such restrictions apply. This is bad news for Islam in general, and for the Palestinians it is beyond bad news. There are many Palestinians who know this to be true. In the week after Sheik Ahmed Yassin's death, the Palestinian Authority issued an appeal for passive resistance that amounted to a repudiation of the suicide bombing. The question remains, however, of how much authority the Palestinian Authority exercises over the fanatics. Our own absolutist half-wits need to realize two things. Al-Qa'eda would go on attacking the democracies even if the Palestinians achieved justice tomorrow. And the Palestinians will never achieve justice if they go on attacking Israel. Both crimes are abetted by bad literature, and to produce bad literature of our own adds fuel to the fire. To that extent, the seductive idea that we are all guilty is exactly right.

Sunday Times, 28 March 2004

Postscript

Even when devoted to dispelling myths instead of creating them, international opinion-peddling on the subject of the Middle East has little value beyond making the participants feel better. Intellectuals who think they can influence events by argument are usually making a mistake. Their only influence can be on the preservation or the further erosion of the complex truth. Those who imagine that there can be such a thing as a useful lie are joining a bad company. A less bad company, but still sad, is formed by those who believe that by clarifying the case they can affect its outcome. The humanities, of which political analysis is a branch, must be pursued for their own sake. Any thinker who can't live with that imperative is doomed to die of disappointment. Our own experience of reading, however, tells us that a thought launched into the void is not necessarily going nowhere. When Albert Camus wrote 'Tyrants conduct monologues above a million solitudes' he changed my life, even if he did nothing to change the minds of a million admirers of Stalin. That might seem a small reward for his effort, but probably the best reason for trying to say things well is that they might travel further, beyond the gravity field of automatic indifference. Thinly spread through space and time, there has always been a community of the receptive, glad to be confirmed in a view they already held, or at least to be reassured that they are not alone. On the Middle East, in my opinion, the reiteration of a commonplace – that anti-Semitism is the enemy of the Palestinian cause – is still worth it. But it is only just worth it. Remotely located pundits who have managed to persuade themselves that the clock can be put back beyond 1948 without generating a mushroom cloud aren't going to have their minds changed by mere reasoning.

What really matters is the opinions of the people on the spot. In that regard, I got a quick education at the Wellington Festival in the following year, when the highly talented Israeli writer Etgar Keret told me that he not only understood what I was saying, but that it scarcely needed saying anyway, since every young person in the area, whether Jew or Arab, understood it perfectly, as long as they had an IQ in triple figures. In other words, there were no opinions left to be thrashed out: only the politics. Meanwhile there was a life to lead. In his marvellous stories, the youngsters lead it, with all the usual dancing to flashing lights. Some of the flashing lights are bombs going off, but that's the way it is. Nevertheless it is surely permissible to be stunned by the sheer number of commentators on the international scene who think they know something that Amos Elon, Amos Oz and David Grossman don't. All three want a Palestinian state. None of them believes in retaining the Occupied Territories. By what feat of mental gymnastics can they be regarded as imperialists? Yet they are so regarded. Now that the international left intelligentsia is united in the opinion that Israel is America's cat's-paw, the Israeli liberals, as if they didn't have enough trouble with their own right wing, find themselves calumniated as stooges of imperialism, simply because they want the State of Israel to continue. Those of us who have lived long enough will hear a bell ringing, and remember the days when the Kremlin labelled liberal democrats as Social Fascists. In the Germany of the 1930s, it was one of the reasons why the Nazis came to power. Since Nazi power made the foundation of the State of Israel inevitable, it makes more sense to blame the Russians than to blame the Americans. But it makes more sense still to blame nobody. The eternal search for a scapegoat is where the whole thing started.

NO WAY, MADAME BOVARY

The first thing to say about *Madame Bovary* is that it's a terrific story. Other comparably great and famous novels aren't, but it is. Everyone should read it. Everyone *would* read it, given a free taste. The plot fairly belts along from the first page. Young Charles Bovary clumps into school to be laughed at by the other kids for his awkwardness. In no time he is a medical student, then a doctor. The beautiful Emma Rouault is his second wife. He wins the right to her hand after setting her father's broken leg. It's a simple job but it gets him a reputation for competence. Fatally he believes this too. Stuck with him in the depths of nowhere, Emma gradually realizes that she has married a chump. Longing for excitement and a classier way of life, she falls for a charming poseur called Leon. Their incipient affair is a stand-off. But with an upmarket louse called Rodolphe she finds sexual fulfilment, and plans a future with him. Sharing no such plans, Rodolphe dumps her. She collapses. Nursed back to health by the unsuspecting Charles, she hooks up again with Leon. This time it really happens. But the extravagance of her double life, financed by money stolen from Charles, gets her into ruinous debt. The loan-shark closes in, Leon backs out, and Emma has only one way to go. On a shelf in the pharmacist's shop nearby is a bottle of . . . but I won't say how it comes out, because some of you might not yet have read the book.

Some purists would say you can't. They would say that Flaubert's prose style is the essence of his art, and too near perfection to survive being translated. But we have to ask ourselves what we mean by the word 'style'. Undoubtedly there is a rhythm and a cadence to Flaubert's prose that only a fluent reader of French can appreciate, although the fluent reader of French had better *be* French. We are always better judges of tone in our first language than in a second or third. To turn things around for a moment, late nineteenth-century French critics were under the impression that Edgar Allan Poe was not only a spellbinding tale-teller but also a great master of English prose, and in the twentieth century it was widely assumed in the French literary world that the leading stylist of the English literary world was Charles Morgan, a dim bulb now long extinguished. If we are learning a foreign language, we tend to admire writers in it who are easy to read. One of the early bonuses attached to learning Russian, for example, is that all the standard European fairy tales were transcribed by great writers. So within a few weeks you are reading Tolstoy, whose name is on the title page of *The Three Bears*. It isn't all that long a step to reading *Anna Karenina*, because Tolstoy's sentences are never very tricky at however high the level of exposition. The temptation is to call Tolstoy a stylist. But in Russian, Turgenev was the stylist. Turgenev was the one who cared about repeating a word too soon. Tolstoy hardly cared at all.

It can safely be assumed that Flaubert's prose makes music. More important, however, is that it would be impressive even if it didn't. This is where the second, and richer, meaning of the word 'style' comes in. You need only rudimentary French to spot that Flaubert never wastes a word. Every word is to the point, especially in the descriptive passages. In his landscapes, trees are sometimes trees and leaves leaves, but when it matters he can give everything a specific name. Within four walls, he gives every object a pinpoint particularity. If he is looking at things through Emma's eyes, he adds his analytical power to her naïve hunger. Emma's wishes might have been blurred by her addiction to sentimental novels, but her creator, never sentimental for a second, keeps her perceptions sharp. Early in the story, there is a ball at a grand house: an episode that awakes in Emma a dangerous taste for the high life. In a few paragraphs, using Emma's vision as a camera, Flaubert captures the sumptuous glamour with a photographic scope that makes us think of those lavish get-togethers in *War and Peace*, in Proust or in *The Leopard*. Dickens could lay out a scene like that, too, but would spend thousands of words on it.

Minting his every phrase afresh, Flaubert avoided clichés like poison. 'Avoid like poison' is a cliché, and one that Flaubert would either not have used if he had been composing in English, or else flagged with italics to prove that he knew it came ready-made.

Martin Amis's War Against Cliché is nothing beside Flaubert's, who waged his with nuclear weapons. (He died waging it: his last book, *Bouvard et Pécuchet*, was about no other subject.) It follows that any translator must be unusually alert to what is alive or dead about his own use of language, or else he will do an injury to Flaubert's style far more serious than merely failing to reproduce its pulse and lilt. When Flaubert seems to be saying that Charles's off-putting first wife is long in the tooth, the translator had better be careful about calling her long in the tooth, which in English means old: Flaubert is just saying that her teeth are long. The translator needs to keep an eye on his own prose. Unfortunately the evidence continues to accumulate that we are now past the time when more than a few jobbing writers knew how to do this. In the second-last stage of our language's decay, it was enough to write correctly in order to gain a reputation for writing well. Now we are in the last stage, when almost nobody knows what it means to write correctly. Among ordinary pens for hire, it is no longer common to write without solecisms; even those who can are likely to bolt phrases together with no real attention to their derivation; and in too many cases the language is utterly emptied of the history that brought it into being. This is a very depleted gene-pool in which to go fishing for a translator of any foreign writer at all, let alone Flaubert. One can only salute the boldness of a publishing house still willing to give it a try. For safety's sake, however, it might be wise not to let the salute progress far above the shoulder until we have made sure that what we are acknowledging is a real contribution.

*

It might only look like one. Perhaps to mark the fact that one of the supreme achievements of French literature is being once again done into English, Oxford's physically handsome new translation of *Madame Bovary* by Margaret Mauldon bears on its cover James Tissot's *Young Woman in a Boat*, dating from 1870. Tissot, after quitting France that very year, spent the rest of his life being claimed by the English as one of their painters, so the invocation of his name can be counted as a nice cross-Channel touch. But *Madame Bovary* was first published in 1857. Considering that women's fashions scarcely stayed frozen in those thirteen years, a pedant might have wished that a French painter of a slightly earlier period could have been called in, but the young lady certainly has a sensual mouth, which can be said to fit. Already, though, it is hard to suppress a suspicion that in the matter of historical fidelity things are out of kilter, and the suspicion intensifies once the book is opened. Professor Malcolm Bowie, who wrote the informative introduction, makes much ado in his back-of-the-jacket blurb about Flaubert's precision, which the professor assures us is matched by Mauldon's brand-new and meticulously accurate translation of the actual work. Any reader wishing to believe this is advised to start on page one. He had better not open the book accidentally at page 178, on which we find Emma's lover Rodolphe justifying to himself his decision to ditch her. Rodolphe is certainly supposed to be a creep, but surely he never spoke the French equivalent of late-twentieth-century American slang. 'And anyway there's all those problems, all that expense, as well. Oh, no! No way! It would have been too stupid.'

*

Just to be certain that Rodolphe never spoke like a Hollywood agent, we can take a look at the same line in the original. '*Et, d'ailleurs, les embarras, la dépense . . . Ah! non, non, mille fois non! Cela eût été trop bête!*' The perfectly ordinary, time-tested English idiom 'No, no, a thousand times no' would have fitted exactly. The awful possibility arises that Mauldon has never paid much attention to English idioms like that. Instead, she thinks 'No way' is perfectly ordinary. We can take it for granted that she knows the French language of Flaubert's era inside out. (She has already translated, for the same series of Oxford World's Classics, works by Zola, Stendhal, Huysmans, Constant and Maupassant.) But she has a crucially weaker knowledge of how the English language of her own era has been corrupted. You might say that the English language has always advanced through corruption, but 'No way!' is an idiom so closely tied to the present that it can hardly fail to weaken any attempt to summon up the past. In Alan Russell's translation of *Madame Bovary* first published by Penguin in 1950, there is no 'no way'. Probably the phrase did not yet exist, but almost certainly Russell would not have used it even if it had. What he wrote was 'No, no, by Heaven no!' Not quite as good as 'a thousand times no!' perhaps, but certainly better than 'No way!': better because more neutral, in the sense of being less tied to the present time.

This is not to say that such glaring anachronisms are frequent in Mauldon's translation. On page 23, when Charles Bovary is seeking Emma Rouault's hand, Emma's father thinks of him as 'a bit of a loser', where Russell has 'a bit of a wisp of a man' – which, as well as being less of a jazzy put-down from the late twentieth century, happens to be more accurate: a *gringalet*, according to my French–English dictionary, is a 'little undersized fellow'. But apart from a few moments like that, Mauldon is safe from being accused of outright barbarism. What she isn't safe from is the question of whether her translation is really an improvement on Russell's. Why try to improve on it, if all she can offer is a prose that sounds – purportedly sounds – less dated? Isn't a dated prose style what we want? Admittedly Russell translates '*nègre*' as 'nigger'. If only for justice, that one word was demanding to be changed; and Mauldon changes it, to 'black man'. But I can't find even one other word in Russell's translation that sounds dated in the wrong way. All the rest of it sounds dated in the right way, i.e. closer to Flaubert in time. It must also be said, alas, that most of it is closer to Flaubert in possessing a sense of movement. Mauldon might say that accuracy precluded an easy stylistic flow, but if she said that, she would have to prove herself accurate. Despite the heavy endorsement from Professor Bowie, her accuracy is not always beyond cavil.

The cavilling starts early in Part One, Chapter One, where we get this sentence about Charles's parents. 'His wife had been wild about him at first; she had treated him with an amorous servility that had turned him against her all the more.' According to Flaubert, '*elle l'avait aimé avec mille servilités qui l'avaient détaché d'elle encore davantage*'. Where did the 'thousand' go? Russell has the wife 'lavishing on him . . . a thousand servilities'. You could say that the word 'lavishing' is put in – but what Mauldon has left out might matter: the wife did a lot of specific things, not just one. And as so often happens with translators, a deadly knack of weakening points by being untrue to the text is accompanied by an even deadlier knack of missing them altogether by being true to it. Later in the opening chapter (during which Charles grows to manhood in only a few pages of hurtling compression) there is a quick summary of his dissipations at medical school, culminating in a clause in which he 'learned how to make punch, and, at long last, discovered love'. Thus Mauldon – and indeed all Flaubert says is that he '*sut faire du punch et connut enfin l'amour'*. But Flaubert doesn't just mean discovering love, he means learning to make love. Flaubert is talking about sex. Russell does better by juicing the text: young Charles 'took lessons in making punch, and finally in making love'. So the older translation is more frank, and thus more true to a novel whose frankness about these things, in the great gallery of nineteenth-century novels, puts Flaubert beside Tolstoy, and ahead of both Dickens and Henry James.

In Part One, Chapter Three, Flaubert pulls off a fatefully resonant effect when Emma drains her glass of curaçao while Charles watches. Flaubert's micrometrically particular style is watching her as well: '... *le bout de sa langue, passant entre ses dents fines, léchait à petits coups le fond du verre'*. Mauldon's version ('the tip of her tongue ... delicately licked at the bottom of the glass') misses the repetitive movement. Russell missed it too, but he might have deliberately dodged it, having spotted the pornographic element in those multiple dartings. They are a forecast of that astonishing single-paragraph set-piece in Part Two, Chapter Nine, when we can tell what Rodolphe has just done to Emma because the whole landscape has an orgasm. Ever the keen student, Mauldon is well aware that with Flaubert, the man who invented the *style indirect libre* (although he himself never used the term), any description of anything can relate to the interior lives of the characters in the scene. She is aware of it, but all too often she doesn't spot the way it works.

Even with the direct style, where emotions are stated up front, there is a lot that she can miss, especially when it depends on an apparently minor point of grammar and syntax. There is a telling example at the end of Part One, Chapter Five, when Charles, after a night in bed with his beautiful wife, goes riding off to work, 'his heart full of the night's bliss'. But once again, Mauldon might have done better to observe the difference between the singular and the plural. Flaubert has Charles's heart *'plein des félicités de la nuit'*. Emma has more to offer than an abstract noun. Sensibly and more sensitively, Russell goes with the numbers: 'the joys of the night'. As with the thousand servilities, the joys of the night are separable events. She did this, she did that: her husband remembers as he rides.

In Part One, Chapter Seven, Emma finally admits to herself that her marriage is boring her to metaphorical death. Real death is still the length of the book away, but here is a portent. *'Pourquoi, mon Dieu, me suis-je mariée?'* Russell, perhaps redundantly but at least faithfully, doubles the invocation of the Deity into 'O God, O God'. Inexplicably, Mauldon switches it to the mundane. 'Why in the world did I ever get married?' This seemingly tiny emendation counts as a heavy loss when you consider Emma's habitually blasphemous relation to the Church. In her downhill phase she will use the House of God as a trysting place for adultery. If we count as a poem any length of writing that can't be quoted from *except* out of context, then *Madame Bovary* is a poem. We might monkey with its language, but we mustn't monkey with its internal consistency.

Strangely enough, on the face of it, an amateur literary stylist is less likely to do that than a professional scholar. But really it is not so strange. From before World War I until well after World War II, in the long heyday of the gentleman translators, the key practitioners were not always supported by a cheering squad from the academy, but they could write a confident prose of their own, however daunting the foreign model. Among them they had most of the big languages covered, and almost all of them were casually at home with French – which, in an era when Greek and Latin still dominated the syllabus, was more commonly acquired on vacation than in the schoolroom. C. K. Scott-Moncrieff's Proust eventually needed upgrading as to accuracy, but Terence Kilmartin, who wrote an elegant prose himself when moonlighting from his job as literary editor of the *Observer*, was properly respectful of the standard Scott-Moncrieff had set in matching Proust's flow; and in the final stages D. J. Enright, another part-timer, was properly respectful of Kilmartin. There is unlikely to be a further advance on the Proust that Kilmartin and Enright gave us, although there will probably be no shortage of boondoggles like the recent group effort by which various translators took on a section each, thus to prove inadvertently that a single voice was the only thing holding the original together. 'Either you got the voice,' said the great soprano Zinka Milanov, 'or you don't got the voice.'

The amateurs had voices of their own with which to pay respect to the foreign voices they loved. In the decade after World War II, the well-connected bunch of translators who were grouped around Roger Senhouse, a Francophile who raised dilettantism to the level of a profession, did a collective job of translating Colette that will brook no superseding, mainly because the collective job was composed of individual spare-time efforts, each answering to a passion. Even more wonderful than her books about Chéri, Colette's masterpiece *Julie de Carnheilan* will never need translating again, because the job was done for keeps by the prodigiously gifted Patrick Leigh Fermor while he was cooling down from his wartime adventures. In the same fruitful few years of recovery from the physical battle against barbarism, the petite nineteenth-century French novels that buttressed the achievement of *Madame Bovary* and sometimes even preceded it – Benjamin Constant's *Adolphe*, Maupassant's *Bel Ami*, Alphonse Daudet's *Sappho* – were translated by people who saw fidelity to them as a delightful but temporary duty, not as part of a long slog to corner a market. Most of those translations showed up in the prettily handy post-war series from Hamish Hamilton called the Novel Library. Now long defunct as a commercial proposition, the series is catnip for collectors in second-hand bookshops all over the planet. One of the Novel Library's particular jewels was the 1948 translation of *Madame Bovary* by Gerard Hopkins, who had the elementary tact to render '*mille fois non*' as 'a thousand times no'. (I could as easily have used his renderings as Russell's in the task of measuring Mauldon's, but the Penguin translation is the one most of us in the old British Empire grew up with, just as most Americans grew up with Francis Steegmuller's translation.)

The impulse behind the great wave of amateur translations – and this was especially true in the immediate aftermath of World War II – was a generous desire to bring foreign cultural treasure within reach of ordinary people. It was the era when patricians, having seen civilization dragged to the brink of ruin, still thought it might be preserved if enlightenment could be spread more equally. Booklovers who knew that their multilingual education was a privilege wanted to share it with people less lucky. The work was aimed directly at the public, not at the academy. Presumably Mauldon is looking to the public too, but her pages of notes at the end of this book are looking to Professor Bowie: they are proof of academic diligence. To put it bluntly, recent translations tend to be busywork, and earlier ones tend to be the real tributes, even when inaccurate by scholarly standards.

No doubt this new translation of *Madame Bovary* is a labour of love. But affection and affectation don't sit well together. In his introduction, Professor Bowie quotes his protégée's translation of the paragraph about Rodolphe that contains the most famous thing Flaubert ever wrote about human language. According to Mauldon, Flaubert said it was 'like a cracked kettledrum on which we beat out tunes for bears to dance to, when what we long to do is make music that will move the stars to pity'. Well, it certainly sounds precise. But it isn't, quite. In his introduction to the first, 1950, edition of his translation, Alan Russell revealed that he thought *Les liaisons dangereuses* was a seventeenth-century novel – wrong by a hundred years. (He quietly corrected the blunder for later editions, but it remains a pretty noisy blunder to have made.) He knew, however, that a *chaudron* isn't a kettledrum. Back in Sydney, in the First Kogarah Company of the Boys' Brigade, I played the kettledrum often enough to know that its barrel can be pretty seriously cracked and it still won't yield a dud note. It does that when its skin is split. If Flaubert had meant a kettledrum, he would have said so. What he meant was a kettle. Russell rendered the word that way, and so did Gerard Hopkins.

So much for accuracy as a fetish: it is bound to lead you into trouble when you stray into the territory of stuff that won't stay still to be researched. And in that territory lie the things of the mind. As his learned admirers, from Francis Steegmuller to Julian Barnes, have had so much constructive fun telling us, Flaubert would go to any lengths in the quest for factual precision. But Flaubert was a creative genius: he was putting his research to work, in aid of psychological perceptions that were uniquely his. One of those perceptions was that he himself was Madame Bovary. No wonder he loved her. Loving her, he gave her novel everything he had. Henry James thought that *Madame Bovary* was as good as Flaubert ever got. James was wrong to believe that the book was a tract against immorality. If it was, then its own author notably failed to heed the lesson. But James might have been right to believe that everything Flaubert subsequently wrote added up to a decline. Even Proust thought that *le mot juste* made a totem out of what should be taken for granted. The Monty Python crew translated *Wuthering Heights* into semaphore, and incidentally proposed that in a novel, story comes before language. So it does, even when the language is a miracle.

As a story, *Madame Bovary* is fit for worship, but it should be worshipped critically, as if it were man-made, and not a sacred text. At one point, Emma confides her sexual frustration to her maid, Félicité. But nothing comes of it. Flaubert might have had the idea of making Félicité part of the action as Emma's confidante. If he did, he forgot about it, and then forgot to take that bit out. It was a big uncertainty to leave in. There is no uncertainty about the style, but there again, the wrong kind of worship leads to myopia. Blinded by the dazzle, Mauldon just doesn't seem to see the absurdity of leaving some of the French as French. Various periodicals are read by the characters in the novel. Mauldon leaves their titles untranslated. So did Hopkins, but Russell was daring enough to give rough English equivalents. The tacit claim behind leaving French words as they are is that your sense of accuracy is so highly developed that if you can't find an exact equivalent, the word should be left inviolate. But in that case, why translate the thing at all?

The question is all too well worth asking, alas. Judging from its introduction and appended apparatus, this translation is looking for a home on the kind of university syllabus in which students are encouraged to believe that they can absorb foreign literatures without ever bothering themselves with the languages in which they were written. In that regard, America's economic dominance of the earth has made the English language imperialistic beyond the dreams of the people who invented it. No doubt it had to happen. Most of the amateur translators were already primed with at least one of the two ancient languages when they arrived at university, after which they acquired three or four of the modern languages as easily as if dipping themselves in paint. Those times won't be coming back. Nor will the once universal assumption among the literate that their time at university was merely the beginning of an education that would last for the rest of their lives.

But surely some of the effort put into the illusory omniscience of today's comfortably monoglot students could be put into teaching them at least one foreign language as a compulsory subject; and surely, in that case, French should be the first on the list. One doesn't ask for perfection. Anyone, even starting late, can learn enough French to know that Flaubert didn't actually sound like any of his translators, no matter how accurate. Using Proust as my handbook, I spent fifteen years learning to read French, and I still don't read it much less haltingly than I speak it. But I can read enough of Flaubert's *Madame Bovary* to know that a translator who can't carry the reader with her own style will put that marvellous book further away, even while she strains every nerve to bring it close.

THE BATTLE FOR ISAIAH BERLIN

Lecturing at the time of the Franco-Prussian war, Jacob Burckhardt told his history students that the revolutionary age from 1789 onwards had been *lehrreich*: rich in teaching. The greatest spirits of a hundred years before were now looking short of knowledge, but only because of what had happened since. Modern students should not attribute virtue to themselves just because they could see so much that their mental superiors had not foretold. It is worth remembering Burckhardt's principle when we come to deal with another great lecturer, Isaiah Berlin. He was once famous for understanding everything about the age he lived in. There is still reason to believe he understood a lot. But if today he is starting to look a bit less penetrating about it all, it could be because things have moved on.

Though Berlin wrote comparatively little about the twentieth century's worst horrors, there wasn't much he didn't know about them. The question is how much he usefully wrote about them: a question worth trying to answer, because on the answer will eventually depend how much we can usefully write about him. On the level of personal publicity, his renown as an amiable sage goes on increasing after death. Mainly due to the beavering diligence of his editor Henry Hardy, compilations of Berlin's essays have continued to appear, making him seem more productive than when he was alive. Michael Ignatieff's finely proportioned biography, a model of the genre, summarizes and clarifies Berlin's themes with a terseness that might lead its readers to skip through the subject's own compositions when it is found that they are seldom as tightly written. But *The Proper Study of Mankind*, a concentration of the compilations, provides sufficient evidence that Berlin's best prose was something more weighty than the distilled monologues of a fascinating talker: as a set book it is likely to go on being a touchstone of

liberal thought for many years to come. Thus attended by curators
and commentators, Berlin continues to enjoy a bustling second life,
like the city of the same name. Yet somehow it has become necessary
to assert, instead of just accept, that he had deep feelings about what
was going on in modern history, because all too often his written
response sounded shallow.

As the bright young son of a bourgeois family that sensibly fled
Riga to escape the Bolshevik revolution, he took with him, as part
of his baggage, memories of Cheka arrogance that made him suspicious for life about any concept of freedom that presumed to
impose itself through political coercion. But even on the subject of
the Soviet Union, he would later write much more about the
repression of individual artists than the mass obliteration of ordinary people – which, as Michael Burleigh has tried to remind us, is
the thing to concentrate on, not gloss over. And the depredations
of Nazi Germany scarcely figure in Berlin's writings at all, even
though he played an honourable part in fighting Hitler. He spent
much of the war in Washington only because he had been sent
there on a diplomatic posting, not because he was playing for
safety. If he had been caught in Britain, he would undoubtedly have
shared the fate of millions of other Jews had the battle been lost.
Silence about Mao's China might be understandable – the full story
emerged late in his life – but how was it that the global aggregate
of totalitarian mania failed to take a central place in his treatment
of recent history? Does his eloquent advocacy of liberalism take the
full measure of the forces ranged against it? We are not necessarily
in contravention of Burckhardt's principle if we say that the twentieth century's seismic outbursts of irrationality were its defining
events. There were plenty of thinkers who thought so at the time.
But if Berlin thought so, he was reluctant to say so; and if he starts
looking weak there, then doubts are bound to creep in about the
strength of his contribution to his main field, the history of ideas
in the Enlightenment and the nineteenth century. If he could say
so much about the preparation for the main event, but so little
about the main event, how good was he on the preparation? Perhaps the first defence against so subversive an enquiry would be to
say that a later superficiality doesn't necessarily erode an initial
seriousness. If it did, Bertrand Russell's recommendations for unilateral nuclear disarmament would have made nonsense of *Principia*

Mathematica. But a better defence would be to show that Berlin's superficiality was only superficial.

This would be easier to show if this whopping first volume of his collected letters had not been published. Wilfully complete – it was Berlin himself, and not, for once, his editor, who wanted everything included – the book begs for belittlement, which it has duly received from some reviewers, especially if they placed a high value on his more formal work. With a lot more to come, the letters cover his active life from the late 1920s, in which the young refugee from revolutionary Russia became almost immediately assimilated into the English *beau monde*, through to 1946, by which time he was established as the most dazzling Jewish social asset since Disraeli, and without being baptized. The contemplative life, however, is largely absent, which is probably the reason why some of the reviewers reacted as if to the diaries of Chips Channon, or of Harold Nicolson at best. Certainly there is an awful lot about grand houses, dinner parties whether in London or in Washington, and – this above all – academic politics in all their bitchy intricacy, as if recorded by a less ponderous and more cultivated version of C.P. Snow.

But 'cultivated' is the operative word. Although the letters might give the impression that Berlin was always at least as interested in the power struggles going on within Balliol and All Souls as those going on within the Foreign Office, the US State Department, the Wilhelmstrasse or the Kremlin, the knowing gossip is enriched by the intensity of his enthusiasm for the arts and for civilized institutions. Indeed he treats British institutions as works of art in themselves, as if endorsing Chesterton's idea that democracy was another name for the sum total of humane traditions. In that crucial regard, this book of letters – and further volumes are bound to confirm the impression – is a sumptuous demonstration of one of his key principles, and ought to be valued as such. The principle is no less valuable because Burke thought of it first: a tolerable polity is an inheritance, and too multifariously determined by the past to be altered comprehensively in the present without the risk of its lethal disintegration. Later on, Karl Popper, in exile in New Zealand, would do the theoretical work establishing the imperative that any imposed social change should be aimed only at the correction of a specific abuse: the theoretical work that decisively identified revolution as the enemy of an open society. Berlin might have elaborated the same theory earlier, if he had had the time. But he was too busy embodying its truth. Sixty years later, nearing death after a happily fulfilled life, he was right to demand that none of his early letters should be left out, because they registered all the different ways he could function, as a free and thoughtful human being, in the full and complicated texture of an historically continuous society, an order which he thought needed no fundamental reordering. If he failed to notice some of its failings, it was only because he was enjoying so many of its virtues. The Jew out of nowhere was in demand everywhere, and he can be excused for loving every minute of it. To call him profoundly conservative hardly meets the case. He thought even the frivolity was part of the bedrock. The ideal guest, a fountain of scintillating chatter to match the fountain in the courtyard, he would gladly have revisited Brideshead every weekend.

Sexually inoperative but incorrigibly flirtatious, he loved the high-born ladies, who loved him right back, although his paucity of physical response – a desert under the ocean of talk – led several of them to despair, and one of them to the mad-house. On this evidence, his appeal was no mystery. Clever young beauties with hyphenated surnames found themselves being adored for their cleverness as much as their beauty. A single letter to Cressida Bonham-Carter is peppered with references to Beethoven, Tolstoy, Kafka, Racine, Henry James, Debussy, Proust, Bartok, Berg and St John of the Cross. It probably went down a storm. Certainly she didn't ask him to lay off the erudition, because his next letter to her mentions Diderot, Balzac, Maupassant and Turgenev, while commending her for agreeing with him about the attractions of his admired Herzen, whom Berlin himself had discovered only recently, while researching his monograph on Karl Marx. Herzen's magnanimity – in such sharp contrast to Marx's vengeful rancour – had bowled him over. ('There is no writer, & indeed no man I shd like to be like, & to write like, more.') These letters to Cressida were written in 1938, by which time it must have been obvious to him that the old world he had already seen coming apart was showing few signs of putting itself back together. Clearly he thought, as Herzen did, that it could be put back together spiritually, in a *convivio* of civilized minds favoured by the seemingly unshakeable social cohesion of Britain, his land of exile.

It hardly needs saying that there were plenty of intelligent native-born people at the time who thought that the social cohesion was bound for well-deserved ruin. But he noticed that they were almost all well connected. To join the Communist party, he observed, was mainly a way for guilty liberals to feel serious. A more serious liberal than that, he firmly recommended, not least by his behaviour, the inherited political stability that enabled subversive opinion to be expressed safely in the first place. If his success as an adornment of grand dinner tables looks a bit cosy in retrospect, we should not forget that he had small reason to question the impenetrable exclusiveness of a social structure's upper works if they were penetrable and inclusive enough to allow his own ascent to favour. He was the living proof of what he proposed as a necessary condition for liberalism: hang on to what works, *pas de zèle*, no root-and-branch solutions for the problems of a civil order that was something far more complicated than a tree. Left-leaning intellectuals who thought that society was on the point of ceasing to work altogether had good reason for despising his attitude as a voluble incitement to do nothing. So it was, but it arose from an acute apprehension of what might happen if the wrong things were done.

From this distance, the apprehension looks like a perception. There were many intellectuals of comparable status who could not accept until many years later that the society they already lived in was the only reliable source of any alterations that might improve it. Berlin took that for granted: so much so that he didn't write much on the subject. Professionally, he didn't yet feel obliged to. His little book on Marx was a one-off, although its attendant prodigies of research would serve him well in his post-war future. Throughout the thirties – and indeed right up until the famous wartime Atlantic crossing when he had his change of heart in the unpressurized belly of a bomber – he was nominally a philosopher, not an historian of ideas; and the philosophers of the day were already well set on the hermetic course that would separate their *métier* from any obligations to interdisciplinary wisdom. But significantly, he didn't write much on the subject in his letters either. Not only was society unquestioned: so were its questioners. Stalin gets only a few lines of the index, and Hitler fewer still. There is a whole column for Maurice Bowra. ('on Forster as bore, 104;' 'hates Connolly, 142;' etc. and *ad inf.*)

Apart from Berlin's sharply expressed objection to his aristocratic friend Adam von Trott's apologetics for the Nazi legal system – a system that would later reward von Trott by hanging him from a hook – the paucity, in the letters, of Berlin's written reaction to the global disaster that emanated from Hitler's Germany would be continued after the war, when, no longer a formal philosopher, he began producing the long string of lectures, broadcasts and essays that gave him his enduring lustre as an intellectual. Hardly any of his public writings impinged directly on that subject; an omission we can safely postpone examining until after taking account of the considerable amount he wrote about the Soviet Union, because there would also be an omission in that, and one that might provide a generally applicable clue. Some of the later letters in the book evoke his celebrated meeting with Anna Akhmatova in Leningrad in 1945. It was one of the key episodes in his life, and, indeed, in Akhmatova's. (Understandably self-obsessed after years of mental torture, she thought that her meeting with Berlin – 'the guest from the future' – was the cause of the Cold War.) His correspondence on the topic presaged the post-war wealth of his writings about Russia in general (to be found in the 1978 collection *Russian Thinkers*) and the Soviet Union in particular. To a certain extent they had been presaged by his book on Marx, but by now he knew that Stalin was the man to contend with.

In *The Soviet Mind*, the latest posthumous collection of Berlin's dispersed papers, it's Stalin who gets the whole column in the index. Maurice Bowra gets a single mention, and there is nothing frivolous even about that. Bowra, an early translator of some of Akhmatova's poems, had spoken of her as someone not heard of since World War I. When Berlin found her still alive at the end of World War II, he made a lot of it. Her beleaguered career under the Soviet Union is at the heart of the book. There is reason to believe that her survival led Berlin to a false conclusion, but there are plenty of true conclusions to consider first. In 1957 he wrote that Stalin's repression of 'ideas as such' had had a destructive effect even on the sciences, whether pure or applied. He could have taken this line further, and certainly much further back: Solzhenitsyn took it as far back as the fate of the engineers when Stalin first came to power. But at least the point takes care of what happened to Russian genetics under Stalin's pet crackpot Lysenko, a triumph for charlatanry which ensured that anything left of Soviet agricultural expertise after the ravages of collectivization was reduced to a terminal impotence. Berlin was capable of assessing the effects of Stalin's dead hand in fields other than the arts, so when it comes to the arts it is no surprise to find him being acutely sensitive to the desperate position that the serious Russian writers were in, at a time when prominent Western writers still felt no shame about accepting invitations to Moscow so that they could spend the blocked roubles of their royalties. Akhmatova and Boris Pasternak emerge from these pages as giants harried by swarming pygmies. It turns out, from Berlin's text and the editor's notes to it, that when Zhdanov, in 1946, infamously characterized Akhmatova as 'half whore, half nun', he was lifting a tag that had already appeared in the *Soviet Literary Encyclopedia* in 1930, and was not new even then. The party apparatchiks had always had boundless powers to suffocate the creativity of their intellectual betters. The ability to pick which head merited the application of a pillow was a kind of intellectual qualification in itself. (Solzhenitsyn said it was called 'the Moscow talent': the talent to frustrate talent in others.) There was never any danger that Berlin would regard such persecution as a mere cultural quirk. He clearly loathed it. But what he says about the Mandelstams makes you wonder if he really took in all the implications.

In her two great books *Hope Against Hope* and *Hope Abandoned*, Nadezhda Mandelstam was talking about a lot more than personal losses among the intelligentsia. She was talking about an impersonal bloodbath: in that regard, her writings rank her with Evgenia Ginzburg and Shalamov, and join her with Solzhenitsyn and Robert Conquest in tracing the whole catastrophe all the way back to Lenin. For her, the death of her husband was at the centre of a far bigger story. Berlin, too, was appalled by Osip Mandelstam's fate. But one of the points Berlin made about him in the 1965 essay 'A Great Russian Writer' is oddly conciliatory towards the regime that murdered him. 'No socialist society has (or at any rate, should have) anything to fear from unfettered powers of creation ... Perhaps like other *maîtres cachés* he too will be allowed to emerge into the light of day.' It could have been that Berlin, with Stalin safely out of the picture, was tempering his opinions in the hope of the essay being read in the Soviet Union and having a helpful effect. It even might have done so. Mandelstam's poetry, like Akhmatova's, was indeed officially republished while the regime was still running. But again like hers, it was in a censored edition. Pretty in its blue binding but devoid of an historical context, the Mandelstam volume was a Potemkin Village in printed form, with no hint in its supposedly scholarly introduction that the poet had fallen victim to much more than an unfortunate accident. Compared with the three-volume collected works that had already been published in the West, it was an insult added to an injury. Certainly it did nothing to contest Josef Brodsky's resonant opinion that true lyricism, which embodies the ethics of a language, is always intolerable to a tyranny. Strangely enough, Berlin elsewhere seemed to be of the same mind: he traced Stalin's repression of the independent intellect back to Napoleon's belief that all critics, of anything, should be silenced, lest they start criticizing him. But Osip Mandelstam wasn't just silenced: he was murdered. Berlin talked about him as if he had lived on in spirit – which was true – but made much less out of the recalcitrant fact that he was dead. And in general Berlin preferred to talk about the Russian writers who had stayed alive, almost as if they had done so by will power. Nowhere in this book can he be heard going quite so far as the opinion attributed to him by Ignatieff, who says that Berlin learned from Akhmatova that 'history could be made to bow before the sheer stubbornness of human conscience'. (According to Ignatieff's footnote, Berlin said something like this in a letter to his friend Jean Floud, which we will probably be getting in the next volume.) But he did seem to believe, or want to believe, that the hounded artists could somehow choose to resist. The facts, however, say that the only choosing was done by Stalin, who chose whether they would live or die.

As Berlin learned later to his horror, his meeting with Akhmatova put her in danger. Her few remaining privileges were revoked and she even ended up losing her union card, which meant that she was no longer, from the official viewpoint, a writer at all. But there had been scores of moments since the Revolution when she might have lost her life, like her husband, or been locked away, like her son. She stayed alive because of Stalin's arbitrary decision, which could just as easily have gone the other way. Among the artists, it had gone the other way many times. Frantic to get her son out of the Gulag, Akhmatova eventually wrote poems in praise of the regime. Her subservience was obtained in the same way that Bukharin's confession had been obtained in 1938. (They didn't have to torture him. All they had to do was threaten his children.) And there had never been any time when, if her existence had been thought useless, it would not have been ended. After the regime fell, Isaac Babel's confession was found in a filing cabinet in the Lubyanka. There was dried blood on it. That was the extent to which history bowed before his stubborn conscience: no extent. Babel's fate gets precisely one mention in this book. Meyerhold's gets two. But even had Berlin talked at length about them and about many other artists and intellectuals equally unfortunate, he would still have been a prisoner of his illusion that the regime's powers of repression were actuated by some variety of rational logic, however ruthless. Yet there was plenty of evidence that the whole thing had been irrational from the beginning. The evidence had been pouring out of the Soviet Union since before Stalin even came to power. After he did, his arbitrary decision went the other way millions of times. Berlin should have seen the sufferings of his living artists in the context of a multitude of less important people – more than all the people alive in Australia when I was a boy – who were dead for no good reason, or even for a bad one. Some of his living artists tried hard enough to tell him, but somehow he didn't get it. It's the somehow that should concern us.

The anomaly may well have arisen from Berlin's fondness for seeing history always in the context of ideas. For him, political propensities, up to and including the propensity for mass murder, arose out of the ideas leading up to them. He rarely considered that the ideas might have been preserved, and given lip service, only to serve the propensity. In 'Soviet Russian Culture' (1957) he correctly noted that under the Soviet Union the Russian intelligentsia had been reduced to 'silence and total submission', but he added a revealing sentence. 'Mere intimidation, torture and murder should not have proved sufficient in a country which, we are always told, was not unused to just such methods and had nevertheless preserved a revolutionary underground alive for the better part of a century.' Even at the time, when Khrushchev himself, who had been an energetic participant in the slaughter, had just finished pointing out that there had been nothing 'mere' about it, Berlin's proposed continuity between the relatively selective barbarities of Tsarist absolutism and the Soviet Union's unrestricted warfare against its own population should have struck him as a touch glib. There was, however, an even more revealing sentence to follow. 'It is here that one must acknowledge that Stalin achieved this by his own original contributions to the art of government.'

Alas, Berlin was being only half ironic. One of the original contributions he specified was the Artificial Dialectic, a term he attributed to O. Utis. For security reasons, Berlin was as yet unable to reveal that 'O. Utis' had been a code-name for himself, when he was sending reports back from Moscow to London at about the same time that George Kennan, code-named 'X', was telling Washington why Containment was the only feasible policy. The notion of Containment had many fathers: nobody who had witnessed the Soviet Union's homicidal activities in Poland could doubt its necessity. The notion of the Artificial Dialectic was all Berlin's, and in retrospect it looks too sophisticated to be true. According to Berlin, Stalin's rhythm of purge and relaxation had always been precisely calculated to maintain the system. One's first objection would have to be that Stalin's purge of Red Army officers on the very eve of Operation Barbarossa might have been calculated to bring the system to an end. But there is a wider objection: the theory makes Stalin a Soviet Mind, a thinker – and therefore a student of history, like Isaiah Berlin.

It seems doubtful. The mark of intellectuals is, or should be, their ability to reach conclusions that don't suit their prejudices. However much Stalin read, he took nothing in that didn't suit his disposition. Dossiers were brought in bundles to his desk that proved Hitler was about to invade him. Those who brought them ran the risk of getting shot. His mind was made up that there would be no invasion. When it happened, he collapsed into bed, giving his colleagues a chance to bump him off that they unforgivably let slip. His debacle convinced even him that he would have to listen to other voices if he wanted to win the war. Listening only to his own, as he usually preferred to do, he would have lost it in the first six months. In the use of his unlimited powers, Stalin was too irrational even to defend the most pressing interests of the regime he ruled. Just as Hitler, with Nazi Germany fighting for its life late in the war, went on diverting manpower and precious rolling stock into the self-imposed task of wiping out Jews, gypsies and homosexuals, so did Stalin, earlier in the war, when the Soviet Union was fighting for

its life, go on diverting manpower and precious Studebaker trucks –
sent to him by the Americans on convoys which he mentioned only
when they were late – into the self-imposed task of resettling his
own populations, with all the usual obscenities attendant on that
pointless activity. The Soviet Union was an asylum with the most
violent patient in charge. Berlin advised London that it was best
dealt with by making no threats, and that it would probably last for
as long as it liked. Kennan was closer to the mark when he advised
Washington that its belligerence could be contained only with armed
strength, but that its irrationality would set a term to its life. The
terminus proved to be another forty-five years in coming, but it
came. Berlin was not the only student who thought that the vast
mechanism might go on maintaining itself indefinitely. I. F. Stone,
with the credentials of an ex-Communist, argued persuasively that
the security services were geared to keep their omnipotence in
perpetuity. With even better credentials, the expelled sociologist
Alexander Zinoviev wrote a series of closely reasoned essays – much
more impressive, in retrospect, than his gigantic satirical novels –
showing how the control mechanisms worked, and how the upsurge
of dissident literature might even be one of them. Not just on the
bien pensant Left, a considerable intellectual investment went into
crediting the Soviet Union with unearthly powers of reasoning.

To do him credit, Berlin rejoiced when the expectation finally
proved false. His essay 'The Survival of the Russian Intelligentsia',
written in 1990, is practically a chorus from *Fidelio*: the prisoners
emerge blinking from their cells into the light of day. But here again,
there is a false note. 'My impression was that what remained of
the true intelligentsia was dying. In the course of the last two years
I have discovered, to my great surprise and delight, that I was
mistaken.' Mistaken, he might have said, mainly in neglecting to
note that what did not remain of the true intelligentsia was already
dead ten times over. Going on to celebrate the vindication of his
friend Andrei Sakharov, he sings this *kaddish* above his grave: 'Nor
was he alone. The survival of the entire culture to which he belonged,
underneath the ashes and rubble of dreadful historical experience,
appears to me a miraculous fact.' More than miraculous, one would
have thought: illusory. The entire culture survived? Tell it to Babel.

But impatience is out of place. Berlin was right enough about the
Soviet Union to help ensure that, in Britain at any rate, those who

were entirely wrong could not have it all their own way. It could have been, however, that Britain was simply better prepared to take a realistic view than, say, France. It was Berlin's French equivalent, Raymond Aron, who published, in 1955, the single most penetrating analysis of Communist ideology, *The Opium of the Intellectuals*. But Aron's message was lost on the *gauchiste* intelligentsia, which continues to this day to behave as if all the atrocities added up to something respectable. *Le livre noir du communisme*, a new Book of the Dead which counts the innocent victims in their many millions, was reviewed in France as if it had been written by the Plans division at Langley, Virginia. Another philosopher who, like Berlin, graduated to political history, Jean-François Revel, in his *L'obsession anti-americaine*, has done a convincing job of tracing fashionable anti-Americanism to this long-lingering reluctance to accept the facts about the new world order that was supposed to replace the depredations of capitalism with something beneficial. (The more *chic* Bernard-Henri Levy, recently in the news for taking the same line on this point, is really piggybacking on an effort that Revel has been putting in for decades.) But is it really a reluctance? Following the rule that we should put the best possible construction on the motives of our opponents, perhaps we should consider the possibility that the facts have been accepted, but can't be fully faced, because the cost of reconstructing a world view would be too painful. Berlin's own – much lesser, but still striking – shyness on the matter suggests this might be so. His view of history depended on the assumption that large-scale events, however terrible, came about as a result of minds deliberating. He would have had to rethink his position altogether if he were to admit the possibility that there could be large-scale events into which minds didn't enter. So there might have been inertia to go with the revulsion. But there can be no doubt about the revulsion. Berlin was a man of feeling. Those giant totals of dead on the page – lines of zeros like strings of bubbles – might look meaningless to the insensitive. But to the sensitive they can be devastating. They mean too much.

Which brings us to the European empire of Nazi Germany, where so many of the bubbles represented Berlin's fellow Jews. There could have been several reasons why Berlin said so little. He called it 'the most fearful genocide in history', but beyond that he offered no illumination, as if the subject were too dark to admit light. The first reason might have been that he didn't know what to say. Thomas Mann – not a Jew but married to a half-Jew, and prominent on Heydrich's personal list of illustrious absentees with Jewish sympathies who should be dealt with promptly if they ever returned to Germany – started broadcasting from America as early as 1942 about what he knew the Nazis were up to in the East. (He didn't need access to the Ultra decrypts to get the facts: they were in the Swiss newspapers.) But after the war, when the full statistics of the Holocaust came out, his reaction was to work on *The Confessions of Felix Krull*. Berlin, too, probably knew all about it from an early date, but perhaps he found himself equally short of adequate things to say when the full magnitude of the horror was revealed. One of the revelations was that both of his grandfathers had been murdered immediately when the Nazis occupied Riga in 1941. He barely mentioned it, and the best explanation is that he was traumatized, and that the trauma was intensified to a paralysis by the realization – imagination overload – that the extinguished multitudes were his grandfathers multiplied by millions.

Another reason could have been that other people did the job, notably Raul Hilberger and Martin Gilbert, and that anything he had to add would have been rhetoric. (He said this to Ignatieff, who might have been slower to report that Berlin 'actively despised the Holocaust industry'. The Holocaust industry has never produced as much toxic waste as the Holocaust Denial industry, and if there are too many books, too few of them have reached even Vienna, let alone Cairo and Riyadh.) Yet another reason might have been guilt for one of the two roles he had played in wartime Washington with relation to Zionism. A Zionist himself, he was a personal friend of Weizmann. Berlin used his connections to smooth Weizmann's path to Roosevelt and a possible endorsement for the Zionist cause. But as an emissary of Britain's Ministry of Information, Berlin was also obliged – unless he resigned – to promote his government's official line on Palestine, based on the infamous White Paper that denied refugee Jews entry to what was, for many of them, the only possible sanctuary from Hitler. It couldn't have been long before Berlin realized that this made him party to a crime. Ever the diplomat, Berlin sided with Weizmann in the conviction that a Jewish entity of some kind would eventually emerge after the British had been talked into modifying their mandate – sided, that is, against David

Ben Gurion, who thought that the Jewish state would have to be established unilaterally, if necessary with resort to force. Berlin always thought that reason might prevail in the matter. (In a letter written home in 1943, we find him opining that the cause would be best promoted 'by means of private conversations on the part of sensible persons'.) Ben Gurion knew better: or, if you like, worse.

*

Born to a concerted Arab attack, the State of Israel grew up in the middle of a war, which has not yet ended. For the rest of his life, Berlin remained committed to Israel, although he was always careful not to offer advice from outside, in case it was thought patronizing. Ignatieff records that Berlin felt guilty about not having said anything publicly in favour of Peace Now. It was a pity he didn't, because the emphasis that Peace Now places on giving up the Occupied Territories is a potent argument for the only possible means by which Israel can preserve itself as a democracy. Berlin's agreement would have been useful to the young soldiers: long on bravery, they were short of clout. But generally, throughout Israel's short and threatened history, Berlin seems to have had the right opinions, even when he didn't voice them in public, and the Israelis valued him as a star of the diaspora, the Jewish equivalent of a Righteous Gentile. In 1979 he was awarded the Jerusalem Prize as a mark of respect. To actually live in Jerusalem, however, was never part of his plans. At one time or another Ben Gurion, Abba Eban and Teddy Kolleck all asked him to move there. He preferred Oxford. He already had his sanctuary. But of course he had always had his sanctuary. He was a Jew who had never needed to make it to the new home. His guilt must have been tremendous for the many who had needed to, and didn't. To where they went, there was no boat: only a train.

The train takes us to the best reason. Apart from his epic visions of domination and destruction, Hitler had few ideas on his mind. As a consequence, Nazi Germany gave the historian of ideas little to talk about. In *The Proper Study of Mankind*, the two essays grouped under the heading 'Romanticism and Nationalism in the Modern Age' stop well short of Hitler's rise to power, as well they might, because Hitler was truly interested only in the power. The German right-wing intellectuals had already discovered this to their embarrassment while he was still a long way from the Reichstag. In 1922 a bunch of them called the June Club invited him to address one of their meetings. Their idea was that they would treat him to their combined scholarly wisdom before he spoke. He made it clear that he wasn't interested in what they had to say, and used the time gained to speak longer, boring some of them into the floor but convincing others that they had been wasting their lives: brutality, that was the thing. (He had the same effect on Goebbels, a proud bookworm before he met his action hero.) Even the anti-Semites found him incurious about the subtleties of their philosophy, as indeed he was, because for him anti-Semitism was a passion, not an argument. Though various ideological dingbats were allowed to pursue their researches on the government payroll, the Nazi regime reflected Hitler's hatred of ideas in all of its departments. Hitler admired Mussolini personally and copied his methods along with Stalin's. But Hitler and most of the other top Nazis thought that Fascism as a philosophy was a waste of time: too many intellectuals.

Hitler rigorously divided action from thought. Thought had to be under the control of action, not vice versa. The action came from his propensities, which were psychotic from the start. Almost all of his early successes depended on initiatives so bizarre that nobody sane could anticipate them. After the Battle of Britain had been lost, his second big failure, in Russia, came about mainly because he preferred to maltreat people who had suffered under Stalin rather than enlist their aid. Making territory he had already conquered ungovernable was no sane way to conquer more of it. Even Himmler could work that out, but Hitler didn't listen. He couldn't, because it involved conciliation, which was a true idea, as opposed to mass murder, which was an expression of emotion. Though it is tempting to believe that Hitler, after absorbing a few nutty anti-Semitic pamphlets in Vienna, read nothing except Karl May's western sagas about Old Shatterhand, the truth is somewhat different. He fancied himself as a philosopher and could drop the names that backed up the claim. In that unintentionally comic masterpiece *Monologe in Führerhauptquartier 1941–1944*, we can find him, on 19 May 1944, telling his nodding audience that throughout the Great War he had carried the full five volumes of Schopenhauer everywhere he went. Since he got the Iron Cross as a runner in the trenches, he must have been running with a handicap. But there is no reason to doubt he carried them, or even that he read them. Nor, however, is there any reason to believe that he critically weighed a single word. Like Stalin, he sought in texts nothing but pretexts for his actions. To bring ideas under scrutiny was not his purpose.

Since it was Berlin's, we have a right to ask how well he did it. The first answer has to be that he did it very well. Though a worthy assemblage of his more heavyweight efforts, *The Proper Study of Mankind* is a bit misleading about how delightful he could be; and as so often happens with writers on serious topics, it is when he is at his most entertaining that he is most informative. He didn't really write all that brilliantly. Most of his prose pieces were transcripts of his talk boiled down from draft to draft, which is not the same process as the *ab initio* concentration necessary to yield a cogently nuanced text that reads like speech. He himself called his talk 'an avalanche', and he seems to have had little gift for the aphorism. That might have been one of the secrets for his continuing success at glamorous dinner tables. With his salon-wise wife Aline to manage his diary, he went on dining out until he had to be carried. Dr Johnson, in his own old age, told Boswell that he wasn't much invited anymore, because his unanswerable sallies silenced the table. Berlin was careful not to make the company feel stupid. On the night I saw him in action, he engaged in a tremendous competition with the political journalist Frank Johnson to name and evoke, with sound effects, every second-rate opera in the world. They were at each other like Joe Louis and Jersey Joe Walcott, to hilarious effect: titled ladies were spitting pheasant. At his best, he could get the same sparkling treasure into his writings. To take just one compilation, *Against the Current*: there is wealth of incidental truth in it. 'Benjamin Disraeli, Karl Marx and the Search for Identity' is the ideal introduction to both men and makes you wonder how they would have got on. (Not very well, probably: we learn that Marx called Lassalle 'the Jewish nigger'.) 'The "*Naïveté*" of Verdi' is a classic restatement of Schiller's principle of the difference between the naïve and the sentimental: saturated with Berlin's infectious love of music, it should be on the first-year course of every student in the country. Best of all, there is the essay about Montesquieu, which comes in handy when we try to give the second answer.

The second answer had to be that he missed a lot out, and some of it has proved to be of lasting importance. Here we should remember Burckhardt's principle. Berlin was already getting old before it started to emerge that totalitarianism had been so poisonous that the collapse or reform of the governments that imposed it would be no guarantee of its disappearance. If the first thing we now see about Nazi Germany, the Soviet Union, Maoist China and the other totalitarian states is their irrationality, it could be because of the growing evidence that totalitarianism can live without a state, and even without having a new state in mind. In that respect, even Saddam Hussein was obsolete, because he was a student of Stalin. Osama Bin Laden doesn't need to be a student of anybody except Andreas Baader, Ulrike Meinhof, the *Brigati Rossi*, Ilich Ramirez Sanchez (usually glorified as 'Carlos') and whichever Japanese terrorists attacked the El Al desk at foreign airports because they had no Jews of their own. Irrationality, we can now see, is a force in itself, and scarcely in need of a brain. Already there is not just an equivalence, but a blend, between the Islamism that condemns the Western liberal democracies and the international pseudo-left intelligentsia that condemns them as well. The anti-Semitic arguments of those Muslim groups – whether terrorist organizations or, less openly, states – who think Israel can be made to disappear are only just crazier than the pseudo-left arguments proclaiming America's responsibility for every injustice in the world. In fact the Arab arguments might even be more sane: the Palestinians can scarcely have a parallel state while suicide attacks against Israel continue, but sacrificing the Palestinians has always suited the Arab nations, and meanwhile Israel, under that degree of pressure, can be relied upon to go on gravitating towards an extremism of its own; although what the Arabs expect the Israelis to do with their atomic bombs should the point arrive when Israel caves in is difficult to judge.

We can be certain, however, that the performance of the Western intelligentsia has never been worse. Before the collapse of the Warsaw Pact regimes, the intelligentsia was merely deluded. After the collapse of the World Trade Center, it has gone haywire. Essentially a branch of the home entertainment industry, the left intelligentsia circulates, almost entirely for its own consumption, opinions even more contemptuous of ordinary people than used to prevail on the right. At least Kissinger, when he gave the green light for the toppling of Allende and the hideous events that predictably followed, could be reasonably sure that Chile's standard of living would go up. When fashionable intellectuals pour scorn on Iraq's provisional government as American stooges, they effectively ally themselves with the fanatics who would like to kill its every minister, with special treatment for the women. As Abba Eban once suggested, a consensus is an opinion shared by people who wouldn't dare to hold it individually. Loathe their own societies as they might – and there is plenty to loathe, even for those of us who realize that a free nation is bound to be full of things we don't like – even the most uninformed Western intellectuals are smart enough to see individually that President Bush didn't order the attack on the Twin Towers: if he had, the Golden Gate bridge would have fallen down instead. But collectively they are ready to agree that it doesn't matter what lies are told as long as a greater political truth is being served. They are unfazed when it is pointed out that the same assumption was a point of agreement between Hitler and Stalin. The totalitarian attitude to the truth, with history being rewritten not just retroactively but as it happens, has become standard. This could be an instance of decay through inheritance. Studying the institutionalized opportunism of states ruled by unalleviated mendacity, a previous generation of students caught the bug. In their separate death throes – spasmodically sudden in the case of the Third Reich, gruesomely prolonged in the case of the USSR – the totalitarian powers were dying patients who infected the doctors: a clear case of the original virus being sucked up into the syringe. The antibiotics have become toxic, like Harry Lime's penicillin. Measuring their virulence, we get a good idea of how lethal the disease was that they were originally employed to cure.

But we can't ask philosophers to predict events. What we can ask of them is that they should illuminate realities. The big reality that Berlin did not illuminate was the force of evil. His original background among the analytical philosophers, none of whom liked abstractions, may have stuck to him even after he broke away. Wittgenstein, by whose linguistic scrupulosity Berlin was buffaloed, said nothing about the Nazi assault on the Jews until it was all over. He had to see the photographs of the liberated death camps before he finally realized that the Nazis had meant what they said: a late and hard way to find out that death really is an event in life. For most of the philosophers, evil was a word: too large a one, and thus lacking in specificity. But evil is a reality, as Berlin's fellow philosopher Stuart Hampshire discovered. Hampshire didn't reason his way to that conclusion. He arrived at it emotionally, when he interrogated Kaltenbrunner at Nuremberg. Wedded to ideas, Berlin missed the opportunity to develop his political theories from his feelings. His love of music might have given him the hint. Quality is art's equivalent for the truth: Aron said that. Berlin didn't, but he felt it. When it came to great music, Berlin was alive to the composer's all-comprehending tragic sense that made it great.

When it came to history, he had the tragic sense, but somehow he never got it into his writings. It went the way of his grandfathers, into a mental realm where threatening facts are received but not attended to, like brown envelopes from the Council piling up on the hall table. There are prose writers, stretching from Thucydides and Tacitus onward, whose plain language gives us the thrill of poetry because they can face the full rage of chaos and still use its power to reinforce their sense of order. The passage in Tacitus about Sejanus' daughter is an uncanny forecast of the girl who gave her age to the German sergeant of engineers at Babi Yar. What Tacitus says would drive us to despair if it had not driven him to a perfect sentence. There is a gravitas beyond eloquence. Montaigne is often like that. From more modern times, Burckhardt is invariably like that, even when going wild about the arts. (As Berlin did, Burkhardt loved Verdi – after the premiere of *Aida* he had to calm himself down with beer – but he could give you the same lift when he talked about Torquemada.) From Berlin's own time, we can read Golo Mann's essays and the section of his *Deutsche Geschichte* dealing with the Weimar Republic and the Third Reich; we can read the book reviews Lewis Namier wrote after the war, when the German generals were cranking out the autobiographies that proved they had known Hitler was a madman even though they had known nothing about what he did; we can read the paragraphs that sympathetically but decisively discredit Georg Lukács in the third volume of Leszek Kolakowski's *Main Currents of Marxism*; we can read the chapter of Benedetto Croce's *Storia d'Europa nel secolo decimonono* that devastatingly analysed the Soviet Union as early as 1931; we can read Abba Eban's *Personal Witness*, a diplomatic memoir that leaves Metternich's sounding simple-minded; we can read a lot of prose like that and get the same thrill. Not always sprightly but always dense with implication, it is the unmistakable and addictive music made by those who have felt on their own skins, even if only as a flash of heat from the far horizon, the full destructive power of human history and are still wedded to making sense of it. Berlin could hear it in his beloved Herzen. He could not, however, quite produce it himself, and it might well be because he couldn't let thought give way to feeling. But feeling is thought's wellspring. The clue was staring him in the face, in his essay about Montesquieu.

What the great humanists have, and learn to overcome, is an apprehension that humanity might be worthless. Berlin lacked that apprehension, and it would be quixotic to regret it. It might have eroded his gusto, which is one of his most lavish gifts to us. Nobody who ever heard his booming burble in the lecture hall as he delivered an unbroken hour-long extravaganza from notes written on a tram ticket will ever forget his incarnation of benevolent mental energy. An invention from the ground up, like the Wolfson College he created in his later years, he was part of the landscape. But he paid the sure penalty for being in the swim. As a theoretician, his chief concerns were not the threats to democracy from without, but the conflicts within. Most of what he said about those was bound to become unremarkable. His celebrated distinction between positive and negative liberty is now the common debating point between and within all the main political parties. Every parent knows that you restrict liberty if you ban smacking. Every child knows that you increase it. There is nothing thought provoking about the dichotomy because there is nothing except the dichotomy. The same applies to his celebrated pluralism. In a free society, what else is there? Dangerously, he left in the air the question of whether good ends could be reconciled. The missing answer left the way open for the suggestion, recently popularized by Donald Rumsfeld, that some ends might have to be pursued by bad means: a tempting idea that Berlin got from Machiavelli.

But it is only an idea. Its refutation was formulated by Montesquieu. Berlin's essay on Montesquieu is a good candidate for the most resonant piece he ever wrote about anything, but even then he stopped short conceptually of the conclusions he was on the point of reaching by instinct. He gives a detailed account of how Montesquieu's pluralism valued all cultures; and then a further account of how Montesquieu, seeing the danger, wanted to leave room for some cultures being more valuable than others; but he made comparatively little of the device by which Montesquieu furthered the concept of an absolute morality that would apply even in the world of relative values that he had done so much to celebrate. Yet the device was right there in Montesquieu's prose, and Berlin actually quoted it. 'Justice is eternal, and doesn't depend at all on human conventions.' Berlin thought Montesquieu had merely deepened his problem by saying that there could be universal laws in a relative world. But Montesquieu wasn't saying that there were universal laws instinctive to all men. He was saying that there were eternal laws instinctive to some of them. Montesquieu argued that it didn't matter who says torture might be necessary: our better nature, if we have one, tells us it is wrong. He was, in other words, a good man by instinct. The implication is that there were good men among the first men, and bad men too. If Berlin had faced the likelihood that his own goodness, like the evil of Stalin and Hitler, stemmed from a time when there was no idea in mankind's head except where the next meal was coming from and how to kill it, he might have been better equipped to deal with modern malevolence in its full horrific force. There was an Isaiah Berlin in the cave. He just had less to talk about at dinner, and the food was terrible.

TLS, 3 September 2004

Postscript

After this piece appeared, the correspondence columns of the *TLS* were predictably bombarded by professional philosophers who seemed annoyed that an amateur had strayed on to their turf. I could summarize their letters, but perhaps their opinions are more digestibly evoked by the collective reply that I sent to the editor in the hope of seeing them off. Apparently it worked.

Sir,
    In his reaction to my piece about Isaiah Berlin, David Boll (10 September) attributes to me a belief that I do not hold. I am not one of the 'promoters of evil as the universal explanation'. I merely believe that a conception of evil is necessary, or else there will be explanations that are doomed to be inadequate. Perhaps

(as Dan Jacobson has reminded me in a private letter) I should not have left it open to be inferred that I think Hitler and Stalin had nothing at all going on in their heads. I think they had plenty. But I also think that their ideas, such as they were, were held in order to further their proclivities, which had the primacy. As for Mr Boll's assumption that I have no 'worries over American policy', would that it were true. If only for their triumphs in Abu Ghraib, I would like to see George W. Bush deposed from office and Donald Rumsfeld made a subject for study in a mental institution. Will that do? But this is not an argument about what I think; it's an argument about what Berlin thought, or anyway about what he said. From that viewpoint, Mr Boll's apparent belief that Berlin had no obligation to write in detail about totalitarian atrocities reveals a strange set of assumptions about what an historian of ideas might be called upon to account for. 'He wrote on plenty of other matters, besides which he made it plain enough what he thought of the horrors.' Yes, but he didn't actually say much.

Tim Congdon (17 September) assures us that Berlin did actually say a lot, in the case of the Soviet Union. But when I called Berlin's book about Marx a one-off, I had hoped to make it clear that the book was unique in the context of his pre-war activities. His detailed writings about the Soviet Union came after the war, as I said. I don't see how Mr Congdon could have misread me on that point in any way except wilfully, but perhaps I should try harder with my prose next time. It is hard to see, however, that any degree of effort on my part could have staved off Mr Congdon's ability to find 'deeply offensive' my account of the fate of the Jewish refugees who were shut out of Palestine. I can think of other subjects that I have been flippant about in my time, but not that one. This might be the moment, however, to repeat my opinion that anti-Semitism is a disaster for the just cause of the Palestinians in claiming their own state, because the suicide bombings can only deliver Israel into the hands of its own fanatics. Why Berlin said so little in support of the Peace Now dissidents is a question at the heart of the mystery I was trying to crack open. Michael Ignatieff tells us that Berlin was guilty about his silence on the point, but doesn't a true philosopher turn his internal conflicts into a subject?

It could be said that Berlin was not trying to be a philosopher.

Those of us who believe, however, that he made his exit from formal philosophy in order to say more about the world are bound to wonder about those occasions on which he seemed to be struck dumb. After all, he was free to speak, untrammelled by the kind of analytical concentration on language that leaves it with no subject beyond itself. That can be a valuable subject, of course, but meanwhile the world is left waiting. Joseph Gonda (17 September) brings his expertise as a professional philosopher to bear on my use of the word 'instinct', saying that it 'explains too much and thereby too little'. But the word 'instinct' explains a reasonable amount when you oppose it to the word 'idea'. It means something you've got, not something you thought of. Since we will always need the conception of an innate disposition antecedent to reason, it is hard to see that the word 'instinct' can ever be 'as conceptually dodoesque as phlogiston'. (Wittgenstein, who seldom mixed a metaphor, must be wondering what went wrong up here.) Phlogiston was never dodoesque: i.e. it was never alive. It was a wrong theory that became scientifically superseded. Whatever some philosophers might think, words do not become scientifically superseded. Mr Gonda's accusation that I was perverting Montesquieu might well be right, but his attendant complaint ('it is no accident that James does not quote or refer to Montesquieu's writings while doing so') is a bit steep. Berlin, in his essay on Montesquieu to which I was referring the reader, does quite a lot of quoting, including the sentence from *Lettres Persanes* that I translated: '*La justice est éternelle, et ne dépend point des conventions humaines*'. But if Mr Gonda wants to hear Montesquieu quoted directly by me, let me give him a sentence from *De l'esprit des lois*, Chapter XVII. After conceding that the practice of torture might suit despotic governments, and that it was normal for the Greeks and Romans to torture slaves, he trails off with an ellipsis before saying this: '*Mais j'entends la voix de la nature qui crie contre moi.*' Now what could he have meant by that?

Stephen Pain (17 September) can't imagine how much I would be pleased if it were thought that I had 'descended to the Dame Edna level of criticism'. That great lady has enviable powers of analysis, especially when it comes to skewering the kind of stuffed shirt who thinks Australians are funny when they try to use hard words. But the major point of his letter is by far the bigger insult, because it depends on an almost inspired distortion of the argument I was most careful to make. 'I do dislike,' he writes, 'this awful form of ethnocentricism that insists if a person is Jewish then they must have something to say about the Holocaust.' But I didn't say that he should have said something because he was Jewish. I said that he should have said something because he was a thinker about history, which was on fire all around him, yet for some reason he preferred to talk about how the house had been built, at the very moment when it was burning down.

Dan Jacobson's private letter was, of course, the one that mattered. When you have a genuine case, it can never really be overstated, but there is always a temptation to understate the possible objections. Hitler and Stalin regarded themselves as monuments of the intellect, and were so regarded by their followers: so it was foolish of me to allow the suggestion that their actions might have been unaccompanied by mental activity. *Mein Kampf* amounted to a consistent, if not reasoned, presentation of a case, and was unreadable only in the sense of being repellent. There were intellectuals outside Germany – most conspicuously Harold Nicolson – who read it and not only saw what Hitler was on about, but guessed what he might do. And Stalin's *Short Course*, which he supervised even if he did not write it, marks the culmination of a Marxist-Leninist tradition, even if it also marks its final descent into sclerosis. But I hold to the conclusion that it was their desire for a certain kind of action that made them think that way in the first place. A stronger objection to that conclusion – an objection which none of the philosophers made, strangely enough – would have been to say that Mao Zedong began by trying to put his principles into action through comparatively benevolent means. He became murderous only later on. When he did, he became more murderous than anybody, but the objection remains. In his case I wouldn't pretend to have an answer to it. Philip Short, in his excellent biography of Mao, doesn't have an answer either. I suppose one possible explanation is that the idea of dealing with an opposing view by killing everyone who holds it, or even might hold it, can enter the head at any time. Nor does the person so inspired necessarily have to be in charge of a state. Tacitus, talking about

Tiberius, gave us everything we need to know about what the despot can do if the mood takes him. The despotic actions adduced by Tacitus were repeated with depressing regularity all the way down to Pol Pot. But the characteristic genocide of more recent times – one thinks, or tries not to think, of Rwanda and Darfur – is a different matter. Now we must deal, or fail to deal, with genocide *instead* of a state, with mass killing as a mode of being; and the focal field of study for that might be in modern terrorism, which, for all but sentimentalists who think there can be no irrationality without a reason, so clearly raises the question of whether someone might not want to perpetrate an evil for its own sake, and even against his own nominated political interests.

Trying to answer that question leads us into an area beyond nihilism, which at least had a kind of purity. But counter-productive terrorism looks to be mixed up with the dubious attractions of celebrity, self-realization and the desire of its practitioners to appear on screen, even if wearing a mask. The political analysts of the next generation, whose task one doesn't envy, might have to face the possibility that the glamour-boy terrorist does what he does, not because he has a definite cause to pursue, but because he is exercising his one and only talent: the one talent which it would be death to hide, but which unfortunately expresses itself in the form of random death to others. This seems likely to have been true in the pioneering case of Ilich Ramirez Sanchez, whom the press foolishly continues to romanticize with the name of Carlos, thereby infantilizing itself along with him. One Sunday afternoon Sanchez threw a grenade into the drugstore in Saint-Germain-des-Prés. He killed two people and wounded thirteen more. Apparently his reason for doing so was that the proprietor was a Jew. There is no reason to think that Sanchez's anti-Semitism is any more fervent than his Marxism. Yet there are convinced anti-Semites who would never do such a thing. We can even distinguish his achievement from that of the Jewish ultra-orthodox madman who, when he massacred thirty defenceless Arabs in a mosque, was at least angry about something. Though putatively enraged by the unholy alliance between the US and Zionism, Sanchez has probably never been angered by anything except the occasional woman who turned him down. Few of them seem to do so. As of this writing, his French lawyer, a clear case of the sophisticated nincompoop, plans to marry him. It is hard not to hope that he will finish her off with suitable casualness when he moves on to his next triumph. Hard, but necessary. If we aren't capable of seeing that the benefit of justice means nothing unless it is extended to those who are too stupid to be worthy of it, we should join the other side.

SAVE US FROM CELEBRITY

A speech delivered at the Australian Commercial Radio Conference,
16 October 2004

I met Andy Warhol only once, and I wasn't sure it was happening even then. Theoretically he was still alive at the time, but he had the handshake of a ghost. It was beyond limp – just a cellophane sack full of liquid, like the water bombs we made in school. But the hand was a miracle of vitality compared to his face. Transparent of skin and with the eyes of a salmon on a marble slab, he would have made Lazarus, emerging from the family vault, look more animated than Billy Crystal. Our encounter happened in London, not Palestine, but there was something biblical about the features thinly painted on the front of that balsa skull, under the canopy of stark white fibre-optic hair. There was a post mortem solemnity there, an intimate knowledge of the world beyond the tomb. Perhaps, after he had been shot a few years earlier by one of his bedraggled platoon of untalented actresses, he had journeyed through the netherworld while on life support. His smile – a computer-generated rearrangement of crumbling tissue – seemed to suggest that he had met me down there, and was as glad as a zombie could be to see me again. It was kind of him, because he had no idea who I was. And of course I wasn't anybody. Everybody Warhol knew was a celebrity. Therefore he did not know me.

For a fleeting moment I felt bad about that. I didn't want it to be such a comedown for the man who had lunch with Jackie O to be having his hand squeezed by Clive Zero. Besides, I quite admired him. I didn't think much of his paintings, which struck me as sheets of stamps designed by the semi-gifted daughter of a Third World despot. I couldn't see why a silk-screen photograph of the electric chair should be more interesting than the actual electric chair, which at least transmits some kind of thrill, even if fatal. But I had been impressed by his much-quoted prediction that everyone in the future would be famous for fifteen minutes. The prediction was so obviously already coming true. And he had said it well, and saying something well is almost as good as doing something. Somewhere in what passed for my brain in those days, I was already struggling towards the conclusion that if somebody did something they had a right to be somebody, but merely being somebody meant nothing if being somebody was the only thing that somebody did. I wonder if I've made myself clear. Let me expand on that point, as the bishop said to the actress. No, wait a second, it wasn't what the bishop said to the actress. It was what the Governor of Tasmania said to the Queen of the Netherlands.

Not long after our encounter, Andy Warhol made another trip to the beyond, and this time to stay. He expired somewhere in the centre of a tangle of plastic tubes, most of them supplying his body with fluids it had never had in the first place. It wasn't the way I want to die – I want to be knifed to death in an Elle McPherson lingerie commercial – but as I read the news of his passing I had already achieved my own fifteen minutes of fame and had started to wonder whether it was worth the trouble. I wasn't world famous, which was the only degree of fame that had ever interested Andy. To be world famous you first have to be famous in America, which I would probably never have managed even had I desired to. Not that I have anything fundamental against America. I have detailed criticisms, but I don't see how you can have those if you hate the whole place: if everything is always wrong, there is nothing they can change. And you have to admire a country so democratic that a mentally handicapped man can become President.

Incidentally, I was in New York the weekend before last, having arrived just in time for the first debate between Bush and Kerry. Watching the debate with a deepening sense of awe, I thought: there is the spectacle of the two most highly qualified men in a great nation contending eloquently for the right to occupy its highest office, and then there is this. It wasn't surprising that Kerry was generally thought to have won the contest. Being more articulate than George W. Bush is no challenge. So is my cat. In the debate, Bush once again proved that it is too early in America's history to have a president for whom English is not his first language. Once again you could see the truth of the remark (I think it was my remark but other commentators have been borrowing it) that the British Prime Minister Tony Blair's great advantage as a world statesman is his gift for putting President Bush's thoughts into words. It's even possible that President Bush has no thoughts at all, only emotions. When he searches for a word, he feels fear, and his face shows it. When he finds one, he feels triumph, and his face shows that. Almost always, the word he finds is the wrong one, but his look of relief arouses sympathy in the audience, as when a child, sent to fetch a spoon from the kitchen drawer, comes back with a fork. I was especially sympathetic when he announced that the 'group of folks', by which he meant the insurgents in Iraq, were fighting us 'vociferously'. 'That's why they're fighting so vociferously.' He must have meant 'viciously' or perhaps 'ferociously', but he could scarcely have meant 'vociferously'. If all that the insurgents were doing was shouting loudly they would be less of a problem. But Bush's premature senile aphasia wasn't the real story of the debate. The real story was that Kerry, even with his opponent disappearing into a semantic black hole, still managed to win only by a hair. In fact he won only by a hairstyle. Kerry's hairstyle is worth a short digression, because it represents the chief reason why I could never have been famous in America.

How did Kerry's hair get like that? We must presume that it is real, or the Bush campaign would already have suggested that he received it as a bribe from Kim Jong-Il. And indeed Kim's bouffant coiffure must be some kind of technological creation, separated from his elevator shoes by the length of a short lunatic. Kerry's hairstyle, on the other hand, almost certainly started its life on top of his own head, instead of in the same laboratory that refines the uranium for North Korea's atomic bombs. But Kerry's hair would be far less frightening if it were fake. As all you women in the audience know, the amount of hair on top of a mature man's head is governed by the amount of testosterone he secretes, but the proportion is not direct. The proportion is inverse. Testosterone attacks the hair follicles. It fries and shrivels them like noodles in a wok of acid. As a potent man comes to maturity, the testosterone begins to kill off the hair on top of his head. As he advances into vigorous middle age, his head rises through his remaining hair like a shining symbol of his virility. Meanwhile the displaced hair-growing capacity moves steadily down his body, cropping up, if that's the appropriate phrase, in the strangest places, for which a healthily curious woman is glad to search. As a result, nothing excites an adventurous woman more than a bald man. Tom Jones may be pelted with women's underwear, but the women's underwear that used to be thrown at the bald actor Telly Savalas still had the women inside it. The American entertainment industry permits itself only one bald male star in a generation, and Telly Savalas drew the lucky card. Exercising the resulting sexual privilege to the full, he died with a gleam on his lips, and I hope to do the same. Ladies, I'll be ready to discuss this theme in more detail later on, up in my hotel room with a bottle of Roederer Cristal and mixed sandwiches, but for now let's just agree that Senator Kerry's luxuriant hairstyle is incontrovertible proof that he doesn't have a drop of testosterone in his body.

Does the American army really want a man like that leading them into battle against millions of vociferous religious extremists? President Bush may be without a brain, but Senator Kerry lacks a gland that most men would agree is even more vital to existence. The only other possible explanation is that he has had a transplant. Perhaps the first plugs of extra hair were inserted during the Vietnam war, when he made his mystery trip into Cambodia. Somewhere beyond the Mekong Delta, a communist hair-scientist was waiting for him, ready to do a deal if he would go home and oppose the war. But the job could have been done in America, bit by bit over the course of all those years when we weren't hearing a lot about him. What was he doing? He was growing younger.

American cosmetic technology can restore to an ageing man everything he ever had, except credibility. In a recent issue of *Vanity Fair* there was a two-page spread devoted to Ralph Lauren products which featured a photograph of Ralph Lauren himself. A man of a certain age, he could be said to be wearing well. An Egyptian mummy wearing that well would still be walking. His hairstyle, an extravaganza in spun silver, looked as if it had been lowered onto his head by a crane. It reflected the light, and looked as if it could reflect bullets. The message being that if you buy clothes with his label on them you will look as casually stylish as he does. You and I might think that Ralph's stylishness looks no more casual than that of Louis XV dressed for his coronation, but clearly the American consumers are convinced. Very thin American men, frantic with worry because their latest boardroom embezzlement is about to be discovered, wear Ralph Lauren clothes on the weekend in order to seem relaxed, just as very fat American men who can swallow a Big Mac like a canapé wear shorts and trainer shoes in order to seem athletic. Since their only conceivable means of rapid unassisted locomotion would be to roll downhill, the trainer shoes are purely symbolic.

Why do the Americans find the incredible plausible? Sufficient to answer that they do. In the society that began the dubious work of raising the cult of celebrity to a world-conquering ideology, the intention is taken for the deed. It's the nicest thing about America, even if it is also the most dangerous. America is the most ritualistic society since Japan was ruled by the Tokugawa shoguns. In America, every event is a ceremony, nobody is allowed to be alone, and everyone thinks that a heart worn on the sleeve must be more sincere instead of less. The result is a superabundance of courtesy. When Americans are not busy bombing the wrong village, shooting down the wrong airliner or wiping out their allies with friendly fire, they are busy being polite. The waiter really does feel it incumbent upon him, when he delivers your main course, to issue the instruction: 'Enjoy your meal.' My sincere answer to that would be 'Only if it's good,' but he would call the manager if I said so. Ritual must be observed. Worse, it has only to be observed in order to be taken as truly meant. To finish with the hair theme for the moment, take the case of that great actor William Shatner. In real life, William Shatner is a smart, funny and delightfully ironic man. But his real life is not his public life. The public William Shatner, after he left *Star Trek*, found that the hair on his head was growing thin. Instead of sensibly concluding that his abundance of testosterone was eating into his thatch, he must have decided that it was being eroded for another reason, perhaps because the stimulating effect of warp engine radiation had been switched off. Whatever his reasoning, when he came back to the screen as T.J. Hooker he was wearing on top of his head what is known in America as a 'piece'. Three times as big as any natural hairstyle he had ever had, the piece looked as if a live dog had been nailed to his skull. You could have thrown chunks of raw meat to that thing. Yet somewhere underneath that ludicrous construction, he still had the same sharp brain. He must have known that he looked like a man crushed by a falling fox terrier. But he also knew that he was in America, where it is sufficient to make the claim in order to fulfil the expectation. Even unto death, an abundant head of hair is a requirement, along with a set of perfect teeth. If the hair is taken from an animal, even if it is the whole animal, and if the perfect teeth are blatantly a set of caps that jar with the tucked face like two rows of white plastic tombstones in the graveyard of a ruined church, still the requirements have been met. They are the requirements of celebrity, and to that extent millions of anonymous Americans behave as if they were famous. We must not let this happen to us.

But it is happening to us, through the worldwide spread of reality television. Reality television actually started in Britain, when a series called *Sylvania Waters* elevated an otherwise painfully ordinary Australian family to tabloid fame. But now the Americans are doing it too, and when America does something everybody does it. One of the many nice things about being at this radio conference is that it's much harder to do reality television on radio. I believe in popular culture, and I even believe that beyond a certain point it is useless to argue with public taste. Popular culture is one of the key transmitters of ethics to the young. After the school playground and the influence of parents, if they have any, children get their principles from popular culture. Hence the importance of keeping it within the bounds of civilized decency. Even when it has a foul mouth, it should not be allowed to speak evil.

On a flight across the Atlantic last week, I was characteristically unable to operate the multiple choice in-flight entertainment system, and got stuck with a screening of the latest Harry Potter movie. I hadn't seen the previous ones because Monica Bellucci wasn't in them, and I expected to be bored. But I was thrilled. It was terrific: inventive, complex, witty and in the best sense fantastic. No wonder the kids love it, and play scenes from it to each other, and can recite every word. But imagine if such a mind-forming creation were preaching, say, racism. In Britain it has been black commentators, not white ones, who have been vocally worried about how so many hip-hop lyrics preach gun-nut violence, so I can safely say that anyone who is unworried about the effect of popular culture when it turns sour is living in a dream. But reality television is not as toxic as all that. Most of the people who appear on it seem to have the same problems with verbal communication as George W. Bush, but the relationships they form between themselves are often quite human and sometimes even touching. On a recent instalment of Britain's biggest reality television show, called *Big Brother*, a young woman who in all her life had read nothing but magazines met a young man who had actually read a book. The look of wondering admiration in her eyes is with me yet. Her life was changing right there, and only a snob would begrudge the transformation.

But the downside can be depressing. Just before I caught the plane here, the British tabloids were front-paging a story about two unfortunate young celebrities whose marriage was breaking up. The two young celebrities were identified by their first name – I think they were called Jane and Wayne, but it could have been Jean and Dean. They had met as participants on one of those reality TV shows in which a houseful of people chosen for their psychological disorders vote each week to expel one of their number. Basically the format is a re-run of a Nazi atrocity but without the machine-gunners waiting outside. In the future, and probably the near future, the machine-gunners will be waiting outside, but we haven't quite reached that point yet, although if the current contestants only knew it, the newspaper editors and book publishers waiting outside will have exactly the same effect as a belt-fed MG-42 manned by the Waffen SS. Anyway, Jane and Wayne, or Jean and Dean, were either the first to be ejected or the last, I forget which. Perhaps one of them was the first and the other was the last. Whether in disappointment or triumph, however, they had cemented the profound relationship they had formed on the show by getting married immediately afterwards. Now the marriage was over. Since the whole of the front page was occupied by their photographs – she looking as if her car had been stolen, he looking as if he had stolen it – I had to turn to pages two, three, four and five to get the facts, which were scattered in tiny gobbets of prose among yet more photographs of the two quondam lovers in their chosen setting, a house whose decor aspired to the taste of Donald Trump, plus overtones of one of Saddam Hussein's palaces as yet unlooted, with all its gold bathroom fittings still in place. This was the paradise they had built for themselves, and from which they would now be cast out. Apparently the pressure of fame had been too much for them. You could hardly get a more poignant case of people who had done nothing believing they were somebody. The only element of reality was the bit about the pressure of fame. They had certainly felt that.

They had become famous for having met each other on screen and fallen in love. This event was agreed by both themselves and the press to have been some kind of miracle – a conjunction, defying the laws of chance, of two soulmates who might otherwise never have found each other. Actually nothing could have been more ordinary, because each of them meets someone exactly like the other every day of the week. It would be impossible for them not to. By now, in the Britain that Tony Blair inherited from Margaret Thatcher and has somehow managed to make worse, there are millions of young people who, without qualifications for attaining to the luxurious life of which they dream, nevertheless believe, and it is the only belief they have, that if they could find their way to the right tree, it would have money growing on it. Money and celebrity. The press, keen to supply them with both those things, closed in. The pair of helpless young inadequates soon found that the press, once it closes in, is slow to go away until there is nothing left drifting down through the pink water except bones. The likelihood that married bliss would be temporary was intensified by the attentions of friends, acquaintances and the general public. Jane and Wayne, to the extent that they had ever had lives, now found that their lives were not their own. Even the closest friends became enemies, because fame breeds envy the more it is unearned, and if you have done nothing at all to earn it, absolutely everybody is dying to see it taken from you. Nobody looks at a photograph of Jesus Christ on the cross and asks 'Why not me?' because they know the answer: you haven't been crucified. Every one of Jean and Dean's friends looked at their photographs and thought, correctly, that they could have been famous too. Thus the friends became betrayers, the acquaintances became informers, and the general public became delighted ghouls at the scene of the inevitable disaster. The only remarkable thing was that the classic dynamics of celebrity were being applied to absolute nonentities.

Perhaps it was a good thing, a necessary sacrifice. Because Andy Warhol understated the case. He should have said that in the future everyone will not be famous for fifteen minutes, they will be famous all the time. And indeed fame is by now not only what almost everybody wants, it is what almost anybody can get. If you want to be famous, urinate on the shoe of someone who is already famous. You will be given your own television series. In Britain at the moment there is a famous couple you may have heard of called David and Victoria Beckham. David plays football very well some of the time and Victoria sings very bravely all of the time, but there is some reason for their celebrity. There is no reason for the celebrity of a young woman called Rebecca Loos except that she managed to sleep with David. By all accounts this feat is rather less taxing than to square the circle, but Rebecca has the plus value of looking rather more upmarket than Victoria. She might look it, but Victoria, were the positions reversed, might have been less likely to sell her story to the press. Rebecca sold her story, and is now a TV star. The historian George Grote brought his monumental, multi-volume history of Greece to an end at the point when, as he explained, the Greeks no longer realized they were slaves. We may have reached the point when people who sell the story of their love-lives no longer realize they are nonentities. Having come into close contact with the famous, they convince themselves that they have caught fame, as they might catch crabs. The age we live in is the apotheosis of the parasite. So far there are few formal studies of this phenomenon, but let me recommend Bob Dylan's fascinating new autobiography, which will soon be published. Judging by the extracts I have seen, it is the work of a master deceiver. He would have us believe that in order to escape the pressure of fame, he made bad albums deliberately. He would have us believe that his early songs were never meant to lead his listeners on the path of social rebellion, and that he was appalled when they did. I suppose that's why he wrote the song with that haunting refrain, 'The times they are a-changing, more's the pity.' But the stuff about how being one of the world's biggest celebrities turned his private life into a misery is obviously all too true.

It isn't a matter of celebrity getting out of control. Celebrity is out of control by its nature. Everyone who becomes famous is convinced beforehand that his fame will be different. All of them find out that it is bound to be the same, because no human being is naturally supplied with the defence mechanisms that can ward off universal attention. Every beautiful woman who becomes famous, for example, acquires at least one stalker. If we think some of them don't, it's only because they have so far managed to avoid having to take out a restraining order. We found out about Nicole Kidman's poet when she went to court to get rid of him, or anyway try to. At the moment he is defending his human rights in the Hague, one of his human rights being the right to make Nicole Kidman admit that she is in love with him. In reality, she awaits his inevitable reappearance with dread. She could put up with the poems he sent her, although if you read a few of them you wonder how she did. She could even put up with his haunting her doorstep with a new bunch of fresh roses every morning. But when he offered to take her children to school in his car, she had to call in the cops. You might have thought that she already had her work cut out, being married to a miniature Scientologist. Incidentally, in her latest movie she mistakes a ten-year-old boy for her late husband. It makes you wonder if she ever mistook Tom Cruise for a ten-year-old boy. But being married to a fellow celebrity was something she chose. She did not choose her stalker. Her stalker chose her. And there is a stalker for almost every celebrity: for all the women and even for most of the men. The penny dropped for Bob Dylan when he realized that not only he himself was incurably famous, the weirdo who was cataloguing his garbage had become famous too. Dylan's garbage-collector was sorting the garbage in order to write a book about Dylan, and then somebody wrote a book about the garbage collector. Jodie Foster won't allow interviewers to question her about the man who shot Ronald Reagan in order to impress her. But all her interviewers mention that they are not allowed to mention it, and here I am mentioning it now. Something she never did is stuck to her for life, and the achievement of a serious artist is ineradicably branded with the action of a psychotic. The Jodie Foster jokes will always be there. In 1982, some comedian said that Ariel Sharon invaded the Lebanon to impress Jodie Foster. It was a good joke, but it was on her. The stalker never goes away. Yoko Ono is not a woman high in my affections. I listened to one of her songs once and suffered irreversible damage not only to my hearing but to my left foot, because the radio was beside the bath and I tried to turn down the volume with my toes. But Yoko Ono is currently living with the knowledge that the man who shot her husband is scheduled to be set free on parole. No doubt the prospect has already encouraged her to rethink her original position on the coercive power of the state. I truly sympathize with her, but her best chance of life resides in the fact that the man who shot her husband is now world famous himself, and thus quite likely to inspire an assassin of his own, in the way that Lee Harvey Oswald was the inspiration for Jack Ruby.

But the chance of getting murdered is only the most spectacular question of life and death that fame raises. Leaving out the malevolence of the mentally disturbed, and the professional cynicism of the press, there is quite enough extreme behaviour from ordinary people to make the everyday life of someone famous scarcely worth living. This is the main reason why the famous actually need the biggest income that they can get, because they will have to spend a large part of it on protection from people who are otherwise clinically sane, but who, faced with the dazzle of someone they admire, temporarily lose all conception of the privacy of others. Julia Roberts needs her twenty million dollars a picture, because she needs nineteen million dollars' worth of perimeter defence in order to stop the fans entering her house and sitting down with her to dinner, each of them convinced that she is as lucky to meet them as they are to meet her. And of course she would have the same chance of dining undisturbed in a public restaurant as Napoleon had of successfully invading Russia. That was why he invaded Russia, in fact: to get away from the press. On the island of Elba, he spent most of his time giving interviews. And that's a true story. When he got tired of giving interviews in exile he would reappear in Europe to fight yet another last battle. It was like Cher's farewell tour, but with fewer lighting effects.

*

Unwanted attention is the real reason why stars isolate themselves, and by doing so they pay another penalty. At any big premiere, or even in any small nightclub, there is a special roped off area reserved for stars. It isn't just so that they can meet their next wife, or so that their current wife can meet Salman Rushdie, it's so that they won't be talked to death by normal people like you and me. Each of us has something interesting to say, but the stars can't afford to listen, or they will be worn out. Nor can they sign every autograph they are asked for, or carpal tunnel syndrome will end their careers early. The late George Harrison, when asked for his autograph, used to say: 'I can't. It's Tuesday.' On Wednesday he would say: 'It's Wednesday.' It was years before anyone noticed that he never gave his autograph. He had the technique worked out for remaining reasonably private in public, although those techniques availed him nothing when a screwball got into his kitchen. The British comedian Eric Morecambe, one of the best-loved faces in the country, was woken up on the stretcher after his first heart attack by one of the stretcher-bearers, who said his daughter would never forgive him if he didn't get an autograph. And these are ordinary people whose obtuseness should be forgiven because for them the encounter with the famous one is unique, and it never occurs to them that for the famous one it would happen a thousand times a day if there were no haven. Yet the cost of being in the roped-off area is that the press will hate you, and so a new layer of harassment is added, by which people who have been raised up by fame are given the reputation of being above themselves.

The natural result of this inexorable process is a well-founded wariness, which is bound to look like aloofness when seen from the distance at which they must keep the rest of us if they are to survive. Even the most magnanimous and naturally gregarious celebrities are bound to ration their supply of bonhomie if they are to get through the day, and if we catch them at it, we are equally bound to think that they are putting on airs. And of course some of them really do. In many cases, talent arises from an unstable personality, and if the talent brings fame then the instability is less likely to be assuaged than exacerbated. But even the most normal artist can be forgiven for enforcing the contract to the letter. Robbed of everyday life, you don't want to be robbed in your professional life as well. One of the many nice things about Mel Gibson is that he can laugh at the hoo-hah: he has retained a degree of Aussie dinkumness that armours him against the hype. While filming a TV special about him in Los Angeles, I went with him to a TV show on which he was promoting one of his movies, and I was pleased at the way he laughed at the outrageous size of the fruit basket that had been put in his dressing room. For most stars, the fruit basket can never be big enough. But if there had been a small fruit basket, we would have seen the Passion of the Mel. When I was doing my first TV series at Granada television in Manchester, Robert Wagner and Natalie Wood were both there to tape a production of *Cat on a Hot Tin Roof*. Their lawyer measured the dressing room that had been provided for them and it turned out to be two feet narrower than the width specified in the contract. The builders were called in, and for several days rehearsals were interrupted by the uproar of pneumatic drills. When I was introducing a Frank Sinatra concert for the opening of Sanctuary Cove, Sinatra's lawyers went down on the floor with a tape measure to make sure that the fasteners holding down the red carpet were no more than the specified eighteen inches apart. I have seen these things happen with my own eyes. And these are the sane people.

Luciano Pavarotti is sane too: the most delightful group of men you could hope to meet. But he has his requirements. When he guested on my New Year's Eve show in England, he had to be flown in from Italy on a private jet, and the private jet had to be big. It wasn't precisely a Boeing 747, but it was big enough to carry a football team. Luciano was a gifted footballer in his early days, by the way, and you kind of wonder why later on the Italian team didn't ask him to keep goal. They would have been impossible to defeat. The car we sent to meet Luciano at the airport had to be a BMW 8 series because although he can fit into a 7 series, he doesn't want to be seen struggling to get out of it. All this was understandable, as was his refusal to descend the stairs on our set. Since the set would obviously have descended with him, we went along with his requirement to walk on from the side. But he also refuses to sit down on set without a table on front of him. When we tried to cheat and put in a table made of glass, the lawyers arrived. Luciano sincerely believes that if the set is correctly arranged, he will look as thin as a reed. He has been encouraged in this belief by his entourage.

The entourage for Diana Ross look like the remaining brothers of Malcolm X. They are there to ensure that Miss Ross will not be expected to do anything not specified in the contract, which includes singing. Instead, she mimes to playback. Not even one improvised musical phrase during a conversation is permitted. I could go on about Barbra Streisand for the rest of the night. I could go on for as long as she kept me waiting, which was five hours. Fame has turned her into a monster of control. Fame has convinced Bono that he is some kind of economist. But these are talented people, and talent should be forgiven anything. And yet it is sad to see how the fame earned by talent can affect the personality. Robert Redford is always, on principle, an hour late for any meeting with anybody. If he ever has a cardiac arrest from the accumulated strain of having his face-lifts lifted, he had better hope that the doctors in the emergency unit aren't working to the same timetable as he is.

Did my own small measure of fame affect my personality? I don't think so. I was always paranoid. I was paranoid in Class IB at Kogarah Infants School, when I won the spelling bee but Laurie Ryan was still given the first early mark just because he had kacked his pants earlier in the day. Next day I beat him to it. But my own small measure of fame did affect my expectations, especially when I travelled. When I went down the jetway into the aircraft, I got far too used to turning left. At the destination, I got far too used to looking for the limo driver holding a card with my name on it. I got far too used to never booking my own tickets, to being greeted by the hotel manager as if I had just arrived from Stockholm after receiving the Nobel Prize for Physics, to getting the suite instead of a room, to the bathroom with enough towels for a symphony orchestra. But above all I got far too used to being recognized, until one day, far too late but better late than never, it occurred to me that being recognized is not the same as recognition. In that regard, television ruins everyone who appears on it. You get used to so many people wanting to say hello. Some of them are coocoo, but most of them are friendly at the very least. And that, I finally realized, is what's wrong. It's a too-easy familiarity. You are being hailed for being somebody, even when you have done nothing.

So a few years ago I fired myself from the small screen and tried to find the path back to normality. I don't claim sainthood for this, and I suppose it could be said that I want it both ways. I want to be well-known enough to be asked to an event like this one tonight, and I want to be anonymous enough to disappear back into the crowd I came from. The two desires are incompatible: I realize that. But I think it's a conflict we're all going to have to face, because we can't go on like this. Our best hope is that the celebrity culture is already discrediting itself. We should help it on its way downhill, and do our best to get back to a state where fame, if we have to have it, is at least dependent on some kind of achievement. If people want to be somebody, they should do something first. There is no excuse for my generation of Australians not knowing the difference, because our early youth was spent in a land without television, and the sharp division between earned fame and pointless celebrity could be heard, if not seen, every week. It could be heard on the radio.

For me it was the difference between Bob Dyer and Jack Davey. Bob Dyer was the Americanized host of *Pick a Box* and my mother and I were agreed that he didn't do very much except shout. Actually it is no cinch to run any kind of game show and in retrospect I can see that Bob Dyer was quite skilful at marshalling the human traffic, but it's equally certain that he had no particular verbal prowess beyond yelling 'Happy motoring, customers' and cranking up the tension as he gave the quaking punter the tantalizing choice between the money or the box. 'The money . . . or the box?' shouted Bob Dyer. Then he would whisper it. 'The money . . . or . . . the box?' The box could have the big prize in it: a Westinghouse refrigerator, a Lotusland inner-spring mattress, or a diamond-encrusted J. Farren Price wristlet watch from Proud's. Or the box could have the booby prize in it: a packet of Bonnington's Irish Moss gum jubes, containing petroloxymel of garagene, from a rare seaweed washed up on the coast of Ireland. But both my mother and I were agreed that for a real booby prize, the box should have had Bob Dyer in it. We were Jack Davey fans and that was that. It was because Jack Davey did something. He made the language live.

Sitting in front of our Stromberg Carlson radio set, which was bigger than the Kosi stove, I was introduced by Jack Davey to the concept of word play, which is essentially the interplay of the expected and the unexpected, and therefore a matter of construction far more complex than a mere pun. Almost anyone can make a pun, which is why we flee those who do. Hardly anyone can do word play. Jack Davey's writers could, and he knew exactly how to deliver it. In the show's tightly written script, it was established that the woman who lived next door was seeking Jack Davey's affections. It was further established that she was large and powerfully built. In one programme, she said to him, 'I'm going to chuck you under the chin.' This announcement was followed by a sound effect of a body whistling through the air and landing heavily at some distance, with a clattering of tin cans. 'Struth,' said Davey, 'she chucked me under the house.' It might not sound like a great joke now, but my mother and I laughed for a week. I had no idea how he did it. I presumed that he had written the line himself. Actually he hadn't, but he easily could have. Jack Davey could think like lightning on his feet. Later on, in another programme, he introduced me to the concept of the educated joke – the joke that depends on a certain cultural sophistication in the audience. This time it was a quiz show, and Davey was improvising, picking up on unexpected things, a knack that can't be scripted. You can script the link material, but to interact verbally with the contestant you have to look up from the page and snatch the opportunity out of the air. In the final, hard round of the quiz, Davey asked a contestant the name of the supporting actress in a certain film, and the contestant gave the wrong answer, i.e a name that could not have been on Davey's script of questions and right answers. The contestant said 'Mercedes McCambridge.' There was the briefest pause before Davey said: 'Mercedes McCambridge? Sounds like a well educated Scotsman in a sports car.' My mother and I laughed for another week, and when I look back on it, I realize that it was then that I discovered my stock in trade. Actually I hadn't really understood the joke at the time. It had gone over my head like a frisbee. But I had been delighted by its flight. That was the thing I would do, if I could.

I would like to think that it was the thing I did on television, some of the time anyway. But most of the credit I got was just for having my face there. It was never much of a face in the first place, and as you can see, it has by now achieved the same condition as Pompeii. To pay myself what compliments for realism I can muster, I never tried to spruce it up. I never had my eyes enlarged or my teeth replaced, and above all, to use precisely the right phrase, I never tried to conceal the ravages of my excess testosterone. One of my producers had a wig designed for me but I never wore it. Later on it was given its own talk-show, which is still running. But my face got famous anyway, just for being there, and I finally realized that there was something wrong with that. By that measure, anyone can be famous, and that's madness. We have to get back to sanity. It will be a battle, but Australia is probably the best place to fight it.

Australia, partly by geographical luck and partly because of the much-underestimated collective wisdom of its political class, has so far managed to avoid both the worst excesses of Britain's uniformly squalid tabloid press and America's demented obeisance before anyone who claims to be unique. Australia, considered as a culture, is held together more by radio than TV, and radio has much less of this madness about glamour. Whatever you might think of John Howard's policies, the population that elected him proved by their votes that they had not yet succumbed to the delusion that a politician should look like a film star. Among Australia's flourishing community of left-wing commentators, there is even a rumour that the young John Howard looked like Ben Affleck, but the Liberal party's cosmetic surgeons went to work on him to make him more electable. If that proves to be a fact, we should rejoice in it. We should rejoice that ordinary Australian people can still pay heartfelt respect to those who have done something, and grant them a further existence beyond the necessarily brief period of their initial glory. In Adelaide earlier this year I was invited to tea by the Governor of South Australia, Marjorie Jackson. It pleased me that the Lithgow Flash had been granted lasting recognition for her achievements. To respect achievement is the only antidote for being poisoned by glamour. But the antidote must be taken before the poison. People should do something before they are allowed to be somebody. Getting back to that reality will be a struggle, but we should make a start now, while we are still sane enough to see that our world is going mad. The prize is a life that our children will find worth living. For that we must fight, and for once an adverb by George Bush applies exactly. We must fight vociferously.

Postscript

My audience on the Gold Coast consisted entirely of people working in Australian commercial radio. Most of them were still in shock from John Howard's recent election victory. If they had been working for the ABC, the country's public service broadcasting network, it wouldn't have been a matter of 'most'. It would have been all of them. Australian media personnel, like the intelligentsia as a whole, tended to believe that Howard could have won only by fooling the electorate, and that the electorate, therefore, had become increasingly easy to fool. These were not opinions I shared, but I was there to entertain, rather than argue, so I thought it best to steer clear of the subject. I also tried to keep an even hand on the question of the forthcoming Presidential election in America. Once again, it was believed that a consensus of the publicly concerned would determine the outcome, and that George W. Bush was therefore doomed to defeat. I didn't share that opinion either, but I could lampoon the incumbent with a whole heart, because I thought that, unlike Howard, Bush deserved to be consigned to oblivion if only it could be arranged. Howard, though the Australian progressive consensus would rather be hanged than grant him any mental quality beyond a certain low cunning, is more than clever enough to be a fit Prime Minister. Bush is not a fit President, and as the leader of the Free World he is a liability, not least because he is so ignorant that he can inadvertently insult even his allies. A man who believes that World War II began with Pearl Harbor should not be delivering a State of the Union address. He should be delivering pizza. Going on what I had seen of the Presidential debates, however, I saw no reason to believe that Senator Kerry would easily defeat him.

Luckily I wasn't called upon to make a political prediction. My nominated subject was the so-called Celebrity Culture, and I felt justified in sticking to that. The subject is quite political enough, and would go on being so whoever occupied the highest office in Australia, Britain or the United States. Fast food doesn't necessarily drive out slow food – for every new branch of McDonald's, a good ethnic restaurant opens somewhere – but it certainly increases the weight of people who eat nothing else, and sooner or later, if you do a lot of travelling, you will find yourself sitting between a couple of them on an aircraft. Similarly, there are alternatives to reality television, but anyone who believes that it doesn't increase the total stupidity in a given culture is simply dreaming. President Bush can't see that the privatization of the benefits system will turn life insurance into a lottery, but that is because he is too obtuse to know the difference. Intelligent people, and intellectuals above all, should realize that the Celebrity Culture is the free market run rampant, and if they can't see how it can be curbed without infringing liberty, should at least think how it can be offset by argument, so as to provide their fellow consumers with a less debilitating ideal. Satire is one way, but the satirists become celebrities too. I don't pretend to know the answer, but I can honestly report that when I delivered this address I got a thoughtful response for having asked the question. The jokes, when successful, might even have helped in this: people are often ready for a new thought after they laugh, just as they are ready for a fresh breath after they sneeze. The joke about the retiring Governor of Tasmania depended on the knowledge being fresh in everyone's memory that he had been a diplomatic catastrophe. William Shatner's hairpiece, however, was a hit even with those who had never seen it. The image has been passed down through the generations. It's no bad thing: the iconography of show business is a frame of reference, and there is virtue in being able to name all the actors who played the Magnificent Seven. I even know which one of them saved Frank Sinatra from drowning. (It was Brad Dexter.) But when the ice-skater Tonya Harding started showing up on television to explain her motivation for taking out a contract on her rival's kneecap, it was time to wonder, and if Lynndie England gets a book deal it will be time to panic.

The word 'book', however, reminds me to be honest, even if it hurts. When it comes to the less popular arts, a high media profile pays off. Unless you can wangle a subsidy, you need publicity. My books of essays would be less likely to earn out their advances if I were not a recognizable name on television and radio. In the US I am not that, and they don't. In the US a writer can be a recluse, but he has to be a famous recluse – Thomas Pynchon, J. D. Salinger – if his books are to stay in print. In Britain and Australia, a writer, no matter how talented, can't be a recluse for long, or he will lose his publisher. Now that I have enough free time to attend the festivals when invited, I attend them all, and do my best to put on a show, as well as hit all the associated radio and television shows that my publisher can arrange. Except in rare cases, I find it excruciating to sit for newspaper profiles, but my publisher would suffer worse pain if I turned them all down. In addition, when there is a new book to push, I accept guest spots on any talk shows that don't require me to wear a funny hat or discuss the uses of a motorized pink dildo with a man who streaks his hair. I would like to think that my book of collected poems, *The Book of My Enemy*, would have paid its way unassisted. But it didn't hurt to recite a poem on air to Richard and Judy, and another poem to Posh Spice and David Bowie on *Parkinson*. So it could be said that I am against the Celebrity Culture for everyone except myself. But I still prefer to think that if I had only myself to promote, and not a body of work, I would have no excuse for being in the limelight. There was a day, admittedly, when I sought the limelight for its own sake. But I was young at the time, and there were far fewer crazy people doing the same thing. A brief way of putting it, and perhaps a fitting conclusion to this book, is that I care enough about writing poems and essays to want other people to read them. They aren't private forms, although any writer who believes they are will have no trouble demonstrating his conviction.